# STATESWOMEN

# STATESWOMEN

## A CENTENNIAL HISTORY
## OF ARKANSAS
## WOMEN LEGISLATORS
## 1922-2022

Lindsley Armstrong Smith
and Stephen A. Smith

FOREWORD BY JANINE A. PARRY

THE UNIVERSITY OF ARKANSAS PRESS

FAYETTEVILLE

2022

978-1-68226-215-3 (cloth)
978-1-68226-216-0 (paper)
978-1-61075-784-3 (e-book)

26 25 24 23 22   5 4 3 2 1

Manufactured in the United States of America
Designed by April Leidig

♾ The paper used in this publication meets the minimum requirements of the American National Standard for Permanence of Paper for Printed Library Materials z39.48–1984.

Library of Congress Cataloging-in-Publication Data
Names: Smith, Lindsley Armstrong, 1963– author. | Smith, Stephen A., 1949– author.
Title: Stateswomen: a centennial history of Arkansas women legislators, 1922–2022 / Lindsley Armstrong Smith and Stephen A. Smith.
Description: Fayetteville: The University of Arkansas Press, 2022. | Includes bibliographical references and index. | Summary: "Stateswomen celebrates the centennial of women serving as members of the Arkansas General Assembly. The book features concise biographies of all the women legislators who have served in the assembly to date, situating their political activity within the history of the expansion of the role of women in the public sphere"—Provided by publisher.
Identifiers: LCCN 2022006948 (print) | LCCN 2022006949 (ebook) | ISBN 9781682262153 (cloth) | ISBN 9781682262160 (paperback) | ISBN 9781610757843 (ebook)
Subjects: LCSH: Arkansas. General Assembly—History. | Arkansas. General Assembly—Biography. | Women legislators—Arkansas—History. | Women legislators—Arkansas—Biography. | Women—Political activity—Arkansas—History. | Arkansas—Politics and government. | LCGFT: Biographies.
Classification: LCC JK5166 .S65 2022 (print) | LCC JK5166 (ebook) | DDC 328.767/09—dc23/eng/20220427
LC record available at https://lccn.loc.gov/2022006948
LC ebook record available at https://lccn.loc.gov/2022006949

*This project was supported by the University of Arkansas Diane D. Blair Center of Southern Politics and Society.*

Dedicated to the memory of
Diane Divers Blair
1938–2000

Friend, scholar, educator, public servant,
and advocate for women

———

# Contents

Foreword xi

Acknowledgments xv

Obstacles and Opportunities:
Securing Space in the Public Sphere 3

## The Stateswomen

Frances Hunt 101

Nellie B. Mack 102

Erle Chambers 104

Elizabeth Thompson 105

Florence McRaven 107

Mary B. Wigstrand 108

Maude Brown 109

Ethel Cunningham 111

Ella B. Hurst 112

Alene Word 114

Helen Buchanan 115

Lera Rowlette 116

Mattie Hackett 118

Willie Oates 119

Bernice Kizer 121

Doris McCastlain 122

Dove Mulkey 124

Gladys Martin Oglesby 125

Dorathy Allen 126

Vada Sheid 128

Lucile Autry 129

Shirley Meacham 131

Carolyn Pollan 132

Gloria Cabe 134

Sarah Jane Bost 135

Irma Hunter Brown 136

Judy Petty 138

Norma Thompson 139

Peggy Long Hartness 140

Charlie Cole Chaffin 142

Nancy Balton 143

Myra Jones 144

Wanda Northcutt 146

Charlotte Schexnayder 147

Gladys Watson 149

Christene Brownlee 150

Jacqueline Roberts 152

Judy Smith 153

Josetta Wilkins 174

Dee Bennett 176

Ann Bush 177

Barbara Horn 179

Marian Owens Ingram 180

Evelyn Ammons 181

Lisa Ferrell 183

Peggy Jeffries 184

Becky Lynn 186

Sue Madison 187

Bobbie L. Hendrix 189

Pat Bond 190

Rita Hale 191

Dianne Hudson 193

Sandra Rodgers 194

Martha Shoffner 196

Wilma Walker 197

Sarah Agee 199

Cecile Bledsoe 200

Jo Carson 202

Joyce Dees 203

Mary Beth Green 205

Brenda Gullett 206

Jan Judy 208

Barbara King 209

Mary Anne Salmon 210

Shirley Borhauer 212

Joyce Elliott 213

Sharon Trusty 215

Ruth Whitaker 217

Judy Pridgen 218

Linda Chesterfield 220

Marilyn Edwards 221

Janet Johnson 223

Betty Pickett 224

Sandra Prater 226

Susan Schulte 227

Shirley Walters 229

Pam Adcock 230

Nancy Duffy Blount 231

Dawn Creekmore 233

Stephanie Flowers 234

Wilhelmina Lewellen 236

Beverly Pyle 237

Lindsley Smith 239

Sharon Dobbins 241

Toni Bradford 242

Joan Cash 244

Donna Hutchinson 245

Tracy Pennartz 247

Johnnie Roebuck 248

Charolette Wagner 250

Kathy Webb 252

Ann Clemmer 253

Jody Dickinson 255

Jane English 256

Debra Hobbs 258

Karen Hopper 259

Andrea Lea 261

Stephanie Malone 262

Barbara Nix 263

Tiffany Rogers 265

Mary Lou Slinkard 266

Linda Tyler 268

Lori Benedict 269

Linda Collins-Smith 271

Mary P. "Prissy" Hickerson  272

Missy Irvin  274

Sheilla E. Lampkin  276

Betty Overbey  277

Leslee Milam Post  278

Mary Broadaway  280

Charlotte Vining Douglas  281

Deborah Ferguson  283

Charlene Fite  284

Fonda Hawthorne  286

Patti Julian  287

Sue Scott  288

Camille Bennett  290

Mary Bentley  291

Karilyn Brown  293

Jana Della Rosa  294

Vivian Flowers  296

Michelle Gray  297

Robin Lundstrum  299

Julie Mayberry  300

Rebecca Petty  302

Laurie Rushing  303

Nelda Speaks  305

DeAnn Vaught  306

LeAnne Burch  308

Sonia Eubanks Barker  309

Sarah Capp  311

Frances Cavenaugh  312

Carol Dalby  314

Breanne Davis  315

Nicole Clowney  317

Cindy Crawford  319

Denise Garner  320

Megan Godfrey  322

Tippi McCullough  323

Gayla H. McKenzie  325

Jamie Scott  326

Denise Jones Ennett  328

Joy Springer  329

Jill Bryant  331

Delia J. Haak  332

Ashley Hudson  334

Bibliographic Essay  337

Appendices  347

Notes  355

Index  379

# Foreword

When most people think of women's progress in American politics — the central actors and pivotal developments in this slow-motion revolution — they do not think of Arkansas. This is a pity, as it is a place of a surprising number of both firsts and rares. It extended statewide (if partial) suffrage rights to women two years in advance of the ratification of the Nineteenth Amendment, for example, making it the first southern state to do so. It also was the first of *any* state to elect a woman to the US Senate. Although Senator Hattie Caraway's service began in the usual way — as a temporary stand-in for a dead husband — it ended with election to a full six-year term in 1932, followed by *re*election in 1938. Other Arkansas politicians include Maud Dunlap Duncan, elected mayor of Winslow (on an all-woman ticket) in 1925; Joycelyn Elders, the second woman (and first Black American) to serve as the US Surgeon General; Little Rock mayor Lottie Shackelford, among the earliest Black women in this role; and Blanche Lincoln, the first woman to chair the US Senate's powerful Agriculture Committee. Arkansas also, of course, was the longtime residence of Hillary Rodham Clinton, the first woman to win a nationwide popular vote (if not to assume the presidency).

If most of these figures have been somewhat overlooked, the nearly 150 women (as compared with thousands of men) who have served in the state General Assembly have been all but invisible. Such an oversight is not unique to Arkansas. Despite being the central decision makers for education, public health, transportation, and criminal justice policy in the fifty states, state legislators are everywhere unheralded, and — frankly — unchronicled. For observers of women in politics, this gap is particularly vexing because American women have had (relatively) greater success accessing these posts as compared with those of higher profile. A handful of political scientists leveraged the uptick in women legislators in the late twentieth century to explore if, and how, a "lady lawmaker" might be different from the traditional sort. And a few enterprising historians have introduced us to the very earliest trailblazers in our respective states. But detailed, comprehensive accounts of which women make it into these overwhelmingly masculine spaces, and what they do when they get there, have been too heavy a lift.

Enter Lindsley and Stephen Smith's *Stateswomen: A Centennial History of Arkansas Women Legislators, 1922–2022*. A monumental contribution in several respects, its most obvious significance lies in the lively, attentive treatments afforded each lawmaker. Readers — whether dutifully proceeding from the first entry to the last or sampling them at random — will quickly spot patterns in the women's experiences. These include the exceptionally long resumés of volunteerism and social activism they built prior to legislative service; the hurdles — legal, cultural, economic, and personal — they had to navigate to serve their communities in this rather radical way; and the importance of family connections to their victories (a characteristic of southern politics long before women could benefit from it).

In addition, the introductory essay is of tremendous scholarly value in its own right. Rather than merely situating the collection in the context of the contemporary climate (which they do efficiently and well), Smith and Smith deliver a probing, original examination of the "long history of resistance to full citizenship rights for women in Arkansas." Indeed, they devote considerable real estate to documenting "the social, cultural, and political forces that previously prevented and presently perpetuate the lack of gender parity in Arkansas" and, of course, nearly everywhere else. They also document, with unparalleled tenacity and care, the very earliest figures to challenge such obstacles successfully: the postmistresses, notaries public, and — most fascinatingly — the General Assembly's engrossing clerks, who ran sophisticated, months-long campaigns for the votes of male legislators *before women could vote*.

None of these matters have been examined nearly enough when you consider how glacial this aspect of fully realized self-governance has been. Not only was simple enfranchisement a nearly century-long battle — meaning we expressly excluded at least half of the population longer than we have included it — but extending to women access to the complete menu of rights and responsibilities also has followed a torturously winding path. All manner of obstacle — from sluggish economic and educational development to rigid religious and other cultural proscriptions, nearly always costumed as something other than straight-up discrimination — blocked the way.

Still, if Arkansas continues to linger under the national average in the proportion of women lawmakers serving in its legislature (23 percent, as compared with 31 percent, both shamefully low), things would be worse if not for the fierce, patient, deft, strident, calculating, bull-headed, demure, strategic, and *determined* women chronicled throughout this book. As Smith and Smith observe, few could contemplate women as fully autonomous political actors (can we now?). So, their subjects—a hundred years ago and now—had to challenge "the dominant domestic ideology and to overcome its social and institutional obstacles. Consequently, their public presence shaped a new social reality, transforming their own lives and attitudes, developing a sense of themselves as competent political actors in what was previously an exclusively male domain, moving from the galleries to the smoke-filled committee rooms, while also opening opportunities for other women in a variety of paid and influential governmental roles." Documenting this transformation, and its ongoing effects, is the central achievement of this painstakingly well-researched book. In doing so, Smith and Smith make a significant contribution to the study, and the practice, of the largest, longest experiment in self-governance the world has yet known . . . one that is still unfolding before our very eyes.

*Janine A. Parry*

# Acknowledgments

The research for and writing of this book was a rewarding and enlightening experience, not only because of the fascinating lives of the women legislators we came to know but also because of the incredible support we received from the many people who assisted with the project and helped make it a reality. Initial funding for conducting the interviews and preparing the transcripts was provided by a grant from the University of Arkansas Women's Giving Circle, with additional funding and support from the Diane D. Blair Center of Southern Politics and Society. Dr. Todd Shields, professor of Political Science, then director of the Center and later dean of the UA Fulbright College of Arts and Sciences, provided continuous support for the project from the beginning.

Our colleagues in the University of Arkansas Department of Communication were uniformly supportive of our research. The students in our courses on political communication and rhetoric of American women shared, or at least tolerated, our enthusiasm for the stories of women politicians and their unique contributions to the legislative process. Several students conducted oral history interviews with women legislators, transcribed and analyzed their observations, and discovered the joys of exploring historical accounts on microfilm.

We are also grateful for the public service of Arkansas women legislators and are especially indebted to those who agreed to be interviewed for this book or completed detailed questionnaires on their personal and political history. Bernice Kizer offered advice on structuring the interviews, and Johnnie Roebuck assisted with design of the questionnaires. Representative Roebuck and Senator Ruth Whitaker also encouraged their colleagues to participate in the interviews and donate campaign materials for the project. Representative Donna Hutchinson conducted the interview with Representative Shirley Borhauer, and Matthew Haas interviewed Senator Judy Pridgen.

Henry P. Jones III, grandson of Representative Frances Hunt, generously shared his personal memories of the state's first woman legislator. Additional biographical information on former women legislators drew on the personal reflections by their relatives, including Neva Buchanan, Helen Buchanan

Crust, Carol Hendrix, Nancy Thompson Herdlinger, William P. Thompson, Senator Jim Hill, Marilyn Horn, Ann Lane, Ann Sugg, and George Anna Hurst Tow.

We are always in awe of librarians and particularly so for all they have done to facilitate our research. Robin Roggio at the University of Arkansas was always on call and cheerful. Melinda Shelton at the Birmingham Public Library provided technical assistance, helpful critiques, and constant encouragement. Shannon Rodriguez, Monticello Branch manager with the Southeast Arkansas Regional Library, is a true detective. Eric Pumroy, director of Special Collections at Bryn Mawr College, graciously provided permissions and photographs from the Carrie Chapman Catt Papers.

Dr. David Ware, director of the Arkansas State Archives and former capitol historian, provided essential materials for this book and delightful conversations over the years. Elizabeth Freeman and Lauren Jarvis, also with the Arkansas State Archives, were helpful in providing photographs from the extensive collection. Additional photographs appear courtesy of the Arkansas House and Senate, with appreciation to Cecillea Pond-Mayo, Ann Cornwell, and John Reed.

We had the support of Dr. Janine Parry from the inception of this project. We are much obliged for all we have learned from her and grateful for her providing the foreword to this book. Our understanding was also informed and enriched by the scholarship of Jay Barth, Diane Blair, Cherisse Branch-Jones, Ann Henry, Frances Mitchell Ross, and Jeannie Whayne. Mike Bieker, David Scott Cunningham, and Janet Foxman at the University of Arkansas Press shared our enthusiasm for the project, offered helpful suggestions, and made our words into this book, which also benefitted from the insightful editing by Michelle Flythe.

Other folks who made significant contributions to our thinking and research effort by providing good leads, helpful suggestions, personal contacts, welcomed encouragement, and other support were Kay Arnold, Harold Coogan, Patti Cox, Tom Dillard, Revis Edmonds, Keith Emis, Jimmie Lou Fisher, Cathy Foraker, Denise Garner, Wes Goodner, Hershel Hartford, William Higgs, Irina Hofstee, Jenn and Bill Horton, William B. Jones Jr., Robert Keenan, Rita Kirk, Guy Lancaster, Angie Maxwell, Rex Nelson, Tim Nutt, Jared Pack, Lynn Parker, Bubba Powers, Tom and Lorna Pryor, Bob Razer, Maylon Rice, Bobby Roberts, Skip Rutherford, Estella Smith, Joe Wasson, Glenn Whaley, Dina Wood, and Joshua Youngblood. Thank you.

# STATESWOMEN

# Obstacles and Opportunities

## SECURING SPACE IN THE PUBLIC SPHERE

This book is an introduction to the 146 women who have served as members of the Arkansas General Assembly during the past century. This centennial year of women first serving in the General Assembly provides the opportunity to address the missing history about how women began serving in office in Arkansas, mapping the path for their service in the highest legislative offices in the state. This book is also intended to recognize the impediments that Arkansas women have overcome to make significant contributions to politics and public policy, as well as to celebrate their indomitable success in doing so. The centennial of the first women legislators also offers an opportunity to reconstruct a broader and more useable political history for women and to share that narrative with others interested in history, government, gender, and public policy.

While the brief biographical entries of the women legislators in this book are primarily descriptive, they also reflect the symbolic and substantive influence that representation by women leaders entails. Most were married, but others were single, divorced, or widowed. Most were mothers. Their age when first elected to the legislature ranged from twenty-three (Lera Jeanne Rowlett) to seventy-four (Shirley Borhauer). The median age for freshman women legislators was higher than for men legislators, because many women legislators were the primary caretakers of their children and waited to enter politics until later in life. Their occupations included homemakers, attorneys, farmers, teachers, business owners, librarians, social workers, probation officers, journalists, mayors, county officials, realtors, insurance agents, landlords, state employees, restaurateurs, office managers, nonprofit organization officers, military veterans, nurses, and other medical professionals. They represented urban areas, small towns, and rural locations. They held high school diplomas and doctorates. They have been Black American, Native American, and white American. They were Democrats and Republicans, heterosexual and lesbian, and most were congregants of various Christian denominations.

The women legislators' personal pathways to office and the issues they chose to address are instructive. Even without comparative statistics, it becomes obvious that most of these women had already devoted their time and attention to voluntary public service before assuming public office, and they generally had more formal education than their men colleagues. Many had family members who had been in politics, which increased their awareness of the possibilities for involvement in public affairs and offered sources of encouragement and support for their own participation. Once in the legislature, women representatives and senators brought new perspectives and raised issues that had been, and otherwise would have been, ignored by their men colleagues.

While we were conducting research for this book, dozens of current and previous women members of the Arkansas General Assembly graciously shared their time and testimony describing their experiences in election campaigns, offering their insights into navigating the legislative culture, and discussing the unique contributions that women bring to making public policy. We found these interviews both helpful and enlightening. While the space and format of this book do not allow the opportunity to share all of these wonderful stories, we have made these interviews available for interested readers and future scholars to hear about the legislators' lives and experiences firsthand. Our research began as a project of the Diane D. Blair Center of Southern Politics and Society and was funded by the University of Arkansas Women's Giving Circle. The transcripts and digital versions of the interviews were donated to the David and Barbara Pryor Center for Arkansas Oral and Visual History, where the materials are available for public access.[1]

We anticipate that the biographical sketches of women legislators presented here will also be a starting point for more detailed and extended scholarship on the political contributions of women to Arkansas history. And we hope that the stories of these committed trailblazers will be an inspiration for women and girls to seek public office and reach new horizons for women leaders. Moreover, a greater recognition of the accomplishments of women legislators can inform everyone and encourage allies in helping support better public policies.

During the first century of the Arkansas territorial and statehood experience, women were discouraged from expressing their opinions on important public issues, ignored or dismissed when they did speak out, and prohibited from even voting for public officials. Arkansas women were forbidden from helping draft our state's fundamental constitutional documents, under which they lived, and they were denied the right to vote to ratify or reject any of the five constitutions that enshrined the state's political patriarchy. The last century has seen an incremental but remarkable presence of women in public office and their emerging role in legislative influence. Five decades after the first women legislators were elected in 1922, only twenty-one women had successfully breached the barriers that hindered their entry to membership in the legislature. It is noteworthy and somewhat astonishing that more women were serving in the Arkansas General Assembly in 2020 than the *total* number who had done so before our state celebrated the sesquicentennial of Arkansas statehood in 1986.

Including the twelve women who have served in both the House and Senate, only twenty-one women have been elected to the Arkansas State Senate, and 137 women have held seats in the House of Representatives. In recognizing and honoring their service and achievements, we must also acknowledge that Arkansas currently ranks in the bottom ten states in percentage of women legislators serving, and it has never reached the national average of 31 percent female representation in state legislatures.[2]

Before presenting information from Arkansas women legislators about their political experiences, we examine the long history of resistance to full citizenship rights for women in Arkansas and provide background to more fully comprehend the current political environment that limits the number of women seeking and holding seats in the state legislature. We think it important to identify and document some of the social, cultural, and political forces that previously prevented and presently perpetuate the lack of gender parity in Arkansas politics. Arkansas was ranked fortieth among the fifty states on the 2020 Women's Empowerment Index, considering seventeen key indicators of gender equality.[3] At the same time, it is essential to discover and describe the courageous voices that resisted repression and to study their strategic efforts to subvert the imposed limitations on women's full participation in the public sphere.

In Arkansas, the conversation was initiated by Miles Ledford Langley, the minister of Pleasant Hill Baptist Church in Clark County, who was a delegate to the constitutional conventions of 1864 and 1868. During the final week of the 1868 Constitutional Convention, Delegate Langley proposed an amendment to the Bill of Rights that read: "All citizens, twenty-one years of age, who can read and write the English language, shall be eligible to the elective franchise, and entitled to equal political rights and privileges."[4]

Delegate Robert Grant of Prairie County, one of the two antagonists to Langley's proposal, facetiously moved to refer the proposal "to Mrs. Lucy Stone," the noted abolitionist and woman's rights advocate. Langley persisted and laid out the premises for his amendment. "Progress is an unchangeable law of nature. This is an age of improvement. Reform is the order of the day," he began, as he offered his vision for state government after the Civil War.

"We must reconstruct the government of our country on radical principles—universal freedom, impartial suffrage, and equal rights."[5]

Langley then raised the central question in the debate, "Shall woman, created the equal of man, be entitled to the same political and legal rights as man? This is the question; and it is destined to be the question of questions, the great question of the age, the question of the country for years to come." Answering that question, he said, "I affirm that woman is by nature endowed with equal rights, social, political, and legal, with man."[6]

After grounding his argument in natural rights philosophy, Langley turned to utilitarian justification for the proposed policy. "For men to make and enforce laws which deny women their political and legal rights, is usurpation, tyranny, injustice, and wickedness," he said, because "the right of woman to vote and hold office is demanded as a matter of good policy." After enduring ridicule and personal attacks from Delegate Jesse Cypert of White County, Langley replied, "My wife is as well qualified to vote as I am. We have women in our country who are better qualified to hold any civil office, however responsible, than are the men who oppose female suffrage." Moving on, he added, "Say what you will, but the sphere of woman is the sphere of man," he asserted, "And woman will yet be admitted to all the political rights of man. It is only a matter of time."[7]

Langley's proposal was tabled, and the convention soon adjourned. Explaining his efforts and his disappointment with "a sad heart but an approving conscience" in a letter to Susan B. Anthony the following week, he described his arguments "of which I am not ashamed. I was met with ridicule, sarcasm, and insult." For his efforts "to guarantee to woman her God-given and well-earned rights of civil and political equality," he said, "the democrats are my enemies because I assisted in emancipating the slaves. The republicans have now become my opponents, because I have made an effort to confer on the women their rights. And even the women themselves fail to sympathize with me."[8]

Twenty years before Miles Langley brought the conversation to Arkansas, the nation's first woman's rights convention had been held at Seneca Falls, New York, in 1848. Called "to discuss the social, civil, and religious condition of woman," it adopted a Declaration of Sentiments that articulated the sources of discrimination against women citizens and resolved, "That it is the duty of the women of this country to secure to themselves their sacred right to the elective franchise."[9]

The constitutional proposition offered by Langley in 1868 was that women should have the right to vote, have the right to hold public office, and have the constitutional guarantee of equal rights with men. Despite his courageous effort, it would be more than fifty years before Arkansas women had the right to vote and hold office. They still do not have a constitutional guarantee of equal rights. Fifty years later, the proposed Arkansas constitution of 1918 provided, "male and female citizens shall enjoy equally all civil, political, and religious rights and privileges," but the proposed charter was rejected by the voters.[10] The proposed constitution of 1980 recognized "the equality of all persons before the law," providing that "no person should be denied the equal protection of the law on account of . . . gender" and that the legislature "shall not grant or deny to any citizen or class of citizens privileges or immunities which upon the same terms shall not equally belong to all citizens," but that document was also rejected by the voters.[11] Finally, although public opinion polls show that Arkansas residents overwhelmingly support the proposed federal Equal Rights Amendment, it has never been ratified by either chamber of the Arkansas legislature since ratification was first proposed in 1973.[12]

Although Langley's arguments were logically compelling as a matter of justice and policy, like other southern states, there was powerful resistance in Arkansas to full citizenship rights for women. We will discuss some of the ways that geography, religion, official historical narratives, economic opportunity, and prevailing cultural assumptions about the separate spheres for men (public and political) and women (private and domestic) undermined women's agency and delayed their opportunities to vote and hold office well into the twentieth century. The vestiges of those assumptions remain impediments to women political candidates and public officials in the twenty-first century. What is revealed is the overwhelming strength of the many Arkansas women who fought for the ability to vote and to serve in public office, despite the resistant cultural and legal barriers. They demanded full rights of citizenship, won a seat at the government table, were eventually accepted and appreciated as policymakers, and finally became an integral part of the Arkansas General Assembly.

## The Geography of Space and Place in a Rural Southern State

Sparse settlement patterns and the regional identity of those who settled the state combined to inhibit the development of a progressive political culture that could empower women and give them a voice in public affairs. Arkansas was admitted to the Union in 1836 as a "slave state" on the southwest frontier, and the majority of the new settlers came from other southern states.[13] By 1860, the enslaved population reached 111,115, approximately 25 percent of the state's total population, and this would have a lasting impact on the power dynamics of race, class, and gender into the twenty-first century.[14]

One reason, of course, is that the women's rights movement developed from women involved in the anti-slavery movement, recognizing that their deprivation of rights was in many ways analogous to that of the enslaved people in the United States.[15] The American Anti-Slavery Society, organized in Philadelphia in 1833, had two thousand chapters by 1840. None of them were in Arkansas, and few southern women spoke out against slavery as did Sarah and Angelina Grimke, who were ostracized and exiled from South Carolina for expressing their views.[16]

The *Arkansas Gazette* made clear that "an Abolitionist is a fanatical intermeddler in the institutions of the South seeking their overthrow by incendiary and nefarious means," but thought, "Hanging an abolitionist now and then, will not in our opinion, do much good, for very few of these zealous fools will risk their precious persons amongst us."[17] One reason for such reluctance was the 1850 Act, sponsored by state senator Napoleon Bonaparte Burrow, a Pine Bluff enslaver and attorney, to prohibit the publication, circulation, or promulgation of abolition doctrines by speaking or writing, subject to one year in jail and a fine of $500.[18]

Patriarchy and white supremacy were enshrined in the Arkansas political and legal structure since before statehood. In 1870, the 77,195 white males of voting age constituted 15.9 percent of the population and historically held 100 percent of the state and county offices. Like all such systems, it operated by design to maintain the status quo; it resisted demands by other citizens, differing in race, gender, or class, for the right to equal participation in the democratic process and equal protection under the law.[19] It would be eighty-six years after statehood before the first women would serve in the Arkansas General Assembly in 1922; it would be an additional fifty-eight years before the first woman of color would be elected to the legislature in 1980.

Arkansas remains a part of the southern political culture that is less supportive of women's rights. While it is often noted that Arkansas was the second southern state to ratify the federal Susan B. Anthony Amendment for women's suffrage, only two others (Texas and Tennessee) did so before the Nineteenth Amendment was added to the United States Constitution in 1920. The other eight states of the old Confederacy finally voted to ratify between 1952 and 1984. Likewise, only three southern states have ratified the Equal Rights Amendment, which would ban discrimination on the basis of sex and guarantee equality for women under the United States Constitution. Texas and Tennessee ratified in 1972 and Virginia in 2020. The Tennessee legislature later voted to rescind its ratification. The Arkansas legislature consistently failed to ratify the Equal Rights Amendment between 1972 and 2019.[20]

Women of Arkansas were barred by law from political participation as voters and candidates, but other aspects of civic participation, such as voluntary association and nonprofit organizations, required convenient contact and communication for effective organization. However, the overwhelmingly rural state of Arkansas lacked the population density that could provide an intellectual and economic infrastructure to foster civic participation.

Moreover, larger communities are generally more tolerant of eccentricity and new ideas and apply less social pressure for conformity than do rural communities.[21] A snapshot from the 1870 census illustrates the particular challenges. The state had a total population of 484,471, with 97.4 percent classified as rural. Little Rock, population 12,380, was the only town with more than 2,500 residents, while only five towns (Helena, Fort Smith, Pine Bluff, Camden, and Hot Springs) had a population exceeding one thousand.[22] Organizing and sustaining a movement to enfranchise women was difficult without a critical mass of women and allies to confront the opposition and change the political culture.

Historically, the state government, dominated by the planter class and rural counties with disproportionate representation in the legislature, had an aversion to taxes on agricultural property and invested almost nothing in public education or other intellectual opportunities. In 1870, there were only six local libraries with a total of 250 books; by contrast, Minnesota with a smaller population had fifteen public libraries with 9,981 volumes, and Rhode Island with less than half the population of Arkansas had ten public libraries with 15,198 volumes. Furthermore, there were fifty-six newspapers in Arkansas with a total circulation of only 29,830, and among the population above ten years of age, 32.7 percent could not read and 39 percent could not write. While broadcast media in the twentieth century and broadband internet service in the twenty-first century would transform the information infrastructure, most Arkansas residents in the years before adoption of the Nineteenth Amendment in 1920 had only limited access to information, ideas, and national policy arguments.

By 1900, four western states had adopted full woman suffrage (Colorado, Utah, Wyoming, Idaho). There are numerous reasons why these states were the first to provide women with the right to vote in all elections, while Arkansas did not for another twenty years, but population distribution was one especially influential contributing factor. Arkansas had a population of 1,311,564 in 1900, greater than the combined population of the four suffrage states. However, Arkansas's population distribution was 8.5 percent urban (towns greater than 2,500) and 91.5 percent rural, compared with the urban populations of 49.3 percent in Colorado, 38.1 percent in Utah, and 28.8 percent in Wyoming.[23] When Arkansas ratified the enfranchisement of women in

1920, the state's urban population had grown to 16.6 percent and had forty-one towns with population above 2,500.

The contrast between urban and rural counties in Arkansas has continued to reflect the difference in recruitment and election of women legislators. Pulaski County, with about 13 percent of the state's population, has elected 22 percent of the women who served in the House and 23 percent of the women senators. The twenty most populous counties account for 104 (71 percent) of the women who have served in the General Assembly. By contrast, the thirty least populous counties have elected only twenty-one women (14 percent), and sixteen of those counties have never elected a woman legislator. There are statistical outliers to the correlation between population and propensity to elect women legislators. White County, ranked ninth in population, and Independence County, ranked twentieth, have never sent a woman to serve in the state legislature. On the other hand, Monroe County, ranked seventy second in population, has elected one senator and three representatives, and Drew County (thirty-eighth) and Bradley County (fifty-ninth) have each elected three women to the House.

## Religion

Arkansas's early and enduring perceptions about women in leadership positions were similar to those held nationally, but Arkansas had few defenders of women in such positions, compared to northern states, and an entrenched culture, including religious, of opposition. Meeting in the Wesley Methodist Chapel at Seneca Falls, the first women's rights convention in the nation adopted a Declaration of Sentiments and Grievances that rebuked the androcentric theology and the religious policies and practices that assigned subservient roles to women in most Christian religious denominations. Specifically, the document charged, "He allows her in Church as well as State, but a subordinate position, claiming Apostolic authority for her exclusion from the ministry, and with some exceptions, from any public participation in the affairs of the Church," and, by doing so, "has usurped the prerogative of Jehovah himself, claiming it as his right to assign for her a sphere of action, when that belongs to her conscience and her God."[24]

Male officials of church and state have proscribed the role of women in religious leadership at least since 1637, when Anne Hutchinson was banished from Massachusetts Bay Colony, in part for leading Bible discussions in her home, "a thing not tolerable nor comely in the sight of God nor fitting for your sex."[25] Hutchinson asserted authority under Paul's Epistle to Titus (Titus 2), but Governor John Winthrop declared it contradicted by Paul's first letter to

Presentation of a League of Women Voters Proclamation in the 1995 legislative session. Representatives Irma Hunter Brown, Dee Bennett, Marian Owens Ingram, Lisa Ferrell, Judy Smith, Charlotte Schexnayder, Carolyn Pollan, Wanda Northcutt Hartz, Jacqueline Roberts, Myra Jones, Josetta Wilkins, Ann Bush, Sue Madison, Becky Lynn, Barbara Horn, and Evelyn Ammons. *Courtesy of Josetta Wilkins.*

the Corinthians. In 1853, Antoinette Louisa Brown Blackwell was the first American woman ordained into ministry by a local Congressional church in Butler, New York, without the approval of the Congregational General Conference. The minister's ordination sermon drew on Galatians 3:28, "There is neither male nor female, for ye are all one in Christ Jesus."[26] Olympia Brown, ordained by the Universalist Church in 1863, was the first woman to be ordained with official denominational authority.[27] Both Blackwell and Brown became active suffragists, as did Anna Howard Shaw, who was granted a local preacher's license in 1873 but was refused ordination rights by the Methodist Episcopal General Conference in 1880.

The influence of organized religion often enforces traditional gender role socialization and represses women's political consciousness by confining them to the domestic sphere.[28] Jean Friedman argues that the pervasive fundamentalist religion was a greater impediment to organizing for women's rights and social reform in the rural South than was the impact of slavery and its aftermath of virulent racism, which would leave Arkansas women decades behind the Northern feminists seeking equality.[29] Nevertheless, as Michael Dougan observed, there were women who resisted and "never accepted the inferior roles evangelical Christianity and conservative rural legislators tried to press down upon women."[30]

For those denominations that insisted the King James Version of the Bible was inerrant and to be literally interpreted, two specific passages in the Pauline Epistles supported the subordination of women and were held to exclude them from ordination as ministers. "Let the woman learn in silence with all subjection. But I suffer not a woman to teach, nor to usurp authority over the man, but to be in silence," wrote Paul in 1 Timothy 2:11–12. In his first epistle to the Christian church at Corinth, Paul said, "Let your women keep silence in the churches: for it is not permitted unto them to speak; but they are commanded to be under obedience as also saith the law. And if they will learn anything, let them ask their husbands at home: for it is a shame for women to speak in the church," 1 Corinthians 14:34–35.

Arkansas women, including the suffragists Lizzie Fyler, Clara McDiarmid, and Fannie Chunn, would challenge the prevailing interpretations and assert that other biblical passages supported a leadership role for women. However, who stands in the pulpit and leads the congregation can be a much more powerful argument than the hermeneutical parsing of isolated passages of scripture. The predominant Methodist and Baptist denominations in Arkansas accounted for 74 percent of the church members in 1870, and neither would continence the ordination of women. Like the state government, they were conservative citadels of patriarchy that enforced "conformity to the notion of white supremacy and to the dominant economic, political, societal, and religious orthodoxy" that denied public leadership roles for women.[31]

James Philip Eagle was a Baptist minister, President of the Arkansas Baptist State Convention for twenty-one years between 1880 and 1903, a four-term state representative, and Speaker of the House in 1885, when he led the Arkansas delegation to the Southern Baptist Convention, meeting in Augusta, Georgia. He would later serve two terms as governor (1889–1892) and three terms as president of the Southern Baptist Convention (1902–1904).[32] Among the seven Arkansas delegates that year were two women.[33] These Arkansas women, by their delegation status in the state, would bring the debate to the national stage at the convention. Mary Kavanaugh Oldham Eagle was president of the Arkansas Woman's Central Committee on Missions and wife of Elder Eagle. Margaretta Adelaide Dudgeon Goldsby "Dottie" Early, a teacher, was corresponding secretary of the Arkansas Woman's Central Committee on Missions, and the wife of Reverend Marshall Daniel Early.[34] While their marriages to prominent leaders of the denomination were essential to their election as Arkansas delegates, Mary Eagle and Dottie Early would soon discover that family connections could not overcome the prevailing gender bias among the other delegates to the Southern Baptist Convention.

When the Arkansas delegation presented the credentials of the delegates, qualified by the requisite contribution of funds as well as election and certification by the Arkansas Baptist State Convention and expecting to be seated as members, objections were immediately raised against recognizing women delegates by two former Confederate chaplains. The opposition was led by Reverend John William Jones of Virginia, "the evangelist of the Lost Cause,"[35] claiming that women never had been and never were intended to be delegates, despite the silence of the Southern Baptist Convention's Constitution.

Reverend Early advocated seating the women, asking, "Shall the Baptist ladies of this country, who have sent more money into the vaults of this Convention than the men, be excluded from a part in its deliberations?" Reverend Eagle argued that Article III of the Southern Baptist Convention Constitution spoke only of the delegates as "members," and the convention should follow its own charter. Reverend James Boardman Hawthorne of Atlanta's First Baptist Church warned against allowing women any role and feared that if admitted as delegates, they could even be president of the Southern Baptist Convention. The debate then turned personal and acrimonious, with aspersions and derision from Hawthorne directed toward Reverend and Mrs. Eagle and loud laughter from the male delegates.[36] After being denied recognition for a point of personal privilege to respond to Hawthorne, Elder Eagle requested leave to withdraw the names of the elected women delegates. The two Arkansas women were in the balcony and not allowed to speak for themselves, although Mary Eagle was a skilled parliamentarian and a forceful debater. The convention then amended the constitution by a vote of 131–42, to specify only "brethren" would be eligible to serve as delegates thereafter.[37]

The Methodist position in 1885 was represented by Dr. Augustus R. Winfield, editor of the *Arkansas Methodist*, who extrapolated from scripture to condemn woman suffrage. "The people of Arkansas are not ready for Woman's Rights or Woman's Suffrage and we hope they never will be," he wrote. "St. Paul . . . thought the women would do better at home. So we think."[38] This sentiment was also espoused by Reverend James Robert Moore, a Methodist minister, in an 1891 commencement address, "Woman's Sphere," at Galloway College in Searcy. He warned the young women, "To be happy, we must fill the place God designed for us and designed us for. To get out of our place is to get out of harmony with God." Moore said that the husband is the head, "because God says so," even though God failed to offer any explanation why. "Some silly folks desire 'obey' left out of the marriage ceremony," he remarked, "but what would it avail since God put it there?"

Moore then moved from marriage to politics, noting that "the heart of the question is reached when we inquire for woman's sphere." He mocked "Woman's Rights," claiming the proponents of this unreasonable party "want to give women the right to do anything that men can do, to be leaders in the professions, the managers of business enterprises, candidates for public office, and therefore the right to vote — and shriek for whatever cause may be nearest their hearts and ambitions. These women want to unsex themselves, to do what God says . . . they cannot, shall not do."

Women who seek to be equal are less appealing to men, Reverend Moore said, and those who earn a decent income outside the home shame their husbands. Perhaps women have been burdened by unfair laws, he admitted but declared, "Chivalry is more reliable than legislation" for feminine, modest, and meek southern ladies. As an example, Moore argued, those states with the most legislation for the rights of women "have the most old maids, grass-widows, and weary wives and mothers standing up in street cars."

"If woman votes, she must also hold office, and if she holds office she must contend for it as men do and against men," Moore warned. He also claimed that if "all women would vote, there would be more bad than good votes cast." Furthermore, appealing to blatant racism as a handmaiden to his sexism, Moore promised that these sweet southern ladies going to the polls would put them on the same level as "some burly son of Ham." Instead, he advised the young graduates that women should be satisfied to have "the right to be a woman, to be what God made her. The right to be loved and comforted, and kept in the blessed bonds of matrimony."[39]

When challenged on his position, Moore doubled down. Sister Hattie Copeland of Rector, a suffragist because she was a prohibitionist, said women elected to the legislature would vote to protect their homes and children, whereas men have failed.[40] Moore replied her argument was a utilitarian one of expediency, and she had failed to show that his position was "contrary to the Word of God."[41]

Reverend Boone Keeton, Methodist minister at Monticello, responded that his position had changed on woman's suffrage, and women should vote if they wanted. He refuted Moore's dire claims about the consequences. "Wherever the right of voting has been granted her, she has used it with as much dignity and discretion as have the men," he observed, "and the predictions, or assertions, that the women if permitted to vote, would unsex themselves, neglect home, besmirch their characters, degrade the ballot, etc., have been refuted by the facts — the irrefutable logic of events."[42]

Reverend Moore shot back that women didn't want to vote. "The great mass of women are content. They are the true, conservative, womanly, motherly women. That there are restless, dissatisfied souls who are angry because they would gladly change things if they could, is freely admitted. And it is obvious that they propose more than the mere investment of women with the ballot," he opined. Then turning from invective, Moore revealed that his real concern was maintaining power. He held up Frances Willard as someone who was advocating that women should be admitted as delegates to the general convention and ordained as ministers. He then attempted to discipline Reverend Keeton for saying that the women's wish for suffrage is more important than the word of God and for "carrying gallantry over into the territory of blasphemy."[43]

The women of the Arkansas Equal Suffrage Association were not buying the arguments of the preachers who were using the Bible as a cudgel against women's rights and suffrage. At their annual convention in 1893, they resolved, "That as the churches are mainly made up and supported by women, we will use our influence against the employment of ministers who are opposed to our movement, and pray the Almighty Father to keep them from our midst."[44]

Former Arkansas bishop Robert Kennon Hargrove, in an 1896 article in the *Methodist Review*, provided an extensive and laudatory review of women's contributions to the work of the Methodist Church, from teaching children to funding parsonages. Nonetheless, he emphasized, "It is not irrelevant here and now to say that the Methodist Episcopal Church, South, makes no place for women in its Conferences as such, and ordains no women to its ministry, and that whoever invites into its pulpit a woman, ordained or unordained by others, offends against the authority and order of this Church, and against the teaching of the holy oracles, as understood and accepted by us."[45] It is remarkable, then, that in November 1896, Sarah Martha Babcock of Searcy, wife and daughter of Methodist ministers, became the first woman even allowed to speak at a Methodist conference in Arkansas, not as an official delegate but when she presented the report of the Woman's Parsonage and Home Mission Society to the White River Conference at Paragould.[46]

In October 1897, Reverend Jesse James Mellard, a young minister at Hatton in Polk County, published a column in the *Arkansas Methodist*, inquiring, "Shall Women Preach?" Calling it a question of "profound importance," he asked, "If God tells her to preach, who can forbid it?" Requiring women "to bury their talent and put their light under a bushel, . . . we turn upon her like a cruel tyrant and with a weapon that pierces like a dagger into her soul, we say, 'Let your women keep silence in the Churches.' And we insist that this had a literal meaning." After anticipating and answering the objections to women's ordination, Mellard concludes, "We know that a house divided against itself cannot stand. O let us be careful in silencing women, we become usurpers in the sight of God. . . . And if God says for her to preach, who can afford to take upon himself the fearful responsibility to say she shall not preach?"[47]

During the next month, his question drew responses from several Methodist ministers who unanimously answered in the negative. Reverend William Jasper Hearon, of Asbury Methodist Church in Little Rock, wrote, "My Brother, some woman suffragist must have hold of you, and your mental equipoise has not yet been recovered." Hearon said none of the women in his flock ever had any interest in becoming ministers, and such an experience would be "rather novel for this Southland of ours." Furthermore, "God has indicated in more ways than one that it was not his purpose for a woman to preach," he contended. "It is evident that God intends the home to be the throne of womanhood, the quieter and gentler duties of life to be her sphere of activity."[48]

Reverend William Pearson Whaley of Benton thought "it is possible for the devil himself to put this question before the Church and the world." He said that women could not preach as well as men, and there was no necessity for women to preach. Whaley asked, "Why should woman preach now? Is man a failure in that position?" After quoting former Arkansas bishops R. K. Hargrove and Oscar Fitzgerald on finding no scriptural support for women ever having been anointed as priests, Whaley concluded, "This being true, we are not justified in licensing a woman to preach, though she have the three marks by which we decide a man is called to preach."[49]

The most emphatic rejection came from Reverend James Robert Moore of Stephens, presiding elder of the Camden District, who had already expounded on his ideas of woman's sphere. "In the face of nearly two thousand years of unbroken acceptance of the belief that God does not call women to the ministry, we should be slow to accept any radical change," he said. "A call to the ministry carries with it the government of the church, the administration of the ordinances, the feeding and overseeing the flock of God. That woman should do these things is plainly repugnant to reason, propriety and common sense, and a perversion of the word of God. It is blasphemy."[50]

The Churches of Christ, the third largest Protestant denomination in Arkansas, also opposed women in the ministry and church governance, as well as their participation in civil government. Without a central state or national governing body over local congregations, David Lipscomb, who became editor of the *Gospel Advocate* in 1866, had more influence on the denomination's churches in the South than any other minister for the next fifty years. He preached a sermon in 1872 at the Christian Church in Little Rock, but his real influence in Arkansas was with the ministers and congregants reading the *Gospel Messenger* and his other publications.[51]

Lipscomb was adamant that the words of Paul against women speaking in church were plain and simple and could not be explained away.[52] Moreover, he held that scripture forbade women speaking publicly on any subject and taking any public role in society, including participation in the Woman's Christian Temperance Society and certainly practicing law or holding public office. First, he said, "In all the historic accounts of the kingdom of God and human government no account is found of affiliation of the pure woman with human governments," and more importantly, "all public teaching and speaking on any subject at any place puts woman out of place, out of her God-given work."[53]

"Woman's work in life is to bear and train children. No higher, holier, more sacred work has ever been committed to human beings. This is her chiefest work in life," Lipscomb contended. "Public speaking in any of the callings of life that demand a constant strain on the mind, a constant anxiety and care in reference to the public affairs of church or state, an excitement of the ambitions for place and power, not only destroy her taste for and cause her to neglect the home and family duties, the duties of wife and mother, but such a strain on the mind destroys the ability for childbearing."[54]

These were the religious environments constructed by male clergy for Arkansas women in the three largest Protestant denominations before they were allowed to vote and hold office. Not only did it restrict the roles women might imagine for themselves in the public sphere, but it also shaped the views of men who were in a position to vote and legislate on suffrage and later consider women candidates for public office.

In the twenty-first century, the Southern Baptist Convention, the Churches of Christ, and the Catholic Church, as well as others, have a majority of women members, and none authorize women to be ministers or priests or to have authority over men in church affairs. The Southern Baptist Convention, at its 1918 meeting in Hot Springs, amended its constitution to allow women to be messengers (delegates), and the Methodist Episcopal Church, South, amended its constitution in 1922 to grant women the right to serve as lay delegates to their General Conference. Individual ministers and congregations can hold diverse views on the role of women, and bold women have made the case for greater participation in church affairs, but the controversy continues to inform the attitudes of a large number of Arkansas citizens and potential women candidates for public office.[55]

Among the four largest religious denominations in twenty-first century

Arkansas, the United Methodist Church is the only one that allows women to serve as ministers and in the highest positions in church leadership; Southern Baptists, Catholics, and Churches of Christ do not. In what was declared by nineteenth century Arkansas Methodist ministers to be blasphemy, the United Methodist Church granted full clergy rights to women in 1956. Reverend Everne Hunter of Batesville, a granddaughter of a nineteenth century circuit-riding Methodist preacher, was in 1964 the first woman minister ordained by the North Arkansas Conference of the United Methodist Church. In 1996, Reverend Janice Riggle Huie became the first female bishop of the Arkansas United Methodist Church.[56]

Nonetheless, differing scriptural interpretations continue to shape the views of different religious traditions about women in the public sphere. The Little Rock Conference of the United Methodist Church passed a resolution in 1977 urging the Arkansas legislature to ratify the federal Equal Rights Amendment, following the 1976 resolution of support by the General Conference stating, "The Gospel makes it clear that Jesus regarded women and men as being of equal worth. Nowhere is it recorded that Jesus treated women in a different manner than he did men." In 1978, the Arkansas Baptist State Convention passed a resolution opposing the ERA, holding that equality of men and women is contrary to the roles and positions ascribed in the Bible and would undermine homes and families.[57]

Despite religious opposition, women from all four of the state's largest religious denominations have chosen to run and have been elected to serve in the Arkansas General Assembly. One indication of the continuing perceived importance of religion to politics in the Arkansas General Assembly is that the religious affiliation of members has been included by the government since the first directories in the 1880s and continuing through the 2022 House and Senate websites with member biographies.[58]

## The Lessons of History

Women have always been an important part of the Arkansas past, and our political, economic, social, and cultural history have all shaped and been shaped by women.[59] However, women have not always been part of the Arkansas story, because women's influence, voices, and contributions to the state's history have been minimized, misinterpreted, or completely ignored in Arkansas history textbooks for generations. And political history always has been particularly resistant to considering the role of gender or the contributions of women.[60]

State-approved Arkansas history textbooks represented the state-sanctioned version of civic truth, and the cultural transmission of these womanless historical narratives in public school textbooks assumed that what women had done was trivial. The message was that men were the important political actors, while women were politically marginal and contributed little beyond the domestic sphere.[61] Such persistent narratives have socially constructed the "appropriate" roles for both women and men and have played a role in legitimizing gendered power relationships that sustain the persistence of patriarchy. As Joan Kelly argued, "It has been a strength of patriarchy in all its historic forms to assimilate itself so perfectly to socioeconomic, political, and cultural structures as to be virtually invisible,"[62] and one contributing factor to its success is to make women invisible in the official historical narrative.

In an Arkansas history textbook published after ratification of the Nineteenth Amendment granting women the right to vote, the author admitted, "The most important chapter of Arkansas history has never been written and probably never will be. It is the part the noble women have played in the making of the state."[63] As a review of Arkansas history textbooks from 1889 to 1966 indicates, that chapter was neither written nor available for generations of Arkansas school children. Although a few women might make cameo appearances, playing roles within ascribed limits, only in the last decades of the twentieth century would the actions and aspirations of Arkansas women become an integral part of the public narrative.

*A History of the State of Arkansas: For the Use of Schools* (1889) by Fay Hempstead was the earliest Arkansas history textbook. The listing of "Distinguished Citizens" were all white males recognized for institutional success in arenas denied by law and social norms to women. No women were mentioned by name in the text, and there was no indication of any meaningful contributions by Arkansas women. There was no explicit discussion of the suffrage movement in Arkansas, but the text listed among fringe political parties between the Prohibition Party and the Greenback Party was the "'Equal Rights Party,' to give the right of voting to women."[64] Otherwise, Arkansas women were nowhere to be found in the official historical narrative.

*The History of Arkansas: A Textbook for Public Schools, High Schools, And Academies* (1898, 1900, 1905), was written by Josiah Shinn, former state superintendent of Public Instruction, who said he "endeavored to be fair and impartial in the treatment of all political questions, and to present every feature of our state growth with accuracy, clearness, and force." The first chapter on "Indian Occupation" mentioned that women made pottery and selected the sites for tents, but they were otherwise unnoticed.

In a discussion of the Whig election campaign of 1840, Shinn reported that fifty unnamed women from Batesville came to Little Rock for a campaign event. The men organizing the event brought a large canoe on wheels for a parade "and filled it with ladies to represent the twenty-six states then comprised in the Union." That they were prevented by law from voting was not mentioned. The section on the 1857 Mountain Meadows Massacre mentioned that Sarah Dunlap, one of the survivors, was later a teacher in the school for the blind.

Women were recognized for their agency in lobbying the legislature to pass an appropriation for the state's participation in the Columbian Exposition at Chicago in 1893. Mentioned by name were Mrs. J. P. Eagle and Mrs. R. A. Edgerton, appointed members of the Board of Lady Managers for Arkansas, and alternates were Mrs. J. H. Rogers (Mrs. Rogers declined the appointment, and Mrs. W. C. Ratcliffe was appointed in her place) and Mrs. W. B. Empie. Ida Joe Brooks was named one of the jurors for exhibits. After a discussion of the size and design of the Arkansas building, Shinn added that "Miss Fannie Scott endeared herself to all visitors, both from Arkansas and from abroad," as hostess and manager of the Arkansas building. In addition, it was mentioned that women were allowed to sign petitions against the sale of alcohol in designated areas.

Although recognized for their roles as potters, campaign props, teachers, petitioners, and fair managers, none of these women or their contributions were included in the comprehensive review for testing at the end of the text. Those questions were for important events like war and politics, finance and transportation, bench and bar, and the answers were always about the contributions and accomplishments of men.[65]

Professor John Hugh Reynolds, in the preface to *Makers of Arkansas History* (1905), was quite clear about his assumptions when he said, "The author wishes to see the children of Arkansas as familiar with the leading men of their own State as they are with the great men of the Nation." The text is the story of ruling white men and includes a section on "Sketches of Prominent Men," but not a single woman is listed in the index. In a later revised edition, the state constitutional amendment for woman suffrage was dispassionately explained, "Under this amendment the poll-tax requirements were retained and were extended to include women, as eligible to vote in conformity with the provisions of the 19th Amendment to the Constitution of the United States."[66] All in all, it totally excluded women from the narrative of Arkansas history, which must have been a disappointment to his wife, Margaret Harwood Reynolds, first vice president of the Faulkner County Suffrage Central Committee.[67]

In 1922, almost immediately after women had won the right to vote and hold office and as they were being elected, the Arkansas History Commission published *The Highlights of Arkansas History*, described as "a handy manual of the really significant facts concerning the history of the State." There was neither a mention of the successful suffrage movement nor of the Woman's Christian Temperance Union, the largest organization of women in Arkansas. Recognition was given to other women's groups, including the United Daughters of the Confederacy, the Daughters of the American Revolution, and the United States Daughters of 1812, all devoted to glorifying the military achievements of men. A nod to the political engagement of women appeared in discussing the Arkansas Federation of Women's Clubs founding in 1897. After mentioning that the early work "was of a literary character" later libraries "and even politics came to be considered, broadening the scope of club work and adding to their usefulness." The section on the pearl industry exceeded the entire portion devoted to women's contributions.[68]

*A School History of Arkansas* (1924), written by Reverend John H. Moore, minister at the First Baptist Church of Pine Bluff and a paid national lecturer for the Ku Klux Klan, went through ten editions as an adopted textbook for Arkansas schools. Controversial for his overtly racist interpretations, his sections on women were more complicated. Pioneer Arkansas women were, he said, "queens of the forest, the spinning wheel, the loom, the plantation, the school, the church, and the home," by which he meant only white women and restricted to that limited domestic sphere. Among the few women mentioned by name were Willie Hocker, who won the DAR contest for a state flag that was adopted by the legislature in 1913, and Eva Ware Barnett, who wrote a state song adopted by the 1917 legislature. He also listed the usual women's civic and patriotic organizations, including the United Daughters of the Confederacy, and noted ratification of the Nineteenth Amendment. "Two women were elected members of the Legislature of 1923," Moore then said, departing from the usual textbook formula but not mentioning them by name. "The women of Arkansas now have the right to vote and hold office, and it is certain that they will stand for everything which pertains to making better homes, better schools, better churches, better citizenship, and for everything else which will help make Arkansas the brightest star in the blue of Old Glory."[69]

The first textbook authored by a woman was *Arkansas Yesterday and Today: A History of Arkansas for Elementary Grades* (1935/1947). Faith Yingling Knoop had been teaching Arkansas history as a fifth-grade substitute teacher in the Little Rock public schools and found the current textbook to be out of date. After moving from Nebraska to Arkansas in 1929, she had traveled the state with her husband and collected information from chambers of commerce for the book, which read like a boosterism pamphlet. While chapters were devoted to such subjects as "Livestock of Arkansas," United States senator Hattie Caraway is the only woman included in the index. Dr. James R. Grant, a geographer and president of Ouachita Baptist College, was added as a co-author. The book was adopted by the state Textbook Commission in 1935 and remained on the approved list for over a dozen years.[70]

*The Arkansas Story* (1955) is another textbook that minimizes the agency of women, yet it does give some attention to their political empowerment. In discussing the accomplishments of Governor Charles Brough, the authors credit the legislature with passing an act that "extended to women the right of suffrage in primary elections," and they note that an act passed during Governor Thomas McRae's administration gave "women the right to hold office." Hattie Caraway is allotted part of a portion of a paragraph as "having the distinction of being the first woman elected to the United States Senate." Caraway's 1932 election is also listed in a six-page appendix of "Outstanding Events," suitable for memorizing for an examination, but nowhere in this textbook or any of the other history textbooks examined was there any mention of Pearl Peden Oldfield and Effiegene Locke Wingo, two Arkansas women who were elected to Congress before Senator Hattie Caraway.

Other events in the appendix, of which women are recognized for their collective contributions, are organizing the Arkansas chapter of the Daughters of the American Revolution in 1893 and the Arkansas Federation of Women's Clubs in 1897. Ratification of the Nineteenth Amendment in 1919 is listed, as is legislation creating a girls' industrial school (reformatory for white girls) in 1917 and the State Farm for Women (penitentiary for white adult women).[71]

*Our Arkansas* (1958) contained no mention of the woman suffrage campaigns, ratification of the Nineteenth Amendment granting women the right to vote, or women's participation in politics, with the exception of United States senator Hattie Caraway, not regarding her election or contributions but noting her political defeat in 1944. Among the other women mentioned by name was Isabella DaVila (Isabel de Bobadilla), who was never in Arkansas but merited six mentions as the wife of the conquistador Hernando de Soto. In addition, the female exemplars mentioned by name included three women opera singers, five women painters, six women writers, and the outlaw Belle Starr, who never lived in Arkansas.[72]

*Historic Arkansas* (1966), published and adopted 130 years after statehood, discussed the woman suffrage movement on a single page and devoted another page to the contributions of women's organizations, including the Arkansas Federation of Women's Clubs, the Business and Professional Women's Clubs, and various women's patriotic organizations. The women meriting mention by name and the roles they represented were the outlaw Belle Starr, local color author Octavia Thanet, Miss America pageant winner Donna Axum, the state poet laureate Rosa Marinoni, and opera singers Mary Lewis and Mary McCormic. Significantly, this was the first textbook to mention the contributions of a Black woman, the politically active Daisy Bates, who was an advocate for working class labor rights, equal rights regardless of race, and the end of segregation.[73]

Fred Arthur Bailey has discussed the treatment of race and class in other Arkansas history textbooks and elucidated the influence of the Arkansas United Daughters of the Confederacy in critiquing, revising, and approving state adopted history texts during the first half of the twentieth century.[74] Not unrelated, the imposition of the Lost Cause mythology in Arkansas textbooks also embedded perceptions about the appropriate role of women and the cult of true (southern, white, Christian) womanhood.[75]

The state's history was also commemorated and expressed in public monuments, including four that were given places of honor at the state and national capitols. The Confederate Soldiers Monument (1905) and the Monument to Confederate Women (1913) were both funded primarily by legislative appropriations and are located on the Arkansas capitol lawn in Little Rock. The first honors the white men who waged war against the United States in defense of slavery or "the Southern way of life." The second honors white women who supported the Confederacy and, according to the inscription, "whose patriotism will teach their sons to emulate the deeds of their sires."[76] The statues of two white men have represented Arkansas in National Statuary Hall for more than a century. Uriah M. Rose, a founder and president of both the Arkansas and American Bar Associations, was honored for his eminence in a profession that barred women when his statue was placed in 1915. The other was of James P. Clarke (1917), a former governor and United States senator, who was elected before women could vote and was an opponent of woman's suffrage.

We should continue to ask and consider what aspects of Arkansas history are extolled and which facets are obscured or absent from popular renditions of the state's political narrative. What are the historical narratives we teach the next generation, and have they distorted and systematically denied the possibility that women can be competent political leaders? What are the practical consequences of ignoring the suffrage narrative, the political contributions, and the other aspirations of women in popular memory? How can women find a useable past that affirms their role in public affairs? How did these historical narratives shape the attitudes of the men and women who taught the classes and the boys and girls who studied them?

The fact that influential women and their stories were omitted from our collective memory sent a message to both boys and girls that the contributions of women don't matter, and that stereotype presented obstacles for women seeking public office.

## Economic Opportunity

The women who met at Seneca Falls in 1848 were well aware of their exclusion, by law and practice, from participating in and benefiting from the economic life of the nation. Specifically, they declared, "He has taken from her all right in property, even to the wages she earns. . . . He has monopolized nearly all the profitable employments, and from those she is permitted to follow, she receives but a scanty remuneration. He closes against her all the avenues to wealth and distinction, which he considers most honorable to himself. As a teacher of theology, medicine, or law, she is not known." In consequence of those restrictions, they resolved that "the speedy success of our cause depends upon the zealous and untiring efforts of both men and women . . . for the securing to woman an equal participation with men in the various trades, professions, and commerce."[77]

The prevailing economic and gender systems combined to limit women's full participation in society, leaving them with less personal autonomy, fewer resources, and little influence over decisions that shaped their lives and affected their pursuit of happiness. Arkansas married women often found themselves without legal personhood and assigned to a domestic sphere where the demands of "unwaged and unacknowledged work" prevented them from participating in the commercial economy dominated by men.[78] Unmarried women faced different but difficult obstacles. As one contemporary observer noted, "The narrow means and necessarily contracted habits of the woman who remained unmarried made her an object of silent contempt, not from any fault of her own, but because outside of wedded life and the interests of rearing a family there was no industry that offered a worthy compensation for her work."[79]

Men, on the other hand, had many options for independence and advancement. The church and the military were both open to Arkansas men, as were positions in banking and business, medicine and higher education, the bench and bar, and, of course, public offices. Legal restraints and social norms prevented women from pursuing those rewarding careers.[80] Moreover, these professional disabilities and exclusions prevented women from the experiences that were seen as qualifying citizens to hold public office and from developing the networks of influence necessary for election.

The US census of 1870 presents a snapshot of the economic opportunities available to Arkansas women at that time. Of the 166,543 women over ten years of age, only 9.5 percent were employed in income-earning jobs, and the other 90 percent were working in the household and homemaking domestic sphere in nonwage jobs. Of those women who were earning wages, 89 percent of those were either agricultural labor or domestic servants. Among the other 1,719 employed women workers were 140 nurses, 266 teachers, and 907 laundresses. There were no women physicians, dentists, pharmacists, nor attorneys. None.

### BUSINESSWOMEN

Few women in Arkansas were engaged in the commercial sector as proprietors.[81] There were some exceptions, and business success often reflected or led to interest in political and public affairs.[82] Clara Alma Cox McDiarmid (1847–1899), who had been a schoolteacher in Kansas, married Major George W. McDiarmid, a Union officer stationed in Little Rock, when she was eighteen. Her husband would practice law, be elected Pulaski County clerk, and serve as chairman of the Arkansas Republican Party, and her father was appointed receiver for the US Land Office in Little Rock. McDiarmid soon began selling and developing real estate, and she was quite successful. When she built a commercial building on Markham Street across from the state capitol in 1889, she offered two rooms on the second floor for offices of the Arkansas Equal Suffrage Association, of which she was president, and the Woman's Christian Temperance Union, of which she was a state officer. McDiarmid was also a frequent contributor on suffrage issues in the columns of the *Woman's Journal* and the *Woman's Chronicle*.[83]

McDiarmid has often been referred to as having been an attorney, but she was never admitted to the bar. Contemporary accounts suggest she attended law lectures at the University of Michigan from 1889 to 1890 while her son was an undergraduate there, and her son also lived in her home while attending Arkansas Law School (1893–1895).[84] Undaunted by being statutorily denied the opportunity to practice law, McDiarmid presented a paper on "The Law and the Lady" at a suffrage meeting in Little Rock, and she posted a sign outside her business office advertising "legal services rendered to any woman free of charge."[85]

Mary Belle Mizell Murrell (1857–1954), the wife of a Little Rock physician, was twenty-two when she was elected engrossing and enrolling clerk for the Arkansas Senate in 1879. The following year she organized the Ladies Building Association, recruited a board of local businessmen, and served as secretary. She managed the savings and loan for ten years. Said to be the only woman in the nation to have successfully established a building society, she

Clara Cox McDiarmid.
*Courtesy of Carrie Chapman Catt Papers,*
*Bryn Mawr College Special Collections.*

was invited to address the World Congress of Building Associations at the Columbian Exposition on "Woman's Place in the Building Association."[86]

Rhoda Philena Munger (1843–1915) had already been active in the temperance and suffrage movements in Michigan and a contributor to the *Woman's Journal* before she moved to Little Rock and opened her news agency at 324 Main Street, selling newspapers, books, and stationery. In 1877, she presented two public lectures on "Woman Suffrage" at the Christian Church and Centennial Methodist Church, also addressing equal pay for women teachers and criticizing the Arkansas Legislature. She continued to publish items in the *Woman's Journal* on suffrage, domestic violence, and custody decisions that she thought wrongfully decided because the father could vote for the judge and the mother could not. Munger represented Arkansas on the American Woman Suffrage Association Executive Committee, was treasurer of the Ladies Benevolent Association, opened a circulating library in 1879, and collected books for a prison library. She briefly operated a store in Conway in 1880, then moved to Kansas, where she taught school, ran as a Prohibition Party candidate for city council and county superintendent, and was able to exercise full suffrage after 1912.

## EDUCATORS

Arkansas women found it much more difficult to enter the professions.[87] Indicative of the prevailing dismissiveness of their aspirations, a column in the *Fayetteville Weekly Democrat*, purporting to be humor, in 1869 wrote, "An editor, alluding to the demand for female suffrage, female doctors, and female clergymen, remarks that another want presents itself—that of female women."[88] While there were 2,558 women public school teachers by 1900, the average monthly salary for women teachers was $35.52 compared with $49.22 for men.[89] Few were in administrative positions, none served on school boards, and none could even vote in school elections. Women were also found on the faculty of colleges and the state university. The emergence of women in professional roles was personally rewarding for those who were able to overcome the barriers facing women, and their presence in the public sphere served to undermine the false assumptions about their abilities and open other avenues for their full participation in society.

### HEALTH PROFESSIONS

G. Neill Hart, owner of Hart's Drug Store in Pine Bluff, presented a paper on "Women in Pharmacy," advocating the profession of pharmacy for women, at the 1893 convention of the Arkansas Association of Pharmacists. In 1895, Belle Hart, his sister and a student at Galloway College, was admitted to membership in the association.[90] Mary Fein, who became the Association's stenographer in 1897, was enrolled as a member in 1905 and served for many years as secretary-treasurer. She was a suffragist and later was the second woman Governor McRae appointed as a notary public, a candidate for state representative in 1932, and an officer in the Arkansas Democratic Women.

In 1903, only one woman was among the twenty-four applicants for the state pharmacy examination, rare enough for the newspapers to remark that there were less than a half-dozen female registered pharmacists in the state. In 1904, Marie Lizzie Squires Cole (1861–1932) of Fort Smith became a registered pharmacist, and Mattie Crenshaw Winston Anderson (1866–1934) of Dermott became a member of the Arkansas Association of Pharmacists. Anderson's daughter was married to Harvey Parnell, who as governor (1928–1933) appointed Hattie Caraway to the United States Senate in 1931.[91] Maud Dunlap Pearce Duncan (1873–1958) of Winslow became a registered pharmacist in 1906 and operated the M. D. Pearce Drug Store. She was later editor of the *Winslow American*, where she frequently editorialized for woman's suffrage. In 1925, Duncan was elected mayor of Winslow for two terms with a full council of women.[92]

Published in 1922, Dallas T. Herndon's *Centennial History of Arkansas* mentioned not a single woman in the chapters on "Bench and Bar of Arkansas" or "The Medical Profession."[93] Although women were no longer prohibited from practicing those professions in 1922, Herndon's omission of women in his book was indicative of how few women had been admitted to those professions, as well as how little attention was paid to their contributions and achievements. Women were statutorily excluded from the legal profession in Arkansas until 1917, much later than most other states. Female medical professionals encountered fewer restrictions but still faced opposition from continuing social stigma, professional associations dominated by men, and medical school admissions committees.[94]

Dr. Fannie Matthews Cooper (1869–1912) was the only female graduate in the class of 1891 at the Ohio College of Dental Surgery, affiliated with the University of Cincinnati. She moved to Little Rock and joined her husband, Helena native Dr. Thomas Y. Cooper, in a practice at 601 Main Street. Dr. Cooper quickly moved in suffrage circles, joining with the writer Lura Brown and *Woman's Chronicle* associate editor Mary Burt Brooks to assist Clara McDiarmid in hosting a reception for Dr. Ida Joe Brooks, a recent graduate of the Boston University School of Medicine. Like McDiarmid, Cooper was also active in the Christian Church and the Educational Aid Society. Dr. Cooper presented a well-received paper on "Women in Dentistry" at the 1895 Atlanta Exposition. After twelve years of practice in Little Rock, she was still said to be "the only lady dentist in the Southwest."[95]

Elizabeth Blackwell graduated from New York's Geneva Medical College in 1849, becoming the first woman in America to earn the MD degree. The following year, two women were admitted to the Medical Department of the Memphis Institute, an institution that regularly advertised in Arkansas newspapers, including the *Washington Telegraph*. In reprinting a sardonic editorial from the *Evansville Journal*, William Etter, editor of the *Washington Telegraph*, removed the supportive comments and focused on complaints that husbands would be vexed by having to care for children while their doctor wives were making house calls and the assumption that young men would not "spark any she doctor," being so repulsed by thoughts of what their lovers might have touched or seen while treating patients. "Bah! it is perfectly disgusting! Then to call on your love, and find that she has just gone to minister to diseased flesh, and not for philanthropic motives, but for filthy lucre."[96] The objection to women physicians was not that they were unqualified but that their professional fulfilment and earned income would make them less romantically desirable and would inconvenience their husbands.

Arkansas women had always been the primary caregivers and more concerned with the illness of family and friends.[97] The first woman physician in Arkansas was Helena Mellia Maxwell Cady (1849–1929). Her family was living in Pulaski County when she married Henry Cady in 1870. After having six children, she enrolled in the Homeopathic School of Physicians and

Surgeons at St. Louis, graduated in 1882, and opened her practice in Little Rock at 502 Main Street. She was certified as an approved MD by the Pulaski County Clerk in May 1882. In addition to her office practice, Dr. Cady volunteered at the Free Dispensary operated under the auspices of the Ladies Homeopathic Aid Society, giving her attention to the diseases of women and children. During the winter of 1883–1884, she spent several months in Boston for additional study of women's health issues.[98] Lizzie Fyler reported in 1885 that Cady had "a large and successful practice, which will compare favorably with that of any physician in the State." In addition to a successful medical practice and raising a family, Dr. Cady hosted meetings in her home of the Quapaw Chautauqua Literary and Scientific Circle and the meeting of the King's Daughters that organized the Little Rock Woman's Exchange.[99]

Dr. Cady moved to Louisville, Kentucky, in 1891, where she resumed her practice, presented papers at state medical society meetings, and was an active member of the Episcopal Church, King's Daughters, the Woman's Christian Temperance Union, the Woman Suffrage Association of Louisville, and president of a circle of the Ladies of the Grand Army of the Republic.[100] She returned to Little Rock in 1903 and later moved to Texarkana, where she continued her practice.

While Dr. Cady demonstrated that women could successfully practice medicine in Arkansas, admission of women to the University of Arkansas Medical Department was still an impediment. Almost forty years after Dr. Elizabeth Blackwell graduated from medical school in New York, Ida Josephine Brooks (1853–1939) was denied admission to the University of Arkansas Medical Department in 1887 because of her gender. Brooks held undergraduate and graduate degrees and had an impressive career in teaching in the Little Rock Public Schools and at Little Rock University, and there was no argument that she was not otherwise qualified. She was admitted to the Boston University School of Medicine, receiving her MD degree in 1891 and completing a residency in psychiatry at the Massachusetts Mental Hospital in Middleborough. After returning to Arkansas in 1906, she had a private practice in Little Rock. After being denied admission to the Arkansas Medical Society, she organized the Women's Medical Club in 1913. Dr. Brooks became the first female faculty member at the University of Arkansas Medical Department in 1915 and held the rank of associate professor of psychiatry. She had been active in the suffrage movement since the 1880s in Arkansas and Massachusetts, and she was the Republican nominee for State Superintendent of Education in 1920, but she was not allowed to run because she was a woman.[101]

The first woman admitted and the first female graduate of the Medical Department of the University of Arkansas was Ann Adelia Annette Ryerse

Dr. Helena Maxwell Cady.
Willard & Livermore, *American Women*, 1897.

Cutting Shoppach (1859–1949). She was a widow with two children in Michigan when she married James Henry Shoppach, a widower with six children, and moved to Little Rock in 1896. Her husband was a Confederate veteran and had held various political positions, including Saline County clerk; 1868 Constitutional Convention delegate; House journal clerk; and state representative 1887–1888, later serving as a clerk in the State Treasurer's Office and as deputy Pulaski circuit clerk. After the admissions committee changed the rules, Annie Schoppach was admitted to medical school in 1897 with academic credentials far less impressive than Dr. Ida Brooks and graduated in 1901. She maintained a successful clinic and maternity hospital at her home at 1401 State Street, sharing a practice with her son, Dr. Herwald Cutting, who would later marry the daughter of suffrage leader Bernie Babcock.[102]

## LADY LAWYERS

While Arabella Babb Mansfield, licensed by the Iowa bar in 1869, became the first female attorney in the United States, it would be almost fifty years before the first woman was admitted to the Arkansas bar. In Illinois, Myra Bradwell had been editor of the *Chicago Legal News*, and she passed the state bar examination, yet Illinois refused to grant her admission to the bar. She appealed the state court decision to the United States Supreme Court, which ruled against her 8–1 in 1873.

The court ruled that Bradwell's desire to practice law was not a fundamental constitutional right. A concurring opinion by Justice Joseph Bradley went much further, holding that both law and nature "recognized a wide difference in the respective spheres and destinies of man and woman," and the "proper timidity and delicacy which belongs to the female sex evidently unfits it for many of the occupations of civil life." Beyond that, Bradley said the family structure was "founded in the divine ordinance," and women properly belong and function only in the domestic sphere, because "the family institution is repugnant to the idea of a woman adopting a distinct and independent career from that of her husband." The unholy idea of women practicing law was, in his mind, also a transgression of a higher law that declared the "paramount destiny and mission of woman are to fulfil the noble and benign offices of wife and mother. This is the law of the Creator."[103]

While Arkansas law since 1837 had been gender neutral regarding a license to practice law, the Arkansas legislature intentionally denied women the opportunity to pursue a legal career. The same year the *Bradwell* decision came down from the Supreme Court, Representative Christopher Thrower, an attorney from Camden, introduced legislation to exclude women and limit admission only to *male* citizens, and it became Act 88 of 1873.[104]

Speaking to the Arkansas Bar Association in 1883, Arkansas Supreme Court associate justice William Wright Smith articulated the reasons that admission to the bar was essential for political power, acknowledging that "lawyers constitute an active and influential class, [who] have more to do with shaping the destinies of this country than any other class in the community." Women who sought to become involved in the public sphere were well aware of this and did not need to follow his suggestion to "consult the rosters of our Presidents and their Cabinets, our Senators and Representatives in Congress, our Governors and Legislatures, with a view to ascertain of what calling our rulers have been." Women arguing for the right to vote and shape public policy already knew that "the bar is the avenue to political distinction."[105] Moreover, they sought to remove the barriers that prevented them from drafting, sponsoring, enacting, and interpreting laws that advanced policies affecting women.

After the national publicity about Belva Lockwood's long fight and eventual admission to practice before the United States Supreme Court in 1879, Arkansas women expressed interest in a legal career.[106] Eliza Ada "Lizzie" Dorman Fyler (1850–1885), a native of Massachusetts and a graduate of Ripon College, moved from Kansas City to Eureka Springs in 1880. Inspired by a visit from attorney and suffragist Phoebe Couzins, Fyler organized the Arkansas Woman Suffrage Association and became interested in practicing law. After reading law in Eureka Springs, she submitted an application in 1882 to join the Arkansas Bar Association. The Executive Committee informed her that the association's constitution requiring members to have been admitted to the Arkansas bar prohibited her membership, but she was invited by Associate Justice John Rogers Eakin to attend the next annual meeting.[107] She drafted legislation to amend the statute and allow women to be admitted to practice but was unable to find a legislative sponsor in the 1883 General Assembly.[108] Fourth Circuit judge John Middleton Pittman of Fayetteville, on his own motion, had allowed her to assist clients in trying cases in Carroll County with "all the privileges of an attorney." Judge Pittman was aware of her interest in law, her abilities, and her favorable reputation with the local lawyers, and it is likely as a young man he was acquainted with her aunt, Sarah Northrup Ridge, who had lived in Fayetteville.[109] Fyler's address at the 1884 National Woman Suffrage Association convention in Washington, DC, was a well-received discussion of *Gantt's Digest* of Arkansas laws that affected women and her own experience practicing law.[110] Her death at age thirty-five was mourned in the local, state, and national press.

Amanda Rivers Brown (1857–1924), the daughter of Union County judge Henry Epps Brown, was a schoolteacher who had read law with her father and been elected House enrolling clerk in 1883. In 1885, she sought admission to the bar from circuit judge Benjamin Franklin Askew, who denied her admission because she was a woman and "the organic law of the land prohibited women from thus speaking in public."[111] Brown roundly criticized Judge Askew's decision in a letter to the *El Dorado Eagle*, arguing that he had misconstrued the statute and that "in other states, and in the United States courts in Washington City, females are permitted to practice as attorneys."[112] The controversy was then taken up in the state press in a lively debate among editors.

The *Arkansas Methodist* called it "a strange case." The editor, Reverend August R. Winfield, said, "We think the judge was exactly right and acted in accordance with the law. Stick to teaching, ladies." In the next issue, Winfield referenced the writings of St. Paul and said he agreed that "the women would do better at home."[113] In response, a front-page editorial in the *Arkansas Democrat* replied, "When the cruel intolerance which would confine women to the school room and the nursery is exposed, the only reply is that woman suffrage and woman's rights are contrary to the teachings of St. Paul." Instead, the *Democrat* editor said he "would open wide the avenues of honorable employment to all women. The irreligion, bigotry and superstition of the world have kept them enslaved long enough. Man's inhumanity to man is sad to contemplate, but his inhumanity to woman is a thousand-fold more oppressive. We talk glibly about liberty and equality, the right of all human beings to the pursuit of happiness, and yet, with strange inconsistency, we cut off from one-half of the world nearly all the avenues by which happiness is to be attained."[114] Likewise, the *Quitman Light* added, "If a woman would prefer to practice law rather than to sew on patches or teach school, let her do so by all means. We have no right to prevent any woman from any honorable occupation that her desires may lead her to select, and if there is a law that admits of such a distinction as the above case would imply, it is not founded upon justice."[115]

The powerful arguments against denying women the right to practice law in Arkansas were of no avail with the legislature, and it would be more than three decades before the statute was changed and women were admitted to the bar. Kate Delaney Cleveland (1863–1900), a Judsonia teacher and the wife of an attorney, gained status as a claims agent licensed to handle cases for disabled veterans and widows of service members before the Bureau of Pensions within the US Department of the Interior. The *Arkansas Democrat* called her "the only lady pension lawyer in the state and a prominent notary public," but she was not an attorney.[116] As an agent and solicitor for claimants, she did not have to have formal legal training but had to have a certificate authenticated by a federal judge attesting to her character, reputation, and ability to provide valuable representation to clients in gathering evidence, and preparing documents.

Erle Rutherford Chambers (1875–1941) worked in a law office for several years, then attended the Arkansas Law School, where she made her first speech for woman suffrage at the law school's Goar Lyceum. While she was a student, the Goar Lyceum also hosted a debate on "Shall Women Be Allowed to Practice Law in the State of Arkansas," which was decided in the negative. Chambers became the first woman graduate of the law school and ranked first in the graduating class of 1912. All of the male graduates in her class were granted automatic admission to the bar, an opportunity that she was denied. Chambers spent an additional year of study at the University of Chicago Law School but declined a position with a law firm in Milwaukee. Instead, she was persuaded by her friend, Adolphine Fletcher Terry, to return to Arkansas and work with the Pulaski County Juvenile Court. She was an active suffragist and later a charter member of the Arkansas League of Women Voters. Chambers never practiced law, although she enacted laws as a member of the House of Representatives from 1923 to 1926.[117]

Other prominent Arkansas suffragists also earned law degrees and used their knowledge to shape legislation and elections, including Laura "Lollie" Davis Fitzhugh (1873–1948), who inherited and managed her family's six-square-mile cotton plantation in Woodruff County and was president of the Fitzhugh-Snapp Mercantile and Fitzhugh Gin Company. She was a graduate of Ward Seminary in Nashville, had a master's degree from Vanderbilt, earned a law degree from Northwestern, and did additional coursework at the University of Chicago and the Sorbonne, University of Paris. She was president of the Augusta Political Equality League, vice president of the Arkansas Woman Suffrage Association, and served with Minnie Rutherford Fuller on the AFWC Legislative Committee. Her aunt, Sallie Calvert Davis, a schoolteacher in St. Francis County and later vice president of the Arizona Territorial Suffrage Association, was the mother of United States Senator Carl Hayden. Fitzhugh was elected to the Augusta City Council and was a candidate for the Arkansas House in 1926. She was especially effective in urging the appointment of Hattie Caraway to the United States Senate in 1931 and securing her election to the Senate in 1932. Fitzhugh served as president of the Arkansas Democratic Women, a delegate to the Democratic National Convention, and the first female vice chair of the Arkansas Democratic Central Committee."[118]

Another rural suffragist was Minnie Ursula Oliver Scott Rutherford Fuller (1868–1946) of Magazine, a graduate of Sullins College, a Methodist women's school in Virginia, and who did graduate and law study at the University of Chicago, the University of Leipzig, Harvard University, and the University of California. She was president of the Arkansas WCTU, a founder of the Political Equality League, vice president of the Arkansas Woman Suffrage Association, legislative chair of the Arkansas Federation of Women's Clubs, and a frequent legislative lobbyist on behalf of suffrage and other issues.[119]

Fuller was an officer in the Southwestern Women's Bar Association, and she drafted legislation in 1911 allowing women to be admitted to the bar. Senator Charles Jacobson of Little Rock introduced it as Senate Bill 121, arguing that the state had outgrown the maudlin sentiments that warp our understanding of women's rights and that they should be able to hold office as well as practice law. Senator Alfred C. Martin of Conway agreed that women were as entitled to practice law as they were to preach, teach, and practice medicine. Others speaking in support of the bill were Senators John H. Keel of Newport, Gus Clerget of Morrilton, and Elmo M. Carl-Lee of Augusta, who would later serve on the advisory board of the Augusta Political Equality Board at the invitation of Laura Davis Fitzhugh. The leading opponents were Texarkana lawyer Emile Friedell, who moved to postpone it indefinitely and argued that "we have not yet reached the point when women should be given the right to practice law, as it would lower her in the esteem of man who is her natural protector." Senators James T. Robertson of Marianna also spoke against the bill, as did Senator Webb Covington, a lawyer and coal operator from Johnson County, who argued that women should be supported by their husbands. "If any man does not support his wife, so that she wants to practice law," he said, he would "get her a divorce without cost, so she could marry someone else" who would support her.[120] The bill did not pass.

In 1913, Senator Thomas C. White of Pine Bluff secured passage of Senate Bill 154, allowing women to practice law, by a vote of 14–12. Earlier in the day, Senator Carl-Lee had passed a resolution for a proposed constitutional amendment for woman suffrage by a vote of 19–9.[121] However, neither were enacted by the House. The 1915 legislative session again had the opportunity to change the law and allow women the right to practice law. Freshman representative Oscar E. Ellis, a twenty-two-year-old lawyer from Salem, introduced a House bill to that effect, but it was referred to the House Judiciary Committee, chaired by Representative Sam Rorex, and was reported out with a recommendation that it do not pass.[122] In many ways, the effort to pass legislation for women to be admitted to the bar tracked the struggle for securing the right to vote from 1911 to 1917.

A Perry County schoolteacher wrote a thoughtful article for the *Arkansas Gazette* in 1916, expounding on the rationale for woman suffrage and confirming that women want the vote. "Maybe they have other wants," she added, "for instance: That women may practice law in Arkansas. That a woman may be a notary public. In another state, a businesswoman of my acquaintance was a capable notary public for five years. On crossing the state line of Arkansas, she mysteriously became incapacitated for any such office."[123]

During the 1917 legislative session that also approved legislation granting women the right to vote in party primary elections, Senator George Franklin Brown, an attorney from Rison, introduced Senate Bill 52, again attempting to authorize women to practice law. It passed the Senate with only one dissenting vote, that of Senator Ivison Cleveland Burgess of Russellville. The *Malvern Record* was among the newspapers endorsing the legislation, holding that women would make good lawyers, and many of them were smarter than some men they know, so "let 'em practice law or . . . anything they want to." Minnie Rutherford Fuller issued a call for women to contact House judiciary chairman Ben McFerrin of Newton County. She reiterated the arguments of expediency regarding the contributions of women attorneys in juvenile courts, but she closed with an appeal to "fundamental justice, which would suggest to any fair-minded person that any human has the right to engage in any honest occupation as a means of livelihood for which that person is fitted."

The House Judiciary Committee reported out the bill with a do pass recommendation, and it passed the House with little discussion by a vote of 44–18. Representative E. Newton Ellis, an attorney from Pocahontas who had opposed the suffrage bill, added his support with a tone of resignation, "You have let the women vote, and you might as well let them practice law."[124] Act 362 of 1917, signed by Governor Charles Brough, authorized women to practice law in Arkansas, and the first women were admitted to the Arkansas bar in 1918.

## Subverting the Spheres

The restrictions on women's rights in nineteenth century Arkansas—religious, economic, legal, and political—were created and reinforced by the dominant social and cultural mores of the period. The overarching source of repression was the widely accepted notion of separate spheres for men and women as extrapolated by men from the Bible and repackaged as conventional wisdom.[125]

The concept permeated the publications and the thinking of the period. Articulated by Baltimore minister George Burnap in his 1841 *Lectures on the Sphere and Duties of Woman*, "it was intended by God that they should move in different spheres," and that God "knew the sphere in which each of them was designed to act." For women, he said, their sphere was "the care of home, the preparation of food, the making of clothing, the nursing and education of children." Assuming that all women should exult in these prescribed roles, Burnap declared, "We now see woman in that sphere for which she was originally intended, and which she is so exactly fitted to adorn and bless, as the wife, the mistress of a home, the solace, the aid, and the counsellor of that One, for whose sake alone the world is of any consequence to her."[126] Men, so adored and pampered, would attend to the public sphere of politics, pulpit, and commerce.

Maintaining the woman's place in her sphere relied not on legal penalties but employed the traditional social mechanisms. In a study of antebellum women's magazines, religious literature, and other popular publications, Barbara Welter identified a zeitgeist that she labeled, the cult of true womanhood, with "four cardinal virtues—piety, purity, submissiveness and domesticity." Anyone who might question or challenge these central tenets or resist the prescribed role for the virtuous woman would be publicly and immediately shunned from polite society as "an enemy of God, of civilization and of the Republic."[127] These omnipresent frames were not descriptive of reality but were socially constructed and propagated by men as a reaction to social changes that threatened the privileges of patriarchy.

Even prominent women sometimes appeared to be complicit in reinforcing their own exclusion from the public sphere. For example, the erudite Hannah Mather Crocker, who was familiar with the writings of Mary Wollstonecraft, in 1818 published *Observations on the Real Rights of Women*. Botting and Houser contend that Crocker sought to "normatively defend and gently extend American women's ongoing informal political participation in the post-revolutionary era and challenged the separate spheres discourse that aimed to restrict it."[128] Nonetheless, Crocker held that "it would be improper, and physically very incorrect, for the female character to claim the statesman's birth or ascend the rostrum to gain the loud applause of men, although their powers of industry may be equal to the task." Furthermore, Crocker said, "it would be morally wrong and physically imprudent for any woman to attempt pleading at the bar of justice as no law can give her the right of deviating from the strictest rules of rectitude and decorum."[129]

In Arkansas and the Southern states that had seceded and lost the Civil War to preserve chattel slavery, the myth of the lost cause that was socially constructed by the United Daughters of the Confederacy was equally as powerful in reinforcing the separate spheres ideology by propagating a false narrative about the Old South. The myth of moonlight and magnolias was invented in the last half of the nineteenth century to promote white supremacy, excuse lynching and disenfranchisement of Black Americans, and project a vision of white womanhood as the southern belle on a plantation pedestal maintaining the mansions with social graces. The reality of antebellum life for Arkansas women was quite different. The quarter of women who were enslaved, bought, forced to work the fields, abused, and often involuntarily separated from their children, had no place in the myth, nor did those white women living on hardscrabble farms in the hills and timberlands.[130]

The myth did not even reflect reality for the few white women of property and standing. Matilda Nowland Fulton, the wife of territorial secretary, governor, and United States senator William S. Fulton and the mistress of Rosewood Plantation, was often at home alone and running the farm on her own. While her husband was in Washington on official business during the winter of 1832, she butchered nine hogs two days before giving birth to her sixth child.[131] Disregarding facts, the collective effort to justify the state's participation in the Civil War, glorify those who fought for the Confederacy, and venerate the women on the home front brooked no dissent from the myth of the lost cause.

It was within this intellectual environment that Arkansas women struggled to assert their individual agency and assume public positions of responsibility, and they did so creatively with limited resources and options for changing the conversation. As they began to engage public policy questions, insist on their rights, and demand the ballot to secure them, women in the late nineteenth century found helpful male allies but also faced opposition from preachers and politicians who "yearned nostalgically for the mythical separation of spheres that had served to keep women from explicitly challenging men in the public realm."[132] Although they overcame many of the barriers they faced, entered the public sphere, secured the franchise, and finally saw women elected to the Arkansas legislature, the same separate spheres ideology, gender stereotypes, and role-congruity prejudice still persist to some degree for women in politics today.[133]

In the five decades between Miles Langley's opening salvo in 1868 and the election of the first women to the legislature in 1922, Arkansas women subverted the separate sphere in a number of ways. They formed and participated in organizations; they spoke and invited speakers; they created their own publications and gained access to the pages of major newspapers; they formed beneficial relationships with men in the power structure; and they directly lobbied the legislature on issues of importance to women and their families.

Largely because women in early Arkansas depended on leveraging the social and political power of their families, and those wielding such power were white men, the story is one of white, middle-class women seeking political equality for themselves. This telling employs standpoint theory, an epistemically privileged approach that foregrounds the role of women without ignoring the role of men.[134] However, this viewpoint also operated to blind these privileged white women fighting for gender equality to the intersectional experience that marginalized the perspective of race and class and impaired the agency of other women. The experiences of Black American and poor white women are not unimportant, but their contributions were ignored. Their voices and efficacy in gaining political agency were limited even further by race and class discrimination with financial barriers, educational limitations, poll taxes, intimidation, white primaries, assorted Jim Crow laws and local ordinances, systemic racism, and other restrictions to oppress the aspirations of different races and classes.[135] Yet, all women were aware of their power and its limitations, engaging in organizing, building communities, educating, lobbying, and attempting to modify the institutions that obstructed their path to voting and holding public office. The efforts for racial justice were delayed, and it would be more than sixty years after ratification of the Nineteenth Amendment before the first Black woman would be elected to the Arkansas General Assembly.[136]

## WOMEN ORGANIZING

Nationally, the woman suffrage movement emerged from previous organizational experience in the temperance and abolitions movements in the Northeast and Midwest. There were no abolition societies in antebellum Arkansas to raise public awareness of analogous oppression of women, but temperance organizations would serve as the first vehicles for women joining together to affect public policy. Couching their efforts in terms of the effects of alcohol consumption on family safety and financial security, they could be seen as extending the concerns for the domestic sphere.

Temperance organizations had existed since territorial times in Arkansas, and some of them included women members. The first legislative action to recognize the important role of women in affecting public policy was the "Three Mile Law," enacted in 1875, allowing residents to petition the county court to prohibit the sale of liquor within three miles of a school.[137] It was introduced by Senator Benjamin F. Forney, an attorney from Lockesburg. It was amended in the Senate Judiciary Committee by Senator George William Norman, an attorney from Hamburg, to strike "legal voters" and substitute "adult residents," effectively allowing every woman above the age of eighteen years to vote by petition. Regarding his strategy, Norman later explained that "as there was then some qualms lingering in the public conscience about woman suffrage, I thought it best to disguise my object by using the words 'adult residents.'"[138]

Women actively participated in circulating and signing the petitions, and attorneys representing liquor interests in one case complained that "four or five hundred of the persons whose names were attached to [the petition], were women and girls." The Arkansas Supreme Court rejected those objections and held, "There is no good reason why women and girls, if adults, should not join in such petitions. They are as deeply interested in removing temptations to dissipation and vice from pupils of schools, and preserving good morals in communities where such institutions of learning are located, as men are."[139] Praising the legislation, Lizzie Dorman Fyler, president of the Arkansas Woman Suffrage Association, wrote, "This act confers equal power, without too suddenly overturning ancient prejudices and customs. Throughout the State it has met with a hearty response, and the feeling of responsibility and power that it has brought to women is preparing the way for the fuller life which is slowly but surely coming."[140]

In 1879, the Arkansas Woman's Christian Temperance Union was organized at Searcy.[141] It quickly became the first statewide woman's organization, bringing women into contact with others around the state who shared their views, including opinions on woman suffrage. Emma R. Colwell was an Arkansas delegate to the 1884 WCTU national convention at St. Louis that adopted a resolution to support woman suffrage. In 1885, she "read a paper advocating woman suffrage before the State Convention of the Arkansas WCTU, and made many converts," although there was still considerable opposition to the idea among the membership.[142] Women interested in suffrage would often remain after the state convention and plan suffrage work. Frances Willard and Susan B. Anthony came to Arkansas speaking for both temperance and woman suffrage in 1889. By the 1894 state WCTU convention—with Fannie Chunn, Bernie Babcock, and Clara McDiarmid as officers of both the state WCTU and the Arkansas Equal Suffrage Association—the organization had been captured, and in 1895 the Arkansas WCTU adopted resolutions and a platform supporting woman suffrage.[143]

There were numerous other women's clubs in almost every town in Arkansas. There were literary societies and philanthropic groups that were seen as furthering the domestic concerns of women without briskly exceeding the boundaries of their sphere. However, there was also a subversive function that empowered women by providing an acceptable forum for discussing ideas and practicing parliamentary procedure, while also helping them recognize their strengths and gain confidence in their capabilities.[144]

These groups also intentionally advanced the interests of women. The Little Rock Woman's Exchange, organized by Dr. Helena Cady and the King's Daughters service club in 1887, operated a consignment shop where women could sell their products made while at home, items ranging from baked goods to clothing and sewing services. In 1890, the group organized a fundraising performance of the "Court of Famous Women." Based on biographical sketches from the book, *Our Famous Women*, Lura Brown adapted speeches into a script that was performed by women in costumes representing such notable women as Frances Willard, Lucretia Mott, Elizabeth Cady Stanton, Margaret Fuller, The Doctors Blackwell, Clara Barton, and Susan B. Anthony.[145]

Arkansas women, led by Mary Kavanaugh Oldham Eagle, were instrumental in securing legislative funding for the 1893 Columbian Exposition in Chicago and organized Columbian Clubs throughout the state for additional funding and discussion of world issues. Clara McDiarmid, who was one of the state lady managers, praised the work of the "Columbian Club movement, which is bringing women in touch with public interests, often for the first time. The ladies who attended the opening at Chicago came back converted

Mary Kavanaugh Oldham Eagle.
*The Congress of Women*, 1894.

to suffrage."[146] Eagle was the chair of the Committee on Congresses, of the Board of Lady Managers, inviting the speakers for the Congress and editing its proceedings with texts of the speeches and short biographical information about the speakers.[147]

Arkansas club women became an even more powerful public presence with the formation of the Arkansas Federation of Women's Clubs in 1897.[148] Beginning in 1899, they engaged in a legislative lobbying campaign for a constitutional amendment granting woman suffrage in all school elections, arguing, "It is absurd to employ women as public teachers, to give more than two-thirds of the schools to them, and yet not permit them to vote in levying school taxes or in the selection of school officers."[149] Among their chief advocates were Virginia "Jennie" Carter Halstead Beauchamp and Bernie Babcock. Like the Arkansas WCTU, the leadership of the Arkansas Federation of Women's Clubs was soon dominated by leaders of the suffrage movement. At the 1915 state convention in Fayetteville, urged by Florence Brown Cotnam, president of the Little Rock Political Equality League, and Alice Sankey Ellington, Arkansas vice president of the Southern States Woman's Suffrage Conference, the AFWC unanimously endorsed woman suffrage.[150]

Florence Brown Cotnam.
*Courtesy of Carrie Chapman Catt Papers,*
*Bryn Mawr College Special Collections.*

In addition to the support for woman suffrage from women's clubs and the temperance union, Arkansas also had suffrage organizations. These were most effective in raising awareness of the possibilities for enfranchisement for Arkansas women, many of whom were uninformed or apathetic in the nineteenth century, and in sharing the arsenal of arguments grounded in justice and utility. They also offered a network for committed suffragists who were assured that they were not alone in their efforts. The first was organized by Lizzie Dorman Fyler at Eureka Springs in 1881. As president of the group, she announced, "The Arkansas Woman Suffrage Association has been organized for the purpose of securing such legislation as shall secure to woman all the rights and privileges which belong to citizens of a free republic."[151] While the group might not have had members beyond Eureka Springs and lasted only until her death in 1885, Fyler had a platform in the pages of the *Woman's Journal*, a column in the local newspaper, and an opportunity to speak at a national convention.

Clara McDiarmid organized the Arkansas Equal Suffrage Association in 1888 at Little Rock, and there were affiliated groups at Hot Springs and

Conway. She was a convention delegate to the National American Woman Suffrage Association, and regularly contributed suffrage essays to the *Woman's Chronicle* and the *Woman's Journal*. A successful businesswoman, McDiarmid also provided free office space to the suffrage association in one of her office buildings on Markham Street across from the state capitol. After her death in 1899, the organization dissolved, and there would not be another suffrage organization in Arkansas for more than a decade.[152]

The Political Equality League was organized in February 1911, during the legislative session in which a proposed constitutional amendment for woman suffrage had been introduced in January. The initial meeting included sixty-seven women and eight men. In March, President Mary Fletcher, Olive Gatling, and Minnie Rutherford of Magazine testified before a House committee considering the amendment. By 1914, the Little Rock Political Equality League called a meeting of its affiliated suffrage groups from Pine Bluff, Fayetteville, Hot Springs, Augusta, and Magazine. A statewide association was organized as the Arkansas Woman Suffrage Association. Alice Sankey Ellington of Little Rock was elected president, and Minnie Rutherford of Magazine was vice president. After passage of the Riggs Primary Suffrage Bill allowing Arkansas women to vote in party primary elections, the twenty-nine local suffrage groups organized the Arkansas Equal Suffrage State Central Committee. After achieving ratification of the Nineteenth Amendment, under the leadership of President Florence Brown Cotnam, the group became the League of Women Voters in December of 1919.[153]

### SPEAKING UP AND SPEAKING OUT

The significance of women's organizations concerned with woman suffrage was in part the result of internal organizational communication among the members, building their credentials and capabilities while recruiting new adherents to the cause. To share the message with a wider and uncommitted audience, including public officials with the power to change the constitution and laws, it was important to utilize all of the available means of information and persuasion. That, of course, included public speaking, which presented a challenge for many women without the experience necessary to develop their rhetorical skills and faced with a culture that still frowned on women platform orators discussing public affairs. The solution was to recruit courageous women and men who did possess those skills.

The first public lecture in Arkansas on suffrage and women's rights was delivered by Phoebe Couzins, a St. Louis suffragette and twenty-seven-year-old law student at Washington University Law School. She spoke on January 3, 1870, in Little Rock City Hall, upon the public invitation of leading

Officers of the Arkansas Woman's Suffrage Association. Front row: Minnie U. Rutherford, Alice Sankey Ellington, Franke V. Land; Back row: Margaret Murphy Cunningham, Lota West Drake, Florence Brown Cotnam, Catherine Vanson Henry. *Arkansas Democrat*, October 15, 1914.

members of the Arkansas bar.[154] In March of 1876, Massachusetts native Mary Livermore—an abolitionist who had supported Abraham Lincoln, a Unitarian, and an editor of suffragist publications—presented lectures at Little Rock and Hot Springs. One of her topics was, "What Shall We Do with Our Daughters?" The speech opened with discussions of Margaret Fuller's influence on her thinking, the long repression of women's life options, and a demand for better education.[155]

Rhoda Munger, a Little Rock bookshop owner who had been active in suffrage campaigns in Michigan, gave lectures on "Woman Suffrage" in 1877 at the Christian Church and Centennial Methodist Church in Little Rock. Frances Willard gave several speeches in Little Rock, Hot Springs, and Texarkana in 1881 and others in 1882 and 1889. Susan B. Anthony spoke in 1889 on woman suffrage at Fort Smith, Helena, and Little Rock, where she was introduced by Governor James P. Eagle.[156]

The Little Rock Eclectic Society held a debate in 1883 on the topic, "Should the Right of Suffrage Be Granted to Woman? Is It Desirable?" Arkansas Supreme Court justice John Eakin and federal district judge Henry Caldwell, both suffragists, argued for the affirmative. Judge Caldwell also gave a speech advocating woman suffrage at a temperance convention at Little Rock in 1884.[157] These presentations could have had a wider influence among lawyers and lawmakers.

Other nationally known women speakers who addressed woman suffrage in Arkansas were Lide Parker Smith Meriwether, a suffrage leader from Memphis in 1896, and Martha Allen, president of the Woman Suffrage Society of Tennessee in 1911. Florence Kelley spoke at Little Rock on "Woman Suffrage" in 1912, and Mabel Vernon from the Congressional Union spoke in 1914. Jean Gordon, president of the Louisiana Woman Suffrage Association, spoke to an overflow crowd at the Old State House in 1913, and Kate Gordon,

Erle Rutherford Chambers (third from right) with Alice Paul (second from right) and Mabel Vernon (center) at Old State House in Little Rock during organization of the Arkansas Branch of the Congressional Union for Woman Suffrage, January 25, 1916. The "We Demand" banner was from the 1913 suffrage parade in Washington, DC. *Courtesy of National Woman's Party Records, Manuscript Division, Library of Congress.*

president of the Southern States Woman Suffrage Conference, spoke at Little Rock High School in 1914. In 1916, both Alice Paul of the National Woman's Party and Carrie Chapman Catt, president of the National American Woman Suffrage Association, spoke at public events in Little Rock as public interest in woman suffrage was growing.[158]

An important voice during the decade that no suffrage organization existed in Arkansas was Reverend Athalia Johnson Irwin (1862–1915). A native of El Dorado, she was the first ordained woman minister in Arkansas, serving the Universalist Chapel at Little Rock, 1904–1908. Reverend Irwin delivered two sermons in March 1907, that received extensive coverage in the newspapers. In "St Paul and Women in the Ministry," she contextualized and refuted reliance on 1 Timothy 2:12 and 1 Corinthians 14:34–35 to prohibit preaching by women and require their silence in the public sphere. Her sermon, "Woman's Place in the World," was one of potential and possibilities. "Woman's place in the world of today is any place and every place she can and wants to fill, from legislative halls and court rooms to the parlor and kitchen; from counting room and council chamber to laboratory and studio; from school room and

Reverend Athalia Johnson Irwin.
*A Bouquet of Verses*, 1905.

university to college matron and chambermaid; from the plow handles and cotton fields, if she will, to the pulpit and the press. This I say is the place in my opinion of woman in the world of today."[159]

Stepping outside the domestic sphere and moving from being passive observers of political campaigns to support political candidates at the polling places was called "a novel approach" to political contests during the Hot Springs municipal elections in 1906. Several members of the two leading women's clubs, the Lotus and the Fortnightly, were at all the polling places, carrying banners and urging the voters to support the Citizens' Improvement Union reform ticket against the local machine slate. When the *Hot Springs Daily News* commented favorably on the influence of women at the polling places, it brought a response from Elnora Monroe Babcock, superintendent of presswork for the National American Woman Suffrage Association. "Now the question arises in the minds of thinking people," she posed, "why in the name of common sense not let the women go a step further and add to their influence (which all agree is for good) the power of the ballot? Influence plus the ballot is certainly far more effective than influence alone. Does it not seem strange that people will praise women for working to influence men to vote right, but condemn them if they manifest a desire to drop their opinion in the ballot box for themselves."[160]

The Political Equality Leagues of Little Rock and Hot Springs obtained booths near the entrance to the State Fair in 1913 and 1914, mixing traditional speaking for suffrage by Florence Brown Cotnam with "voiceless speeches" by Mary Fletcher Drennen that drew considerable attention. Women would stand silently in the booth while flipping large placards with simple yet poignant suffrage statements, making their arguments for suffrage while nonverbally mocking the prescribed submissiveness of woman's sphere.[161] The league also hosted a large Suffrage Day rally at the Old State House in 1914, featuring dozens of prominent supporters presenting five-minute speeches.[162]

New voices began joining the conversation, supplementing the protests from suffrage leaders with participants in popular culture. The actress Lillian Russell, in Little Rock for a stage performance at the Kempner Theater, gave a newspaper interview declaring and detailing the rationale for her strong support of woman suffrage.[163] The growing public discussion and support for woman suffrage was especially evident among the younger generation that was less reticent. The House and Senate literary societies of Little Rock High School hosted a debate in 1911 on the resolution, "That the Granting of the Full Rights of Suffrage to the Women of the United States Would be an Advantage to the Nation."[164] Nora M. Brown read her essay on "Woman Suffrage" at her Stuttgart High School graduation in 1914.[165] The following year, two young men on the Ouachita College debate team defeated the team from Centenary College, arguing for the affirmative on the resolution, "That women in the United States should be granted equal suffrage."[166]

## THE PUBLIC PRESS

Arkansas suffragists frequently contributed to the *Woman's Journal*, published in Boston by Lucy Stone, Henry Blackwell, and Alice Stone Blackwell, for the American Woman Suffrage Association. The first Arkansas newspaper published for and by women was Mary Ann Webster Loughborough's *Arkansas Ladies' Journal*, established in 1884. It was later changed to the *Southern Ladies Journal* and had a wide circulation in the region until Loughborough died in 1887. Although it was not a suffrage journal, it did address issues of interest to women and helped build a sense of community. It was said to have had "an entrance into every intelligent household in Little Rock, and is the journal of intelligent Arkansas women."[167]

The *Woman's Chronicle* was first published in March 1888 and announced in the first issue, "Suffrage seems to be the modern stand for the progressive, intelligent woman to take. Women who have any interest in politics usually embrace suffrage."[168] It was edited by three Little Rock suffragists, Catherine "Kate" Campbell Cunningham, Mary Burt Brooks, and Haryot Holt Cahoon. It advocated for suffrage and for the appointment of women to public office. Copies were distributed weekly to the desks of legislators at the capitol during legislative sessions and was educational if not persuasive on the issue of woman suffrage. It ceased publication in 1893.

During the early twentieth century, Arkansas newspapers began devoting pages to issues of interest to women, and suffragists took the opportunity to contribute their views. Adolphine Terry worked hard to spread the message. The *Woman's Journal* commenting on her efforts said, "She furnishes material to 75 newspapers in the State, sending them the weekly press items which are furnished by the National Press Bureau, and she has arranged to send suffrage articles regularly to a newspaper syndicate reaching all of the important papers throughout the Southwest."[169] The *Osceola Times* had a woman's page with national suffrage news in the 1880s, and the *Pine Bluff Graphic* had a regular weekly column, "The Suffrage Department edited by a suffragette." The *Arkansas Democrat* and the *Arkansas Gazette* both devoted space for women's issues. The *Gazette* gave a full page each week for women's news from the clubs in the Arkansas Federation of Women's Clubs.

The first public debate in Arkansas on feminism played out in those *Arkansas Gazette* columns in July and August of 1914.[170] Joining the debate and writing as "New Woman," future state representative Elizabeth Thompson of Helena explained to her antagonist, "You men make the mistake of trying to make of us either goddesses or slaves. As goddesses we will soon fall from our pedestal, as slaves we rebel." She argued that women were men's equals and were intended to "rule with him." That, she said, "is Feminism in a nut shell."[171]

## Office Holders

There were many Arkansans who helped to initiate and chart the path forward for Arkansas stateswomen. Arkansas women were barred by law from voting for and being elected to school, municipal, county, or state public offices; however, appointments to federal and state offices presented opportunities to challenge the patriarchal monopoly on power and positions. Institutional hurdles eliminated traditional pathways to public office for women in Arkansas, but several pioneering Arkansas women and their male allies recognized potential openings and employed strategies that led to women serving in political offices prior to their ability to vote or serve in the Arkansas General Assembly.

The second prong of Delegate Langley's woman suffrage proposal in the 1868 Constitutional Convention was not only that women should have the right to vote but also that they should be eligible to seek and hold public office. "The right of woman to vote and hold office is demanded as a matter of good policy," he said during the debate, then added, "We have women in our country who are better qualified to hold any civil office, however responsible, than are the men who oppose female suffrage." While that right was rejected by the framers the 1868 Arkansas Constitution and neglected by the drafters of the Arkansas Constitution of 1874, the concept was already making headway even before Langley advanced the idea.

The Arkansas Constitution of 1874, declared, "The equality of all persons before the law is recognized, and shall ever remain inviolate."[172] However, other sections state that women, minor children, convicted felons, "idiot"s, and "insane person"s could not vote, and those citizens, along with atheists, were "disqualified from holding any office of trust or profit in this State."[173] Nonetheless, many Arkansas women possessed an informed civic consciousness. They were clever and courageous, compassionate and concerned, competent and connected. These women boldly used the tools they had at the time to overcome political marginalization, notwithstanding the limitations imposed on them by the Arkansas Constitution, the General Assembly, the common law, and the patriarchal political culture of the times.

## UNITED STATES POSTMASTERS

After the Civil War, United States Post Office Special Agent Marcus LaRue Harrison was charged with the appointment of postmasters and reestablishing mail routes in Arkansas, which was a challenging task. In a letter to Governor Isaac Murphy, Harrison said, "It is to be regretted that the people in many localities manifest very little interest in the appointment of postmasters."[174] It was, however, an especially propitious time for Arkansas women, because unmarried women were not, by law, forbidden from holding public office as postmasters. The *Postal Laws and Regulations* (1866) provided, "No person can be appointed postmaster who cannot legally execute an official bond, and take the required oath. Minors and married women are, by law, incapable of holding the office of postmaster."[175]

Moreover, many Arkansas men who might have received these federal appointments were ineligible because they had borne arms against the United States or given aid and encouragement to the civil and military forces of the Confederate States of America or its state governments. The prescribed oath of office for United States Post Office employees required them to "solemnly swear ( or affirm ) that I have never voluntarily borne arms against the United States since I have been a citizen thereof; that I have voluntarily given no aid, countenance, counsel, or encouragement to persons engaged in armed hostility thereto; that I have neither sought, nor accepted, nor attempted to exercise the functions of any office whatever, under any authority, or pretended authority, in hostility to the United States; that I have not yielded a voluntary support to any pretended government, authority, power, or constitution within the United States, hostile or inimical thereto."[176] Thus, with the need to fill the positions of postmaster and the ineligibility of many male Arkansans, there was a unique window of opportunity for the possible appointment of women in these positions.

While married women, who were *femme covert* under common law, were unable to execute the oath of office, single women and widows were eligible for appointment as postmasters and holding this important, highly visible, and relatively well-paid federal office. As postal historian Cameron Blevins noted, "The entry of women into these offices represented a quiet yet important initial foray into public officeholding for women who were eager to take on official roles in government and politics."[177] They captured these offices in the same way that men did, by being clever, ambitious, and having politically connected families in the community.

The first woman to hold public office in Arkansas was Mary Murphy Lowe, the thirty-year-old widow of State Auditor Herald Lowe, appointed postmaster at Batesville in October 1865. She was the daughter of Governor Isaac Murphy, daughter-in-law of former Independence County judge David Lowe, and sister-in-law of State Auditor James R. Berry. Lowe served only one month in that post, but she was the appointed postmaster at Fayetteville from December 1866 until January 1868, when she remarried. By 1868, Arkansas had fifteen women serving as postmasters.

Nancy Howard Tate Newland was commissioned as postmaster at Batesville on January 3, 1866. She was the widow of Dr. Robert C. Newland, a physician who had served as register of the Land Office at Batesville in 1843–1846 by appointment of President John Tyler. Furthermore, she had remained loyal to the Union and had helped supply the federal troops during the occupation of Batesville during the "War of the Rebellion."[178]

Newland served for more than six years, enduring an almost constant campaign against her by William H. Bayne, the young editor of the *Batesville Republican*, published by state senator Robert McChesney. The *Arkansas Gazette* complained "that postmistress having taken the place of a man must share the responsibilities of a man."[179] When Newland, "the old lady who has for some time been postmistress at Batesville," was dismissed in May 1872, the *Arkansas Gazette* cheered, "We congratulate the people of Batesville on this change. We trust Mr. Bayne will be as successful in his administration of the post office of that place as he was in the fight he made on the recent postmistress."[180] It seems that resentment of women being appointed to these federal offices was not uncommon.

However, there was also important support for women in these offices.

Congressman Anthony A. C. Rogers proudly told his constituents that he had been successful in reestablishing postal routes and securing several new post offices in Arkansas. He also proudly reported that Kate Campbell had been appointed postmaster at Pennington's Mill (Woodson). Campbell, twenty-four, was the daughter of former Pulaski County judge William G. Campbell.[181] By 1871, there were thirty-nine women serving as postmasters in Arkansas.

The appointment of postmasters in the larger towns required nomination by the president and confirmation by the United States Senate. As such, these nominations became subject to local and national political fortunes, as well as the forces of party factions. The strong community contributions and social standing of many Arkansas women enhanced their likelihood as successful candidates for appointment. Isabella Clark "Belle" Atkinson Shumard was nominated as postmaster at Fort Smith by President Ulysses Grant on January 29, 1873, and the Senate confirmed the appointment by unanimous consent on February 13.[182] Shumard was from an old Fort Smith family, a thirty-five-year-old mother of two, and widow of Dr. George Getz Shumard, who had opposed secession and then served with the United States Volunteers as a surgeon in the Union Army.

Valentine Dell, editor of the *Fort Smith New Era*, former state senator and chair of the Republican State Committee, launched an attack on Shumard as "one whose every connection and sympathy was ever bitterly opposed to the Republican party, . . . and whose capacity for the duties of the office," involving large sums of money, "not a soul in this town would admit." Despite professing personal regard for Shumard, Dell claimed, "as a public officer, we have the same right to criticize her appointment and public acts as if she belonged to the sterner sex."[183] Senator Clayton recalled her appointment and rereferred it to the Committee on Post Office and Post Roads on March 1. Because President Grant had already signed her commission, Belle Shumard continued to serve as postmaster until she remarried on October 9, 1873.[184] President Grant then nominated Valentine Dell as postmaster.[185]

Two appointments by President Benjamin Harrison in 1889 vividly illustrate the importance of family political connections in the appointment of women postmasters in Arkansas. Emma Clayton, twenty-two, was commissioned as postmaster at Pine Bluff in June 1889. She was the niece of former governor and US senator Powell Clayton, and the oldest daughter of Colonel John M. Clayton, who had been a state representative, state senator, Jefferson County sheriff, Republican nominee for Congress in 1888, and who was assassinated on January 29, 1889, while contesting the election. Emma Clayton had been seeking the appointment as early as February, and her appointment was welcomed by the *Arkansas Gazette* "with more general satisfaction than any other that could have been made."[186] She served until October 1893, when she resigned to marry Jefferson County judge William D. Jones.

Powell Clayton, a member of the Republican National Committee, and the Arkansas Republican State Central Committee were unanimous in supporting Garland County judge John William Howell for postmaster at Hot Springs. The Arkansas Republican establishment was both chagrined and embarrassed when President Benjamin Harrison ignored their recommendation and nominated a Hot Springs schoolteacher. Flora New Harrod Hawes was a thirty-two-year-old widow with little local support beyond that of Dr. William Henry Barry, Garland County school superintendent and former Democratic state representative. Local Republicans bemoaned that Hawes had lived in Hot Springs less than a year, touted the military and party credentials of Judge Howell, circulated a petition calling for withdrawal of the appointment, and promised to fight her confirmation by the Senate.[187]

Flora Hawes proved to be a more adroit politician than Senator Clayton and his allies in the state Republican Party. A native of Indiana, Hawes returned there for a visit in late summer during the 1888 presidential campaign. Among her family and friends were her cousin, former United States treasurer John C. New, chairman of the Indiana Republican Party, delegate to several Republican national conventions, and publisher of the *Indianapolis Journal* who had strongly supported Benjamin Harrison for United States Senator and President. Another close family friend of Hawes, Elijah Walker Halford, had been editor of the *Indianapolis Journal*, until he became private secretary to Senator Harrison. Hawes made another trip home to Indiana during the summer of 1889 then went to Washington, DC, to personally seek appointment as postmaster. She had private meetings with E. W. Halford, now private secretary (chief of staff) to the president, and with President Harrison, which secured her commission in August. She assumed the post in September during the Senate recess, and her formal nomination and confirmation came in December 1889.[188]

When President Harrison and Postmaster General Wannamaker visited Arkansas in 1891, they were welcomed by Governor Eagle, greeted warmly in Little Rock, and heard no complaints about Postmaster Hawes. She served almost four years as postmaster at Hot Springs, supervising a staff of thirteen, four of whom were women, until December 1893, at which time there were 122 women postmasters in Arkansas. Hawes's operation of the office was said to have been "thoroughly satisfactory and successful," and "her splendid executive ability and thorough business tact have been generally remarked by the press throughout the country."[189]

Flora Hawes.
Willard & Livermore, *American Women*, 1897.

Although federal law and postal regulations had changed to make married women legally eligible for appointment as postmasters, the attitudes and practices of government officials in the early twentieth century were still problematic. "Every time a woman is appointed to a clerkship in one of the departments," said one official in 1902, "she lessens the chance of marriage for herself and deprives some worthy man of the chance to take unto himself a wife and raise a family." In that same year, Postmaster General Henry Payne announced that "a classified woman employee in the postal service who shall change her name by marriage will not be reappointed," and he was not inclined to appoint women postmasters, because he thought women should "stay at home and attend to their household duties."[190]

However, in 1906, Postmaster General George Cortelyou wrote that the office of postmaster was an honorable position for women and that there was "something of elation in being closely connected with the operations of a great Government. It keeps her in contact with affairs, gives her prominence, and affords her opportunities . . . to take part in the more active life of her community." However, he continued, "we do not always appreciate the value of the postmistress. And yet, while there are no monuments to her, and while she has not been eulogized in Congress, she is very close to popular affections."[191] Despite the bureaucratic and political resistance they often faced, women postmasters, holding federal public offices more than five decades before they could vote or run for state or local office in Arkansas, were emblematic enthymemes that refuted arguments against women holding public positions of trust. These female political pioneers provided visible examples of public servants that encouraged the aspirations of other women to become involved in politics and the public sphere.

### LEGISLATIVE OFFICERS

Shortly after the adoption of the Arkansas Constitution of 1874, a number of white, middle-class women sought legislative clerkships that moved them into the heart of the political public sphere and presented a nuanced perspective on women's political influence and roles in representation. Specific to Arkansas stateswomen, these legislative offices also moved women in increasing numbers and influence into the Arkansas capitol and the halls of legislative power. Moreover, it mattered not in the obtaining of such jobs whether the woman was married or single. The role of a legislative clerk is central to the working of the legislature, inclusive of supervising record keeping and bill processing, actions that are integral to the success of legislative sessions and the more efficient work of senators and representatives. Senate and House clerks were elected to those positions by members of the House and Senate, so the campaigning and securing support of a majority of male members of the General Assembly was necessary for their appointments.

Since the imaginary separate sphere of domesticity did not contemplate women assuming roles beyond their household, classroom, or church, the women who became legislative clerks had to finesse these norms when challenging the dominant domestic ideology and to overcome its social and institutional obstacles. Consequently, their public presence shaped a new social reality, transforming their own lives and attitudes, developing a sense of themselves as competent political actors in what was previously an exclusively male domain, and moving from the galleries to the smoke-filled committee rooms, while also opening opportunities for other women in a variety of paid and influential governmental roles.

These women seeking legislative clerkships were political pioneers for future female state representatives and senators. They were often from politically involved families, giving them a sense of politics and a familiarity with government. With a modicum of political ambition and the influence of the men in their families, they actively sought these positions. They announced their candidacies as much as four months before the legislative session, received newspaper endorsements, personally lobbied legislators, enlisted the support and assistance of their female friends, won contested elections that usually involved numerous opponents and took several ballots, were sworn into office, received a salary, and often ran for reelection. In office, they further developed an understanding of a broad range of public policy issues, discovered the different interests and arguments on each side of an issue, and observed the process of negotiation and compromise. These bold campaign activities and the presence and effectiveness of these elected female officers within the legislative enterprise provided public affirmation for the aspirations of other women and played an important role in changing descriptive and substantive representation.

Women first breached the legislative precincts in 1874 with the election of Sallie Robertson Reid as House engrossing clerk. By 1883, each chamber had women serving as engrossing clerk and enrolling clerk, and women were being hired to staff positions as committee clerks. The Office of Assistant Sargent-at-Arms was renamed postmistress when the first woman was elected in 1893. The election of women to these offices became a practice and pattern, and the *Arkansas Gazette* noted that by 1906 the three positions in each house were usually held by women.[192]

Sarah Ann "Sallie" Robertson Reid, thirty, was unanimously elected engrossing clerk by the Arkansas House of Representatives on November 20, 1874, and sworn in by Chief Justice Elbert H. English in the House chamber on November 27.[193] She was a graduate of Cane Hill College, a lifelong student of politics, a published poet, the mother of two young sons, and the wife of Charles C. Reid, whom she had assisted voluntarily when he was chief clerk of the House (1873–1874). Her father, Littleberry Robinson, was Johnson County assessor and had represented Johnson County in the House (1860–1862), and her husband, a former major in the 2nd Kansas Cavalry, had served as prosecuting attorney and Johnson County clerk. Sallie Reid was also a good "republican mother,"[194] since her oldest son, Charles Chester Reid Jr., a graduate of the University of Arkansas and Vanderbilt Law School, served as a member of Congress from 1901 to 1911.

Before the beginning of the 1874 legislative session, the *Arkansas Gazette* devoted several columns, with the sole view of assisting the deliberations of the two houses, stressing the important qualifications and duties of the officers. "The engrossing clerk, to whom is entrusted the incorporation of amendments to the bills, should be a man of education and intelligence, as well as a neat and ready writer." Moreover, when members introduced "bills written on all sorts and descriptions of tags and loose ends of paper, and in such handwriting as pleases heaven though it may defy the clerk's skill

Sallie Robertson Reid.
*House of Representatives*, 1881.

to decipher it," the engrossing clerk "promptly and neatly copied, in a large and legible hand, on bill-paper of uniform size," each bill for discussion and debate, then quickly and precisely incorporated any amendments in a limited time frame. The enrolling clerk, "who has the important trust of preparing the final copy of the bill, for the signature of the executive, should be not merely a man of business, and familiar with clerical work, but one in whom entire trust can be placed."[195]

The *Arkansas Gazette* ignored its gendered description of qualifications when pronouncing that Reid's election was in "appreciation of her former efforts. The lady is an excellent copyist, and no doubt will give the utmost satisfaction." At the end of the session in March, 1875, the House passed a resolution of appreciation for Reid, for having "engrossed over two hundred bills, and in some instances a large number of amendments were adopted, to be incorporated in the same on engrossing, requiring great care, skill and proficiency in the discharge of such duty;" and "in addition to the full discharge of her duties as engrossing clerk, has enrolled all the bills except four, during the entire session, and the same having been correctly done, and the execution in a neat and elegant manner." When Reid ran again for the position in 1877, the *Arkansas Gazette* reprinted the House resolution in its endorsement of her candidacy. "Now, men run around to lobby and electioneer for themselves, but public sentiment in Arkansas forbids, and rightly so, too, we think, that ladies should personally advance their claims; but as they make the best clerks, they should not be without champions," said the editor, before stating that she "is an accomplished and talented lady, and the public service will not suffer by her election."[196] Reid was reelected on the first ballot over eight opponents (seven men and one woman, Maggie Garvey), but was unsuccessful in 1879. She was elected by the House again in 1881 and 1883, then ran unsuccessfully for Senate clerkships in 1885 and 1887.

Mary Belle Mizell Murrell, twenty-two, was the first woman to hold a legislative office in the state senate, elected Senate engrossing and enrolling clerk on the fourth ballot over two male opponents in 1879. She was a skilled artist, secretary of the local Methodist Woman's Board of Foreign Missions, organizer and secretary of the Young Woman's Building Association, and the wife of Dr. Thomas Edgar Murrell, a Little Rock physician and medical school professor. The *Arkansas Democrat* endorsed her as "a deserving and competent candidate for the position," and the editor added, "Our friends are invited to call at this office, where specimens of her writing can be seen."[197] Excellent penmanship was a highly valued qualification, because legislative bills were not typewritten until after 1900.

The importance of family connections for candidates was especially evident in 1881. The House enrolling clerk was Frances "Fannie" Ann Ashley, twenty-five, an 1875 graduate of Mrs. Cuthburt's Young Ladies' Seminary in St. Louis, who was active in the Presbyterian Church, the Aesthetic Club, and numerous patriotic societies. In addition, she was politically aware as the granddaughter of US senator Chester Ashley; daughter of former Little Rock mayor and state representative William Eliot Ashley; niece of Little Rock mayor Roswell Beebe; and cousin of Mary Ashley Freeman, who had lived in the Ashley household before her marriage to Chief Justice Sterling Robertson Cockrill. Although endorsed by the *Arkansas Democrat*, Ashley was defeated for reelection in 1883, but she was elected in 1885 as Senate engrossing clerk.

The 1881 House engrossing clerk was Georgia Lydia Knox Faber, thirty-five and widowed. Her father, George Washington Knox, came to Arkansas Territory in 1825 and was the first United States marshal of the Western District of Arkansas. Her grandfather, Horace Boardman Rose, a former US Customs official, founded Roseville in Logan County, and an uncle, Samuel Montgomery Weaver was secretary of state in 1860. She sought the clerkship while living with her sister and brother-in-law, Hugh Thomas French, a former state representative, Confederate congressman, delegate to the 1874 Constitutional Convention, and current state senator. The Senate engrossing and enrolling clerk was Cora Reid Gantt, graduate of the Georgetown Academy for Young Ladies in Washington, DC, daughter of Dallas County planter Thomas Jefferson Reid, widow of Little Rock attorney Dick Gantt, and sister-in-law of Edward W. Gantt. She was reelected by the Senate in 1883 and 1885. Gantt remarried and resigned during the 1885 session, replaced by Bethunia Lea Roane, the daughter of Confederate brigadier general and Arkansas governor John Selden Roane. Among the candidates that Roane defeated was Nellie Bright, a teacher at Peabody School, who would later become state representative Nellie B. Mack in 1922.

Among those elected in 1883 were House enrolling clerk Amanda Rivers Brown, twenty-five, an El Dorado schoolteacher and daughter of attorney and Union County judge Henry Brown, and Senate enrolling clerk Mary "Mollie" Melbourne Borland Beattie, daughter of United States Senator Solon Borland. In 1885, Annie B. Pettigrew of Fayetteville was elected House engrossing clerk. She was the granddaughter of former House member George A. Pettigrew, the daughter of former Washington County sheriff Zebulon Montgomery Pettigrew, the sister of Washington County assessor George H. Pettigrew, and the niece of Confederate lieutenant colonel James Russell Pettigrew, who was an attorney, former state representative, publisher of the *Fayetteville Sentinel*, and journal clerk of the United States Senate, 1879–1882. She was reelected in 1887 and 1889, then was elected Senate enrolling clerk in 1891.

Lillian Eakin was elected House enrolling clerk in 1887. She was the daughter of Supreme Court justice John Rogers Eakin, editor of the *Washington Telegraph*, delegate to 1874 Arkansas Constitutional Convention, early advocate of women's suffrage, and the most progressive jurist on women's property rights in the nineteenth century. The Senate enrolling clerk that year was a former committee clerk, Jean "Jenty" Moore Loughborough, who was educated at Mrs. Cuthbert's Young Ladies' Seminary in St. Louis and attended Monticello Seminary in Illinois and Arkansas Female College and was the daughter of former state senator James M. Loughborough. She would be reelected for the 1889 session. The *Arkansas Democrat* said Loughborough "is a general favorite in Little Rock society, and is well-known as associate editor of the *Southern Ladies Journal*, of which publication her accomplished mother is the founder and principal writer. Miss Jean's work in the enrollment of bills is her best testimonial. The enrolled bills are models of beautiful penmanship, neatness, and accuracy." She would go on to a career as a writer and delivered an address, "The Young Woman of the South," at the Columbian Exposition in Chicago.[198] Willie Kavanaugh Hocker, a Pine Bluff teacher, who would later become a charter member of the Pine Bluff Political Equality League and the designer of the state's first flag, was an unsuccessful candidate for Senate enrolling clerk in 1889.[199]

During the 1891 session, Elizabeth "Bessie" Cunningham Cockrell was elected House enrolling clerk. She was the daughter of Union Labor Party vice presidential nominee Charles E. Cunningham, younger sister of *Woman's Chronicle* editor Catherine Campbell Cunningham, and widow of attorney John Joseph Cockrell, son of US senator Francis Marion Cockrell of Missouri (who had chaired the Senate Committee on Woman Suffrage). She would later hold a position as copyright clerk at the Library of Congress. The Senate enrolling clerk was Willie Pascal Honey of Huntsville, an 1888 graduate of Lindenwood College. Her grandfather, John Shelby Polk, was Madison County judge, 1877–1880, and her stepfather, William Lowry, was Madison County sheriff, 1889–1892. Honey was reelected in 1893, the year she married Edward J. Berry, son of state auditor James R. Berry and grandson of Governor Isaac Murphy. In 1897, she married Houston Watson Johnson of Missouri, state representative, state senator, circuit judge, and chairman of the Democratic Party of Missouri.

Margaret Thomas "Tompie" Toland, twenty-one, of Howard County was elected Senate enrolling clerk in 1895. She was the niece of state senator John Henry Bell. Her brother, Dr. William Henry Toland, would serve seven terms in the House, and her niece was Representative Dove Toland Mulkey, 1961–1964. The Senate engrossing clerk was Lydia Alice Rankin of Morrilton. She was the granddaughter of Anderson Gordon, a former state representative and brigadier general of the Arkansas Militia under Governors Elisha Baxter and Augustus Garland. Endorsing her candidacy, the *Arkansas Gazette* said, "She is a most estimable young lady and is eminently well qualified for the position, and has a strong following for the position she is seeking. No mistake would be made in her election to the position."[200] Later that year, Rankin was the hostess for the Arkansas exhibit at the famed 1895 Cotton States and International Exposition in Atlanta. She was reelected in 1897, but was defeated in 1899 on the sixth ballot in a contest described by the *Arkansas Gazette* as a "battle royal."[201] She served as a joint committee clerk in 1899 and resumed her career as stenographer for the state superintendent of Public Instruction. Bessie Perry, a teacher from Horatio and cousin of Attorney General Edgar B. Kinsworthy, was elected House enrolling clerk for 1895 on the fifteenth ballot. The 1895 House engrossing clerk was Clara Webb, twenty-one, a graduate of Winchester Normal College and a teacher from Forrest City. The *Forrest City Times* published a glowing endorsement of her candidacy, recounting her skills and qualifications, and commended her "honorable and laudable ambition to attain to greater spheres."[202] Webb was unsuccessful in her reelection in 1897, but she served as a committee clerk. At the end of the session, she married Crittenden County representative Frank G. Smith and supported his future political career as a state senator and associate justice of the Arkansas Supreme Court.

The prevailing public opposition to women voting and holding political office was occasionally reflected by some members of the legislature, who introduced various bills between 1886 and 1899 to prohibit women serving as legislative officers and committee clerks. Interrupting the nominations for House engrossing clerk in 1885, Representative John Alden Partridge Bingham, a Saline County farmer, objected to the election of women to House offices, contending the Constitution declared that only duly qualified electors could hold public office. Representative John B. Boykin, attorney of Paragould, quipped, "I dare to say this is the first time I ever heard a constitutional question raised to a man supporting a woman." Colonel William Henry Halliburton, an attorney from DeWitt, contended that Mr. Bingham's position was not well taken. Representative J. P. Roberts of Poplar Grove, explained, "The section of the constitution the gentleman from Saline refers to has reference to offices created by the constitution," then remarked, "I must say that after what I have heard of these ladies, I should vote for one or other of them even in the face of the section." The House ignored Bingham's objection, excused him from voting, and proceeded with the roll call, electing Annie Pettigrew of Fayetteville by 67–27 over Mattie Powell of Hamburg.[203]

The issue of women serving as legislative officers continued to be discussed in future sessions. In 1891, Representative James B. Baker, an attorney from Melbourne, waged a campaign to dismiss committee clerks, claiming that it was an efficiency matter. In defending his conduct against charges published in the *St. Louis Globe-Democrat* and critical comments from his House colleagues, Baker admitted that he previously had been elected as a committee clerk and now thought "the wholesale employment of committee clerks is nothing but legalized robbery of the people's money."[204] The editor of the *Woman's Chronicle* suspected another motive, reporting rumors that he intended to propose legislation barring women from all offices of trust or profit and promising to shame him if he did so. For whatever reason, Representative Baker introduced no such bill.[205]

In 1895, Representative Almus J. Witt, former Randolph County judge and sheriff and a lawyer from Pocahontas, introduced House Bill 344 to prohibit the election of female clerks in future sessions by requiring all legislative officers to be qualified electors. The women employees of the House, three elected officers and six committee clerks, "were thrown into an excited condition" by the proposal to ban women from serving as officers in the legislature.[206] One legislative correspondent observed, "The anxiety of the mother bird is not more manifest, when some Sunday school boy invades the sacred precincts where her little brood is hidden, than was that of the female contingent, when the ominous threat was hurled at them."[207] The manifest opposition from the female staff and that of their male legislative supporters, no doubt, contributed to the failure of Witt's bill to make it out of committee.

Serving as a state senator in 1897, Witt introduced Senate Bill 23, an identical bill that banned women officers of the legislature by requiring all officers to be qualified electors. Since the Arkansas Constitution did not permit women the right to vote, this would effectively end their budding employment at the Arkansas capitol. The legislative debates on the bill and newspaper commentary on the proposed measure offer unique insight to the perceived roles of women and their place in the public sphere. Senator Jerry C. South, an attorney from Mountain Home, proposed an amendment to exempt the second and third assistant clerks in both Houses, which were the class of elected officers that had become those traditionally held by women. Senator Aurelius Gilbert Gray, a farmer from Hickory Valley in Independence County, opposed the amendment, explaining that the purpose of the bill was to replace ladies with well-qualified electors (men), that "running for public office by women took off a certain part of their modesty," and that the unsuccessful candidates lose faith in mankind, when he and others pledge to vote for all of the candidates and then vote for only one. Senator Witt opposed the amendment for the good of Arkansas and the ladies, most of whom, in his opinion, were not capable of filling the positions. Senator Thomas W. Hayes, a Methodist minister from Prescott, supported the Witt bill with a more nuanced argument. He said he remembered the time when women were consigned to the spinning wheel and later teaching was the only professional avenue open to them, but he would not oppose women preachers and did support suffrage. Moreover, he thought women were qualified for the positions; however, he did not think office seeking was an appropriate thing for them to do.[208]

On the argument for women officers, Senator South said women were holding positions of trust all over Arkansas and should have some recognition by the legislature; furthermore, he said he had heard no complaints about the qualifications of the women clerks, and most did a better job than men. Senator Jacob King, a farmer from Mountain View, supported the South amendment and opposed the Witt bill. He said that women were not asking to be treated better than a man but only demanded to be treated with equality, that he did not believe it was disgraceful for women to run for office, and that they enhanced the value of all political gatherings. Senator William P. Grace, a Pine Bluff attorney, supported women officers, declared it was a rank injustice for men to exclude women who had no voice in elections, and said men should support women seeking honest professional employment instead of compelling them "to sling greasy pots and hire out." Senator John D. Kimbell, a Hot Springs attorney and former secretary of the Senate, said that he would not close avenues of honorable employment, that the women legislative officers were well qualified, and that most women candidates were much less likely than men to pursue positions for which they were not qualified and about which they knew nothing. The South Amendment failed 13–15, and the Witt bill passed the Senate, 17–11.[209]

The House quickly took up Witt's Senate Bill 23 to require all officers to be qualified electors and almost as quickly disposed of it. Representative George Naylor of Little Rock, city editor of the *Arkansas Democrat* and former chief clerk of the House, led the opposition and moved that it be postponed indefinitely. Naylor argued that there was no demand for such a law, that it would be unjust and unfair to the women of the state who were amply qualified to hold such positions, and that members should not vote upon their wives, sisters, and daughters such an unfair law."[210]

Eight House members supported Naylor's motion and opposed Senator Witt's bill. Representative James E. Smith, an attorney from Wynne, said he "would be doing an injustice to the pure, innocent womanhood of Arkansas" if he failed to speak against the Witt bill. He "was heartily in favor of seeing women elected to the clerkships, because they added much needed dignity to the legislature and its proceedings." It "would be a shame" to bar them from public service. Representative Thomas Yadon, a Sebastian County farmer, also raised "his voice on behalf of the womanhood of Arkansas," because he had been elected by the influence of his women constituents and would not otherwise be in the House. He discounted the arguments against "the ladies lobbying in the Capital hotel before the convening of the Legislature," but he "had seen nothing there to mar the character of any lady" seeking office. "When we honor the women of Arkansas," he said in closing, "we honor ourselves." The House voted 51–30 for Representative Naylor's motion and killed Witt's bill for the session.[211]

The *Arkansas Gazette* editorialized against the Witt bill after it had passed the Senate, calling it "a step backward" and called for further empowering Arkansas women. "In four states of the Union, women vote and hold office the same as men. They are members of the Legislature, hold state and county offices, and fill any and all positions heretofore held by men only. In these states this departure from the old beaten paths has not proved detrimental to the public weal," it explained. "Instead of curtailing the female privilege in Arkansas, the *Gazette* would like to see it broadened so that women may at least be elected to the position of school directors. This privilege is granted in most of the states, while many others permit women to vote in municipal elections."[212]

A letter to the editor of the *Arkansas Gazette*, signed "An Old Woman," critiqued the Witt bill, offering rebuttal of the supporters' contentions and praise for those members who had opposed it. Then, getting to her own argument, wrote, "Give woman the privilege to labor and study side by side with man, and in a few years, we will see our beloved land blessed with a grand, noble, self-sustaining womanhood. This is not a plea to turn our girls out to heavy manual labor; it is to fit them for toil in intellectual pursuits."[213]

Senator Witt and his legislative colleagues opposed to allowing women to seek and be elected to legislative offices found support from the *Helena Weekly World*. The editorial expressed consternation about the clerkship campaigns, during which, ambitious "women, seeking clerkships, assistant clerkships, etc. and their women friends, boldly invaded hotel lobbies and corridors, button-holed susceptible lawmakers and warmly and persistently urged their claim upon them." The proposed legislation, they asserted, "resulted from a desire to preserve, as far as possible, the women of Arkansas from the temptation of resorting to the ways of the politician, which ordinarily do not meet with unqualified admiration." Continuing the paternalistic analysis and argument against women's assertion of agency, the *World* editorial added, "Theoretically it is all right for a woman to hold office, to take to the stump, to exercise the elective franchise, and to do all those things which her brother is wont to do, but practically it is a sight to excite the sympathy, to put it as mildly as may be, of all men who value her for those qualities which we have been taught to revere, when we see her soiling her skirts and her character in the mire of practical politics." It was beyond the bounds of true womanhood, said the editor:

> When forty young women, with a hundred young lady friends to scotch for them, invade the lobbies, corridors and parlors of the leading hotels; lie in wait for bibulous solons just outside of barroom doors, and exert to the uttermost all their powers of persuasion and fascination in the effort to corral a half dozen clerkships, it is time for some legislator to interpose with a measure like Senator Witt's. It does not avail to say woman has as much right to get a clerkship as a man has; the question is, has a body of gentlemen the right to permit her to come in contact with the dirt of politics.[214]

The final attempt to ban women from elected legislative clerkships came in 1899. Freshman representative Dr. James Osgood Andrew Sullivan of Waldron introduced House Bill 116, specifically prohibiting all females and sons of members from holding positions with the General Assembly. The *Fort Smith Times* endorsed the proposal to "cure what is recognized as a great evil existing."[215] It was considered in the House as a special order of business on January 21. Representative Thomas D. Brooks, attorney from Atkins, unsuccessfully moved to strike "all females" from the text of the bill; Thomas Herrn, an attorney from Evening Shade, successfully moved to strike "son of members" from the bill. Representative Hardin Toney of Jefferson moved to table the bill, and Representative Robert F. Foster of Jefferson moved to postpone it, but both motions failed. Representative Foster then spoke in opposition to the bill, saying it "did not seem fair for members to be allowed to vote their sons and not for their daughters." Furthermore, he "thought if ladies were competent to hold clerical positions in connection with the legislature, common courtesy dictated that they should not be denied the opportunity to do so." Nonetheless, the House approved the ban by a vote of 49–33.[216]

In the Senate, there was less discussion and a different result. Senator George Hillhouse, a Newport lawyer, moved rather quickly to lay the Sullivan bill on the table, and the motion passed 17–10.[217] That action was "greeted with laughter and applause" in the House, as was a later message that the Senate had voted to reconsider the motion to table.[218] The Senate again considered Sullivan's "anti-female bill," as the newspapers were labeling it, placed it on third reading, defeated it by a vote of 9–19, and ended any further attempts to bar women from holding legislative offices.[219]

The election of women officers in the Arkansas General Assembly continued in 1899. Stella Royston, educated at the Arkansas Female College and the University of Michigan and employed at the *Washington Telegraph* in Hempstead County, was elected Senate engrossing clerk on the sixth ballot. The *Conway Log Cabin* called her "one of the shrewdest young politicians in the state," and the *Arkansas Gazette* attributed her election to "the best endeavors of an energetic, cultured, and diplomatic young lady."[220] Her father was the Hempstead County and Circuit clerk. Her grandfather, Grandison Delaney Royston, had been a delegate to the 1836 and 1874 Constitutional Conventions, Speaker of the House in 1837, a state senator, prosecuting attorney, and a representative in the Confederate Congress. She was reelected without opposition in 1901 and served again in 1907.

Royston's friend Annie Elizabeth Bruce was elected Senate enrolling clerk in 1899 and 1901. Educated at Shorter College in Georgia, she was the daughter of Confederate colonel George Washington Bruce, who was an attorney, publisher of the *Conway Democrat*, former state representative, and mayor of Conway. It took twelve ballots to elect Lucy Houston Beavers as House postmistress. Her political awareness was also a family tradition. Her father,

John J. Beavers, had been Grant County clerk, 1889; her uncle, Dr. Benton B. Beavers, was a former state senator and secretary of state; her grandfather, William E. Beavers, had been Saline County judge; and her other grandfather, Samuel Houston Whitthorne, had been an attorney, founder of the *Saline County Courier*, and general of the Arkansas State Guard. Her cousin, Lenora Beavers, was elected House postmistress in 1901.

Women sought these legislative offices in increasing numbers in the early twentieth century, and there is evidence they were developing effective political skills in winning them. In 1903, House enrolling clerk Katherine Clarissa Faust was reelected on the nineteenth ballot in roll calls that extended over two days. The House responded with applause and relief and unanimously adopted a resolution extending a vote of thanks to "the various lady candidates for the uniform polite way in which they conducted their different campaigns." By contrast, the Senate cleared the galleries, locked the doors, and met in caucus to elect Annie May Craig as enrolling clerk. She was a legal secretary and court reporter from El Dorado, and she was the niece of Chief Justice Henry G. Bunn. Craig again made history as being one of the first women to be appointed a notary public by Governor Thomas C. McRae in February 1921.

Fannie Mathews Jones of Redfield was nominated for House postmistress in 1905 by Representative Sidney Hunt of Pine Bluff, and elected on the first ballot, with sixty-four votes against thirty-two for her three opponents. After the session, she married Representative Hunt, and in 1922 became state representative Frances Hunt, the first woman to serve in the Arkansas General Assembly. By December 1906, only seven years after the last attempt to prohibit women from holding legislative offices, the *Arkansas Gazette* noted, "The positions of postmaster and engrossing clerk and enrolling clerk are usually given to women," then listed ten women already announced for those positions in the House in 1907.[221]

Two women who were unsuccessful candidates in 1907 would later be among the most ardent advocates for woman suffrage. Bernie Babcock, a published author and formerly on the editorial staff of the *Arkansas Democrat*, was among seven candidates for House postmistress. She was a leader in the state Woman's Christian Temperance Union, wrote a biography of Frances Willard, was active in the Political Equality League and the National American Woman Suffrage Association, promoted the Chautauqua work of future state representative Florence McRaven, and was appointed director of the WPA Writers Project in Arkansas.[222] Elizabeth "Bettie" McConaughey Wassell was an unsuccessful candidate for Senate assistant journal clerk in 1907. She was later a charter member of the Political Equality League, organized and

Representative Florence McRaven around the time
she worked for the Labor Commission, ca. 1924.
*Courtesy of the UALR Center for Arkansas History
and Culture. Women in Arkansas photograph
collection, ca. 1850s–1980s.*

participated in debates of the League's Weekly Study Club, and was one of
the featured speakers at the 1914 Suffrage May Day Rally at the Old State
House. For her continuing work, Wassell was presented with one of the pens
that Governor Brough used to sign the proposed Equal Suffrage Amendment
in 1919. As historian of the Equal Suffrage State Central Committee, she
wrote "History of Equal Suffrage Movement in Arkansas." Wassell was also
a good "republican mother" of future Little Rock mayor Sam Wassell.[223]

Mary Ellen Campbell Marshall, a successful insurance agent, was elected
Senate enrolling clerk in 1909 and 1911. She was the daughter of Major
William Peyton Campbell, Woodruff County clerk, state land commissioner,
and clerk of the Arkansas Supreme Court. Marshall was one of the speakers
at the Political Equality League luncheon for Carrie Chapman Catt's suffrage
campaign visit to Little Rock in 1916.[224]

Ella B. Hurst, wife of state representative George Abner Hurst of
Fayetteville, was an unsuccessful candidate for House enrolling clerk in 1909,

but she was appointed to a committee clerkship. In a 1911 rematch, she was elected enrolling clerk, which put her in a position to hear her husband, chair of the House Judiciary Committee, lead the fight against a proposed constitutional amendment for woman suffrage. "Women have not been sufficiently educated in the practical ethics and economics of civil affairs to conduct, or assist to conduct, affairs of government," he said. "This bill should be everlastingly killed. The women should not be further encouraged in this equal suffrage foolishness."[225] Nonetheless, Ella Hurst would not only exercise the right to vote but would later become a three-term Arkansas state representative.

Laura B. Jacobson had been encouraged to become politically active by her brother Charles, a member of the state senate, who was previously assistant attorney general and secretary to Governor Jeff Davis. Laura was a House stenographer in 1909 and then a stenographer for Governor George W. Donaghey before she was elected Senate engrossing clerk in 1911 and 1913. She later went to Washington as secretary for United States senator William F. Kirby from 1916–1920.

Dozens of women were elected to these legislative offices, returned to their home communities after the sessions, and provided examples for other women interested in politics and government service. These offices were important to those who campaigned for them and to those who were elected. At the close of the legislative session in 1909, Representative Edwin J. Kerwin, an attorney from Pine Bluff, speaking to the women officers and staff members, praised their contribution and said, "We have not regarded you as servants, either, but as our equals on this floor."[226] Certainly, these women saw themselves as more than mere cyphers. They acquired essential political knowledge working for the legislators, and there is some evidence that they played an active role in advancing policies that empowered women.

In 1915, Emma Reichardt Hoeltzel was an unsuccessful candidate for Senate enrolling clerk, but she was appointed clerk for the Senate Budget Committee. She was from a financially successful and civically involved family, and she and her sister, Eva Reichardt, were both active suffragists. Hoeltzel was a charter member of the Political Equality League that had supported and testified for the proposed suffrage amendment tabled (63–13) by the House in 1911. They made some progress in 1913, losing in the House by a vote of 35–55. However, both chambers approved a suffrage amendment in 1915, although it did not get on the general election ballot. At the close of the session, Hoeltzel, on behalf of the women employees, presented a gift to Senate president Elmer Lundy, who expressed his gratitude for being permitted to cast a vote for an amendment to the Constitution for equal suffrage, and added that someday it will be "Lady President" instead of "Mr. President" in addressing the presiding officer of the Senate.[227]

Martha Lula Scruggs, a North Little Rock music teacher, was an unsuccessful candidate for House postmistress in 1911, 1913, and 1915, but she secured a stenographic position and closely followed the debates on labor issues and woman suffrage. Her aggressive campaign tactics during the voting in 1915 amused the capitol press, but she persisted.[228] Scruggs was chair of the Argenta Branch of the Pulaski County Suffrage Central Committee and dedicated to woman suffrage. She and Florence Brown Cotnam addressed the Arkansas Farmers Union Convention and secured the union's endorsement for a suffrage amendment. During her fourth campaign for House postmistress in 1917, she was elected on the sixth ballot and held that office when the Riggs Primary Suffrage Bill passed. There is little doubt that she had lobbied hard for passage; Governor Brough presented her one of the pens with which he signed the act, and Representative Riggs called her "the cleverest woman politician he had ever met."[229] Scruggs was appointed to the state Minimum Wage Commission, served as a delegate to the 1918 Democratic State Convention, and was reelected House postmistress in 1919, again receiving one of Governor Brough's signing pens for the Equal Suffrage Amendment Resolution. She was reelected in 1921 and in 1923, when she became a part of legislative history. The first motion made by a woman legislator was when Representative Frances Hunt (the House postmistress in 1905) made the motion in 1923 that Scruggs's election be made unanimous.[230]

Legislative pages, elected from congressional districts by the legislature, remained the domain of young men a while longer. The job of these young pages was to assist legislators in their duties during the session, which largely provided a learning opportunity about Arkansas government. Young girls could also benefit from the position, but apparently no one had ever considered it, until 1915, when Clarice Dunaway, twelve, of Little Rock launched her campaign for the position of Senate page. Dunaway's late grandfather, Dr. William N. Hereford, had been mayor of Lonoke and a state representative (1883–1884). The boys seeking page positions were somewhat alarmed, thinking "they would be hopelessly handicapped if opposed by a girl." Since no girl had ever served as a page in the Arkansas legislature, these boys sought an opinion from a veteran senator as to whether it was legal for a girl to be a page. They were informed that there was "no legal bar to a girl serving as page."[231] Perhaps it was the novelty of the idea of a female page that her campaign was unsuccessful.

The first female page was Irene Thompson, thirteen, of Paragould, serving in the House during the 1931 session.[232] Her father, John Edward Thompson,

Representative Nancy Balton with legislative pages.
*Courtesy of Nancy Balton.*

was serving in the House at the time, as had her grandfather and great-grandfather before him. Irene Thompson did not pursue a political career, but her younger brother, Mack Thompson, served in the House (1973–1986). Yet, Arkansas was still advanced on this front nationally thanks to Irene; it would be another forty years before young women were first appointed pages in the United States Senate (1971) and House of Representatives (1973).[233]

It would also be more than ninety years after the first woman was elected engrossing and enrolling clerk and forty years after women were elected to the legislature that women would hold the top elected staff positions in either chamber. Jim Jennie Searcy Childers served as chief clerk of the House from 1969 to 1985, and Sylvia Ann Hindsman Cornwell has served as secretary of the Senate from 1995 to the present.

## NOTARIES PUBLIC

Today, more than 85 percent of the notaries public in Arkansas are women, but that was not always the case. Unlike postmasters, who were federal officers, and legislative officers of the House and Senate, created and elected by the state legislature, the office of notary public is a state office recognized by the Arkansas Constitution and controlled by statutory law. Act 17 of 1874 specified that the governor "may appoint a convenient number of notaries public for each county, who shall be citizens of the county for which they are appointed."[234] The only requirement of the statute was that they be citizens, and it is not necessary that one be an elector in order to be a citizen.[235]

In January 1891, Governor James P. Eagle,[236] received a petition from the circuit judge, the prosecuting attorney, and several attorneys from Chicot County, recommending and requesting the appointment of "a highly respectable married woman," the wife of a leading lawyer from Chicot County, as a notary public. Governor Eagle announced his intention to make the appointment; however, Attorney General William E. Atkinson issued an opinion holding that "women at common law are ineligible to [hold] public office by reason of their sex. Their legal status, and their physical and mental characteristics, were the reason for their exclusion." Since the common law was part of Arkansas law, unless specifically changed by statute, he was "of the opinion that the office of Notary Public cannot be legally filled in Arkansas by a woman."[237]

Shortly after assuming office in 1897, Governor Daniel Webster Jones received a request from a merchant in Nevada County to appoint Ella Phillips (1870–1928), a teacher and bookkeeper at Emmett, as a notary public.[238] Jones replied that if Phillips "was a citizen of good character and possessed the necessary qualifications and $5" for the commission fee, he would appoint her. Governor Jones, having previously served as attorney general and seeing no need to request an official opinion from the attorney general, noted that there was nothing in the statutes requiring notaries public to be electors and said, "A woman is a citizen, and if she is qualified to hold the position, she has the right to be appointed."[239]

Governor Jones, who "manifested a liberal spirit in the appointment of women as notaries public," continued to appoint dozens of women as notaries public during the next four years. The *Arkansas Democrat* approvingly said, "Women are as well-fitted for these positions as men, and there is no reason why they should not share in the honors."[240] Beyond the basic qualifications necessary to notarize documents, many of these women appointed by Governor Jones were from politically active families. Molly Emerson of Magnolia was the daughter of former state senator Reuben Emerson, editor and proprietor of the *Columbia Banner*. Della Dollison, stenographer of Paragould, was the daughter of Jasper W. Dollison, editor of the *Clay County Advocate* and former state representative (Union Labor). Elizabeth C. Pugh of Hamburg was the daughter of the Ashley County Clerk and wife of the mayor.[241]

Soon after Governor Jones began making these appointments, a group of the newly empowered young women were instrumental in founding the Business Women's Club in Little Rock. When Kate Phillips of Little Rock was appointed, the *Arkansas Gazette* said, "She is an expert stenographer and in becoming a notary steps to the front as a self-supporting young lady." She also became editor-in-chief of the organization's monthly newspaper, *Business Women's News*. The associate editors were Batesville insurance agent Clare Neill, daughter of Congressman Robert Neill; Lucy Sanders of Helena, daughter of Circuit Judge Matthew Sanders and stenographer for United States attorney Joseph House; and Edith Black of Fort Smith, an honor graduate of the Fort Smith Commercial College and later chief clerk of the University of Arkansas Experimental Station. The paper's business manager was Ellen Reinhardt, stenographer and secretary of Thomas Cotton Mills. Her brother was Prairie County clerk for eighteen years and a state representative, and her brother-in-law was editor of the *Searcy Citizen*.[242]

The question of women being able to serve as notaries public arose again in 1901. Within a month of taking office, Governor Jeff Davis asked for an attorney general's opinion on the legality of continuing to appoint women notaries public. Attorney General George W. Murphy, after a thorough review of the constitutional infirmity of the appointments, reluctantly replied that women cannot serve as notaries public:

> I have gone through the question and consulted all the authorities attainable. My opinion, given in answer to your request, is based on the plain provisions of our constitution. I have sought to find something somewhere that would justify me in saying that a woman might be a notary public. It seems to me to an unnecessary discrimination against her when we say that she cannot be such; the discrimination is a harsh and arbitrary one, yet the constitution makes it. I answer your question against my personal inclination, by saying that a woman cannot legally hold the office of notary public under our constitution. I beg to say to you further that this restriction ought not to exist. For the gallant fame of our state, it ought to disappear. I trust you will find it convenient to recommend an amendment in this regard.[243]

Murphy's opinion held that the previous acts by the women notaries public were still valid, but their offices must be vacated. In response to the ruling, Representative John Perrin Farrar of Marianna introduced House Joint

Resolution 11, proposing an amendment to the Constitution permitting women to be appointed as notaries public, which was referred to and died in the committee on constitutional amendments.[244] The *Arkansas Gazette*, commenting on the opinion, said, "This is to be regretted, since this office alone is about all the women have been permitted to hold."[245] No one mentioned that while these very competent women were removed from office, Gardner Oliphant, an eleven-year-old boy who had been commissioned by Governor Jones, was unaffected by the opinion and legally would continue to serve.[246]

The issue was again joined in 1913, when Governor Joseph Taylor Robinson appointed Mary Carter Baird Gray, a single mother, head stenographer, and office manager for the law firm of Rose, Hemingway, Cantrell, and Loughborough, as a notary public.[247] When secretary of state Earl Hodges refused to issue the commission on the grounds that she was a woman, George B. Rose filed suit in Pulaski Circuit Court for a writ of mandamus requiring Hodge to issue the commission to Mary Gray,[248] but Judge Guy Fulk ruled against Gray. While the case was on appeal, state senator Elmo M. Carl-Lee, an Augusta attorney, filed Senate Bill 181 authorizing women to be appointed notaries public. It passed the Senate by 25–7 but was defeated in the House by a vote of 36–37.[249]

The Supreme Court of Arkansas delivered its unanimous opinion in *State ex rel. Gray v. Hodges* on March 3, 1913. It rejected George Rose's argument on behalf of Gray that the statute merely required that Gray be a citizen, not an elector, and that, unless there was a specific constitutional provision prohibiting it, a woman could be appointed and hold the position. Upholding the lower court opinion denying women access to the job of notary public, Associate Justice Jesse Cleveland Hart held that "under the common law which was in force in this State at the time of the adoption of our Constitution, . . . the political privilege of voting and holding public office was denied to women." Thus, he concluded, "the law of the State at the time of the adoption of the Constitution, the whole frame and purport of the Constitution itself and the general understanding and the practical construction given to the Constitution by the law makers all support the conclusion that women are not eligible to hold public office, and . . . she would have no constitutional or legal authority to exercise any of the functions of the office of notary public."[250] As such, despite their social and political connections, the support of governors in appointing women to the political office, and their expertise and excellent work, these female notaries public in 1913 were denied office and other women informed that such pursuits were not permitted in Arkansas due merely to their sex.

Governor Charles Brough, a supporter of women's suffrage, in his 1917 inaugural address called for a constitutional convention to include "the just principle of universal suffrage, extended to women as well as to men." Senator Walker Smith, an attorney from Magnolia, and Representative Thomas S. Osborne, a Fort Smith attorney, introduced legislation calling for a constitutional convention, and Representative John A. Riggs, editor of the *Hot Springs New Era*, introduced a resolution for a constitutional amendment on suffrage. Minnie Rutherford Fuller, reporting on the legislative action for the Arkansas Woman Suffrage Association and the Arkansas Federation of Women's Clubs, thought the constitutional convention would be the most likely way to achieve woman's suffrage. "We certainly have never had before the same splendid opportunity to get our wishes crystalized into legislation which we now have, with the governor on our side and a legislature determined to carry out the wishes of the governor," she exclaimed.[251] Governor Brough signed the act on February 16 for a convening of a Constitutional Convention.[252]

Deferring to the Constitutional Convention, Representative John A. Riggs withdrew his proposed constitutional amendment providing for full women's suffrage and introduced a bill providing woman suffrage only in primary elections, which could be done by statute. "I don't think anyone is foolish enough to try seriously to stop the spread of woman suffrage," he said. "The legislature of 1915 went on record for it overwhelmingly."[253] The legislation granting women primary suffrage passed the House by 71–19 and the Senate by 17–15. As such, beginning in 1918, women of Arkansas could vote in primary elections, being the first southern state to do so.[254]

"The climax of a stirring week was the suffrage parade and mass meeting, which finished the day of the passage of the Riggs primary suffrage bill. A long line of gaily decorated automobiles announced to Little Rock that at least half of the adult population was jubilant and many of the most progressive men were with us in spirit, if not in body," reported Minnie Rutherford Fuller at the end of the legislative session. "The parade finished at the Hotel Marion, where a huge audience was assembled to celebrate the partial emancipation of Arkansas's women. I have never attended a more enthusiastic meeting, and the most thrilling moment was that which began the signing of the bill by Governor Brough."[255]

What the Riggs Primary Suffrage Act meant was that white women now could vote in primary elections but not in nonpartisan school or municipal elections, general elections, ballot issues, constitutional amendments, or the forthcoming proposed constitution. Blanche Olive Butler, manager of an insurance agency at Malvern, submitted an application to be a Notary Public and the five-dollar fee immediately after the bill was passed, but was summarily rejected by Secretary of State Thomas J. Terral, citing the decision in *Gray v. Hodges*.[256] Attorney General John R. Arbuckle issued a spate of opinions declaring that women cannot be notaries public, county superintendents of schools, deputy clerks, or judges or clerks for primary elections. Women were also held ineligible to vote in school elections, but they could pay a poll tax if they wanted.[257]

Two days after Governor Brough had signed the Riggs Primary Bill, Franke Lampedo Van Vulkenburgh Land, founding president of the Pine Bluff Political Equality League, attempted to pay her poll tax and was refused by the Jefferson County Collector who said he had no authority to issue a poll tax receipt to a woman.[258] There were laws, and then there was the administration of those laws, which seemed to vary depending on the attitude of various county officials. The following week, Elizabeth "Bettie" McConaughey Wassell, a charter member of the Little Rock Political Equality League, became the first woman in Pulaski County to pay her poll tax. "I am not a recent convert to the cause," said Wassell, a fifty-eight-year-old widow. "My father preached it and three sons, who vote, have always believed their mother as competent to vote as themselves."[259]

Despite continued attempts by some in Arkansas to continue keeping women out of the public sphere, women significantly increased their participation in the political process. It has been estimated that more than forty thousand Arkansas women cast their first votes in the May 1918 Democratic Primary Election. Fifty women were seated as delegates to the Democratic State Convention, which endorsed the federal Susan B. Anthony Suffrage Amendment, and Stella Zanone Brizzolara of Fort Smith, secretary of the Arkansas Equal Suffrage Central Committee, was elected to the Democratic State Central Committee that year. In 1920, seven women would be elected alternate delegates to the Democratic National Convention, including suffrage organizer Josephine Miller.[260] The 1920 Republican State Convention seated six women delegates and elected one woman as an alternate delegate to the Republican National Convention.[261] These trailblazers, due to passage of the act allowing women in Arkansas to vote in primary elections, were successful in advancing women of Arkansas to the national stages of party politics, demonstrating the heart of Arkansas's progressive spirit for women's rights while also providing women and girls additional examples of women in the political sphere.

As to the Arkansas Constitutional Convention of 1918, women were successful in lobbying the delegates to include a suffrage section, adopted with only one dissenting vote, Edmond Penn Watson of Bentonville. Fifty years after Miles Langley had stood alone for women suffrage in 1868, the proposed state constitution of 1918 declared, "The right of citizens of this state to vote and hold office shall not be denied or abridged on account of sex. Both male and female citizens of this state shall enjoy equally all civil, political and religious rights and privileges."[262] It would provide suffrage, eligibility to hold office, and equal rights for all citizens, regardless of sex. Unfortunately, women could not vote for adoption of the proposed constitution, and it was rejected.

Finally, Arkansas women would get the right to vote after adoption of the Nineteenth Amendment to the United States Constitution, which had received unanimous support from the Arkansas Congressional delegation.[263] Governor Brough called a special session of the Arkansas legislature to ratify the Nineteenth Amendment. After passing the Senate by 29–2 and the House by 75–17, Governor Brough signed the Joint Resolution for Ratification on July 29, 1919. In addition, Arkansas voters supporting suffrage for women adopted Amendment VIII to the Arkansas Constitution, passing it with 63.7 percent of the vote in the November 1920 general election. In endorsing the proposal, the *Arkansas Democrat* called it, "a tardy, but complete, recognition of equal rights of men and women in our political life."[264] However, women would soon discover it was not.

In 1920, Dr. Ida Josephine Brooks was nominated for state superintendent of Public Instruction by the Republican State Convention, and Julia Ward Pennington was nominated for state senator by the Socialist Party of Arkansas. Secretary of State Thomas J. Terral refused to certify their nominations. Attorney General Arbuckle issued an opinion that, notwithstanding the fact that women were now qualified electors under the Nineteenth Amendment, "no positive authority is found in the common law guaranteeing the right to women to hold office," and further, "Nowhere in the Constitution or Statutes of this State can we find a provision guaranteeing to women the right to hold office." While this disqualifying political status could be cured by legislation, until then, Arbuckle said, "the Secretary of State should refuse to certify any and all women nominated as candidates to be voted on at the coming general election in November."[265]

Governor Charles Brough had long been an active supporter of women's suffrage. In his farewell address to the General Assembly on January 12, 1921, he urged legislative action to insure that "no citizen, otherwise eligible, shall be disqualified from holding any office on account of sex."[266] Arkansas's next governor, Thomas C. McRae, had an even longer record of supporting women's suffrage—and office holding. He had supported inclusion of suffrage in the Arkansas Democratic Party platform in 1916, and he was a member of the 1918 Constitutional Convention that approved the broad provision for women's suffrage, public office, and equal rights. During his 1920 campaign, his newspaper advertising blasted opponent senator Lamar Smead for voting against the Riggs Primary Bill, and on the stump, McRae said, "A governor should appoint to office men and women of merit and character. That is exactly what I propose to do."[267]

Governor McRae was even more forceful in his inaugural address, pledging, "If it be true that women are not eligible to hold office, I favor a law promoting their equal rights with male citizens. I do not want any discrimination. I have declared repeatedly that I will recognize our women citizens by appointing them to positions upon boards and commissions and there certainly should be no inhibitions against their power and right to hold offices and positions of trust."[268] The following day, Representative Prince R. Andrews of Helena introduced the legislation to allow women of Arkansas to run for and hold public office, and it had easily passed both chambers less than three weeks later. McRae signed it as Act 59 of 1921, providing that "hereafter, sex shall not be a bar to the holding of any public or civil office in this State," and that "women, where otherwise qualified, shall be entitled to hold public or civil office, whether elective or appointive."[269]

Wasting no time, Governor McRae began appointing notaries public on the same day he signed Act 59. The first appointed was Margaret Boyce (1869–1953), who had been a stenographer in the Little Rock office of the Internal Revenue Collector, a stockholder in England Loan and Trust, and currently head of the tax department for Bankers Trust Company after twelve years of government service. She was a graduate of the Commercial College and an officer in the Woman's Club of Little Rock, the Advertising Club, the Athenian Chapter of Delphian Society, the Business and Professional Women's Club, and the Little Rock Federation of Women's Clubs. She and her sister, Grace Boyce, were suffragists and had been among the first women to pay the poll tax in 1917. The second appointment was Mary Augustine Fein (1881–1954), owner of the Public Stenographic and Multigraph Letter Shop, past president of the Little Rock Business Woman's Club, secretary-treasurer of Arkansas Pharmaceutical Association, and on the advisory council of the Little Rock League of Women Voters. In 1932, she was a charter member of Arkansas Democratic Woman's Club and a candidate for the Democratic nomination for state representative.

McRae continued to appoint women to office. In March, he announced that he planned to appoint Erle Chambers to the newly authorized Pulaski

Mary Augustine Fein.
*American Druggist and
Pharmaceutical Record*, 1908.

County Probate Judge position, but then the Arkansas Supreme Court declared the authorizing legislation unconstitutional. Chambers would go on to be elected to the House of Representatives in 1922. When two vacancies opened in the Arkansas House of Representatives, Governor McRae appointed Frances Hunt of Pine Bluff as state representative in April 1922, making her the first woman to serve in the Arkansas General Assembly, and she was elected by the voters to additional terms in 1922 and 1924. For the other open House of Representatives position, Governor McRae appointed Mabel Irene Fowler Wilson (1883–1973) of Warren, a graduate of Ouachita College, a former teacher at Magazine Academy, district president of the Arkansas Federation of Women's Clubs, and vice president of Arkansas League of Women Voters. She was married to John Rufus Wilson, a prosecuting attorney and former state representative, who had served with McRae in the Constitutional Convention and had been on the Suffrage and Elections committee. She declined the appointment, since they were moving from Bradley County to El Dorado. Governor McRae then appointed Nellie B. Mack of Warren to the open Bradley County state representative position in May 1922, the second woman to serve in the Arkansas General Assembly.

Representatives Erle Chambers and Frances Hunt on
the Arkansas Capitol steps in January 1923. *Courtesy
of the UALR Center for Arkansas History and Culture.
Women in Arkansas photograph collection, ca. 1850s–1980s.*

Women were also running for public office, now that they were permitted
to do so. The first woman elected to a public office was Josephine Moore
Jarman, elected Phillips County treasurer on May 24, 1921, without opposition in a special election to fill a position vacated by the death of her husband.
Jarman was elected to three more terms. In the 1926 Democratic primary, she
defeated state representative Elizabeth Thompson for the County Treasurer
position, in Arkansas's first election contest between two female candidates
for public office. In 1922, Representative Frances Hunt of Pine Bluff was
elected for a second term, and Erle Chambers was elected to the House from
Pulaski County.

Although Julia Ward Pennington had been nominated for the state senate in 1920 and Zella Harper of Little Rock announced but did not file for
state senator in 1922, Lois Dale (1889–1934) of Texarkana was the first woman
to run for state senator. She was a graduate of Lindenwood College and
Tulane Law School, a practicing attorney, and treasurer of the Texarkana

Political Equality Club. Dale was endorsed by the Texarkana League of Women Voters, but she finished second among three candidates in the 1922 Democratic primary. Dale later served on the legislative committee of the Arkansas Federation of Women's Clubs and was appointed Miller County and probate judge by Governor McRae in 1924.[270] Although several women, including Representatives Florence McRaven and Ella B. Hurst would run for Senate seats, it would be forty years before Dorathy Allen would be the first woman elected to the state senate.

## Women of the Arkansas House and Senate

After eighty-six years of statehood, the first two women, Frances Hunt and Nellie Mack, were appointed to fill vacancies in the Arkansas House of Representatives by Governor Thomas C. McRae in the spring of 1922. Later that year, the first two women were elected to the Arkansas General Assembly, Frances Hunt and Erle Chambers, after prevailing over male opponents. With no precedent for a legislative body that included women, they were trailblazers, not only for their election victories but also for negotiating the roles that women would play in the Arkansas legislature. They were celebrated for their successes by the League of Women Voters while being treated courteously by their male colleagues as curiosities. Representatives Hunt and Chambers were allowed to choose prime seats on the front row, to the right of the Speaker's dais, which would become the customary seating arrangement for future women legislators.

As we celebrate the centennial of the first women in the Arkansas General Assembly, there now are more women holding seats in the Arkansas House of Representatives than the total number who served during the first fifty years. Only twenty women served in the House between 1922 and 1972, and there were no women legislators during fourteen years of those five decades. No women served in the Arkansas Senate until the election of Dorathy Allen in 1964. No Black American woman served in the Arkansas General Assembly until Irma Hunter Brown in 1981.

These legislative pioneers faced daunting circumstances in being elected and in making an impact in the male-dominated institution. All seemed well aware of the importance of having women's perspectives on legislation, reflected in their contribution to the debates and by the bills they introduced. They also expressed the need for and recognized the benefits of electing more women to the legislature, knowing that their mere presence would raise awareness among their male colleagues that the views of women might be worth considering or at least not so routinely ignored.

Representative Irma Hunter Brown (a 1995 Africa Fund delegate to South Africa, Namibia, and Zimbabwe) travels the United States in April 1996 with Africa Fund delegates Deputy Speaker Edna Madzongwe of Zimbabwe, Deputy Speaker of Northern Province Legislature in South Africa Koti Nyama, and Chairperson of the Management Committee of Mariental in Namibia Lucia Basson.
*Courtesy of the African Activist Archive Project and the Africa Fund.*

After three weeks into her first legislative session in 1927, Florence McRaven published an article, "What I Think of the Arkansas Legislature," commenting primarily on the process and giving her colleagues every benefit of the doubt about their motives. Other than commenting that her perspective on activity in the chamber was quite different from that she had from the balcony as a civilian before her election, there is no expression regarding the influence of gender on her new role.[271] One can only imagine what her views might have been two months later, after joining the contentious floor fight against the Rotenberry anti-evolution bill sponsored by one of her Pulaski County colleagues.

Representative Elizabeth Thompson published *Songs and Sonnets of a Solon* in 1926, as she was completing her term in the House. It was dedicated to her legislative colleagues, but specifically naming and including photographs of Representatives Frances Hunt and Erle Chambers, the two women with whom she served. It opened with a short story in dialect, "Maria at the State Legislature and the Welfare Conference," wherein the narrator makes humorous observations about the loquaciousness of the male legislators and endorses the earnest efforts of women to address the needs of children.[272]

Representative Erle Chambers, first elected in 1922, said she found "that men members pay more attention to the opinions of women members and women constituents than is apparent on the surface." Although she was a single career woman, Chambers said, "The particular service for which women are fitted in public life lies in the fields related to children and the home. Man is essentially a provider for the home, woman is a maternal protector of the home and children. There are many legislative fields which do not come primarily within a woman's province, but there are also others which men are not qualified to handle. There is no essential difference in ability between the two, it's chiefly a question of attitude."[273]

In addition, Chambers discussed the higher standards that voters and the larger public seemed to apply to women candidates and legislators. "Women in public office are subjected to merciless scrutiny, and women themselves will vote down an incompetent woman far more readily than men will vote against an incompetent man," she said. "Because it is so much harder for a woman to be elected to the legislature than a man, the standard set for women in that position will be superior to that set for men for a long time to come." The relatively higher qualifications she recognized necessary for women as candidates and legislators generally continue to hold true in the twenty-first century.[274]

Representative Ethel Cole Cunningham, who represented Yell County and was the only woman in the House in 1931–1933, appears to have met that standard with her constituents and her legislative colleagues. The *Arkansas Gazette* mused, "Feminine politicians are a continual source of amusement, apparently, to the cartoonists of the country, but judging by the great courtesy and consideration with which Mrs. Cunningham is treated by her associates in the legislature, it would seem that masculine politicians themselves have the greatest respect for her."[275] One reason might have been that Representative Cunningham was handily elected in 1930 over five male opponents and was reelected in 1932, defeating ten male opponents. She would then go on to serve sixteen years on the board of trustees for Arkansas Polytechnic College by appointment of four consecutive governors.

It is difficult to miss the irony in Representative Ella B. Hurst's election to the first of three terms in 1934. Her husband, former representative Abner Hurst, had led the fight in the House against a proposed woman's suffrage amendment in 1911, arguing that women were not clamoring for suffrage

Front row: Representatives Ella B. Hurst and Ethel Cunningham, Arkansas First Lady Tera Futrell, and Arkansas Second Lady Rachel Cazort. Back row: Representatives Erle Chambers and Maude Brown. January 1935.
© Arkansas Democrat-Gazette *File Photo.*

and that many would not vote. "This bill should be everlastingly killed," he said, and "women should not be further encouraged in this equal suffrage foolishness."[276]

Ella Hurst, of course, *did* vote and was elected to the legislature, leading the Washington County Democratic primary ticket over eight men opponents and avoiding a runoff. She also expressed regret, being the only woman in the House during her first term, that there were not more women members in the legislature, but she "confidently expected the day to come when 50 percent of the membership will be composed of women."[277] That day has not yet arrived. The state senate had a record eight women members (22.9 percent) during the 2011 session. The House briefly had twenty-eight women members in 2020 after three special elections to fill vacant seats. With seven women in the Senate that year, the General Assembly reached a record of thirty-five women (25.9 percent) in December 2020. In the centennial year, female representation declined slightly to 23 percent, with seven Senators and twenty-four Representatives.

Other women who had served in the legislature agreed with Hurst that Arkansas would benefit from having more women in the legislature to give a more favorable balance of perspectives. Representative Maude Brown of Clarendon thought Arkansas would be an even better place to live if there were more women in the legislature. "Women are prompt, sincere, conscientious, and conservative, and they make good legislators," she said at the 1929 United States Good Roads Association in Memphis.[278]

Those early women legislators were not as optimistic as Representative Hurst that the percentage of women in the House would ever be so high. So far, their doubts have been confirmed. Representative Brown expressed doubt that women would constitute a significant portion of the legislative membership for many years and that "women can hope for nothing more than to grow slowly in their new-found fields of opportunity. This, I think, is a very fortunate thing for us," she said, hedging on her earlier views, "because it will allow us to grow and become equal to the responsibility, rather than to have it thrust upon us before any considerable women are equal to the work of conducting public affairs." Representative Ethel Cole Cunningham agreed that most women in Arkansas were "not yet aroused to the responsibility of citizenship and that no greater injury could be done to the cause of feminine independence than to place them prematurely in positions of prominence and importance." While such characterizations of women citizens might appear dismissive, it was not unfounded at the time nor until the impact of second wave feminism on women's political consciousness.[279]

Women in Arkansas were working tirelessly to make sure women *were* "aroused to the responsibility of citizenship." Blanche Collins, legislative chair of the Little Rock Business and Professional Women's Club, in 1937 said women must recognize their "right to a place in the political sun [and] be recognized as a unit of our body politic." She lauded the ongoing effort "to put as much emphasis as possible on the development of the business and professional woman as a well-informed individual who knows her community." Collins echoed the proposition that there are "certain types of legislation which come naturally to be referred to women for the simple reason that they deal with subjects of primary interest to women." Credit for the recent success in passing legislation "to make both business and politics responsible for the welfare of workers and minors, and to introduce humanitarian legislation" must go to women, for "they first thought them out then fought them out," and "we cannot overlook the large part our women legislators have played."[280]

Collins praised the success of Representative Ella Hurst for passage of the "Pure Elections Law," in 1935. Hurst had lost a Senate election in 1936, but she was back for a second term in the House in 1943. She was perhaps more amused than chagrined when male legislators began their floor speeches with the salutation, "Gentlemen of the House," and she was still advocating to women's political groups for the recruitment and election of more women in

Representative Ella B. Hurst was an accomplished sidesaddle
equestrian and popular part of University of Arkansas homecoming parades. She is pictured here at the 1949
homecoming parade. *Courtesy of Ann Sugg.*

the legislature.[281] In 1945, Hurst was joined in the House by Alene Word of
Mississippi County and Helen Buchanan of Nevada County, marking the
first time in twenty years that three women were serving simultaneously.

During a period of four years with no women in the Arkansas General
Assembly, the *Arkansas Democrat* named Pauline Hoeltzel as the 1949
Arkansas Woman of the Year. As a young girl, she had marched in suffrage
parades with her mother, the suffrage leader Emma Reichardt Hoeltzel; as
an adult, she worked with the Arkansas Democratic Women's Club to recruit
and elect women to the Arkansas legislature. The newspaper also published
a feature article in 1950 headlined, "Women Have Assumed Vital Role in
Politics in Short 52 Years." Governor Sid McMath, in a keynote speech to the
statewide Senior Girl Scout Conference in 1951, said he wished that the legislature had a few women in it right now. Explaining his reasoning, he said, "If
we had some women legislators in the special session now, we wouldn't have

the trouble we are having in getting extra revenue for the schools," because "women just naturally recognize the need for providing adequate money for the school children."[282]

In 1952, Lera Jeanne Rowlette was elected from Miller County and would be the only woman in the House for the 1953–1954 session and is still the youngest ever. She was a twenty-three-year-old lawyer who had defeated two men, including the incumbent, and advocated for more women in politics. She said she thought that "women of serious purpose are likely to be more conscientious in public office than men." In a telling comment that reflects a continuing tendency to focus on appearance over ability, the *Arkansas Democrat* felt compelled to describe her as a pretty, five-foot-seven, 120-pound, blue-eyed blond when asking how she felt about being the only woman in the House, although there had been no comparable physical accounts of any male legislators or inquiries during the last four years as to their feelings about being among the 135 male legislators.[283]

A female reporter for the *Arkansas Democrat* later wrote that Representative Rowlette represented "the American career girl at her best." Nell Cotnam, the daughter of suffrage leader Florence Brown Cotnam and a former suffragist herself, wrote a feature for the *Arkansas Gazette* reporting that Rowlette said "if all women would make up their minds and vote according to their beliefs instead of asking their husbands to make up their minds for them, they could put across any kind of legislation they desire." To Rowlette, "It is quite all right for husband and wife to be in accord, but she believes in women doing a little thinking on their own."[284]

Rowlette served only one term before being defeated for reelection in 1954, followed by four more years without a woman in the legislature. When representatives Mattie Hackett and Willie Oates were elected in 1958, the *Arkansas Gazette* pronounced it a good thing, not for their political perspectives or political platforms, but because the "House, frequently a rowdy, playful body, will have the calming influence of at least two women members."

When Bernice Kizer, Doris McCastlain, and Dove Mulkey joined Hackett in 1961, they set a record for having four women members in the House. When Representative Hackett died in office in 1963, she was replaced by Gladys Martin (later Oglesby), the first instance of a woman being replaced by another woman since 1927. The first rendition of a women's caucus was formed in 1963, when Doris McCastlain organized and chaired the state chapter of the National Order of Women Legislators (OWL).[285] In 1964, Dorathy Allen became the first female state senator in Arkansas, forty-two years after women first served in the House. Representative McCastlain resigned in 1965, advising future women legislators that "men still think politics is a man's

Willie Oates files for state representative at the Pulaski
County Courthouse in 1958. *Courtesy of Butler Center for
Arkansas Studies, Central Arkansas Library System.*

Representative Mattie Hackett at her desk in the House of
Representatives Chamber in 1959. *Representative Mattie Hackett
ECD559.01, Arkansas State Archives, used with permission.*

Representative Doris McCastlain with Representative
Albert Hayes. *Courtesy of Doris McCastlain.*

game," and that "women are wanted in the legislature about like mice are
wanted in the kitchen."[286]

Vada Sheid, first elected to the House in 1966, became only the twentieth
woman in Arkansas to hold legislative office. She would serve twelve years
in the House and eight in the Senate, becoming the first of twelve women
to serve in both chambers. An article by Sara Alderman Murphy, "Distaff
Note: The Ladies of the Legislature," was based on interviews with the four
women members of the 1967 General Assembly about their perceived roles.
All agreed that they would like to see more women run and win legislative
office, but they acknowledged that both men and women said women should
not be in politics. Representative Martin said when hearing objections from
women, "I always answered that women are needed in the legislature for
balance and stability. Since women play such a big part in electing officials,
I think they should also be elected to office." Representative Sheid reported
that one woman constituent said she "would not vote for her because she had

Senator Dorathy Allen, Arkansas First Lady Alta Faubus, and Representatives
Bernice Kizer, Gladys Martin Oglesby, and Doris McCastlain, 1963.
*Courtesy of Doris McCastlain.*

to stay home and do housework." Having been housewives themselves, the
legislators felt even more strongly that more women should become involved
in politics.[287]

Senator Allen, who was already well-acquainted with the men in the
Senate for working there when her husband served, said she had wondered
how she would be accepted as the first woman senator in 130 years of the
state's political existence. Representative Oglesby was aware of the possible
backlash against assertive women and said, "We try not to push ourselves
out front and hog the show." Representative Kizer also acknowledged the
demands of role expectations, and believed to be effective, women legislators
should maintain "the dignity that men like to see in a woman. It is important
that we think and act like women. It's not a matter of taking a man's place, it's
a matter of working with men. Everything we do reflects on the next woman
who comes to serve in our place."[288]

These women were well aware of the conundrum facing women political
leaders. In persuasion and debate, it is important to be knowledgeable and

informed, but one element of political power is "the necessity for a show of strength."[289] This is often a delicate balance of perceptions about gender role expectations for women in politics, finding the lacuna between the degree of assertiveness and passionate argument routinely admired in male legislators and exercising that same forcefulness without being labeled aggressive and emotional. Nonetheless, they told Murphy they hoped their examples of running hard-fought campaigns and winning over male opponents would encourage more women to run for the legislature and increase the influence of women's perspectives on public policy.[290]

Senator Sheid, later reflecting on her long career in politics, revealed how she navigated the obstacles facing women in politics during the last half of the twentieth century. When she first filed to run for Baxter County treasurer in 1956, she said, "Some laughed and some thought I was out of place." During her second and successful campaign for the office, seeking the support of one influential man in county politics, she recalled him telling her that "he didn't think politics was any place for a woman, and he didn't approve of me seeking the job."[291] Even after having been a county official and having served quietly and very effectively in the House and Senate for two decades, during her unsuccessful 1984 Senate campaign for reelection, she found that still, "they were making fun and ridicule . . . of the very notion that a woman could be a leader in state politics." Sheid knew that women were expected to be "docile, demure, and deferential," but she had always seen her best qualities as being "opinionated, independent, and persistent." When newspaper columnists or her political opponents called her "fluffy," weak, and ineffective, her response was revealing of her choices for being successful in serving her constituents and bringing significant infrastructure projects to her district:

> Well, of course I worked behind the scenes. Of course, I batted my eyes and looked helpless when I was trying to get the men of the Legislature—and the Congress and the White House—to pass the bills and acts my people needed. What the devil else was I supposed to do? For a few short intervals, I was the only woman in the game. There was no way they were ever going to take me seriously. I couldn't even let myself care about that. I only cared that they did what I needed done. If I had to cajole, flatter, simper, pretend helplessness, pretend to be a damned lunatic, it didn't matter. I wasn't there to make myself a power broker. I was there to get things done. So, I did what I had to do. I played the game of politics, and I played it well.[292]

Legislative reapportionment and the move toward single-member districts offered more opportunities for women legislative candidates. In 1975,

Representative Vada Sheid speaking on House floor.
*Courtesy of the Arkansas Senate.*

Representative Carolyn Pollan of Fort Smith became the first Republican woman to serve in the House, continuing to be reelected and serving there for twenty-four years (still the record for female legislators) until her retirement due to term limits. Another effect was the election of Irma Hunter Brown of Little Rock in 1980, the first Black woman legislator to serve in the House and later the first in the state Senate. In 1983, with a record seven women serving in the legislature and still finding themselves excluded from many "back room" discussions, the first bipartisan and bicameral women's caucus was organized. Among other legislative policy concerns, the caucus addressed the long-standing inequity of a private restroom for the convenience of male legislators, while women legislators had to leave the chamber to find a public restroom for women.[293] In a legislative culture that had long been white, male, and dominated by a single political party, the concept of a caucus was unfamiliar and unappreciated, but it seemed to be an effective move for women legislators to discuss and voice their issues and concerns.

This period also ushered in women members who had developed skills in the political environment and with party activities before being elected. Representative Judy Petty was steeped in Republican Party organizations since high school and had already made her first campaign for Congress, when she handily defeated a ten-term House Democratic male incumbent in 1980. She began working in politics as a secretary for Governor Winthrop Rockefeller, at a time when, she said, "a lot of young ambitious women were

Representative Judy Petty with a page at the
Arkansas Capitol. *Courtesy of the UALR Center for
Arkansas History and Culture. Women in Arkansas
photograph collection, ca. 1850s–1980s.*

wearing those buttons that said *I Make Policy, Not Coffee.* I made so much
coffee, so willingly, poured coffee, refilled coffee cups, didn't mind doing it.
It put me in where things were going on, and I tried to be like a sponge. I
tried to absorb, how are decisions made, what are the considerations of the
people who really do make policy."[294] Representative Gloria Cabe had been
president of the Arkansas League of Women Voters and had been the organization's lobbyist for ratification of the Equal Rights Amendment, as well as a
paid political staffer for Bill Clinton's gubernatorial campaigns. She declined
running for reelection in 1990 to manage Governor Clinton's reelection campaign, then became his chief of staff. Both Petty and Cabe would later hold
high-level political appointments in Washington, DC.

The Arkansas legislative culture in which women legislators must function
has been slow to change. Exclusively the domain of men from 1836 until

1922 and remaining dominated by male legislators constituting more than 75 percent in 2022, the old ways and operative assumptions only slowly adapt to integrate the women interlopers. The legislative culture and its disdain for activist women in the 1960s came to be represented by Representative Paul Van Dalsem, a rural legislator first elected in 1936. In a program sponsored by the Arkansas Chapter of the American Association of University Women (AAUW) in 1961, Van Dalsem complained that interest groups corrupted the legislature and that the average legislator gets more propositions than a beauty contest winner. And among those groups, he charged, "the worst ever to come before the legislature are the woman's organizations such as the American Association of University Women, the Women's Voters League, the Library group, and others."[295]

In 1963, when the League of Women Voters and the AAUW sent members to testify in committees and lobby legislators to support a bill to abolish the poll tax and to oppose a literacy test amendment, Representative Van Dalsem was annoyed that they had successfully persuaded several legislators to oppose the literacy test and complained it just showed "how pretty women can excite people." In a speech to the entirely white male Little Rock Optimist Club after the legislative session, Van Dalsem derided the "frustrated" women lobbyists and said he had seen as many as thirty of them on the House floor at one time. Then he uttered the remarks that would stigmatize the Arkansas legislature well past his retirement in 1976. "We don't have any of these university women in Perry County, but I'll tell you what we do up there when one of our women starts poking around in something she doesn't know anything about. We get her an extra milk cow. If that don't work, we give her a little more garden to tend to. And then if that's not enough, we get her pregnant and keep her barefoot."[296]

Women say they are generally treated courteously by their male colleagues, and none reported being openly rebuked for their gender or sincere interest in politics. Nonetheless, several examples offer obvious evidence that women legislators are not always accorded the same acceptance and respect indicative of equal status. During the 1995 legislative session, Nap Murphy was presenting a bill on the House floor that made substantial changes to the probate code, something he knew little about and could neither explain nor answer questions. Representative Becky Lynn raised several questions, and Murphy replied, "Well, Sweetie, we'll just leave that to the lawyers." Representative Lynn maintained her composure and said, "Well, Mr. Murphy, I *am* a lawyer, and I'm trying to understand how this is going to affect the law." Laughter erupted. She let it pass at the time, because she thought, "I couldn't do the women lawyer thing and crucify him, because then he would have gotten the

Senator Charlie Cole Chaffin in committee.
*Courtesy of the Arkansas Senate.*

sympathy vote." Representative Lynn was known, in jest, for several years as "Representative Sweetie."[297]

During her first term in 2009, Representative Stephanie Malone, thirty, was sitting next to another legislator while waiting for a committee meeting to begin. A member of the staff approached the older legislator and said, "Excuse me, representative, your daughter isn't allowed to sit at the committee table." Malone, surprised by the comment, remembered, "I will never forget hearing that sentence only two weeks into my first term in the Arkansas legislature, and realizing they meant *me*, mistaking me as the daughter — rather than the colleague — of another state representative." Although she was the youngest woman in the House that year, several of the male legislators were even younger, yet, she noted, "I'd be willing to bet they never had to deal with anything like that."[298]

Women were making gains in representation in the late twentieth century, but the number of female House members dropped from twenty-two in 1997 to fourteen in 2001, and in 1999, Arkansas was the only state without a woman in the state senate. During the first two decades of the twenty-first century, the number of women legislators in 2011 (thirty) had tripled in the two decades since 1991 (ten), affirming the contention that when more women run, more women win election to office. Some of these woman legislators were advocates for the equal treatment of men and woman and participated in organizations supporting the women's movement; others would eschew the label of feminist. All, however, were beneficiaries of the nation's second wave of feminism that raised the awareness of obstacles and opportunities for women in politics. Although as usual, Arkansas was slower in experiencing national trends, but more women were becoming involved in politics and political party activity, more were being recruited as candidates, more were seeing themselves as capable and competent leaders, more were running for public office, and more women were being elected to the Arkansas legislature.

Women legislators were becoming better educated than their female predecessors as well as their male colleagues. They were entering the legislature at an earlier age, with previous political experience and with business and professional experience beyond unpaid housework and childcare, and they were still more likely than their male colleagues to have considerable volunteer experience.[299] Another significant change that reflected the state's political shift was that since 2015 there have been more Republican women than Democrats. Although all brought a woman's perspective to their work, they do not have identical voting records. Political partisanship often trumped gender considerations. Support for ratification of the Equal Rights Amendment and restrictions on women's reproductive health care are but two examples.

The fact that the Arkansas General Assembly, like in other states, was a male-oriented institution by law prior to the early 1920s, created an enduring culture that privileged male legislators and their effectiveness, even as women were being appointed and elected to serve. Despite this male-dominated culture, which endured throughout the twentieth century and in some ways into the twenty-first century, we find no evidence that women legislators served with an intent to change that culture. Through their service, however, the culture evolved, both in greater acceptance of their presence in the legislature and in the minds of voters who increasingly accepted and elected women into the state's highest legislative offices. As Senator Ruth Whitaker remarked, "It is still a good-old-boy's network, but there are some that are now coming around and not being as condescending to us. I think we were an oddity when I was elected." She added, "I think politics for centuries has been more of a man's world. It has been an unspoken thing. But as more and more women become better educated, and more financially independent, it is opening up many doors."[300]

In running her first campaign, Representative Jacqueline Roberts encountered, as did other female legislative candidates, an electorate unsupportive

Peggy Jeffries testifies against Governor Bill Clinton's education
reforms, as First Lady Hillary Rodham Clinton listens,
October 17, 1983. © Arkansas Democrat-Gazette *File Photo.*

and unwilling to picture women in such elective office. "I had people ask me,
'Why are you trying to take a man's job?'" She responded, "I'm not trying to
take a man's job. I'm trying to do a job that a woman or man can do that's
qualified."[301] Garnering the support of the electorate and changing that culture is the first step, and necessary for securing women in public service.
Representative Joyce Dees found that "Women in the Legislature are the
hardest working people in the world. We researched issues, met with agencies, advocates, and many, many, special interest groups. Our time was dedicated to the people of the State. It was a job that we took very seriously."[302]
Representative Barbara Nix said, "As a woman, I felt we had to work harder
to win the respect of not just male legislators, but others who represented
companies, special interest entities such as those who worked to lobby legislators. It was important to understand the 'good-old-boy' mentality in order
to be effective as a legislator and not just as a 'female legislator.'"[303] Roberts
regretfully added, "So they don't think you're supposed to be there in the first
place. That's the number one strike. And the number two strike: you're there,
and we don't like it because you are here."[304]

The Women's Legislative Caucus sponsored a program, "Celebrating Women in the General Assembly—Past to Present," in the capitol rotunda during Women's History Month in 2010. Representative Lindsley Smith presented the keynote address on "Sheroes of Arkansas History." Former women legislators were represented by Charlotte Schexnayder, who spoke about her House experiences from 1985–1998, and Senator Irma Hunter Brown spoke "about and memorialized the contributions of deceased women legislators." State Treasurer Martha Shoffner, the first woman legislator elected to a constitutional office, presented the Proclamation of Arkansas Women's Legislative Day, and Henry Jones III, the grandson of Representative Frances Hunt, shared his memories in "Reflections on the First."[305] Almost all of the living women who have served in the Arkansas General Assembly were present, and each stood as they were individually recognized and honored for their service.

Led by Representative Sarah Capp, women in the Arkansas House initiated #ARGIRLSLEAD in the ninety-first General Assembly. Representative Capp was inspired to organize the project after talking with students at a high school in her district, and two young women told her it was personally empowering to meet and get to know a woman legislator. To promote positive image and leadership for young girls across the state, several women legislators recorded unscripted video presentations, sharing their own vulnerabilities and encouraging girls and women to become involved in state politics and consider running for office. The project maintains an online social media presence that includes YouTube, Facebook, and Twitter accounts.[306]

During Women's History Month in 2019, Representative Charlene Fite introduced House Resolution 1056, Celebrating Women in Public Office Day, and calling upon "the citizens of Arkansas to unite as we support the success of women who serve in public office." Among the self-evident truths declared in the resolution were that: (1) women who serve in public office are essential to ensuring that women in Arkansas are well-represented; (2) while the twentieth century was a pivotal time of growth for women entering politics, women remain underrepresented in male-dominated fields, including politics, and thus providing opportunities to support women who serve in public office is imperative; and (3) recognizing women who serve in public office will raise awareness of the fundamental necessity of their work and will inspire young people to serve their communities. It was adopted by the House of Representatives without dissent and ignored in press coverage of legislative activities that day, whether because it was noncontroversial or because it was considered unimportant is unclear. The argument that seeing more women in

Governor Bill Clinton signing bill with sponsors and supporters. Women legislators are Representatives Wanda Northcutt Hartz, Charlotte Schexnayder, Nancy Balton, and Shirley Meacham. *Courtesy of Nancy Balton.*

public office motivates other women to participate in politics is an important truth.[307]

We hope that this book helps provide a greater appreciation for the long history of struggle by women for political citizenship in Arkansas, a subject that has often been ignored and remained untold. It has been a joy to research and bring to greater public attention the lives of the 146 women who have been members of the Arkansas General Assembly. Their stories are an inspiration in themselves and are instructive of the many paths to public service by women from varying backgrounds and personal experiences.

We believe that these 146 women legislators have enriched Arkansas's political history and that their stories need to be told and remembered. The brief biographies included in this book should be only a starting point for empirical investigations that explore such issues as voting records and issue analysis, campaign strategies, committee work and floor debate, indeed, all aspects of initiating and enacting public policy. Because so little has been written about Arkansas women legislators, there is much more to explore and explicate.

Visibility is vital, or in the popular vernacular, "if you can see it, you can be it." Our greatest hope is that the biographical entries of the women legislators in this book will tell a new story and that its reception will inspire more girls and women to become involved in politics and public affairs, to run for public office, and to bring their unique insights and leadership abilities to improve the lives of all who call Arkansas home. As Representative Wanda Northcutt remarked in her speech on women in Arkansas politics in March of 1993, "The history of women in Arkansas politics may be neither as detailed nor as extensive as we would like. It is a history, though, that is being built rapidly during this century. And it is a history that will become more compelling, more involved, and more comprehensive in the century to come."[308]

# THE STATESWOMEN

# Frances Hunt

FROM: Pine Bluff, Jefferson County
PARTY: Democratic
BIRTHPLACE: Des Arc, Arkansas
DATES: June 6, 1874–August 23, 1958
EDUCATION: Des Arc High School
OCCUPATION: homemaker

*Photo courtesy of Arkansas Secretary of State.*

Frances Hunt—born Frances Rowena Mathews and known to her family as "Fannie Dear"—was educated in the Des Arc public schools and learned the printing trade at her father's newspaper, the *Des Arc Citizen*. While working at a newspaper in Benton in 1899, she married Henry Pearce Jones, a young attorney. Henry Jones died less than a year later, and Hunt, a pregnant widow, moved to Redfield to live with her family.

In November 1904, Hunt began a campaign for postmistress of the Arkansas House of Representatives, and she was overwhelmingly elected on the first ballot in January 1905. In October, she married Representative Sidney Jackson Hunt, a prominent Pine Bluff attorney who represented Jefferson County in the Arkansas House of Representatives 1905–1908.

Frances Hunt was an active clubwoman in Pine Bluff. She was secretary of the Young Ladies Club of the First Methodist Church and vice president of the Woman's Christian Temperance Union. Hunt was also a member of the Democratic Women's Club, as well as the David O. Dodd Chapter of the United Daughters of the Confederacy and the Pine Bluff Chapter of the Daughters of the American Revolution.

On April 11, 1922, Hunt became the first woman member of the Arkansas House of Representatives, appointed by Governor Thomas C. McRae to fill a vacancy created by resignation. Less than a month later, she announced her candidacy for reelection to a full term, securing nomination in the Democratic primary and winning unopposed in the general election.

On the first day of the 1923 session, Representative Hunt introduced legislation to curtail the activities of "labor agents" recruiting sharecroppers and farm laborers for better jobs in the North, a process that undermined the low wage farm economy and the Jim Crow system in the South. She was named chair of the Committee on Confederate Soldiers and Widows.

Hunt was reelected in 1924. During the 1925 session, she became the first woman to preside over the House, when she took the chair during a temporary absence by Speaker Thomas Hill, her Jefferson County colleague. She proposed a pension fund for destitute single mothers, financed by a three-dollar fee on marriage licenses. Hunt successfully passed legislation to create the Board of Cosmetic Therapy to license beauticians and inspect cosmetology schools and beauty shops.

Choosing not to seek reelection in 1926, Hunt continued to be involved in public affairs and was employed as a field inspector for the Board of Cosmetic Therapy. For twelve years she traveled the state inspecting beauty shops and occasionally prosecuting unlicensed beauticians. She retired in 1938 to raise her grandson, Henry P. Jones III, whose mother died in childbirth.

# Nellie B. Mack

HOUSE: 1922
FROM: Warren, Bradley County
PARTY: Democratic
BIRTHPLACE: Antioch, Tennessee
DATES: October 1857–July 24, 1931
EDUCATION: Public schools in Fayetteville and Nashville, Tennessee; Edgefield High School (Nashville, TN), 1875; Edgefield Female Academy, 1876
OCCUPATION: insurance agent, teacher

*Photo courtesy of the authors.*

Nellie B. Mack (born Ellen DeMoville Bright) was the eleventh of fourteen children born to William Hall Bright, a prominent farmer, and Elizabeth Eppes DeMoville, a homemaker. Her family was politically prominent in Tennessee, where her great-grandfather, William Hall, was a member of the state house (1797–1805) and senate (1821–1829), governor (1829), and congressman (1831–1832). Her grandfather, James Bright, was Lincoln County circuit clerk (1810–1826), and her uncle, John Bright, served in the Tennessee house (1847–1848) and the US Congress (1871–1880).

After completing her education, Mack taught primary grades at the Main Street School in Nashville and was a teacher in the North Edgefield Baptist Mission Sunday School. She moved to Little Rock in 1882 and taught at Peabody School until 1885. During her time in Little Rock, she attended suffrage debates at the Eclectic Club and socialized with the Ten Pin Club, was nominated for enrolling clerk of the Arkansas state senate, was said to be "one of the leading lights of Little Rock society," and the *Arkansas Gazette* called her "a lady of culture and refinement." In 1885, she married local businessman James Russell Barnett, and they had two children before his death in 1889.

Moving to Morrilton to be near her younger sister, Mack continued to teach and became an insurance agent. She was a candidate for Morrilton postmistress in 1892, was an active debater in the Pathfinder Club, and was on the executive committee of the Arkansas Federation of Women's Clubs. Her brother-in-law was William Lewis Moose, the leading attorney in Morrilton, president of the state senate, circuit judge, and later attorney general of Arkansas.

In 1903, Mack married William Francis Mack, a Confederate veteran and former Bradley County judge, and moved to Warren. She was a teacher of primary classes at the West Ward School and became active as vice president of the First Baptist Church Women's Missionary Society, publicity chair of the Warren Woman's Christian Temperance Union, and state chaplain of the Knights and Ladies of Honor. Her son married the daughter of William E. Atkinson, former attorney general of Arkansas (1889–1893) and Fifth Circuit chancery judge (1921–1935).

In 1921, Mack announced as a Democratic candidate for Bradley County treasurer. However, following the death of Representative Byron L. Herring, Governor Thomas C. McRae appointed Mack as state representative on April 24, 1922. Serving for eight months, Representative Mack was the second woman member of the Arkansas House.

# Erle Chambers

HOUSE: 1923–1926
FROM: Little Rock, Pulaski County
PARTY: Democratic
BIRTHPLACE: Germantown, Tennessee
DATES: July 25, 1875–January 9, 1941
EDUCATION: Little Rock public schools;
University of Arkansas Law Department,
1912; University of Chicago Law School
OCCUPATION: executive secretary

*Photo courtesy of Arkansas Secretary of State.*

Erle Rutherford Chambers and her family moved to Little Rock in 1881. Her father, Thomas Chambers, was a prominent attorney and was the 1890 Union Labor Party nominee for Arkansas attorney general.

After graduating from Peabody High School, Chambers obtained a teaching certificate and taught in the Little Rock public schools for nine years, then worked as a legal secretary for the firm of Moore and Smith. Graduating first in her class from the University of Arkansas Law Department in 1912, she studied an additional year at the University of Chicago Law School.

Chambers was appointed chief probation officer for the Pulaski County Juvenile Court in 1913 and successfully lobbied the state legislature to establish a Boys Industrial School and a new Girls Industrial School. In 1917, she began a twenty-four-year career as executive secretary of the Arkansas Tuberculous Association.

Chambers served as treasurer of the Little Rock Professional Women's Club and on the judicial and legislative committees of the Little Rock Federation of Women's Clubs. Governor George Hays appointed Chambers as the state's representative to the Southern Conference on Woman and Child Labor, Governor Charles Brough appointed her chair of the Commission of Charities and Corrections, and Governor Thomas McRae appointed her as probate judge for Pulaski County.

Chambers gave her first speech on "The Woman Movement" in 1910. She was a founding member of the Arkansas Women's Political Equality League in 1911 and the Arkansas League of Women Voters in 1920. She helped conduct citizenship schools for newly enfranchised women voters in 1920, and was recruited by the League of Women Voters as a candidate for the Arkansas House in 1922.

Chambers was nominated for one of the four Pulaski County House seats in the August 1922 Democratic primary and was unopposed in the general election. She was reelected for a second term in 1924. Representative Chambers chaired the Labor Committee during both terms. The first bill she passed was to authorize state participation in the Sheppard-Towner Maternity and Infancy Protection program, funded by the US Children's Bureau. She sponsored appropriations for the Arkansas Illiteracy Commission, the Board of Health, and the School for the Blind, and legislation abolishing curtsey rights of husbands and making competent testimony of women in certain criminal cases. Chambers was floor manager in making Arkansas the first state to ratify the proposed federal Child Labor Amendment.

After choosing not to seek reelection in 1926, Chambers continued to be involved in public service. She was secretary of the Arkansas Negro Tuberculosis Sanatorium Board and a member of the Board of Trustees of Arkansas AM&N College. In the community, she was a member of the Arkansas State Interracial Committee, Arkansas Council of the Association of Southern Women for the Prevention of Lynching, Urban League of Greater Little Rock, and the Little Rock Housing Association. She ran unsuccessfully for the Arkansas House in 1932.

# Elizabeth Thompson

HOUSE: 1925–1926
FROM: Helena, Phillips County
PARTY: Democratic
BIRTHPLACE: Kingston, Georgia
DATES: January 8, 1872–October 19, 1960
EDUCATION: Clarendon public schools;
Galloway Women's College
OCCUPATION: teacher, newspaper reporter

*Photo courtesy of Arkansas Secretary of State.*

Elizabeth Thompson (born Elizabeth Gatewood Hooper and known as Bessie) grew up in Clarendon in a politically active family. Her father, a Confederate veteran and attorney, was Monroe County judge and her brother was county clerk. After graduating from Galloway College and teaching at Clarendon High School, she married Phillips County planter Frank Thompson and moved to Midland Crossing.

Thompson was an active clubwoman, including dramatics chair of the Twentieth Century Club, chair of the Authors and Composers Society for Phillips County, and District Education Chair and Legislative Council of the Arkansas Federation of Women's Clubs. As president of the Phillips County League of Women Voters, she led the group in demanding "clean and fair elections" and the appointment of women as election judges and clerks and positions on the Democratic Central Committee. She published three collections of poetry that brought her wider literary attention. In 1914, she engaged in a debate in the *Arkansas Gazette* defending feminism. In 1922, she was an Arkansas delegate to the National League of Women Voters convention and the Pan American Conference of Women.

In 1924, Thompson became a candidate for the Arkansas House. She had the support of a wide network of women, the Young Men's Democratic Club, Representative John Sheffield, and "the straight Democrats." She was opposed by the local Ku Klux Klan. Thompson finished first among four candidates, defeating the Klan candidate, who finished third, by more than five hundred votes.

During the 1925 legislative session, Thompson handled local legislation on street improvement districts, police pensions, and securing state lands for support of the levy district. She sponsored legislation on teacher certification and an appropriation increase for the state's library service. She and Representative Erle Chambers sponsored a resolution urging the nation to join the World Court, and they worked to defeat Governor T. J. Terral's plan to abolish voluntary state boards and commissions. After the session, Thompson published *Songs and Sonnets of a Solon*, a collection dedicated to her legislative colleagues, especially Representatives Frances Hunt and Erle Chambers.

After the death of her husband in 1926, Thompson ran for Phillips County treasurer against incumbent Josephine Johnson, the first political contest in Arkansas between two women. Complaining that "pernicious propaganda" by the "Phillips County Political Machine" led to her defeat, she received 43 percent and lost by 399 votes.

Thompson continued her writing and worked as a reporter for the *Helena World* before moving back to Clarendon. She wrote a column for the local papers and served as a correspondent and contributor to papers in Memphis and Little Rock. Thompson founded the Clarendon Public Library and served as the librarian. She remained interested in local government, and at age seventy-seven, she was serving Monroe County as deputy county treasurer and secretary to the county judge.

# Florence McRaven

HOUSE: 1927–1930
FROM: Little Rock, Pulaski County
PARTY: Democratic
BIRTHPLACE: Tate County, Mississippi
DATES: May 11, 1877–October 25, 1975
EDUCATION: Altus public schools;
Hiram and Lydia College
OCCUPATION: labor inspector

*Photo courtesy of Arkansas Secretary of State.*

Florence McRaven (born Emily McGraw) moved to Arkansas with her parents in 1878. Her father, Daniel McGraw, was Franklin County surveyor for twelve years and was superintendent for a coal mining company. McRaven attended Altus public schools then graduated from Hiram and Lydia College with a master of English literature degree in 1895. She married John McRaven, and they moved to Little Rock in 1903.

As a mother of three, McRaven was an officer of the Pulaski Heights School Improvement Auxiliary and the Women's Educational Aid Society. She was a member of the Bay View Club and the United Daughters of the Confederacy, chaired committees of the Little Rock and Arkansas Federation of Women's Clubs, and was appointed head of the County Library Board. She was also an officer in the women's auxiliary of the local Ku Klux Klan.

McRaven attended courses at the Chautauqua Institute in New York. She taught vocal expression at the Little Rock Conservatory and presented oral interpretations of literary work and original poetry to various civic organizations. McRaven was a member of the Little Rock Drama League and president of the Arkansas Authors and Composers Society.

McRaven worked as an assistant juvenile probation officer and served as the coordinator of the fifty School Improvement Associations in the county. From 1923 to 1925, she was an inspector for the state labor bureau and secretary of the Industrial Welfare Commission, working on child labor issues and minimum wage and hour regulations for women.

Announcing as a candidate for the House of Representatives in 1926, she presented a brief for women in public office but said effective legislative leadership depended not upon the sex of the representative but upon "right motives, intelligence, and strength of character." She won that election and was reelected in 1928.

Representative McRaven sought to expand pensions for low-income mothers and extend the wage and hour regulations to women working in cotton mills. She also introduced legislation to abolish the death penalty and limit corporal punishment at the state farm for women. McRaven vigorously opposed the Rotenberry anti-evolution bill and argued for allowing Sunday baseball in Little Rock.

In 1930, McRaven ran for the state senate but was defeated. Through the influence of Senator Hattie Caraway, she was employed on the WPA Arkansas Writers Project, and she later returned to the state labor department until her retirement in 1947.

# Mary B. Wigstrand

HOUSE: 1927
FROM: Mena, Polk County
PARTY: Democratic
BIRTHPLACE: Chicago, Illinois
DATES: September 17, 1856–July 12, 1927
EDUCATION: St. Agnes Academy
(Memphis)
OCCUPATION: juvenile probation officer

*Photo courtesy of Arkansas Secretary of State.*

Mary B. Wigstrand (born Mary Ellen Blackburn) was from a politically prominent Kentucky family. Her father, captain Breckenridge Flournoy Blackburn, moved his family to Memphis and practiced law until his death from yellow fever in 1867. Growing up in Memphis, Wigstrand attended St. Agnes Academy, was a member of St. Peter's Catholic Church, and participated in the annual fundraising carnival for Christian Brothers College.

In 1877, Wigstrand married Amos Walter Jones, an aspiring architect, who died in 1879, and the following year she buried their young son. She remained in Memphis, but she often visited Kentucky while her uncle, Luke Blackburn, was governor, and she moved in the social and political circles of the nation's capital, living there for a time while her uncle Joseph Blackburn served in the US House and Senate.

While living in Laconia, Arkansas, near her Blackburn relatives' plantations, Wigstrand married Fred Wigstrand, a civil engineer from Sweden. Her cousin, Percy Blackburn, was elected to represent Desha County in the Arkansas House (1899–1902). The Wigstrands moved to Mena in 1900. Fred was appointed Polk County surveyor in 1904 by Governor Jeff Davis, and he was elected to the position in 1910.

Wigstrand was involved in her community, serving on boards and holding offices in the School Improvement Association, the Red Cross, the White Oak Cemetery Association, the Women's Literary Club, and the League of Women Voters. She shared her talents by writing and presenting poetry, and she won first place in fine arts for an etching at the Polk County Fair. In 1922, she was a delegate to the Democratic State Convention.

In 1924, Wigstrand was appointed juvenile probation officer for Polk County, and she was a candidate for state representative in 1926. Wigstrand soundly defeated Hatfield mayor William Brewer in the Democratic primary and was unopposed in the general election.

During the 1927 legislative session, Representative Wigstrand enacted legislation to change the name of the Illiteracy Commission to Arkansas Adult Education Commission. She and Representative Florence McRaven co-authored a bill to require the father of an illegitimate child to pay hospital expenses. Although she made a serious effort, she failed to achieve her main goal to establish the Western Agricultural College at Mena.

Mary Wigstrand died shortly after the legislative session adjourned.

# Maude Brown

HOUSE: 1929–1930
FROM: Clarendon, Monroe County
PARTY: Democratic
BIRTHPLACE: Jacksonport, Arkansas
DATES: October 31, 1885–July 19, 1961
EDUCATION: Newport High School
OCCUPATION: switchboard operator, nurse

*Photo courtesy of Arkansas Secretary of State.*

Maude Brown (born Maude Richardson), the daughter of Vaney Elizabeth Taylor and Arthur Ralph Richardson, a Confederate veteran, attended public schools in Newport. After high school graduation, she was a local telephone switchboard operator for Southwestern Telegraph and Telephone and was said to be "one of the most popular operators the local telephone exchange has ever had." In 1906, she married Jesse Brown, a telephone lineman, and moved to Clarendon.

While raising their two sons and caring for her aged parents, Brown received training and certification as a practical nurse, and she was appointed by Governor Charles Brough as the county chair to raise funds for the silver service of the USS *Arkansas*. She was active with the Methodist Church and Red Cross relief work, and she was a member of the United Daughters of the Confederacy and the Daughters of the American Revolution. Jesse became a successful farmer, cotton buyer, and automobile dealer. In 1917, he helped secure the Brinkley Chautauqua "feast of reason," and he was the US county food administrator in 1918.

Jesse Brown represented Monroe County in the Arkansas House of Representatives, 1921–1924. Three years after his death, Maude Brown announced as a candidate for the House in 1928. She was a tireless campaigner and made a special effort to emphasize the contributions of women legislators and to secure support from women voters. She won the Democratic primary over two opponents and was unopposed in the general election.

During the 1929 session, Representative Brown was vice chair of the Charitable Institutions Committee and worked with Brooks Hays, president of the Children's Home Society, to pass legislation for the Arkansas Children's Home and Hospital to become a state agency. She sponsored a bill to restore the Confederate state capitol and cosponsored legislation for the $1.5 million White River Bridge to replace the ferry at Clarendon. At the close of the session, the House of Representatives voted her as its most popular member.

Brown announced for reelection in 1930 but withdrew her candidacy before the election. She served as postmistress of the state senate in the 1931 session and remained in Little Rock while her oldest son was attending medical school there. As an experienced musician in piano, violin, and orchestral performance, she became a member of the Little Rock Civic Music Association and the Arkansas Authors and Composers Society, and she directed the YWCA glee club. In 1936, Brown assumed responsibility for her two nephews after their parents died.

She moved to Detroit in 1940, where her son was a resident at Henry Ford Hospital, and later lived with her sons in Ohio.

# Ethel Cunningham

HOUSE: 1931–1933
FROM: Dardanelle, Yell County
PARTY: Democratic
BIRTHPLACE: Dardanelle, Arkansas
DATES: July 4, 1882–January 1, 1979
EDUCATION: Dardanelle High School
OCCUPATION: homemaker

*Photo courtesy of Arkansas Secretary of State.*

Ethel Cunningham (born Ethel Cole) was from a politically active family that lived in Yell County since the 1850s. Her uncle was county judge and sheriff, her brother-in-law was circuit clerk, and another uncle was sheriff. In 1905, she married Benjamin Cunningham, a doctor from an old Arkansas family, whose father had been a circuit judge and state representative from Yell County.

Before seeking public office, Cunningham was active in church, raising funds for the Liberty Loan campaign during the Great War and for the Red Cross during the flood of 1927, and campaigned for the 1928 Smith-Robinson ticket. As a candidate for representative in 1930, she was endorsed in a news-paper ad by numerous local women and led the ticket over five opponents in the Democratic primary and two in the general election. In her 1932 reelection campaign, she finished first in the primary among ten opponents and was unopposed in the general election.

Representative Cunningham was the only woman in the legislature during the 1931 and 1933 sessions. In 1931, the House adopted a resolution declaring her "the most popular, valuable, and outstanding member of the House." She sponsored legislation to provide for inheritance and distribution of property to single mothers, changed the payment of property taxes to the fall after farmers harvested crops, and voted to raise the gasoline tax to fund highway construction. Cunningham was outspoken against Louisiana Governor Huey Long's plan that no cotton be grown, arguing instead for acreage reduction for employment and to "maintain labor's self-respect."

Cunningham resigned from the legislature in April 1933 to accept appoint-ment to the Arkansas Tech Board of Trustees. She served for sixteen years under four governors, and part of that time was board secretary and chair of the executive committee of the four state agricultural colleges. Among her first acts was naming a new women's dormitory in honor of her friend, Senator Hattie Caraway—Caraway Hall.

Continuing her spirit of service, Cunningham was Arkansas Children's Hospital publicity chair, Christmas Seals campaign state radio chair, and Little Rock Women's Chamber of Commerce public affairs committee chair. She was also a member of the Century of Progress Exposition Commission and the Arkansas Centennial Commission, was a founding member of the Arkansas Democratic Women's Club and served as president, and a delegate to the 1936 Democratic National Convention. She worked as assistant collector of Internal Revenue under President Roosevelt, and in 1963, she became a charter member of the Arkansas chapter of the Order of Women Legislators.

# Ella B. Hurst

HOUSE: 1935–1936 and 1943–1946
FROM: Fayetteville, Washington County
PARTY: Democratic
BIRTHPLACE: Dallas, Arkansas
DATES: June 17, 1885–February 1, 1972
EDUCATION: University High School; University of Arkansas
OCCUPATION: legislative clerk, homemaker

*Photo courtesy of Arkansas Secretary of State.*

Ella B. Hurst (born Ella Blanche Hudgins) was the daughter of Ella B. Petty and Holder Hightower Hudgins, a merchant and farmer. In 1901, Hurst moved to Fayetteville and lived with an aunt and uncle, who owned the local opera house. In 1905, she married George Abner Hurst, an attorney and member of the Arkansas House of Representatives. Hurst was repeatedly elected by the House as enrolling clerk and was later elected Senate warrant clerk. She would later use that experience working ten sessions to bolster her qualifications for office. In the meantime, she was president of the Washington School PTA and member of the Fayetteville Women's Civic Club.

Hurst announced her candidacy for state representative in 1934, pledging to work for the interests of women and children and to support public schools and higher education. She led the field of eight candidates in the Democratic primary and was unopposed in the general election. During the 1935 session, she sponsored House Bill 1, the Pure Elections Bill, to reform voting procedures, legislation regulating the process for legally adopting children, and cosponsored a bill to create a State Library Commission. She voted for creating a Workman's Compensation Commission and supported a state sales tax to support education.

In 1936, Hurst made an unsuccessful campaign for state senate, finishing second of three candidates. She failed to regain her House seat in 1938, finishing fifth of six candidates. Both election losses were less a rejection of her record than a result of litigation that her husband brought against powerful local business interests. She continued to have an interest in local issues as an officer of the local Democratic Women's Club, advocate for the Townsend Plan for old age pensions, PTA officer, and county chair of the Tuberculosis Association fundraising drive.

After her husband was disbarred in 1940, Hurst returned to the legislature. In the 1942 Democratic primary, she defeated County Judge Irvin Rothrock for a House seat, and she was unopposed for reelection in 1944. She announced for reelection in 1946 but withdrew to accept a full-time job with the University of Arkansas Housing Office.

Hurst continued to be active in the Fayetteville Community Concert Association, the Business and Professional Women's Club, and was president of the Chi Omega Mothers' Club. Her interest in politics continued as well. She served two terms as president of the Arkansas Democratic Women's Club and attended the Democratic National Convention as a Delegate in 1960 and an alternate in 1964. After two decades with the university as a housing official and sorority housemother, Hurst turned her home near campus into a boarding house for students, and she became a celebrity for riding her horse sidesaddle in homecoming parades for fourteen years. In 1967, she was awarded the Distinguished Citizen Award by the Washington County Historical Society.

# Alene Word

HOUSE: 1943–1948
FROM: Osceola, Mississippi County
PARTY: Democratic
BIRTHPLACE: Osceola, Arkansas
DATES: August 27, 1906–December 18, 1990
EDUCATION: Osceola High School
OCCUPATION: attorney

*Photo courtesy of Arkansas Secretary of State.*

Alene Word was born in Osceola, Arkansas, to homemaker Nora Lee Davis and Percy B. Word, a building contractor and lumber salesman for Robert E. Lee Wilson, owner of a sixty-five-thousand-acre cotton plantation After graduating from high school, she was employed as a legal secretary in the office of Charles E. Sullenger, a prominent member of the local bar and a former state legislator. She was active in the First Baptist Church, serving as general secretary and teaching the Philathea Sunday school class for young women. In the community, Word was president of the Business and Professional Women's Club and a member of the Civic Club and the Women's Progressive Club.

Having worked in a law office and having read law, Word was admitted to the bar and began a civil practice with Sullenger in 1932. She first became involved with politics that year as the secretary of the Mississippi County Roosevelt-Garner Club and soon was elected secretary of the South Mississippi County Bar Association and secretary of the Arkansas Council of the National Association of Women Lawyers. Word ran unsuccessfully for Osceola City Attorney in 1936, but later that year she was elected as a Roosevelt delegate to the Democratic National Committee.

In 1942, Word was appointed Osceola city attorney and acquired the Osceola Abstract Company. That same year, she ran unopposed for the Arkansas House of Representatives and was again unopposed in 1944. She won with 54 percent against a returning veteran in the 1946 Democratic primary and was unopposed in the general election.

Representative Word was chair of the Committee on Levees and a member of the committees on Judiciary, Cities and Towns, and Roads and Highways.

Among the legislation she sponsored were bills dealing with local courts, allowing municipalities to own and manage electric plants, and requiring automobiles to have liability insurance.

Declining to seek a fourth term in 1948, Alene Word returned to her law practice in Osceola and became the first woman president of the South Mississippi County Bar Association. She later married James H. "Jim" Crain of Wilson, chairman of the Arkansas Highway Commission and former manager of the Lee Wilson Company farming operations. She chaired the Heart Fund drive and continued to be active in politics as a member of the Democratic State Committee and as a delegate to the 1960 Democratic National Convention. Her step-daughter, Nancy Crain Balton, later served in the Arkansas House of Representatives.

# Helen Buchanan

HOUSE: 1945–1946
FROM: Prescott, Nevada County
PARTY: Democratic
BIRTHPLACE: Springdale, Arkansas
DATES: September 2, 1912–April 23, 2006
EDUCATION: Springdale High School 1931; University of Arkansas, BS in home economics, 1936, and MA in sociology, 1954; Pennsylvania State University, EdD in family relations, 1961
OCCUPATION: home demonstration agent

*Photo courtesy of Arkansas Secretary of State.*

Helen Buchanan (born Helen Mae Eidson) was the Nevada County home demonstration agent in 1937, when she married Leslie Buchanan, a World War I veteran and widower with two children. Leslie Buchanan was elected to the Arkansas House of Representatives in 1940 and 1942. He was reelected in 1944 but died on Christmas Eve.

Helen Buchanan expressed her "desire to fill the place left vacant by the passing of my husband," adding, "I feel my qualifications are sufficiently adequate to enable me to fill this office." The Nevada County Democratic Convention nominated Buchanan, a thirty-two-year-old widow with four children, and she was unopposed in the special election on January 24, 1945.

She joined Representatives Ella Hurst and Alene Word, and for the first time in twenty years, three women were serving in the legislature.

Representative Buchanan passed legislation requiring a three-day waiting period between application and issuing a marriage license. She was also the lead sponsor of the Flour and Bread Enrichment Act. She ran for reelection in 1946 but was defeated by sixty-nine votes in the Democratic primary by returning WWII veteran Hillman May.

Buchanan and her daughters moved to Little Rock, where she worked as assistant editor for the *Arkansas Baptist* magazine. In 1949–1950, she was dean of women and professor of sociology at Central College in North Little Rock, and she taught civics and home economics at Springdale High School from 1950 to 1954 while completing a graduate degree in sociology at the University of Arkansas.

After earning her EdD in Family Relations at Pennsylvania State University in 1961, Dr. Buchanan taught at the University of Tennessee. She married Penn State professor Robert Meahl in 1965 and taught at Juniata College and Penn State until her retirement in 1978. Remaining active in the American Association of University Women, she was named Outstanding Woman of the AAUW State College Branch in 1990.

# Lera Rowlette

HOUSE: 1953–1954
FROM: Texarkana, Miller County
PARTY: Democratic
BIRTHPLACE: Oklahoma City, Oklahoma
DATES: June 20, 1929–November 28, 1973
EDUCATION: Texarkana High School, 1945; Texarkana Junior College, 1947; University of Arkansas, LLB, 1951, and BA, 1954; East Texas State Teachers College, MEd, 1957; doctoral coursework at Louisiana State University
OCCUPATION: attorney, professor

*Photo courtesy of Arkansas Secretary of State.*

Lera Rowlette, elected at age twenty-three, is the youngest woman to have served in the Arkansas legislature. After graduating high school with honors at sixteen and graduating from junior college, she enrolled in the University of Arkansas at Fayetteville, taking prelaw and drama classes and serving as secretary of the Arkansas Student Political League. Entering law school as the only woman in her class, she was also the first woman to hold office in the Student Bar Association. While in law school, she was briefly married to John Lonsdale, who had been an unsuccessful candidate for governor in 1948.

Admitted to the Arkansas bar upon graduation in 1951, Rowlette returned to Texarkana and joined a law practice with her father. She was active in the community as president of Beta Sigma Phi, acting in Little Theater, and as a member of the American Association of University Women and the Pilot Club. In 1952, she challenged incumbent state representative Henry "Champ" Turner and led with 49 percent in a three-way contest. Turner withdrew before the runoff, giving the nomination to Rowlette, who was unopposed in the general election.

Representative Rowlette was the only woman in the General Assembly during the 1953 session. She was appointed to the House Rules Committee and successfully passed legislation for payment of legal fees to attorneys appointed to represent indigent clients.

After the session adjourned, Rowlette returned to Fayetteville for classes during the 1953–1954 academic year, earning a 4.0 and a BA in speech and dramatic art. She fared less well in her bid for reelection. Rowlette led the Democratic preferential primary with 41 percent over two opponents but received only 40 percent in losing the runoff primary against John W. Goodson.

After her term expired in January 1955, Rowlette attended East Texas State Teachers College, teaching speech and theater classes while earning her MEd degree. She was chair of the Department of Speech and Drama at Nicholls State College in Thibodaux, Louisiana, from 1957–1963. While teaching speech and business law and directing plays, Rowlette met and married commerce faculty member Jonathan Kelly. She also took coursework toward a PhD in the Department of Speech at LSU and published her first journal article on the Senate speeches of Senator J. William Fulbright. In 1960, she was introduced by Senator John McClellan when admitted to practice before the United States Supreme Court.

In 1965, Rowlette and Jonathan Kelly accepted faculty positions at Ouachita Baptist University, where she was chair of the Division of Business and Economics. When returning to Little Rock from a conference in December 1973, she fell while disembarking the plane, hitting her head on the tarmac. She died the following day in a Little Rock hospital.

# Mattie Hackett

HOUSE: 1959–1963
FROM: Stamps, Lafayette County
PARTY: Democratic
BIRTHPLACE: Buckner, Arkansas
DATES: December 12, 1886–February 17, 1963
EDUCATION: Buckner High School; Tennessee College for Women
OCCUPATION: teacher, saleswoman, librarian

*Photo courtesy of Arkansas Secretary of State.*

Mattie Hackett (born Mattie E. Garner) was the daughter of Olevia Crawford and Dr. George W. Garner, a physician. Her grandfather Augustus A. Crawford was Saline County judge, 1885–1894, and she considered him her tutor in government and politics.

After attending the Tennessee College for Women, a Baptist institution in Murfreesboro, Tennessee, Hackett taught public school in Hope. Within a few years, she became a saleswoman in women's clothing at stores in Fayetteville, Stamps, and Hot Springs, often traveling to New York as a buyer.

While living in Hot Springs, Hackett married William T. Hackett, a former Cleveland Police detective. After his death in 1936, she continued in business and was president of the Hot Springs Business and Professional Women's Club and active in the Arkansas Federation of Women's Clubs.

In 1948, Hackett returned to Stamps, became the town's librarian, and led a successful campaign for a one-mill library tax. She was president of the Stamps Women's Study Club and the Stamps-Lewisville Business and Professional Women's Club. She was an unsuccessful candidate for the Stamps City Council in 1952. The Stamps-Lewisville B&PW named her Woman of the Year in 1958.

Hackett was a member of the Arkansas Democratic Women's Club and was first elected to the Democratic State Committee in 1954. She was elected an alternate to the 1956 Democratic National Convention and a delegate to the 1960 Democratic National Convention.

In 1958, Hackett challenged state representative Pat Robinson, an eight-term incumbent. She finished second in the Democratic preferential primary and won the runoff with 52.4 percent. She was reelected in 1960 with 55 percent over Robinson, and in 1962, she led a three-way primary and won the runoff with 64 percent.

Hackett admitted that her greatest interests, other than politics, were research and writing, and she "was known as a free thinker." At a speech to the Camden Lions Club in 1958, she called for political tolerance, defended intellectuals, and stressed the need for clear thinking and political courage.

Representative Hackett was appointed to the Governor's Commission on Aging and introduced an appropriation bill for county old-age homes. She also sponsored legislation to reduce voter fraud and to authorize Attorney General Bruce Bennett's scheme for governments to lease public facilities to avoid integration.

Mattie Hackett died during the 1963 regular session. Her gravestone in Lakeside Cemetery in Stamps is inscribed, "A Life of Service and Love to Her Fellow Man."

# Willie Oates

HOUSE: 1959–1960
FROM: Little Rock, Pulaski County
PARTY: Democratic
BIRTHPLACE: Arkansas City, Kansas
DATES: January 14, 1918–March 4, 2008
EDUCATION: Arkansas City High School
(Kansas); Arkansas City Junior College;
University of Arkansas, BA in Spanish and
French and a minor in social sciences, 1941
OCCUPATION: homemaker and civic
volunteer

*Photo courtesy of Arkansas Secretary of State.*

Willie Oates (born Will Etta Long) was the daughter of Roberta Fern Jordan and Harry Lee Long, a pharmacist and Republican mayor of Arkansas City, Kansas. Oates was involved in numerous high school and college activities but is most remembered as a Razorback cheerleader, a role she would continue throughout her life. At a Kappa Kappa Gamma sorority event, she took to heart the advice of alumna Roberta Fulbright to pursue a life of charitable and civic work.

In 1941, Willie Oates married medical student Gordon Oates and moved to Little Rock. While raising their two children, Oates proved herself a dynamic organizer and fundraiser. The American Cancer Society, American Heart Association, March of Dimes, MS Society, Muscular Dystrophy Association, and the Arkansas Aids Foundation were just a few organizations and causes that benefitted from her volunteerism. Oates received national awards from United Cerebral Palsy, American Red Cross, and the Salvation Army. She was named Little Rock Woman of the Year in 1955.

Oates was the first female member of the Charter Lion's Club and held leadership positions with many organizations, including Altrusa, the American Association of University Women, the Arkansas Arts Center, and the Little Rock City Beautiful Commission. As president of the Arkansas Federation of Women's Clubs, Oates developed and widely performed a skit, "How to Make the Most out of Being a Woman." Her fondness for colorful hats led to her nickname "The Hat Lady."

Politically active in the Arkansas Democratic Women's Club and a member of the Democratic State Committee, Oates ran for an open House seat in 1958. She led a three-way primary with 43 percent, and won the runoff with 55 percent, attributing her victory to the work of women from fifty organizations of which she was a member.

Representative Oates was vice chair of the House Public Health and Practice of Medicine Committee. She passed motorcycle safety legislation and a bill requiring polio vaccinations for school children. Although Oates withdrew it due to religious backlash, she introduced a bill to repeal the state's 1928 anti-evolution law, believing "legislation against ideas or ideals is wrong." Due to her support for a private high school and votes undermining public education, Oates was opposed by the Women's Emergency Committee and defeated for reelection in the 1960 Democratic primary.

After her legislative term, Oates served on the 1964, 1968, and 1972 Governor's Commission on the Status of Women. She was vice chair of the Arkansas Women's Committee on Public Affairs and continued her involvement with civic and charitable organizations. In 1990, she received the University of Arkansas Community Service Award for outstanding alumni, having been a homecoming cheerleader for fifty years. Governor Bill Clinton presented her the Governor's Volunteer Excellence Award, and she received the Senator David Pryor Award for Seniors Active in the Community and Volunteer Service.

# Bernice Kizer

HOUSE: 1961–1974
FROM: Fort Smith, Sebastian County
PARTY: Democratic
BIRTHPLACE: Fort Smith, Arkansas
DATES: August 14, 1915–January 16, 2006
EDUCATION: St Anne's Academy; Fort
Smith High School, 1932; Stephens
College; University of Arkansas Law
School, LLB, 1947, and JD, 1969
OCCUPATION: attorney

*Photo courtesy of Arkansas Secretary of State.*

Bernice Kizer (born Bernice Corinne Lichty) was the daughter of Opal Shirley Culler, bookkeeper for the family businesses, and Ernest Christian Lichty, an electrical supply store owner who built and operated power plants in rural communities. In high school, Kizer was in the Athenian literary society, on the basketball team, acted in plays, and was homecoming queen. As a member of the debate team, she debated unemployment insurance, and she won the WCTU Gold Medal for Oratory. Hearing Senator Hattie Caraway campaign in 1932 sparked her interest in Democratic politics.

After high school, Kizer worked as a grocery checker, earning money to attend Stephens College. There she was a member of the Book Club, Judicial Council of the Civic Association, and the Stephens League of Women Voters, while working as a waitress to meet expenses.

In 1935, Kizer continued her education at the University of Arkansas, where she was a member of University Theatre, Wesley Players, and an officer of Delta Delta Delta sorority. Returning to Fort Smith, she was the county chair of the Christmas Seals campaign, working closely with state director Erle Chambers. Kizer married Jamie Parker, grandson of Judge Isaac Parker, and they had three children. When he was deployed during World War II, she returned with her children to Fayetteville and earned her law degree.

After the death of her husband, Kizer practiced labor and employment law in Fort Smith, the only female member of the Sebastian County Bar Association, and she was a member of the National Association of Women Lawyers. She married Harlan Kizer in 1959. Bernice Kizer was president of the PEO Sisterhood, Girls' Club, Business and Professional Women's Club, and State Chair for Library Week. She was a member Seroptimist, Pilot Club, and Arkansas Democratic Women. She served on the boards of Cottey College, Old Fort Museum, Clayton House, City National Bank, Sparks Regional Medical Center, and St. Edwards Mercy Medical Center.

Kizer was unopposed in her first campaign for the House in 1960; won contested elections in 1962, 1964, and 1970; and was unopposed in 1966, 1968, and 1972. Much of Representative Kizer's legislation dealt with public education, election law reform, workers' compensation, and economic empowerment of women. She sponsored legislation to create the law school in Little Rock. Kizer was appointed to the 1964 and 1968 Governor's Commission on the Status of Women and the Governor's Commission on Aging.

After fourteen years in the Arkansas House, Representative Kizer was elected Chancery Judge in 1974, the first woman elected to a judgeship in Arkansas, serving 1975 to 1986. After retiring, Judge Kizer was elected to the Fort Smith Board of Directors (1988–1992).

Judge Kizer received numerous honors, including the University of Arkansas Law School Outstanding Alumna Award, Outstanding Woman of Achievement by *Southwest Times Record*, and League of Women Voters of Arkansas Hall of Fame. She was listed in Who's Who in America, Who's Who in American Law, and Who's Who in American Women.

# Doris McCastlain

HOUSE: 1961–1965
FROM: Brinkley, Monroe County
PARTY: Democratic
BIRTHPLACE: Graysonia, Arkansas
DATES: January 23, 1918–October 29, 2009
EDUCATION: Rosboro High School, 1936
OCCUPATION: homemaker and farmer

*Photo courtesy of Arkansas Secretary of State.*

Doris McCastlain (born Doris Wagner) was the daughter of Flossie Meeks, a homemaker, and Earl Leonel Wagner, a lumberman. She attended public schools in Graysonia, Arkadelphia, De Queen, and Rosboro. In 1937, she married Hugh Marvin "Ted" McCastlain, superintendent of Glenwood Schools. In 1939, they moved to Brinkley, where Ted opened a law office and served in the Arkansas House, 1941–1944.

While raising four children, Doris McCastlain was a member of the PEO Sisterhood and active in the community as president of the Woman's Society of Christian Service for Brinkley First Methodist Church, president of the Brinkley PTA, vice president of the Brinkley Business and Professional Women's Club, president of the Brinkley Gli Amici Literary Club, and president of the Brinkley Country Club. McCastlain served as assistant chief clerk of the Arkansas House during every legislative session from 1941 until 1952, when she made an unsuccessful campaign for state representative, losing to a former county judge. When Ted McCastlain died after being elected to the House in 1960, McCastlain ran to replace him and was unopposed in the December special election. She would also be unopposed for reelection in 1962 and 1964.

Representative McCastlain passed legislation creating the Louisiana Purchase State Park, increasing funds for the Jackson Convalescent Center school for handicapped children, requiring reporting of suspected child abuse, and creating the Arkansas Law Enforcement Training Academy. Active in the Arkansas Farm Bureau Federation, she helped them with their legislative package. She was one of the first women to serve on the House Rules Committee and the Joint Audit Committee. McCastlain organized and chaired the Arkansas Chapter of the Organization of Women Legislators, served on the Governor's Commission on the Status of Women, and was legislative chair of the Arkansas Women's Committee on Public Affairs. She was a delegate to the 1964 Democratic National Committee, and she supported her son-in-law, Sheffield Nelson, in his contentious election as state president of the Young Democrats.

In 1965, McCastlain resigned from the House, when Governor Orval Faubus appointed her as Arkansas Revenue Commissioner, the first woman to hold that position and only the third woman to hold a cabinet position. She was named Outstanding Legislator by her House colleagues in 1965 and was listed in Community Leaders of America, Women in American Politics, and World's Who's Who of Women.

McCastlain married Colonel Carl Hinkle, executive director of the Arkansas Industrial Development Commission and former commander of the Little Rock Air Force base, in 1966. After retiring from public service in 1968, Doris McCastlain Hinkle continued to live in Little Rock, where she was active in St. James United Methodist Church.

# Dove Mulkey

HOUSE: 1961–1964
FROM: Nashville, Howard County
PARTY: Democratic
BIRTHPLACE: Mineral Springs, Arkansas
DATES: October 7, 1891–May 7, 1972
EDUCATION: Mineral Springs High
School; Ouachita Baptist College, BM, 1913
OCCUPATION: farmer

*Photo courtesy of Arkansas Secretary of State.*

Dove Mulkey (born Dove Irene Toland) was the daughter of America Frances Compton, a homemaker, and Dr. William Henry Toland, a physician and planter. Dr. Toland was also president of Planters Bank and Trust and president of the State Board of Medical Examiners. In addition, the family was politically prominent. Mulkey's uncle, John Henry Bell, was a Howard County judge and state senator. Her father served seven terms in the Arkansas House of Representatives.

After graduation from college, Mulkey returned home to Nashville, where she was known as "a prominent and popular young society girl." She christened the first Memphis-Dallas and Gulf Coast Railroad train to enter Hot Springs, and she was the Howard County delegation sponsor to the 1914 Arkansas reunion of the United Confederate Veterans in Little Rock.

In December 1915, Mulkey married Faust Everett Mulkey, a Nashville hardware store owner and grandson of a state senator. Mulkey frequently performed vocal numbers at public events, in church, and for civic clubs. She was president of Nashville Garden Club and a member of the PEO Sisterhood, Daughters of the American Revolution, the Tuesday Music Club, and the Woman's Missionary Union of the First Baptist Church.

Mulkey first aspired to be a legislator when she worked during the 1945 and 1949 legislative sessions as the committee clerk for the House Committee on Public Health and the Practice of Medicine, chaired by her father. In 1960, she ran for an open House seat and defeated former Howard County assessor Jim Cowling with 51.2 percent in the Democratic primary. Mulkey was unopposed for reelection in 1962, but in 1964, she drew two opponents and finished last with only 22 percent in the Democratic primary.

Representative Mulkey served on the Committees on Constitutional Amendments, Public Health, Public Welfare, and Publicity and Parks. She pledged to work for middle-class tax relief and securing industry to supplement farming income in Howard County, and she was interested in supporting education and public health. She sponsored legislation to raise the monthly payments to disabled citizens.

Governor Orval Faubus appointed Mulkey to the 1964 Governor's Commission on the Status of Women, and Governor Winthrop Rockefeller appointed her to the 1967 Governor's Committee on Employment of the Handicapped. Mulkey's grandson, Jim Hill, served in the Arkansas House of Representatives from 1993–1996 and in the state senate from 1997–2007.

# Gladys Martin Oglesby

HOUSE: 1963–1970
FROM: Stamps, Lafayette County
PARTY: Democratic
BIRTHPLACE: Stamps, Arkansas
DATES: March 11, 1903–June 24, 1998
EDUCATION: Patmos grade school;
Stamps High School, 1920
OCCUPATION: librarian, newspaper correspondent, bank teller, secretary

*Photo courtesy of Arkansas Secretary of State.*

Gladys Martin Oglesby (born Gladys Naomi Ward) was the daughter of Minnie Ola Nelson, a homemaker, and Francis Leon "Frank" Ward, a real estate and agricultural supply salesman. She married Harry Martin, and they had one son. She worked as a secretary for Davis Construction Company, a teller at Bodcaw Bank, and the office secretary and publicity chair for the Stamps Chamber of Commerce. She was also a bylined correspondent for both the *Arkansas Gazette* and the *Arkansas Democrat* and hosted a weekday morning radio program.

Martin Oglesby and her husband Harry led the efforts of the American Legion and the Women's Study Club to establish the Stamps Public Library in 1935, and both served as librarians for several years. Consistently taking leadership roles in community activities, Martin Oglesby was publicity chair of Stamps Senior Musical Coterie, chair of the Citizenship and Public Affairs committee for Stamps Women's Study Club, president of Stamps-Lewisville Business and Professional Women's Club, secretary-treasurer of American Legion Auxiliary, and secretary of Lafayette County Fair Association. She also taught the women's Sunday school class at First Baptist Church. Twice, Martin Oglesby was named Woman of the Year by the Stamps-Lewisville Business and Professional Women's Club.

Although recently widowed, Martin Oglesby became a candidate to complete the House term of her friend, Representative Mattie Hackett, who had died during the 1963 legislative session. She won the special Democratic primary election against two former state representatives. In 1964, she won the Democratic primary over attorney Nick Patton with 52 percent. She married Lowman Oglesby in 1965 and was on the ballot as Gladys Martin Oglesby when James Compton of Magnolia challenged her in 1966 but withdrew before the election. In 1968, she won the Democratic primary with 56 percent over Nathan Graham, a retired high school teacher. Running for a fifth term in 1970, Martin Oglesby was defeated in the Democratic primary by attorney Don Corbin.

As a legislator, transportation issues were a special concern for Martin Oglesby. She co-authored a bill that established a free ferry across the Red River, secured a $142,000 road project, added fifteen miles of county roads to the state highway system, and required painted white strips on outer edges of highways. She also enacted the school vaccination requirement law. Martin Oglesby introduced legislation to abolish capital punishment, which failed in the House, 19–79. She also served on the 1964 and 1968 Governor's Commission on the Status of Women.

# Dorathy Allen

SENATE: 1964–1974
FROM: Brinkley, Monroe County
PARTY: Democratic
BIRTHPLACE: Helena, Arkansas
DATES: March 10, 1910–May 12, 1990
EDUCATION: Public schools and Sacred Heart Academy in Helena; Macon and Andrews Business College (Memphis)
OCCUPATION: journalist, editor, publisher

*Photo courtesy of Arkansas Secretary of State.*

Dorathy Allen (born Dorathy McDonald) grew up in a prominent Phillips County family. Her father owned extensive timber operations, and her brother was Phillips County circuit clerk from 1933–1956. Allen was the society editor of the *Helena World*. In 1941, she married Tom Allen and moved to Brinkley, where they published weekly newspapers, including the *Citizen* at Brinkley, the *Monroe County Sun* at Clarendon, and the *Woodruff County Democrat* at Cotton Plant.

Allen became known as the "Mother of the Miss Arkansas Pageant," after transforming the Eastern Arkansas Young Men's Club local pageant in 1944. She added talent competition and interviews to the swimsuit contest and became director for a statewide Miss Arkansas Pageant, accompanying the winners as chaperone to the Miss America Pageant in Atlantic City for several years. She served on the Governor's Advisory Committee on Mental Retardation, was president of the Arkansas Hospital Association, president of the Brinkley Business and Professional Women's Club, president of Arkansas Press Women, and president of the Arkansas Association for the Crippled.

Tom Allen was elected to the Arkansas House of Representatives in 1944 and to the state senate in 1952, serving until his death in 1963. On July 28, 1964, Allen ran in a special election for the Senate seat made vacant by her husband's death. She won with 52.2 percent of the vote to become the first woman to serve in the Arkansas Senate. She was reelected without opposition in 1966 and 1970.

In her first term, Senator Allen served on the Agriculture Committee and Legislative Council. Her first speech opposed an investigation of the administration at the Arkansas Children's Colony. She sponsored a resolution encouraging physicians to test newborns for the genetic disorder Phenylketonuria and enacted legislation to create a board for the Arkansas Law Enforcement Training Academy.

During her second term, Allen was considered part of the "Old Guard," legislators who had supported former governor Orval Faubus and were less likely to endorse the policies advanced by Governor Winthrop Rockefeller. She sponsored an appropriation to pay off the bonded debt and end toll charges on the Helena bridge, which was vetoed by Governor Rockefeller. In 1969, Allen sponsored legislation authorizing schools to create early childhood-development demonstration projects. Her legislation creating the Louisiana Purchase State Park was vetoed by Governor Rockefeller.

During the 1971 session, Allen was appointed to the Southern Regional Education Board. As vice chair of the committee on Roads and Highways, she sponsored a nonbinding resolution to end the highway commission's toll charges over the Helena bridge, and the tolls ended soon afterward.

In 1973, Allen was part of the Senate opposition to administration bills proposed by Governor Dale Bumpers, and she supported the maneuvers of Senator Guy "Mutt" Jones to prevent ratification of the Equal Rights Amendment. In 1974, Allen decided not to run for reelection, but she continued working at the capitol as a Senate clerk from 1975 to 1976.

# Vada Sheid

HOUSE: 1967–1976 and 1993–1994
SENATE: 1977–1984
FROM: Mountain Home, Baxter County
PARTY: Democratic
BIRTHPLACE: Wideman, Arkansas
DATES: August 19, 1916–February 11, 2008
EDUCATION: Calico Rock High School, 1934; Draughon School of Business, 1937
OCCUPATION: county treasurer, furniture store owner

*Photo courtesy of Arkansas Secretary of State.*

Vada Sheid (born Vada Peralee Webb) was the only child of Gertrude Reynolds, a homemaker, and John William Webb, a cattle farmer. She developed a love of politics as a young girl accompanying her father to campaign events in Izard and Fulton counties. The family moved to Calico Rock in 1926, and in high school, Sheid was on the debate team and in school plays.

The summer after graduation, Sheid volunteered with a statewide Democratic gubernatorial campaign. At nineteen, she became Izard County welfare director, distributing food to needy families. She graduated from Draughon School of Business in Little Rock then married high school classmate Carl Sheid, and they had one son. She worked for the state senate and secretary of state, then they moved to Mountain Home and opened Baxter Furniture Store.

Always involved in the community, Vada Sheid was active in the American Red Cross, Business and Professional Women, Arkansas Federation of Women's Clubs, and the Baxter County Democratic Committee. She served on the boards of the Baxter Regional Medical Center Foundation, Ozark Regional Mental Health Center, and the Baxter County Fair. She was also a delegate to the White House Conference on Aging.

Sheid made her first run for office in 1956 when she ran for Baxter County treasurer, but she lost to the incumbent by under one hundred votes. In 1958, she defeated the incumbent and served as treasurer from 1959 until defeated in 1964. Undeterred, Sheid ran for state representative in 1966 against two incumbents in a newly redistricted seat, defeating one in the Democratic primary and the other in the general election.

Representative Sheid served five terms in the House before being elected to two terms in the state senate. As a freshman lawmaker in 1967, Sheid said her priorities were "education, welfare, and roads," a platform she continued to pursue throughout her legislative career. She immediately began working to replace two ferries with bridges across Norfork Lake, projects finally realized in 1983. Her commitment to education was realized in legislation she sponsored creating Arkansas State University–Mountain Home and North Arkansas Community College in Harrison.

After eighteen years in the legislature, Senator Shied was defeated in the 1984 general election. She was the second woman elected to the state senate, the first woman in the state senate who did not succeed a late husband, and the first woman to serve in both chambers. In 1987, Governor Bill Clinton appointed Sheid to the Arkansas State Police Commission. She made two more campaigns for the House. In 1990, she lost a runoff to former house Speaker John Miller; two years later she was elected, serving one term before retiring at age seventy-eight. She was honored after more than four decades of public service by the Arkansas State University's Vada Sheid Community Development Center at the Mountain Home campus.

# Lucile Autry

HOUSE: 1968
FROM: Burdette, Mississippi County
PARTY: Democratic
BIRTHPLACE: Lonoke, Arkansas
DATES: October 5, 1903–July 26, 1993
EDUCATION: Lonoke High School, 1922; Arkansas State Teachers College
OCCUPATION: teacher

*Photo courtesy of Arkansas Secretary of State.*

Lucile Autry (born Lucile Sullivan) was the daughter of Rose Mattie Jones and Henry Hays Sullivan, a store clerk and farmer. She began teaching in Lonoke County schools after graduating from high school and attended Arkansas State Teachers College during summer sessions. In 1928, she married Lilburn Hardy Autry, a fellow teacher, and they moved to Burdette, where her husband became superintendent of the Burdette Consolidated Schools. Autry returned to teaching when her children entered school and taught a number of different grades, directed high school plays, and served as librarian, but she especially enjoyed working with first-grade children.

Active in her community, Autry served as chair of the Burdette Heart Fund Drive and chair of the legislative committee of the Burdette PTA. She attended New Liberty Baptist Church and was involved with the Woman's Missionary Union of First Baptist Church, Blytheville.

Autry was interested in politics from an early age. Governor James P. Eagle was her great-uncle, and her younger brother, Hays Sullivan, was a longtime member of the Mississippi County Democratic Committee. Autry worked as a Democratic Party election clerk for the Burdette polling place, and her husband, L. H. Autry, represented Mississippi County for eleven terms in the Arkansas House of Representatives. Following his death in September 1967, she became a candidate to fill his position in the January 1968 special election.

Autry was opposed by Ed Allison, a Blytheville insurance salesman and state chair of the Young Republicans, backed by Governor Winthrop Rockefeller. Autry told voters she had a "thorough working knowledge of the Arkansas legislature, which I attended for many years with my late husband, L. H. Autry, and which I served as clerk of the pages for four sessions. I have only the best interest of Mississippi County at heart and will endeavor to represent the people to the best of my ability." Autry was elected with 56 percent of the vote. She carried the Burdette precinct by 184–1.

Representative Autry served in the February 1968 special session that proposed a constitutional convention and adopted prison reform measures. She announced in March that she would not seek reelection, instead returning to her previous job as clerk of pages during the 1969 session. She served on the Burdette City Council then moved to Lonoke in 1971.

# Shirley Meacham

HOUSE: 1975–1990
FROM: Monroe, Monroe County
PARTY: Democratic
BIRTHPLACE: Helena, Arkansas
DATES: April 17, 1927–December 11, 2010
EDUCATION: Clarendon public schools;
Clarendon High School, 1945; Baptist
Memorial Hospital School of Nursing;
Memphis State University
OCCUPATION: nurse, farmer

*Photo courtesy of Arkansas Secretary of State.*

Shirley Meacham (born Shirley Fay Terry) was born in Helena to Edith Mae Cook, a homemaker, and Tommy Lee Terry, a Standard Oil Company distributor. The family moved to Clarendon when she was four, and she attended the Clarendon Public Schools. One of her earliest memories was attending a political rally for Senator Hattie Caraway in Brinkley City Park, where Meacham and her friends from dance class performed as one of the warmup acts for the speakers.

After graduation from high school, Meacham enrolled in the US Cadet Nursing Corps, training at the Baptist Memorial Hospital School of Nursing and taking classes at Memphis State. She was working for a doctor in Clarendon when she married Kirby Meacham in 1947. Together, they raised three children and farmed 1,800 acres of rice and soybeans.

When their friend, Representative Doris McCastlain, resigned to become Commissioner of Revenue, Kirby Meacham ran for the position in 1966. Meacham quickly mastered the demands of campaigning, and her husband won the Democratic primary after a hotly contested runoff. He ran unopposed thereafter and died in 1974, after being nominated for a fifth term.

Governor Dale Bumpers called Meacham to encourage her to run in the special election to fill her husband's seat. She and three opponents spoke before the District Democratic Convention at the Monroe County Courthouse, and she was nominated on the first ballot with 75 percent of the votes. She was unopposed in the 1974 general election and both the primary and general elections in 1976, 1978, and 1980. She won contested primary and general elections in 1982 and 1984, then was unopposed in 1986 and 1988.

Meacham married Billy Calhoun in 1982 and was known as Shirley Meacham Calhoun while they were married.

Representative Meacham introduced few bills and made few speeches during her eight terms in the House. However, she was especially interested in educational reform and funding because her daughter and daughter-in-law were both teachers, making her well aware of the challenges facing educators. She worked diligently to be informed on every bill and was dedicated to constituent service. Meacham declined to seek a ninth term after redistricting in 1990. She received awards from the Farm Bureau for her support of agriculture, was twice named Woman of the Year by the local Business and Professional Women's Club and was listed in Who's Who in American Politics.

# Carolyn Pollan

HOUSE: 1975–1998
FROM: Fort Smith, Sebastian County
PARTY: Republican
BIRTHPLACE: Houston, Texas
DATES: July 12, 1937–October 23, 2021
EDUCATION: Fishback grade school, 1951; Springdale High School, 1955; John Brown University, BS in radio and television, 1959; Walden University, PhD in education, 1995
OCCUPATION: businesswoman, literacy project director

*Photo courtesy of Arkansas Secretary of State.*

Carolyn Pollan (born Carolyn Joan Clark) is the daughter of Faith Margaret Basye, a medical transcriptionist, and Rex Clark, a poultry farmer. The family moved from Texas to a farm east of Springdale, where Pollan was an officer in the Zion Fishback 4-H Club. At Springdale High, she took classes from former representative Helen Buchanan and was a newspaper reporter, editor of the yearbook, won the journalism award, and was voted Most Likely to Succeed. As an honor student at John Brown University, Pollan worked at KUOA, was a Broadcasting Club officer, and was named outstanding woman broadcaster. She was also yearbook editor and was voted Most Versatile Girl. Moving to Fort Smith in 1959 to work for KFBW radio then Central Airlines, Pollan married George Pollan in 1962 and raised three children while working as bookkeeper for the family business. She was editor of the *Fort Smith Historical Society Journal* and operated the Fort Smith Patent Model Museum.

Becoming interested in public service, Pollan volunteered with Winthrop Rockefeller's campaign in 1968, and she soon became president of the Sebastian County Republican Women, and vice chair of the Republican Party of Arkansas. She was an alternate in 1972 and delegate to the 1976 and 1980 Republican National Conventions.

Representative Bernice Kizer, supporting women over party, encouraged Pollan to run for her open Arkansas House seat in 1974. As a candidate that fall, Pollan was an outspoken supporter of the Equal Rights Amendment, and she continued to work for its ratification until 1982. Pollan won the 1974 general election with 52 percent, becoming the first Republican woman to serve in the Arkansas legislature and later becoming the first woman appointed Associate Speaker Pro Tempore of the House and, after twelve terms, the longest-serving female legislator.

Representative Pollan created and chaired the Joint Committee on Children and Youth. She passed more than 250 bills during her twenty-four years in the House, most reflecting her passion for protecting families and children, including establishing juvenile courts, protecting missing and abused children, childcare facility licensing, notification about sex offenders, victims' rights, child welfare, and at-risk youth. Her work was honored by awards from the Arkansas Advocates for Children and Families, the Children's Advocacy Centers of Arkansas, the League of Women Voters, and numerous other organizations and news media.

Governor Bill Clinton appointed Pollan as chair of Arkansas Child Sexual Abuse Education Commission and to the Governor's Commission on Adult Literacy, and Governor Mike Huckabee appointed her to the Early Childhood Commission. She held regional and national leadership roles as chair of the Southern Regional Education Board, chair of the Southern Legislative Council Education Committee, and member of national advisory boards for the US Department of Labor and US Department of Education.

After being term-limited in 1998, Dr. Pollan served as Governor Mike Huckabee's legislative director until 2003, when he appointed her as the first woman on the Arkansas Oil and Gas Commission. She was also president of the John Brown University Board of Trustees, chair of the Health Policy Board for the Arkansas Center for Health Improvement, and on the Clinton School of Public Service Advisory Board. Pollan was inducted into the Arkansas Women's Hall of Fame in 2021.

# Gloria Cabe

HOUSE: 1979–1980 and 1983–1990
FROM: Little Rock, Pulaski County
PARTY: Democratic
BIRTHPLACE: Pine Bluff, Arkansas
DATES: September 15, 1941–
EDUCATION: Plainview, Cleveland Avenue,
and Gabe Meyer Elementary Schools;
Pine Bluff High School, 1959; Hendrix
College, BA in French, 1963
OCCUPATION: teacher, librarian, and
consultant

*Photo courtesy of Arkansas Secretary of State.*

Gloria Cabe (born Gloria Sue Burford) is the daughter of Eva Elizabeth Owen, a waitress and factory worker, and William Alexander Burford, a civilian employee of Pine Bluff Arsenal. An avid follower of current events from an early age, Cabe read the *Pine Bluff Commercial* daily in grade school and watched television news twice daily. In 1963, she received her bachelor's degree in French from Hendrix College, where she studied political science with Robert Merriweather. She married classmate Robert Cabe, and they had two children. For four years, Gloria Cabe was a teacher of language arts, science, and social studies and worked as a librarian. In 1967, she was a member of the Arkansas Constitution Revision Study Commission.

Cabe was the lobbyist for the League of Women Voters of Arkansas for the Equal Rights Amendment ratification and other issues, and she served as president of the Arkansas and Pulaski County Leagues. Cabe was a paid political staffer for Bill Clinton's gubernatorial campaigns, serving as Pulaski County coordinator from 1980 and as campaign manager in 1990. The early days of the women's movement and efforts to ratify the Equal Rights Amendment inspired Cabe to run for the Arkansas legislature in 1978. She won her first campaign for public office but lost her race for reelection in 1980 by twelve votes to Doug Brandon. Cabe again ran successfully in 1982, serving four terms until 1990.

Representative Cabe was particularly pleased with the bills she helped write and sponsored in the 1983 special session on education, serving as floor manager for Governor Clinton during that important session. Representative Cabe worked on juvenile justice system reform, improving campaign finance oversight, and advocated for Arkansas's ratification of the Equal Rights Amendment. While serving as representative, Cabe was also an unpaid member of Governor Clinton's staff, representing him in several national education venues, including the National Governors Association and Education Commission of the States.

Opting against running for reelection in 1990, Cabe managed Governor Clinton's reelection campaign then became his Chief of Staff. In 1992, she worked for Clinton's presidential campaign, opening and running the Washington, DC, office. She subsequently served as counselor to the Chairman of the United States Export-Import Bank during the Clinton and Bush administrations and as a senior advisor to Secretary Hillary Clinton in the US Department of State Global Partnership Initiative. Cabe later worked extensively in the private sector, including as vice president and chief operating officer of the Corporate Council on Africa, president of Emerging Market Strategies, vice president of the Ridley Group, and with James Lee Witt Associates.

# Sarah Jane Bost

HOUSE: 1980
FROM: Sherwood, Pulaski County
PARTY: Democratic
BIRTHPLACE: Ellis County, Texas
DATES: June 6, 1929–December 25, 2018
EDUCATION: Adamson High School (Dallas, TX); Baylor Dental College, BS in dental hygiene
OCCUPATION: dental hygienist, medical investigator, probation officer

*Photo courtesy of Arkansas Secretary of State.*

Sarah Jane Bost (born Sarah Jane Hightower) and her twin brother were the third and fourth of five children born to Sarah Emily Turner and Hubert D. Hightower, a rancher and deputy sheriff. Moving to Dallas when her father joined the police department, Bost was class vice president at Adamson High School. She married Charles Glasgow, and they had a son before later divorcing. While attending dental hygiene school, she met and married John Lewis Bost, a dental student. In 1959, she moved to Arkansas when Dr. Bost, an Arkansas native, opened his dentistry practice in North Little Rock.

In addition to her work as a dental hygienist, Bost was honored for volunteer work with the Memorial Hospital Auxiliary, was president of the North Little Rock League of Artists, and served as vice president of the North Pulaski County Chamber of Commerce. She worked as a medical investigator for the Medicaid Fraud Unit of the Arkansas Division of Social Services for several years, before resigning to file for state representative in 1978. Bost finished second of three candidates in the Democratic preferential primary but lost with 48 percent in the runoff election. In November 1978, she was elected with 73 percent as a delegate to the 1979–1980 Arkansas Constitutional Convention.

Bost served as probation officer for the Sherwood Municipal Court from 1979–1981. During that time, she was elected as an alternate Carter delegate to the 1980 Democratic National Convention, and she was elected without opposition in a 1980 special election for an unexpired term in the Arkansas House of Representatives. Representative Bost was sworn in on November 20, 1980, and served for seven weeks.

After her brief time as a state representative, Bost was elected vice president of the Pulaski County Democratic Women. She and Dr. Bost retired to Hot Springs, then they moved to Paris, Texas, as family caregivers until their own deaths in 2018.

# Irma Hunter Brown

HOUSE: 1981–1998, SENATE: 2003–2008
FROM: Little Rock, Pulaski County
PARTY: Democratic
BIRTHPLACE: Tampa, Florida
DATES: January 5, 1939–
EDUCATION: Forsyth, Georgia, public schools; Shorter College, AA, 1958; Arkansas Agricultural, Mechanical, and Normal College (UAPB), double major in history and government and education minor, 1960; graduate work at Memphis State University and District of Columbia Teachers College
OCCUPATION: teacher, community organizer

*Photo courtesy of Arkansas Secretary of State.*

Irma Hunter Brown (born Irma Jean Hunter) moved to Arkansas in 1956 to attend college. After graduating and teaching in the Memphis and Washington, DC, public schools, she returned to Arkansas in 1969 with her husband, Dr. Roosevelt Brown. Irma Hunter Brown engaged in community service work in nutrition education and day care options for low-income residents.

After working in several political campaigns, Brown ran for the Arkansas House of Representatives in 1976 but lost to the incumbent in the Democratic primary runoff. She was appointed by Governor David Pryor as chair of the Arkansas Human Resources Commission to promote and protect civil rights, and in 1980 she won an open House seat.

In 1981, Representative Brown became the first Black woman to serve in the Arkansas House of Representatives, where she chaired the Arkansas Legislative Black Caucus. Among the first bills Brown passed was one that increased diversity on state boards, commissions, committees, and task forces. Brown served on the executive committee of the National Conference of State Legislators and the National Black Caucus of State Legislators.

After being term-limited out of the House in 1998, Brown was appointed president of Shorter College. Remaining active in community and public service, she was a member of Rotary International, served on the board of directors of the Little Rock YWCA, was president of the Little Rock Parent Teachers Association Council, served on the board of the Museum of Discovery, and was vice chair of Arkansas Educational Television Network Foundation.

In 2002, Brown ran for the Arkansas Senate, beat the incumbent in the primary, and won the general election. When sworn into office in January 2003, she became the first Black woman to serve in the Senate. Brown chaired the City, County, and Local Affairs Committee for three sessions. She was an outspoken advocate for human rights and sponsored legislation on education, homestead tax exemptions, cancer research funding, rehabilitating abandoned or neglected properties, and to qualify Arkansas for the HUD Fair Housing Assistance Program. She was proud to serve at a time when the legislature cut the sales tax on groceries and increased funding for early childhood education.

For her legislative service, Brown was named the 2007 ACLU Humanitarian of the Year and received the Distinguished Citizen Award from Philander Smith College.

Seeking a third term in 2008, Senator Brown was defeated by former representative Joyce Elliott in the Democratic primary. The Democratic Party of Arkansas Black Caucus created the annual Irma Hunter Brown

Women's Leadership Award. In 2015, Brown was recognized by a plaque on the Arkansas Civil Rights Heritage Trail, and she was inducted into the Arkansas Black Hall of Fame in 2019.

# Judy Petty

HOUSE: 1981–1984
FROM: Little Rock, Pulaski County
PARTY: Republican
BIRTHPLACE: Little Rock, Arkansas
DATES: September 4, 1943–
EDUCATION: Pulaski Heights Elementary School and Junior High; North Little Rock High School, 1961; University of Arkansas at Little Rock, BA in international relations, 1975
OCCUPATION: administrative assistant, teacher, public relations

*Photo courtesy of Arkansas Secretary of State.*

Judy Petty (born Judy Lynne Chaney) is the daughter of Jo Stein Lemming, a Farm Security Administration statistician, and John Totty Chaney, a credit manager. In high school, Petty was a cheerleader and member of the honor society, student council, debate team, Quill & Scroll, and Thespians. She also won the American Legion oratory contest.

Petty first became active in politics in high school as chair of the Pulaski County Youth for Nixon in 1960. As a freshman at Little Rock University in 1961, she was secretary of the Young Republicans Club. In 1962, she left school, married John Dandridge Petty, and they had a daughter. Judy Petty was a volunteer for Winthrop Rockefeller's gubernatorial campaigns in 1964 and 1966, and after her divorce in 1967, she found her first job as a secretary on Governor Rockefeller's personal staff, where she worked with increasing responsibilities until his death in 1973.

Petty was chair of the Arkansas Young Republicans, vice chair of the national Young Republican Federation, secretary of the Republican Party of Arkansas, and a Nixon delegate to the 1972 Republican National Convention. She ran unsuccessfully for the Pulaski County Quorum Court in 1970 and 1972. In 1973, Petty returned to UALR to finish her degree. She supported the Equal Rights Amendment and served as chair of the Arkansas Women's

Political Caucus and on the National Women's Political Caucus Steering Committee.

In 1974, Petty challenged eighteen-term congressman Wilbur Mills and lost with 42 percent of the vote. She was the Republican nominee for state representative in 1976 but withdrew to be regional director of the Ford-Dole campaign.

While teaching junior high social studies, Petty ran for the Arkansas House in 1980, defeating a ten-term Democratic incumbent, and was reelected in 1982, defeating a former Democratic state senator. Among legislation Petty enacted were increased penalties for driving while intoxicated and an opportunity for crime victims and their families to provide victim impact statements in court.

After two House terms, Petty ran another unsuccessful race for Congress in 1984. She then worked for the American Legislative Exchange Council (ALEC) and later as the director of Public Affairs for the National Highway Traffic Safety Administration. In 1985, she married Dr. Robert H. Wolf. After moving to San Antonio, Judy Petty Wolf was senior vice president for External Affairs at the University of Texas Health Science Center. She did volunteer work for George Bush in his campaign against Governor Ann Richards in 1994, and Governor Bush appointed her to the Statewide Health Coordinating Council. Petty and her husband retired in 2006 and returned to Arkansas.

# Norma Thompson

HOUSE: 1981–1982
FROM: Marked Tree, Poinsett County
PARTY: Democratic
BIRTHPLACE: Lepanto, Arkansas
DATES: March 21, 1916–March 16, 2001
EDUCATION: Lepanto High School, 1934; attended Arkansas State University 1934–1935
OCCUPATION: homemaker

*Photo courtesy of William P. Thompson.*

Norma Thompson (born Norma Eileen Cornelison) was the daughter of Myrtle C. Greenwood, a stenographer, and Lewis Franklin Cornelison. Her mother died when Thompson was nine years old, and she grew up in the home of her aunt Dalton, a teacher, and uncle John Weatherly, a banker.

In 1937, she married William Henry Thompson, a cottonseed dealer from Marked Tree, and, as the family homemaker, she cared for the home and raised their six children. While her husband was a member of the Arkansas House of Representatives from 1953 to 1981, Norma Thompson often worked as a member of the House staff during the legislative sessions. She was also an avid reader and enjoyed traveling in the United States and abroad.

Representative Bill Thompson was serving his fourteenth term in the House of Representatives when he died in August of 1981. Thompson decided to run for his unexpired term. "I would like to finish out Bill's term," she said. "Having worked down there for so many years, I think I can go down there and do a good job." She was nominated by a Democratic Convention of Delegates from Craighead and Poinsett Counties on September 10 and was elected without opposition in a special election on October 27, 1981.

Representative Thompson served fourteen months in the House, fully participating in committee work and casting roll-call votes on forty-five bills in the November 1981 special session to consider consumer protection, teacher bonuses, state agency appropriations, utility rate regulation, and transportation legislation.

After moving to Little Rock in 1995 to be near her family, Thompson became a member of the First United Methodist Church of Little Rock, continued her active reading, and enjoyed spending time with her grandchildren. She was survived by fifteen grandchildren and eight great-grandchildren.

# Peggy Long Hartness

HOUSE: 1983–1985
FROM: Monticello, Drew County
PARTY: Democratic
BIRTHPLACE: Monroe, Louisiana
DATES: November 7, 1939–
EDUCATION: Logtown Elementary School; Ouachita Parish High School, 1957; Northeast Louisiana State College (ULM)
OCCUPATION: abstract company owner

*Photo courtesy of Arkansas Secretary of State.*

Peggy Long Hartness (born Peggy O'Neil Long) was a freshman at Northeast Louisiana State College in 1958 when she met and married Bill Hartness, an Air Force veteran and varsity football player from Monticello, Arkansas. Bill became a partner in a home construction firm. Peggy Hartness was a homemaker, raising two children, and teaching Sunday school and playing piano at Union Missionary Baptist Church in Bosco.

In 1964, the Hartness family moved to Monticello, Arkansas, where they helped organize a savings and loan association and opened Hartness Building Supply and a homebuilding business. Hartness kept the financial books and managed the business while raising four children. She was involved in the community, where she served as president of the Monticello Junior Auxiliary, founded the local office of Suspected Child Abuse and Neglect Services, raised funds for the school band, and taught Sunday school at First Baptist Church.

Hartness obtained a broker's license and opened Drew County Abstract & Title Company with her son-in-law, attorney Cliff Gibson. In 1981, she became concerned about county financial practices and planned to run against the incumbent county judge, who suddenly resigned without explanation. After a new judge was appointed, Hartness ran for state representative in 1982, defeating incumbent Vernon Roberts with 68 percent of the vote in the Democratic primary. In 1984, she was unopposed in both the primary and general elections.

Representative Hartness was a vocal opponent of Governor Bill Clinton's educational reform legislative package, but she supported the Monticello location for the Southeast Arkansas Education Cooperative and programs and services to local schools. In both her first and second terms, she tried unsuccessfully to enact legislation authorizing "no trespassing" signs on unfenced timber property. After the session, Hartness received the Drew County Chamber of Commerce Woman of the Year Award in 1983 and the Arkansas Democratic Party's Gressie Carnes Award as the Democratic Woman of the Year in 1984.

After a divorce in 1984, Hartness married Carl Blair, an employee of Sun Oil Company. On October 1, 1985, she resigned from the legislature and moved to New Jersey. She eventually made her way back to Arkansas.

# Charlie Cole Chaffin

SENATE: 1984–1994
FROM: Benton, Saline County
PARTY: Democratic
BIRTHPLACE: Little Rock, Arkansas
DATES: September 13, 1938–
EDUCATION: Malvern High School, 1956;
University of Arkansas, BSE, 1960, and
MEd, 1964; curriculum specialist program
OCCUPATION: teacher

*Photo courtesy of Arkansas Secretary of State.*

Charlie Francis Cole Chaffin was raised in Sheridan and Malvern in a politically active family. Her grandfather, father, brother, and two uncles served
in elective or appointed office, and her mother marched for civil rights with
Dr. Martin Luther King Jr. They were well-read on current events and had
frequent discussions about issues facing Arkansas. "It was almost like a debate
team sometimes," she said.

Before seeking public office, Chaffin taught chemistry and physical science
at Bryant High School for eleven years (from 1970 to 1981). Later, she was a
part-time chemistry lecturer at the University of Arkansas at Little Rock
(1977–1990). After her political service, Chaffin began teaching chemistry at
the Arkansas School for Mathematics and Sciences in 1997.

Chaffin was elected a delegate to the 1979–1980 Arkansas Constitutional
Convention, serving as chairperson of the Science and Technology Committee
and member of the Finance and Taxation Committee. She was one of thirteen women in the hundred-member convention. She stated, "I served on the
Finance and Taxation Committee, because I wanted to be involved in areas
that were not especially associated with women."

In 1982, Chaffin ran unsuccessfully for the House of Representatives against
a two-term incumbent. In 1983, she served on the Education Standards Committee chaired by First Lady Hillary Rodham Clinton. Chaffin ran in a special election in 1984 for the Senate seat vacated by the death of Senator James
Teague and won. She was sworn in by her brother, circuit judge John Cole.

Senator Chaffin was the third woman to serve in the Arkansas Senate and
was the only female senator during eight of ten years in the Senate. In 1992,
senators elected her to the new position of deputy president pro tem. She was

also on the Capitol Arts Commission. Chaffin worked on education, ethics, civil rights, disability, and environmental legislation, such as the bill to create the Arkansas School for Mathematics and Sciences. Chaffin was also a frequent speaker at Girls State.

In 1994, Chaffin won the Democratic nomination for lieutenant governor, but lost to Mike Huckabee. She again ran for lieutenant governor in a special election in 1996, losing to Winthrop Paul Rockefeller. She served on the Arkansas Blue Ribbon Commission on Public Education (2001–2002), and in 2014 was honored as one of the pioneers by Women Lead Arkansas.

# Nancy Balton

HOUSE: 1985–1990
FROM: Wilson, Mississippi County
PARTY: Democratic
BIRTHPLACE: Wilson, Arkansas
DATES: August 27, 1935–May 24, 2018
EDUCATION: Wilson public schools; Ward-Belmont (Nashville); the Hutchison School (Memphis), 1953; Mississippi County Community College, AA in economics, 1981
OCCUPATION: farmer and businesswoman

*Photo courtesy of Arkansas Secretary of State*

Nancy Balton (born Nancy Lee Crain) was the daughter of Mary Edith Siler, a homemaker, and John Enochs Crain, president of Crain Co. and manager of a twenty-five-thousand-acre plantation. Both her father and her grandfather, James H. Crain, served as chairman of the Arkansas Highway Commission. After the eighth grade at Wilson, Balton attended preparatory schools in Tennessee and married John Collins "Jake" Balton shortly after graduation in 1953.

While raising two children, Balton was a member of the Wilson Cooperative Club, president of the Wilson PTA, member of the PEO Sisterhood, and organist at the Wilson First United Methodist Church. She was also a trustee of the Methodist Children's Home, chair of the George W. Jackson and Mississippi County Mental Health Center boards, and chair of the Mississippi County Community College Board.

Balton began her political career in 1968 as secretary of the Mississippi County Young Democrats and a member of the Executive Committee of the

Democratic State Committee. She would later chair the Mississippi County Democratic Central Committee and in 1974 became the first woman to serve as chair of the Democratic Party of Arkansas. In an interview during her term as party leader, she said she "leans to the right," opposed affirmative action and campaign finance disclosure, and took no position on ratification of the Equal Rights Amendment. Balton was a delegate to the Democratic National Convention in 1976, 1984, and 1988, and she was the Democratic National Committeewoman from 1984 to 1990. She received the 1982 Gressie Carnes Award for Outstanding Arkansas Democratic Woman.

In her first race for state representative, Balton lost the 1982 Democratic Primary to eight-term incumbent representative Bill Nicholson. When Nicholson died in 1984, she was unopposed in a June 1984 special election to fill the seat. Balton was unopposed for reelection in 1984, 1986, and 1988. After a federal court mandated redistricting, she did not run for reelection in 1990.

Representative Balton was a member of the House Public Transportation and the Agriculture and Economic Development Committees. She was outspoken against increased taxation and government spending, and she was a cosponsor of legislation awarding tax credits and exemptions to the Nucor-Yamato Steel plant in Mississippi County.

After her legislative service, Balton continued her volunteerism as chair of the Mississippi County Farm Bureau Women's Committee, honorary governor of the Arkansas Northeastern College Foundation Board, and member of the Arkansas State University Foundation Board.

# Myra Jones

HOUSE: 1985–1998
FROM: Little Rock, Pulaski County
PARTY: Democratic
BIRTHPLACE: Belle Fourche, South Dakota
DATES: March 8, 1936–February 20, 2012
EDUCATION: Belle Fourche High School, 1953; Oberlin College Conservatory of Music, BME, 1957; Indiana University, 1958; Drake University, MME in music, 1963; Northern Illinois University, 1965
OCCUPATION: city director, teacher, small-business owner

*Photo courtesy of Arkansas Secretary of State.*

Growing up on a ranch in South Dakota, Myra Jones (born Myra Gutsche) was active in 4-H and loved training and showing cattle. She played clarinet in the school band and joined the Belle Fourche Cowboy Band, a band playing at summer rodeos and events. She often returned to South Dakota throughout her life to play in the band.

Jones taught music in Des Moines public schools, both in the classroom and on educational television. She married Bob Jones in 1961, and they moved to Little Rock in 1966 when Bob was transferred by IBM. She managed three Dairy Queen restaurants that they owned.

Jones served eight years on the Little Rock City Board of Directors (1977–1984), was vice mayor of Little Rock for three of those years (1981–1984), the first female elected to that position, and in 1981 became the first woman elected to the board of a major utility in Arkansas (ArkLa 1981–1990). She was a Little Rock Chamber of Commerce Board Executive Committee member (1981–1984), chairman of board of Junior Achievement of Arkansas (1989–1990), on the UALR Foundation Board (1988–1991), and the National League of Cities Board of Directors. In 1995 Jones joined the Arkansas Women's Leadership Forum and in 1997 became a founding board member of the Women's Foundation of Arkansas.

In 1984, Jones was elected to the first of seven terms in the Arkansas House of Representatives. She chaired the City, County and Local Government Committee, and was a founding member of the Women's Legislative Caucus in 1985. Jones introduced and supported bills relating to local government, education, small businesses, and utilities. Her legislation included extension of the Code of Ethics Act to local officials and lobbyists, eyesight testing for driver's license renewal, the automobile "lemon law," the Medical Waste Disposal Act of 1995, the Telecommunications Regulatory Reform Act of 1997, the Safe Schools Bill, and the Prudent Investor Act.

During her legislative service, Jones was a 1988 Democratic National Convention Dukakis delegate, a 1992 Arkansas Traveler for Bill Clinton's presidential campaign, and a 1992 Democratic National Convention Clinton delegate and Platform Committee member. Jones was selected to Top 100 Women in Arkansas by *Arkansas Business* magazine in 1994, 1995, 1996, and 1997. The Arkansas Municipal League honored her in 1989 as Person of the Year and in 1997 as Representative of the Year.

After legislative service, Jones became a lobbyist for the Little Rock Realtors and continued operating The Hunter, her interior décor and personal shopping business. In 2002, she was honored as Little Rock Rotarian of the Year.

# Wanda Northcutt

HOUSE: 1985–1998
FROM: Stuttgart, Arkansas County
PARTY: Democratic
BIRTHPLACE: Stuttgart, Arkansas
DATES: April 21, 1937–
EDUCATION: Stuttgart public schools;
Stuttgart High School, 1954; Ouachita
Baptist University; University of Arkansas,
BA in biology and minor in chemistry, 1957;
University of Arkansas Medical Sciences,
BS in medical technology, 1959
OCCUPATION: farming

*Photo courtesy of Arkansas Secretary of State.*

Third-generation Stuttgart farmer Wanda Northcutt (born Wanda Hildebrand) is the daughter of Cleda Maria Simpson and Alfred Louis Hildebrand. Northcutt worked at a local drug store in high school and during summers in college. At the University of Arkansas, she was an officer in Pi Mu Delta (pre-med society) and a member of Zeta Tau Alpha sorority. After receiving her medical technician degree in 1959, she married medical student Carl Northcutt, and they moved to Stuttgart. Wanda Northcutt occasionally did lab work at the hospital and was involved in volunteer organizations. She was in PTA, president of the Stuttgart Hospital Auxiliary, president of the Arkansas Hospital Auxiliary, district Girl Scout leader, and district chair of the American Cancer Society. They had four children, two adopted.

When Representative Wayne Hampton announced his retirement in 1984, Northcutt ran for the seat, leading two male opponents in the Democratic primary and winning the runoff. Before the general election, Representative Hampton invited her to Little Rock, introduced her to people, and enhanced her working knowledge of the legislature. She defeated her Republican opponent with 68 percent in the general election. Thereafter, she never had another opponent, serving fourteen years until term-limited in 1998.

Representative Northcutt's major legislation includes the creation of the Office of Rural Advocacy, creation of the UAMS chair for drug and alcohol abuse, passage of the drink tax to build the UAMS biomedical research building, the Arkansas Water Plan, and child support. She is credited for the revival and passage of the 1989 school desegregation legislation the night before the session was to end. Northcutt advocated for conservation and protection of state aquifers and was influential with agriculture and education legislation, serving as co-chair of the House Education Committee. She also served on the House Rules Committee and the Joint Budget Committee.

Northcutt was chair of Girls State, the first woman chair of the Southern Legislative Conference Agriculture Committee, and an organizer for the Arkansas General Assembly Women's Caucus. The Soil and Water Commission recognized her for promoting conservation of water resources. Other honors include the Riceland Foods Friend of Farmer Award, the distinguished service awards from the College of Medicine and Arkansas Municipal League, and the Henry Horizon Tourism Award.

In 1998, Northcutt married Jake Hartz, and after her legislative service was on the Bancorp South Stuttgart Board and the Phillips Community College Foundation Board (PCCUA). She is president of Hildebrand Farm, Inc.

# Charlotte Schexnayder

HOUSE: 1985–1998
FROM: Dumas, Desha County
PARTY: Democratic
BIRTHPLACE: Tillar, Arkansas
DATES: December 25, 1923–
December 11, 2020
EDUCATION: Tillar High School, 1940;
Arkansas A&M; University of Chicago;
Louisiana State University, BA in sociology
and journalism, 1944; graduate journalism
courses, 1946–1947
OCCUPATION: newspaper editor and
publisher

*Photo courtesy of Arkansas Secretary of State.*

Charlotte Schexnayder (born Charlotte Tillar) was the daughter of Bertha Elizabeth Terry, a teacher, and Jewel Stephen Tillar, a furniture store manager. In the seventh grade, Schexnayder published her first newspaper as an English class project and soon decided to become a journalist and own a community newspaper. A Girl Scout trip to meet Eleanor Roosevelt led her to imagine women's political contributions. In high school, she was editor of the Tillar High School *Eagle* and a district finalist in extemporaneous speaking.

At age sixteen years, Schexnayder attended Arkansas A&M, where she was student council secretary and business manager of the *Weevil Outlet* student newspaper. She attended summer school at the University of Chicago, studying public administration with Dr. Leonard White, then transferred to finish her degree at Louisiana State University. She was campus editor of the *Reveille*, named to Theta Sigma Phi (Women in Communication), on the YWCA cabinet, and a member of Pi Beta Phi sorority.

Shortly after graduation from LSU, Schexnayder was hired as editor of the *McGehee Times* in 1944, where she editorialized against Japanese American internment camps. She married Melvin Schexnayder in 1946, and they returned to Baton Rouge, where she took graduate journalism classes and was journalism department secretary. In 1948, they moved back to McGehee, where she was again editor of the *McGehee Times*. The Schexnayders purchased the Dumas *Clarion* in 1954 and made it into one of the leading community newspapers in the state, editorializing in favor of the desegregation of Central High School in 1957.

While raising three children and publishing the newspaper, Schexnayder became a state and national leader in the profession. She was the first woman president of the Arkansas Society of Professional Journalists (1973), first woman president of the Arkansas Press Association (1981), and first woman president of the National Newspaper Association (1991). She was also president of the Arkansas Press Women (1955) and the National Federation of Press Women (1977). Governor David Pryor appointed her the first woman member of the state parole board, and she was president of the Dumas Chamber of Commerce. Schexnayder was on the board of the Winthrop Rockefeller Foundation and helped create the Arkansas Humanities Council.

Schexnayder ran for the Arkansas House of Representatives. She was unopposed in 1984, 1986, 1988, 1990, and 1992, and was reelected in 1994 and 1996, winning the Democratic primaries and being unopposed in the general elections. Her legislative achievements include the Great River Bridge, rural roads, education improvement, economic development, a state ethics act, defending the Arkansas Freedom of Information Act, a high school press bill of rights, establishing a research chair at the University of Arkansas for Medical Sciences, and preventing the removal of reporters from the House chamber.

Among honors Schexnayder received for her careers in journalism and the legislature were Arkansas Journalist of the Year in 1978, induction into the Hall of Fame at Louisiana State University's Manship School of Mass Communication, the League of Women Voters of Arkansas Horizon Award, the Brownie Ledbetter Civic Engagement Award, and inclusion in Who's Who in America. Schexnayder published her memoirs, *Salty Old Editor*, in 2012, and she was inducted into the Arkansas Women's Hall of Fame in 2019.

# Gladys Watson

SENATE: 1988–1990
FROM: Monette, Craighead County
PARTY: Democratic
BIRTHPLACE: Oakland, Arkansas (Marion)
DATES: September 21, 1925–January 11, 1996
EDUCATION: attended Arkansas State University
OCCUPATION: teacher and folk artist

*Photo courtesy of Arkansas Secretary of State.*

Gladys Watson (born Gladys Gilbert) was the only child of Eunice Hollingsworth and Alfred Eugene Gilbert, who were both public school teachers. She attended various public schools where her parents taught in north Arkansas and West Plains, Missouri. They also taught Japanese American children in the school at the Thule Lake Relocation Center in California. In later years, Watson reflected on the unfairness of confiscating the property of American citizens and incarcerating them for no crime and "thought it was a shame."

Following the family tradition, Watson taught school at Milligan Ridge in Mississippi County. She married Tom Watson in 1943, and they had one son. She was a homemaker, took classes at Arkansas State University, and helped run the family farm four miles south of Monette. She was also active in the Monette First United Methodist Church and the Arkansas Federation of Democratic Women.

Watson became well-known in northeast Arkansas for her folk art paintings of scenes of Northeast Arkansas Delta history and often was referred to as the local "Granny Moses" of crafts. She called it "folk art from the cotton patch," with paintings that included a field of cotton, a shed barn, a log house, workers, tenant houses, a church, and a schoolhouse. Watson produced her work in the Cotton Patch Craft Shop on her farm, traveled the craft show circuit, and sold some of her art in the state capitol gift shop.

Tom Watson was a state senator from 1971 until his death in 1988, and Gladys Watson worked each session on the Senate staff supervising pages. She knew the legislators and understood legislative procedures, so she announced as a candidate for her husband's unexpired term. Endorsed by the Arkansas Education Association and backed by Democratic women's groups, she led the Democratic primary with 44.3 percent against Green County judge Jerry Shipman and former representative Andy Shug, then won the runoff by 456 votes over Judge Shipman. Governor Bill Clinton told her, "You were brave getting out there and campaigning. You won a hard-fought victory—nobody gave it to you."

Sworn into office in November 1988, Senator Watson served in the 1989 regular session and three extraordinary sessions that year. She was on the Public Transportation and the Aging and Legislative Affairs Committees. Her voting record reflected support for public education and Governor Clinton's other programs. She did not seek reelection 1990.

# Christene Brownlee

HOUSE: 1991–1994
FROM: Gilmore, Crittenden County
PARTY: Republican
BIRTHPLACE: Jonesboro, Arkansas
DATES: October 16, 1955–
EDUCATION: George Washington Carver, Marked Tree, and William R. Golden public schools; Turrell High School, 1973; Mid-South Community College
OCCUPATION: mayor, business manager

*Photo courtesy of Arkansas Secretary of State.*

Christene Brownlee (born Christene Jackson) is the youngest of ten children born to Fannie Murray Wall, a homemaker, and Tom Edward Jackson, a farmer. She was salutatorian of her sixth-grade class, a cheerleader, and active in her church. She married Billy Earl Brownlee two months before she graduated from Turrell High School in 1973.

While raising three children, Christene Jackson Brownlee was employed as assistant manager at the Liquor Center in West Memphis. In 1986, she was elected the first Black mayor of Gilmore, receiving 57 percent of the vote against two male candidates, including the incumbent. She was elected secretary of the Arkansas Black Mayors Association, and Governor Bill Clinton appointed her to an advisory committee of the Lower Mississippi Delta Development Commission in 1989.

After publicly supporting the Democratic ticket of Dukakis-Bentson in 1988, Mayor Brownlee ran for a House seat as a Republican. In the 1990 general election, she trailed Blytheville alderman Lonnie Middlebrook by thirty-six votes but won by five votes in a recount. After an election challenge, Brownlee was seated by an 88–9 vote of the House of Representatives, becoming the first Black Republican woman legislator to serve in the Arkansas General Assembly. She won a second term in 1992 with 53 percent but was defeated for reelection in 1994, losing by fifty votes to Democrat Joe Harris Jr.

The National Republican Legislators Association named Brownlee the 1991 Outstanding Freshman Legislator of the Year. She was a member of the Legislature's Republican Caucus, Black Caucus, and Women's Caucus. She sponsored HB 2087 to require doctors to provide women state-approved information and alternatives to abortion twenty-four hours prior to the procedure, which passed the House but failed in the Senate committee. Twice she voted against a budget amendment that would have prohibited condom distribution by school clinics, arguing that anti-abortion legislation would be unnecessary if school clinics could provide condoms to prevent unwanted pregnancies. Brownlee joined as a plaintiff in *Turner v. Arkansas*, an unsuccessful federal lawsuit supported by the state Republican Party challenging the Congressional redistricting plan.

Governor Mike Huckabee appointed Brownlee as a legislative liaison for the 1997 legislative session. In March 1997, Brownlee was recruited and elected mayor by the Gilmore City Council to fill an unexpired term. In 1998, she ran unopposed for a four-year term and served as mayor until 2002, when she was defeated for reelection.

Brownlee became a part-time substitute teacher at the Turrell School District and worked to secure grants from the US Department of Housing and Urban Development for a home rehabilitation program in Gilmore. In 2018, she attempted to return to public office, running unsuccessfully for mayor.

# Jacqueline Roberts

HOUSE: 1991–1998
FROM: Pine Bluff, Jefferson County
PARTY: Democratic
BIRTHPLACE: Dermott, Arkansas
DATES: April 30, 1944–
EDUCATION: Greenville Elementary;
Pine Bluff Merrill High School, 1963;
Arkansas Agricultural, Mechanical, and
Normal College (UAPB), BA, 1976;
teaching certificate, 1977
OCCUPATION: apartment management

*Photo courtesy of Arkansas Secretary of State.*

Jacqueline Roberts (born Jacqueline Johnson) is the daughter of Gertrude Colvin and Osie Johnson and the seventh of ten children. When Roberts was a baby, the family moved to Pine Bluff. In high school, she worked at the Greyhound bus station. In 1963, she married Curley Roberts, her high school sweetheart and a track all-American. They had three children.

Jacqueline Roberts's first job out of college was as a third-grade teacher in Warren. Finding that teaching was not for her, she worked as a nursing home dietician, but ultimately became an apartment manager. She was a field coordinator for Arkansas Career Resources and a substitute teacher, was a member of Arkansas Community Organizations for Reform Now (ACORN), and a Jesse Jackson delegate to the 1988 Democratic National Convention. In 1990, her friend representative Henry Wilkins called and encouraged her to run for an open House seat. Roberts won the 1990 Democratic primary with 51 percent and the general election with 88 percent. She was reelected with 62 percent in the 1992 Democratic primary and was unopposed in 1994 and 1996.

In her first session, Roberts was disappointed that one of her first floor speeches was opposing a House civil rights bill, a deceptive Chamber-backed bill giving legislators cover for killing the real Senate civil rights bill. She spoke passionately for a domestic violence bill, informing colleagues of her sister's death to an abusive husband. She was most pleased with legislation on breast cancer, domestic violence, school uniforms, hate crimes, civil rights, and several education bills. "My passion was always children. Any legislation that had to do with youth, that's really what I wanted to be involved in, or women's health," she said. She filed legislation requiring adults to keep loaded weapons locked to protect child safety. She started Youth Enhancement Services, encouraging children to stay in school, and created the first Pine Bluff back-to-school festival.

Representative Roberts was a member of the Arkansas Legislative Black Caucus and chaired the Subcommittee on Hate-Motivated Crimes. In 1995, she received an Honorary Doctorate of Humane Letters from Shorter College. She was a delegate to the 1996 Democratic National Convention, and in 1997 was named to the Minority Health Commission Common Ground Program Committee.

After legislative service, Roberts worked for a year as a liaison for Senator Blanche Lincoln before returning to manage apartments. She was a Jefferson County justice of the peace from 2005 to 2006.

# Judy Smith

HOUSE: 1991–1998
FROM: Camden, Ouachita County
PARTY: Democratic
BIRTHPLACE: Ville Platt, Louisiana
DATES: March 10, 1953–
EDUCATION: Ville Platt school district; James Steven High School, 1971; Grambling State University, BASW, 1974, and graduate coursework; University of Arkansas at Little Rock, volunteer management, 1985
OCCUPATION: nonprofit administrator

*Photo courtesy of Arkansas Secretary of State.*

Judy Smith (born Judy Ann Seriale) was raised by her grandmother, Agnes Watson Bellard, the Creole-speaking political matriarch of Belair Cove, a sharecropping community in Evangeline Parish, Louisiana. Smith picked cotton when not attending school. Smith attended segregated schools until integration her senior year. She credits her high school biology teacher, Beatrice Johnson, for helping her overcome shyness and gain confidence and her civics teacher Mark Latigue for encouraging her to join the Civics Action Club. Smith was, she said, "the first one in our entire family, from the first time one of us got to America, to graduate from high school."

When Smith's Pell Grant and work study applications were rejected, her grandmother took her to a state legislator's office and, in Creole, asked him to help, which he did. At Grambling, she majored in social work, joined a sorority, and was president of several campus organizations. In December 1974, she married Grambling student Sylvester Lee Smith from Camden, Arkansas. Sylvester was a law enforcement officer, Ouachita County coroner, and a funeral director and embalmer. They had two children.

In Camden, Judy Smith worked in the tax collector's office before returning to Grambling for graduate school. She had a child and worked as a behavioral science assistant instructor training medical residents. In 1979, Smith and her family moved back to Camden, where she pursued her social work career with the anti-poverty program Community Action, a substance abuse prevention nonprofit, and the youth organization People are Concerned.

In 1990, Smith ran for the House of Representatives, defeating a twelve-term incumbent in the Democratic primary. Representative Smith continued to be reelected, serving eight years. She was vice chair of the Committee on Children and Youth and sponsored legislation addressing issues of stalking, poverty, public assistance, probation, apprenticeships, grandparents' visitation rights, adult and child abuse, banning corporal punishment in public schools, youths, disabilities, education, kinship foster care, public safety, and increasing the age of sexual consent.

In 1998, Smith was unopposed for the Democratic nomination for Congress in the Fourth District, losing to the Republican incumbent, Jay Dickey, 57 percent to 42 percent. She ran again for Congress in 2000, losing the Democratic primary to Mike Ross, who went on to defeat Congressman Dickey in the general election. Governor Mike Huckabee named Smith to head the Minority Health Commission in 2002. She continued working as administrative director of the Hot Springs Rehabilitation Center and director of transition programs at Arkansas Rehabilitation Services.

Representatives Nicole Clowney and Megan Godfrey during the 2019 legislative session. *Courtesy of Nicole Clowney and Megan Godfrey.*

Current and past female legislators gather for Arkansas Women's Legislative Day at the Arkansas Capitol on March 31, 2010, during Women's History Month. Front Row: Senator Ruth Whitaker, Representative Pam Adcock, Henry P. Jones III (representing his grandmother Representative Frances Hunt, the first woman to serve in the Arkansas legislature); Row Two: Rep. Nancy Balton, Rep. Myra Jones, Rep. Charlotte Schexnayder, Rep. Wanda Northcutt Hartz, Senator Irma Hunter Brown, Senator Charlie Cole Chaffin, Rep. Wilhelmina Lewellen; Row Three: Rep. and Treasurer Martha Shoffner, Rep. Sarah Agee; Row Four: Rep. Lindsley Smith, Rep. Jan Judy, Rep. Barbara King, Rep. Charolette Wagner, Rep. Linda Chesterfield, Rep. Kathy Webb, Rep. Johnnie Roebuck; Row Five: Rep. Marilyn Edwards, Senator Mary Anne Salmon, Senator Sue Madison, Rep. Judy Smith, Rep Joan Cash; Row Six: Rep. Janet Johnson, Rep. Sandra Prater, Rep Sandra Rodgers, Rep. Jacqueline Roberts, Rep. Joyce Dees, Rep. Nancy Duffy Blount, Rep. Debra Hobbs; Row Seven: Rep. Mary Lou Slinkard, Rep. Linda Tyler, Rep. Karen Hopper, Rep. Dee Bennett, Rep. Donna Hutchinson; Row Eight: Rep. Andrea Lea, Rep. Ann Clemmer, Rep. Jody Dickinson, Rep. Barbara Nix, Rep. Tiffany Rogers; Row Nine: Rep. Shirley Walters, Rep. Toni Bradford, Rep. Susan Schulte, Rep. Tracy Pennartz, Rep. Beverly Pyle. *Courtesy of the authors.*

Representatives Michelle Gray and DeAnn Vaught playing for the Arkansas House of Representatives against the Arkansas Senate in the Hoops for Kids' Sake charity basketball game benefitting Big Brothers Big Sisters of Central Arkansas, March 4, 2015. *Courtesy of Michelle Gray and DeAnn Vaught.*

Representative LeAnne Burch served in the United States Army, retiring as a Brigadier General and Commander of the Army Reserve Legal Command. She is pictured in July 2009 with two girls at a local daycare facility in Kabul, Afghanistan, during a Volunteer Community Relations (VCR) Mission. *Courtesy of LeAnne Burch.*

Equal Rights Amendment Resolution sponsor Senator Joyce Elliott and cosponsor Senator Linda Chesterfield present the resolution to the Senate State Agencies Committee during the 2019 legislative session. *Courtesy of* Arkansas Times *and photographer Brian Chilson.*

Representative Nelda Speaks at the Arkansas Women's Primary Suffrage Centennial Day at the Arkansas State Capitol, February 7, 2017. *Courtesy of the Arkansas House of Representatives.*

Representative Carolyn Pollan and her sixteen-year-old daughter, Cee Cee, prior to the 1977 equal rights parade outside the Arkansas State Capitol. *Courtesy of Carolyn Pollan.*

Senator Barbara Horn Highway dedication, August 8, 2016, at the Little River County Courthouse in Ashdown, Arkansas. The dedication section of highway is a portion of Arkansas Highway 41 and Highway 32 south of Foreman, Arkansas. *Photo by Jim Williamson/*Texarkana Gazette, *used by permission.*

Senator Gladys Watson during the 1989–1990 legislative term. *Courtesy of the Arkansas Senate.*

Arkansas constitutional and legislative women gather in January 2019 on the Arkansas Capitol steps prior to the beginning of the legislative session. Front Row: Representative Breanne Davis and child, state auditor and past state Representative Andrea Lea, State Attorney General Leslie Rutledge, Rep. DeAnn Vaught, Rep. Sonia Barker, Rep. Robin Lundstrum, Rep. Karilyn Brown, Senator Joyce Elliott; Second Row: Rep. Deborah Ferguson, Senator Jane English, Rep. Jamie Scott, Rep. Megan Godfrey, Senator Missy Irvin, and Representatives Frances Cavenaugh, Carol Dalby, Nelda Speaks, Sarah Capp, and Laurie Rushing; Back Row: Rep. Cindy Crawford, Senator Cecile Bledsoe, and Representatives Michelle Gray, LeAnne Burch, Denise Garner, Tippi McCullough, Gayla McKenzie, Nicole Clowney, Charlene Fite, Mary Bentley, and Rebecca Petty. *Courtesy of the Arkansas Senate.*

Campaign brochure and billboards for Carolyn Pollan's 1974 campaign for the Arkansas House of Representatives. *Courtesy of Carolyn Pollan.*

Representatives Nancy Duffy Blount (seated), Wilhelmina Lewellen, Stephanie Flowers, and Tracy Pennartz in the House Chamber on March 3, 2010. *Courtesy of the authors.*

Arkansas Women's Legislative Caucus retreat at Couchwood near Hot Springs in October 2005. Pictured are Representative Susan Schulte (front), Representatives Sandra Prater, Betty Pickett, and Wilhelmina Lewellen; Senator Irma Hunter Brown, Representative Pam Adcock, Senator Sue Madison, and Representatives Shirley Walters and Lindsley Smith. *Courtesy of the authors.*

Senator Cecile Bledsoe and Representatives Debra Hobbs and Barbara Nix at a Women's Legislative Caucus gathering in January 2009. *Courtesy of the authors.*

Legislators with Governor Mike Huckabee at 2001 General Assembly Session bill signing. Women legislators are (from left): Representative Mary Anne Salmon, Rep. Pat Bond, Rep. Wilma Walker, Rep. Jo Carson, Rep. Jan Judy, (unidentified bill supporter), Rep. Sandra Rodgers, Rep. Shirley Borhauer, Senator Sharon Trusty, Rep. Barbara King, Rep. Sarah Agee, Rep. Mary Beth Green, Rep. Cecile Bledsoe, Rep. Joyce Dees, and Senator Barbara Horn. *Courtesy of Shirley Borhauer.*

Great friends Charlotte Schexnayder, Wanda Northcutt Hartz, and Myra Jones in September 2007 at the funeral of Charlotte's husband, Melvin. *Courtesy of the authors.*

Representatives Kathy Webb, Pam Adcock, Ann Clemmer, and Dawn Creekmore in the House Chamber on March 3, 2010. *Courtesy of the authors.*

Representatives Nancy Duffy Blount and Beverly Pyle presenting the names of women who have served in the Arkansas General Assembly at the 2010 Arkansas Women's Legislative Day at the Arkansas Capitol. *Courtesy of the authors.*

Representative Myra Jones being recognized at the 2010 Arkansas Women's Legislative Day at the Arkansas Capitol. *Courtesy of the authors.*

Rally for the Equal Rights Amendment during the 2007 legislative session. Rep. Johnnie Roebuck, Rep. Joan Cash, Rep. Wilhelmina Lewellen, Rep. Marilyn Edwards, Senator Sue Madison, Rep. Sandra Prater, Senator Mary Anne Salmon, Senator Irma Hunter Brown, Rep. Lindsley Smith, Rep. Betty Pickett, rally organizer Karen Garcia, and Treasurer and former Rep. Martha Shoffner listen to Governor Mike Beebe's presentation in support of Arkansas ratifying the national Equal Rights Amendment. *Courtesy of the authors.*

Representative Josetta Wilkins, with Representative Jacqueline Roberts in support to her left. *Courtesy of Josetta Wilkins.*

Senator Ruth Whitaker campaign card. *Courtesy of Ruth Whitaker.*

Representative Charlene Fite speaking on a bill during the 2021 legislative session. *Courtesy of Charlene Fite.*

Past Representatives Tiffany Rogers, Kathy Webb, Linda Tyler, and Johnnie Roebuck at an event in the fall of 2019. *Courtesy of Johnnie Roebuck.*

Representative Denise Ennett filing legislation during the 2021 session, wearing her mask during the COVID-19 pandemic. *Courtesy of Denise Ennett.*

Representative Jamie Scott, with Representative Carol Dalby in background, April 2019. *Courtesy of the Arkansas House of Representatives.*

Arkansas House of Representatives, March 2019; Representatives Karilyn Brown, Nicole Clowney, Rebecca Petty, Jamie Scott, DeAnn Vaught, Tippi McCullough, Nelda Speaks, Sara Capp, Carol Dalby, Charlene Fite, Deborah Ferguson, Mary Bentley, Megan Godfrey, Sonia Eubanks Barker, Robin Lundstrum, Frances Cavenaugh, Denise Garner, Cindy Crawford, and Vivian Flowers. *Courtesy of the Arkansas House of Representatives.*

January 2019 in House well: Representatives Michelle Gray, Jamie Scott, LeAnne Burch, Megan Godfrey, Tippi McCullough, DeAnn Vaught, Frances Cavenaugh, Denise Garner, Robin Lundstrum, and Cindy Crawford. *Courtesy of the Arkansas House of Representatives.*

Arkansas women legislators photographed in April 2016 at the Arkansas Capitol with Allison Jensen (sitting), director of membership of the National Foundation for Women Legislators. Legislators are Representatives Betty Overbey, Vivian Flowers, Nelda Speaks, Camille Bennett, Deborah Ferguson, Mary Broadaway, Prissy Hickerson, Karilyn Brown, Jana Della Rosa, DeAnn Vaught, Mary Bentley, Charlotte Vining Douglas, Rebecca Petty, Laurie Rushing, Charlene Fite, Sheilla Lampkin, Robin Lundstrum, and Michelle Gray. *Courtesy of the Arkansas House of Representatives.*

2019 Session. Representatives LeAnne Burch (foreground), Cindy Crawford, Denise Garner, and Nelda Speaks (background). *Courtesy of the Arkansas House of Representatives.*

Legislative Hunger Caucus member Representative Stephanie Malone serving dinner with other caucus legislators at the Governor's Mansion in June 2012 for the Arkansas Hunger Relief Alliance fundraiser. *Courtesy of the Arkansas House of Representatives.*

Representative Lindsley Smith, sponsor of the Equal Rights Amendment Resolution in the 2007 legislative session, speaks before the House State Agencies and Governmental Affairs Committee. STOP ERA campaign organizer Phyllis Schlafly pictured back center. © Arkansas Democrat-Gazette *File Photo.*

# Josetta Wilkins

HOUSE: 1991–1998
FROM: Pine Bluff, Jefferson County
PARTY: Democratic
BIRTHPLACE: North Little Rock, Arkansas
DATES: July 17, 1932–
EDUCATION: Merrill grade school; Sherrill grade school; Merrill High School, 1950; Arkansas Agricultural, Mechanical, and Normal College (UAPB), BSE in elementary education and social studies, 1961; University of Arkansas, MEd in counseling, 1967; Oklahoma State University, EdD in higher education administration, 1987
OCCUPATION: teacher, counselor, college professor

*Photo courtesy of Arkansas Secretary of State.*

Josetta Wilkins (born Josette Edwards) is the fifth of fourteen children of Laura Bridgette Freeman, a homemaker, and James Wesley Edwards, a sharecropper. Growing up in Sherill, Wilkins began working in the cotton fields when she was five years old and at six began walking seven miles to Pine Bluff to attend the nearest public school for Black students. After high school, she worked a year as a domestic servant, then was a dishwasher while attending Arkansas AM&N College as a divorced single mother. In 1953, after changing the spelling of her name, she married Henry Wilkins III.

While raising five children, Wilkins graduated magna cum laude in 1961, taught elementary school, served as president of the PTA, and was a counsellor at Arkansas Rehabilitation Services in the Special Work Program for Disabled Children. After earning graduate degrees, she joined the faculty at the University of Arkansas at Pine Bluff in 1973, and during the next twenty-six years became an associate professor of education and director of University Relations and Development.

Henry Wilkins was elected to the Arkansas House in 1972, serving until his death in 1991. Josetta Wilkins ran in a special election to fill his term, defeating two opponents with 52 percent in the Democratic primary and winning the general election with 87 percent. She was reelected in 1992 with 79 percent in the general election and was unopposed for reelection in 1994 and 1996.

Among Representative Wilkins's most cherished legislative accomplishments were creation of the Martin Luther King Jr. Commission, an act requiring the Department of Education to develop and distribute curriculum materials for teaching character and citizenship, and the Breast Cancer Act of 1997, funding education, mammography, diagnosis, treatment, and research of breast cancer for Arkansas women.

During her legislative career, Wilkins was a member of the state Martin Luther King Jr. Commission and the National Order of Women Legislators, and she was an election monitor in El Salvador. Among the awards she received were the Humanitarian of the Year by the Arkansas Region of the National Conference for Community and Justice, the Advocacy Award from American Cancer Society's Mid-South Division, the National Governors Association's Lifetime Achievement Award in Community Service, the Delta Sigma Theta Outstanding Leadership and Service in Women's Health Award from her sorority, the University of Arkansas at Pine Bluff's Hall of Fame, Local Hero Award from the Susan G. Komen Breast Cancer Foundation, a presidential citation from the National Association for Equal Opportunity in Higher Education, and the Governor's Volunteer Excellence Award. In addition, the Arkansas Department of Health created the annual Josetta Wilkins Award, and the Martin Luther King Jr. Commission presents the annual Josetta Wilkins Courage Award.

After retiring from the legislature, Dr. Wilkins served on the Arkansas Minority Health Care Commission, the Rockefeller Cancer Institute Foundation Board, and the Wesley Foundation at UAPB.

In addition to her husband, Henry Wilkins (House 1973–1991), Josetta Wilkins's brother Jean Edwards (Senate 1991–2000) and son Hank (House 1999–2000, Senate 2001–2006) were state legislators, and her son-in-law, Rodney Slater, was United States secretary of transportation (1997–2001).

# Dee Bennett

HOUSE: 1993–1998
FROM: North Little Rock, Pulaski County
PARTY: Democratic
BIRTHPLACE: Little Rock, Arkansas
DATES: August 20, 1935–
EDUCATION: Dunbar High School, 1952;
Arkansas Baptist College, BA in education,
1956; University of Wisconsin, 1963; State
College of Arkansas (UCA), MEd in sec-
ondary school counseling, 1974; University
of California, PhD in psychology, 1977
OCCUPATION: recording artist, community
activist, teacher and school examiner

*Photo courtesy of Arkansas Secretary of State.*

Dee Bennett (born Mildred Delores Dolphus) is the daughter of Earnestine Marie Goode, a teacher, and Frank Dolphus, a laborer. Bennett and her sister, Jeanne, were part of the gospel group the Dolphus Singers and later formed the popular soul group Jeanne and the Darlings, beginning as backup singers for Stax Records and becoming an influential American musical group, having a Top 40 hit in 1967 among the six singles they recorded for Volt.

She married Berttie Edgar Bennett Jr., minister of Greater Friendship Baptist Church, and they had five children. She became an elementary teacher in the Pulaski County Special School District in 1965 and, after graduate work, returned as a special educational examiner for the district until her retirement in 1989.

Dr. Bennett was president of the Greater Little Rock Operation PUSH in 1979, publicly advocating against racial discrimination, police violence, and the KKK; and for increased voter registration, school programs for at-risk children, hiring more Black teachers, and recognition of a state Martin Luther King Jr. holiday. In 1985, she was appointed by Governor Bill Clinton to the Martin Luther King Jr. Holiday Commission.

After narrowly losing a race for North Little Rock City Council, Bennett was appointed to the North Little Rock City Planning Commission in 1985. She lost another city council race in 1988, the same year that she chaired Jesse Jackson's state campaign, was a Jackson delegate to the Democratic National Convention, and was a presidential elector.

Bennett's first electoral success came in 1990, when she became the first Black member elected to the North Little Rock City Council, winning with 52 percent over four opponents, including the incumbent. Governor Clinton appointed her to the state Civil Rights Commission in 1991. Dr. Bennett ran for the Arkansas House in 1992, winning the Democratic primary with 63 percent. She was unopposed in the general election and was also unopposed for reelection in 1994 and 1996. Representative Bennett cosponsored legislation proposing to enhance penalties for hate crimes, opposed allowing juveniles to be questioned by police without parental consent, and supported the appropriation to construct a large indoor arena in North Little Rock.

While serving in the House, Representative Bennett was executive director of Greater Friendship, Inc., and a full-time volunteer at the Granite Mountain Youth Center. In 1996, Governor Jim Guy Tucker appointed her to the Arkansas Advisory Council on Volunteerism, and, in 1998, she and her husband were honored by the National Parents' Day Foundation. After being term-limited, Bennett ran against the incumbent for a North Little Rock City Council seat in 2000 but lost in the runoff.

# Ann Bush

HOUSE: 1993–2000
FROM: Blytheville, Mississippi County
PARTY: Republican
BIRTHPLACE: Ripley, Tennessee
DATES: April 18, 1935–
EDUCATION: Ripley High School; University of Tennessee at Knoxville, BS in home economics, 1958
OCCUPATION: homemaker

*Photo courtesy of Arkansas Secretary of State.*

Ann Bush (born Ann Holmes) was born in Ripley, Tennessee, to John Acton Holmes, an insurance salesman, and Ruth Barton, who ran a small canning factory and taught kindergarten and first grade. In 1957, she married Allen Bush, and in 1958 they moved to Blytheville to operate the Bush Brothers canning plant.

While raising their three sons, Bush taught Sunday school, was on the county fair board, was president of the PTA, and volunteered for the Red Cross campaign. In 1967, she was named Woman of the Year by the Blytheville chapter of Beta Sigma Phi for her community service. Bush was an unsuccessful candidate for the Blytheville School Board in 1975. She became a member of the Republican County Committee, later serving as its chair. Bush also served as a Mississippi County election commissioner and initiated a punch card voting system for the county.

When Representative Walter Day died in office in 1993, Bush resigned as chair of the Republican County Committee and ran for the open seat in a special election. Bush focused on education, and she stressed her experiences with the church, as an officer in the Arkansas Federation of Women's Clubs, and as state regent of the Daughters of the American Revolution. Her advertising did not mention that she was a Republican. Bush defeated Democrat Marvin Childers with 52 percent and was sworn in that fall. In her 1994 reelection campaign, she won by 55 percent over Democrat Jack Goodman. In 1995, Speaker of the House Bobby Hogue appointed Bush as a Constitutional Convention delegate.

Bush was unopposed for reelection in 1996 and 1998. She was a Bob Dole delegate to both the 1988 and 1996 Republican National Conventions.

Representative Bush specialized in election law, passed legislation to expand the Arkansas Economic Development Act tax credits, supported equal education funding, and opposed the soft drink tax. She cast the sole vote against legislation authorizing advanced-practice nurses to prescribe medication. She argued that election materials should be in English only and for Latin words being removed from the state constitution.

In 1999, Bush was elected to the board of the Historic Preservation Alliance of Arkansas. She also served on the Arkansas Board of Election Commissioners, 2001–2009, by appointment of Governor Mike Huckabee.

# Barbara Horn

HOUSE: 1993–2000, SENATE: 2001–2010
FROM: Foreman, Little River County
PARTY: Democratic
BIRTHPLACE: Mountain Pine, Arkansas
DATES: October 11, 1936–
EDUCATION: Foreman High School, 1954;
Texarkana Junior College, 1955
OCCUPATION: insurance agency owner
and agent

*Photo courtesy of Arkansas Secretary of State.*

Barbara Horn (born Barbara Jean Bell) is the daughter of Hazel Oletta Davis, a homemaker, and Elbert Wesley Bell, an employee of Foreman Cement. She married Hoye Horn in 1955, and they had three children. She worked at First National Bank as a teller and bookkeeper for ten years before becoming an insurance agent and starting Horn Insurance Agency.

She was president of the Little River Chamber of Commerce and was a member of the Ashdown Rotary Club, the Foreman Kiwanis Club, and the Foreman Music Club. She also served as treasurer of the First Baptist Church.

Horn shared an interest in politics with her husband, who served six terms as county judge before being elected state representative in 1988. When he died in 1993 in his third term, she ran for the seat in a special election. She led a field of four candidates with 44 percent in the Democratic primary, won the runoff with 55 percent, and received 59 percent in the general election. Horn was unopposed in 1994, 1996, and 1998.

Representative Horn ran for the state senate in 2000, supported by Republican governor Mike Huckabee in the Democratic primary against Representative Dennis Young. She won the primary with 51 percent, and the Republican nominee withdrew before the general election. Senator Horn was reelected with 60 percent in 2002 and was unopposed in 2006.

In the Senate, Horn sponsored bills limiting liability of nursing homes for abuse and health violations and cutting sales taxes for manufacturers. She supported a timber industry tax break, testified in favor of coal-fired generating plants, opposed regulation of payday lenders, and proposed cutting the minimum wage for restaurant employees. Horn was state chair of the

American Legislative Exchange Council. She also voted against ratification of the Equal Rights Amendment.

Senator Horn was effective in securing appropriations for district projects. She was most proud of legislation to expand rural telecommunications infrastructure and supporting rural health care, as well as sponsoring the Susan Komen Foundation license plate. She was a steadfast supporter of the UA Cossatot Community College, serving seventeen years on its board of visitors and securing funding for the Ashdown campus. In 2010, she was named to Who's Who in American Politics.

After leaving office, Horn was appointed to the Arkansas Workforce Investment Board. She was honored by the designation of the Barbara Horn Highway in Foreman and the naming of the Barbara Horn Civic Center at UA Cossatot-Ashdown.

# Marian Owens Ingram

HOUSE: 1993–1998
FROM: Warren, Bradley County
PARTY: Democratic
BIRTHPLACE: Beebe, Arkansas
DATES: September 17, 1936–
EDUCATION: Cabot and Searcy public schools; Searcy High School, 1954; University of Central Arkansas, ABA, 1956; University of Arkansas at Monticello, real estate courses
OCCUPATION: business owner and realtor

*Photo courtesy of Arkansas Secretary of State.*

Marian Owens Ingram (born Marian Daniel) was born in Beebe to homemaker Arlene McCulloch and William Elvis Daniel, a funeral director, later elected county coroner and White County circuit clerk. At Searcy High School, she played drums in the marching band and tympani during concert season, wrote a school column in the Searcy newspaper the *Daily Citizen*, and attended Girls State. She played the accordion at community events, and was in several organizations, including Girl's Ensemble, Latin Club, Thespians, and Lionettes.

After graduating from high school in 1954, Owens Ingram earned an associate's degree in business at Arkansas State Teachers College. In 1957, she married men's clothing store owner Wayne Owens of Warren, and they settled in

Warren, raised three children, and she operated a ladies clothing shop. Owens Ingram studied real estate and became a realtor, opening her own company, Warren Realty. She served on the Warren Housing Authority Board and eight years on the Warren City Council, becoming its first female member. She was a member of the Rotary Club, Woman's Club, Southeast Arkansas Board of Realtors, Southeast Arkansas Industrial Development Group, Arkansas Realtors Association, and the National Association of Realtors. Wayne Owens passed away in 1990, and she later married Marlin Perry Ingram.

House Speaker John Lipton resigned from the legislature in 1992, and Owens Ingram was nominated to fill the Democratic nomination over two other candidates for the House seat at the district Democratic convention and won without opposition in the general election. In 1994, she won reelection over former county judge Joe Fowler in the Democratic primary and was unopposed in the general election. In 1996, she was unopposed for reelection.

Although it failed to pass, Owens Ingram sponsored legislation to secure capitol doors with security detectors. In 1995, she passed legislation requiring background checks for new teaching applicants. After that session, the *Arkansas Democrat-Gazette* published articles about educators with criminal backgrounds and loopholes in the 1995 law, which helped Owens Ingram pass stronger criminal background legislation in 1997. She also sponsored legislation increasing UAMS freshman enrollment positions and legislation allowing school districts to shift annual elections to the general election in even-numbered years.

After legislative service, Owens Ingram was a realtor in Oklahoma and North Carolina before returning to Hot Springs.

# Evelyn Ammons

HOUSE: 1995–2000
FROM: Waldron, Scott County
PARTY: Democratic
BIRTHPLACE: Ross Creek Community, Arkansas
DATES: October 2, 1937–January 28, 2017
EDUCATION: Waldron grade school; Waldron High School, 1956
OCCUPATION: circuit clerk

*Photo courtesy of Arkansas Secretary of State.*

Evelyn Ammons was working as a secretary in the Scott County office of the University of Arkansas Cooperative Extension Service when she ran for Scott County and Circuit clerk in 1978, winning the Democratic primary with 73 percent of the vote and being unopposed in the general election. She was unopposed in seven subsequent elections, serving sixteen years from 1979 to 1994.

While serving as clerk, Ammons was encouraged to run for an open legislative seat, and she filed for House District 16 in 1994. In the preferential primary, she led in a three-way contest with 49 percent, secured the Democratic nomination in a runoff with 57 percent, and was elected with 58 percent in the general election. The first time she had ever been to the Arkansas capitol was the day she was sworn into office. During her first term, Representative Ammons passed a bill changing the composition of the County and Circuit Clerks' Continuing Education Board and cosponsored legislation to require county governments to bid all purchases above ten thousand dollars.

In 1996, Ammons won reelection with 58 percent in the general election. House Speaker Bobby Hogue appointed Ammons as Assistant Speaker Pro-Tem of the House of Representatives in 1997. She served as chair of the Small Business subcommittee of the Agriculture and Economic Development Committee and was a member of the Public Transportation and Legislative Audit committees. She also was a member of the Arkansas Tuition Trust Authority and the Natural Heritage Commission. Ammons passed legislation to exempt first-time home buyers from the real estate transfer tax.

Ammons won the 1998 Democratic primary with 69 percent against the mayor of Waldron and was unopposed in the general election. During the 1999 session, she served on the committees on Public Health, Welfare, and Labor; Insurance and Commerce; and House Management. She was also elected to the Legislative Council. Ammons secured funds for Sodie Davidson Park in Waldron, attempted to protect streams from gravel-mining operations, and sought several Arkansas attorney general opinions on behalf of the Arkansas Game and Fish Commission.

Representative Ammons retired from the House due to term limits in 2000, feeling that she had listened to her constituents, tried to vote as they would desire, and provided constituent service to solve their problems with state government.

# Lisa Ferrell

HOUSE: 1995–2000
FROM: Little Rock, Pulaski County
PARTY: Democratic
BIRTHPLACE: Conway, Arkansas
DATES: July 16, 1963–
EDUCATION: Immaculate Conception
Catholic School; Mt. Saint Mary Academy,
1981; Smith College, BA in economics, 1985;
Harvard Law School, JD, 1990
OCCUPATION: attorney

*Photo courtesy of Arkansas Secretary of State.*

Lisa Ferrell is the daughter of Olive Burnham-Packham, a homemaker, and William Alfred Ferrell, a Sun Oil Company employee. In high school, she was on the debate team, participated in Model United Nations, was a National Merit Scholar, and worked at the Laman Library in North Little Rock.

At Smith College, Ferrell was elected class president, was active in student government, and was a Truman Scholar. She studied at the Institute de Politique Science in Paris and received a Rotary scholarship to study at the Université de Genève. After graduation, she interned with Senator Dale Bumpers and worked on the staff of Congressman Bill Alexander. She then attended Harvard Law School, where she was on the Law School Council and was named a Kaufmann Fellow.

Returning to Arkansas in 1990, Ferrell was a Pulaski County deputy prosecuting attorney before becoming an associate at the Rose Law Firm. She was secretary-treasurer of the Pulaski County Bar Association and a member of the Arkansas Association of Women Lawyers. In the community, she was on the boards of Big Brothers/Big Sisters of Pulaski County and the Rape Crisis Center.

Ferrell became involved with the Arkansas Women's Political Caucus, was an Arkansas Traveler for Bill Clinton in 1992, and received the Fulbright Award for the "Most Promising New Arkansas Young Democrat." Governor Jim Guy Tucker appointed her to the Crime Victims Reparations Board and to the Child Abuse, Rape, and Domestic Violence Commission.

In 1994, Ferrell ran for the Arkansas House of Representatives, winning the Democratic primary with 66 percent and the general election with 73 percent. She was reelected in 1996 with 73 percent in the general election and was unopposed in 1998. Representative Ferrell was vice chair of the Judiciary Committee and co-chair of the Women's Legislative Caucus. Her major legislation included establishing victim rights, strengthening workforce investment, and additional funding for Meals on Wheels, but she most enjoyed constituent service.

After her legislative service, Ferrell was president of the Board of Central Arkansas Library System, president of the Arkansas Committee on Foreign Relations, and hosted the AETN program, *Bringing It Home: US Foreign Policy in Arkansas*. Governor Beebe appointed her to the Arkansas Economic Development Commission, and she served on the Federal Reserve Bank of St. Louis Real Estate Industry Council. Ferrell continued to practice law and managed a "new urbanism" real estate company that developed Rockwater Village and Marina in North Little Rock. She and her husband, Jim Jackson, have three adopted children.

# Peggy Jeffries

SENATE: 1995–1998
FROM: Fort Smith, Sebastian County
PARTY: Republican
BIRTHPLACE: St. James, Missouri
DATES: June 4, 1940–
EDUCATION: Fort Smith High School, 1958; Hendrix College; Kansas State University, BSE in early childhood development, 1967
OCCUPATION: teacher

*Photo courtesy of Arkansas Secretary of State.*

Peggy Jeffries worked for Head Start and taught at Country Aire Kindergarten and Parker Elementary School in Fort Smith. In the community, she was active as PTA president, chair of the Fort Smith Christian Women's Club, and member of the boards of the Community Rescue Mission and Girl Scouts of America. Jeffries was also very active in the First Baptist Church of Fort Smith, serving on the executive board of the Arkansas Baptist State Convention, teaching Sunday school classes, and organizing the Salt and Light Committee to encourage political involvement by the congregation.

Soon, Jeffries became chair of the Sebastian County Republican Women, vice chair of the Sebastian County Republican Committee, and secretary of the Arkansas Federation of Republican Women. In 1994, she challenged incumbent Republican state senator Travis Miles, because she thought his fourteen-year voting record was indistinguishable from the "opposition party," and she wanted to give people a choice for a conservative Republican. Jeffries defeated Miles in the Republican primary by 57 percent to 43 percent and was unopposed in the general election.

Jeffries served one four-year term, during which she was the only woman in the Senate. She opposed legislation that would give public school teachers binding arbitration rights and legislation requiring home-schooled and private school students to take high school exit exams. Jeffries sponsored bills, none of which were enacted, that required school boards to adopt procedures for students' parents to review the list of books in the school libraries and curriculum; to require the election of Arkansas State Board of Education members; and to require information and a twenty-four-hour waiting period for women seeking abortions.

Senator Jeffries was a delegate to the 1996 Republican National Convention and served on the Platform Committee. She received recognition in 1995 from the Arkansas Christian Educators Association, the Bulldog Award from the Arkansas Family Council in 1995, the Citation for Meritorious Service from the American Legion in 1997, the Senator Doug Brandon Memorial Good Government Award in 1997 from the Eagle Forum of Arkansas, and the Republican Pioneer award in 1998 from the Sebastian County Republican Committee.

After her four-year term, Jeffries decided not to run for reelection in 1998. In 2001, Governor Mike Huckabee appointed her to the State Board of Education. Jeffries also served as executive director of the Eagle Forum of Arkansas and secretary of the Arkansas Club for Growth.

# Becky Lynn

HOUSE: 1995–2000
FROM: Heber Springs, Cleburne County
PARTY: Democratic
BIRTHPLACE: Little Rock, Arkansas
DATES: January 18, 1957–
EDUCATION: Pike View Elementary; Indian
Hills Elementary; Lakewood Junior High
School; Northeast High School, 1975; University of Arkansas; University of Arkansas
at Little Rock, BA in criminal justice and
minor in political science, 1979, and JD, 1982
OCCUPATION: attorney

*Photo courtesy of Arkansas Secretary of State.*

Becky Lynn (born Becky Linz) is the daughter of Peggie Jean Williams, a secretary, and Charles Richard Linz, a pilot and brigadier general with the Arkansas Air National Guard. When Lynn was six, her family moved from Little Rock to North Little Rock. In high school, she was involved in debate, drama, and the speech department, playing Anita in *West Side Story*. She received a drama scholarship to the University of Arkansas as a communication major before transferring to UALR for a degree in criminal justice.

When in college in 1976, Lynn married Jerry Stark, a meat cutter, and they were married four years. As an undergraduate, she worked in the Victim Witness Assistance Unit for the Pulaski County public defender. In law school, she was a legislative assistant to State Representative Bill Sherman and a research assistant for the Arkansas Constitutional Convention of 1979–1980. She married Terry Lynn in 1981, and they opened a Heber Springs law office together in 1982.

Becky Lynn was a member of the Cleburne County Bar Association, Arkansas Women's Political Caucus, and vice president of the Cleburne County Community School Board. She was elected to the Heber Springs City Council and served for eight years (1987–1994). When an Arkansas House seat opened in 1994, Lynn ran and won a two-woman general election race for the seat. She was unopposed in 1996 and beat her Democratic primary opponent in 1998 with 68 percent of the vote to win reelection.

Representative Lynn focused on domestic violence, family law, child support, and orders of protection. She was honored by the Coalition Against

Domestic Violence for her work. Lynn sponsored the bill setting up the registry through ACIC for orders of protection. She also passed legislation allowing sales tax to fund a two-year school, leading to the establishment of Arkansas State University in Heber Springs. Lynn's legislation also included land-owner protection from condemnation for easements, punishment for desecration of a burial ground, rape and sexual abuse protection for institutionalized individuals, and penalization of harassment or threats via computers. She was appointed as Constitutional Convention delegate in 1995.

After legislative service, Lynn continued her law practice in Heber Springs and was a lobbyist for the Arkansas Trial Lawyers Association. She was also appointed to the Arkansas State University Advisory Council.

# Sue Madison

HOUSE: 1995–2000, SENATE: 2003–2012
FROM: Fayetteville, Washington County
PARTY: Democratic
BIRTHPLACE: Okinawa, Japan
DATES: February 10, 1948–
EDUCATION: Lakes High School, 1966; University of Edinburg; Louisiana State University, BS and MS in botany, 1970 and 1977
OCCUPATION: real estate investor and property manager

*Photo courtesy of Arkansas Secretary of State.*

Sue Madison (born Lyda Sue Wood) is the daughter of Lyda Camille Yates, a homemaker, and Lt. Colonel Roy Lee Wood, a career Army officer. The family moved often, but her parents and their families were from Washington Parish in Louisiana. Madison was involved in Young Republicans in high school, campaigned for Barry Goldwater when she was sixteen, and for Robert Kennedy when she was in college.

After high school, Madison attended the University of Edinburg, due to her father's nearby military assignment. When her father retired to Louisiana in 1967, she transferred to Louisiana State University. After receiving her bachelor's degree in botany, she taught freshman labs and earned her master's degree. She married Dr. Bernard Madison, and they moved to Fayetteville with their two children in 1979, when her husband joined the University of Arkansas faculty. Madison became active in the Fayetteville Garden Club, joined the League of Women Voters, worked on several political campaigns, and was active in the Democratic Party. She held office in the local National Conference for Community and Justice and American Association of University Women. Madison also had career in real estate investments and property management.

Madison served on the Fayetteville Planning Commission (1984–1988) and was elected to two terms on the Washington County Quorum Court (1991–1994). She was elected to three terms in the Arkansas House of Representatives and three terms in the state senate.

During her sixteen years in the House and Senate, Madison chaired the House Aging, Children and Youth Committee and the Senate City, County, and Local Affairs and the State Agencies and Governmental Affairs Committees. She sponsored legislation on a variety of issues, including foster children getting drivers' licenses, children and family services, labor, taxes, animal cruelty, property, education, abolishing the office of constable, elections, environmental, juvenile justice, foreign exchange student placement, college textbook costs, and Arkansas history in public schools.

Senator Madison sponsored the Equal Rights Amendment ratifying resolution three times and was the only Arkansas legislator to get the ERA Resolution out of committee and to a floor vote (2005). She was a member of the Arkansas Code Revision Commission and passed bills improving the state's code with important technical revisions. She was chair of Girl's State in both the House and Senate.

Madison helped acquire land for expansion of the national cemetery in Fayetteville, was instrumental in obtaining funding for the veterans' home in Fayetteville, and delivered appropriations to the University of Arkansas for the Center for Advanced Spatial Technologies, the Pryor Center for Arkansas Oral and Visual History, Mullins Library Special Collections, the debate team, and numerous other projects. She successfully fought against UA Chancellor John White's plans to lay off thirty-two physical plant employees and to close the UA Press.

After her legislative service, Madison was appointed to the City of Fayetteville Keep Fayetteville Beautiful Committee and continued working in property management. She was also elected to four terms on the Washington County Quorum Court, serving from 2013 to 2020.

# Bobbie L. Hendrix

HOUSE: 1996
FROM: Antoine, Pike County
PARTY: Democratic
BIRTHPLACE: Mena, Arkansas
DATES: February 28, 1933–March 01, 2012
EDUCATION: Mena public schools; Mena
High School, 1950; Henderson State
University, BS and MS in social work, 1981
and 1988
OCCUPATION: farmer and secretary

*Photo courtesy of Carol Hendrix*

Bobbie L. Hendrix (born Bobbie Lou Lamb) was the daughter of Ida McBee Campbell and George Bernard "Buddy" Lamb. Her parents divorced when she was young, and she grew up in Mena in the home of her grandfather, Dr. Cyrus Campbell, a physician. After high school, she enlisted in the United States Air Force and was honorably discharged in 1954.

She married Gerald C. Hendrix, a banker and rancher, of Antoine in 1952. Together, they were partners in Hendrix Farms, were involved with the Bank of Delight, and raised three sons. She also held secretarial positions with a law firm in Murfreesboro and the Bank of Prescott. Her father-in-law, Olen Hendrix, was a state senator from 1959 to 1982. Her husband served on the Arkansas Soil and Water Conservation Commission for twenty-six years, and she was president of the Arkansas Association of Conservation Districts Auxiliary, receiving its Distinguished Service Award in 1988.

Bobbie Hendrix was interested in local history, serving on the boards of the Pike County Archives and History Society and the South Arkansas Regional Archives at Historic Washington. She researched the history of the Crater of Diamonds and self-published *Crater of Diamonds: Jewel of Arkansas* (1989) on the history of the diamond mine. Hendrix also served on several boards of charitable causes in the southwest Arkansas area, and she was an unsuccessful candidate for the Democratic nomination for justice of the peace in 1988.

After Gerald Hendrix was elected to the Arkansas House of Representatives in 1994, Bobbie Hendrix worked on the House staff during the 1995 legislative session. When her husband died in office in 1996, she was elected without opposition to finish his term of office in a special election on July 30.

Representative Hendrix was sworn in on August 15, 1996, and served five months. She was again a House staff employee during the 1997 legislative session.

Hendrix retired to Mine Creek Village retirement community in Nashville, Arkansas. She continued to be involved in civic and service organizations in the Nashville area and the Antoine Church of Christ until her death.

## Pat Bond

HOUSE: 1997–2002
FROM: Jacksonville, Pulaski County
PARTY: Democratic
BIRTHPLACE: Gladewater, Texas
DATES: August 6, 1938–
EDUCATION: Lewisville public schools; Lewisville High School, 1956; Southern Methodist University; University of Arkansas, BSE, 1960
OCCUPATION: small-business owner

*Photo courtesy of Arkansas Secretary of State.*

Pat Bond (born Patricia Lee Parker) traces her interest in politics and government to growing up "always listening to the news, seeing people read newspapers, reading newspapers, staying up half the night seeing the votes come in. . . . I remember specifically Governor Francis Cherry, when he was running for reelection, standing on our lawn, which was right across the street from the Lafayette County Courthouse, singing "'It's Cherry Pickin' Time in Arkansas.'"

Pat and Tommy Bond settled in Jacksonville in 1966, where they owned a map production company, a construction business, and Bond Consulting Engineers, of which Bond was vice president. Pat Bond focused on raising their three children and was very active in community service, teaching music in kindergarten, working as a substitute teacher, serving as president of the Junior Auxiliary, president of the PTA, president of the hospital auxiliary, and working on committees in the Methodist Church. She chaired the Jacksonville Parks and Recreation Commission, headed the effort to build the Jacksonville community center, and was co-chair of Jacksonville People with Pride Clean-up Coalition.

In 1996, Bond ran for the District 64 seat in the Arkansas House of Representatives. Emphasizing public education and economic development, she won with 83 percent in the Democratic primary and 57 percent in the general election. She was reelected in 1998 with 63 percent in the general election and was unopposed in 2000.

Reflecting on her time in the House, Bond was most proud of legislation for art and music courses in elementary schools, authorizing a school district for Jacksonville, nursing education, tobacco settlement funding, and her work as vice chair of the City, County, and Local Affairs Committee. Bond was honored as a Grand Champion for Children for her legislative record.

Bond ran for the state senate in 2002 but lost to former House Speaker John Paul Capps in the Democratic primary. After her legislative service, Bond continued her community service, including serving as chair of the Jacksonville Chamber of Commerce Board, chair of the Jacksonville Education Foundation, raising funds for Project Wisdom, and serving on the hospital board and the long-range planning committee of her church. Her son, Will Bond, was chair of the Arkansas Democratic Party and served in both the Arkansas House of Representatives and the Arkansas Senate.

# Rita Hale

HOUSE: 1997–1999
FROM: Hot Springs, Garland County
PARTY: Democratic
BIRTHPLACE: Pine Bluff, Arkansas
DATES: September 28, 1943–September 19, 1999
EDUCATION: Pine Bluff High School, 1961; University of Arkansas, BA in English, 1965; University of Arkansas at Little Rock, JD, 1986
OCCUPATION: social worker and attorney

*Photo courtesy of Arkansas Secretary of State.*

Rita Hale (born Rita Norton Rowell) is the daughter of Martha Cummings Norton, a homemaker, and Alexander Hendrix Rowell Jr., an attorney and state senator. At Pine Bluff High School, Hale was the first young woman to be elected student council president, a member of the National Honor Society, and voted Most Likely to Succeed.

While attending the University of Arkansas, Hale married Bennett Clubbs, and they had two daughters. She briefly taught at Rogers High School before living in Puerto Rico and the Philippines while her husband was in the US Navy.

Returning home, Hale was president of the Pine Bluff School Board and served on the Arkansas Advocates for Children and Families board and the Committee Against Spouse Abuse. Governor Bill Clinton appointed her to the Governor's Rape Task Force, and she was vice chair of the Pine Bluff Crime Commission.

Hale was director of Suspected Child Abuse and Neglect (SCAN) in Jefferson County from 1974 to 1976, then the SCAN state coordinator from 1976–1978. She was victim services coordinator for the Jefferson County prosecuting attorney from 1979 until 1986, then was a deputy prosecutor. She married Arkansas state police Lt. James W. Hale and moved to Hot Springs, where she was chief deputy prosecuting attorney in Garland County until 1995.

After beginning a private law practice, Hale was active in Leadership Hot Springs, served on the board of the Ouachita Children's Center, and was on the vestry board of St. Luke's Episcopal Church. In 1996, Hale ran for an open seat in the Arkansas House of Representatives, winning the Democratic primary with 67 percent and the general election with 62 percent of the vote. She was unopposed for reelection in 1998.

Representative Hale was vice chair of the House Judiciary Committee and vice chair of the Women's Legislative Caucus. She considered her most important legislation to be the Arkansas Prenatal and Early Childhood Nurse Home Visitation Program, a program sending nurses into the homes of some first-time mothers to discuss health and parenting issues, home safety, and decision-making skills.

Her legislative career was cut short by a fatal stroke at the age of fifty-five. The *Arkansas Democrat-Gazette* commented, "She was a wonderful mixture of grace and grit, always the lady and always the fighter, personal and personable, formal and warm. In the legislature and out, she showed all of us how it's done."

# Dianne Hudson

HOUSE: 1997–1998
FROM: Sherwood, Pulaski County
PARTY: Democratic
BIRTHPLACE: Little Rock, Arkansas
DATES: November 6, 1939–
EDUCATION: St. Patrick's Catholic School, 1953; Mount St. Mary Academy, 1957; University of Arkansas at Little Rock
OCCUPATION: homemaker, store owner

*Photo courtesy of Arkansas Secretary of State.*

Dianne Hudson was interested in politics from an early age and followed the news about state and local issues and campaigns. Both she and her husband, Freddie D. Hudson, were members of the Pulaski County Democratic Central Committee and delegates to the Arkansas Democratic Convention in 1976.

While raising three daughters and working as the bookkeeper for the family's Sherwood Grocery, Hudson was also involved in school and community affairs. She was president of the North Little Rock Jaycettes, active in the Immaculate Conception Catholic School PTA and Booster Club, and a member of the Sherwood Chamber of Commerce.

Hudson was elected to the Pulaski County Quorum Court in 1978, where she served nine terms. On the Courts and Emergency Service Committee she was particularly interested in oversight of the Sheriff's Office under Tommy Robinson and Carroll Gravett. She then chaired the Finance and Administration Committee for twelve years.

In 1996, Hudson ran for an open seat in House District 63, campaigning for middle-class tax reform, economic development, increased education funding, crime prevention, highway improvements, and grants for rural fire departments. Unopposed in the primary, Hudson was elected to the House of Representatives with 57 percent in the general election vote.

During the 1997 session, Representative Hudson passed legislation to assist counties, to reduce the cost of prisoner telephone services, and to expedite motor vehicle registration. She cosponsored legislation for income tax reform, the ARKids First health-care coverage, the Health Care Consumer Act, and the Enhancement of Crime Victims Rights. After the session, she was recognized by the Arkansas Municipal League for legislation supporting local government and was named Woman of the Year by the Sherwood Chamber of Commerce.

Hudson was a candidate for reelection in 1998, stressing her experience and accomplishments. She was unopposed in the primary but lost in the general election by thirty-six votes after a recount.

Reflecting on her legislative service, Hudson said, "I tried to listen to concerns of constituents, study the issues, and make informed decisions about the policies and programs that affect their lives. Remembering that you are there to enrich their life, not yours."

Hudson considered running again for the House of Representatives in 2000, but she did not. She and her husband retired, traveled, and enjoyed time with their daughters and grandchildren.

# Sandra Rodgers

HOUSE: 1997–2002
FROM: Hope, Hempstead County
PARTY: Democratic
BIRTHPLACE: El Dorado, Texas
DATES: April 9, 1960–
EDUCATION: Laneburg grade school; Laneburg High School, 1978; Henderson State University
OCCUPATION: legal secretary, fiscal officer

*Photo courtesy of Arkansas Secretary of State.*

Sandra Rodgers (born Sandra Dinell Reyenga) is the daughter of Elsie Fay Duncan and James Martin Reyenga, who held various jobs and moved from Texas to Arkansas when Rodgers was three years old. She was raised on her grandparents' farm in Nevada County and attended a small high school where she was a cheerleader and was on the basketball team. She married after high school, had a son, and divorced a year later. Rodgers worked at night at the Nevada County Sheriff's Office in Prescott as a jailor-dispatcher while attending Henderson State University, and she later worked for an ambulance service.

In 1984, she married Danny Paul Rodgers, an attorney. She became his legal secretary and then fiscal officer when he was in private practice, a deputy prosecutor, and a public defender. Rodgers also enrolled at Henderson State University and studied psychology, focusing on child abuse, until their family moved to Hope. When a House seat opened in 1996, Rodgers became the only woman among five candidates. She received 32 percent against three opponents in the Democratic primary, won the runoff, and was elected with 71 percent of the vote in the general election. Rodgers was unopposed for reelection in 1998, and in 2000, she won the Democratic primary with 71 percent and was unopposed in the general election. She described herself as a pro-life Democrat who hunts, fishes, is pro-gun, and is like a Dixiecrat.

Representative Rodgers chaired the Aging, Children, and Youth Committee and was a member of the Judiciary, Education, and Public Health, Welfare, and Labor Committees. She passed legislation addressing the administration of justice, emergency medical services, long-term care facilities, lowering the DWI threshold, and denying drivers licenses to undocumented residents. Rodgers was also instrumental in securing funding for the Clinton Birthplace Home at Hope in her district. She was disappointed that she was unable to secure legislation allowing adopted individuals to obtain an original birth certificate at age twenty-one. Related to her personal and legislative interests, Rodgers was appointed to the Arkansas Trauma Advisory Council.

After leaving the legislature due to term limits, Sandra Rodgers was appointed to a term on the state Board of Election Commissioners. In 2008, she was elected Hempstead County clerk, serving from 2009 to 2016.

# Martha Shoffner

HOUSE: 1997–2002
FROM: Newport, Jackson County
PARTY: Democratic
BIRTHPLACE: Weldon, Arkansas
DATES: July 10, 1944–
EDUCATION: Weldon School; Gibbs
Albright Elementary; Newport High
School, 1962; Memphis State University,
1962–1964; Arkansas State College, 1964–
1965; Northwestern University Kellogg
School of Management, public finance
institute, 2007
OCCUPATION: advertising, assistant to the
state auditor, realtor

*Photo courtesy of Arkansas Secretary of State.*

Martha Shoffner was born to Helen V. Deaton, a teacher, and James Edwin Shoffner, a cotton and soybean farmer, on the family farm near Shoffner, a community settled by her great-grandparents. Her aunt, Irma Shoffner, was Jackson County circuit clerk for twenty-four years. Shoffner often handed out campaign cards for political candidates. At Newport High School, Shoffner won the drama award. She attended Memphis State, where she joined Gamma Phi Beta sorority, and she was chosen Miss Newport in 1963. Transferring to Arkansas State, she traveled and studied in Paris on a study abroad program.

Leaving college in 1965, Shoffner held a summer internship with Governor Orval Faubus, then worked for twelve years at Cranford-Johnson, an advertising firm that handled political campaigns. She worked in marketing for Storer Cable and operated Miss Martha's Tamales, before becoming administrative assistant to State Auditor Julia Hughes Jones for two years.

Shoffner returned to Newport in 1993 and was a realtor with Sink Realty. She held memberships in the Business and Professional Women's Club, Daughters of the American Revolution, Jackson County Humane Society, and Newport Chamber of Commerce and was named Jackson County Woman of the Year. In 1994, Shoffner was a Democratic candidate for the Arkansas House, leading the three-way primary but losing the runoff to longtime Jackson County sheriff Donald Ray. She ran again in 1996, unseating

Ray by five votes in the primary. Shoffner was unopposed for reelection in 1998 and 2000.

Representative Shoffner chaired the State Agencies and Governmental Affairs Committee and was a member of the Joint Budget Committee. Her legislation included issues of municipal and county government, prohibiting minors from purchasing and using tobacco, and preventing domestic abuse. She also served on the Arkansas Alternative Dispute Resolution Commission.

After being term-limited, Shoffner ran for state auditor in 2002 but lost in the Democratic primary. In 2006, she ran for state treasurer, winning the Democratic primary runoff and prevailing in the general election over the Republican and Green Party candidates with 54 percent. Shoffner endorsed and spoke for ratification of the Equal Rights Amendment during the 2007 legislative session, and she was reelected in 2010 with 68 percent in the general election. As treasurer, Shoffner served on the boards for public employee and state teacher retirement systems, and she showcased Arkansas artists with exhibitions in the treasurer's office.

Shoffner received the 2008 Sandra Wilson Cherry Award from Gaines House, the 2009 Business and Professional Women's Friends of B&PW Award, and the 2010 Arkansas Democratic Party's Politician of the Year Award. Shoffner resigned from office in May 2013, after being charged with bribery and extortion related to state bond business.

# Wilma Walker

HOUSE: 1997–2002
FROM: Little Rock, Pulaski County
PARTY: Democratic
BIRTHPLACE: College Station, Arkansas
DATES: March 3, 1938–
EDUCATION: College Station Elementary and Junior High Schools; J. C. Cook High School; GED, 1966; Shorter College, AA, 1970; Philander Smith College, BA in social work and psychology, 1972
OCCUPATION: special school district parent coordinator, business owner

*Photo courtesy of Arkansas Secretary of State.*

Wilma Walker (born Wilma Jean Craig) was born at College Station to Erma Lee Rembert and Lawrence Craig, a lumber mill worker. Walker dropped out of high school at sixteen to marry Amos Greer in 1954. She worked several laundry and housecleaning jobs while raising seven children, and in 1966 earned her GED. Walker was on the dean's list at Shorter College and earned a degree in social work and psychology at Philander Smith.

In 1971, Walker began a thirty-year career as a Title I Parent Coordinator in the Pulaski County School District. While in that job, she also owned a special-events business and a clothing store. In 1976, she married Melvin Walker. She became president of the College Station Progressive League in 1985, and she received the Time to Care Award in 1991 for her volunteer community activities.

Walker ran for the Pulaski County Quorum Court in 1994, leading in the Democratic primary but losing in the run-off. In 1996, she ran for the Arkansas House of Representatives in a six-candidate race, leading in the Democratic primary and winning the runoff with 53 percent. She was unopposed in the general election. She was reelected with 98 percent against a write-in candidate in the 1998 general election, reelected in the 2000 Democratic primary with 62 percent, and was term-limited in 2002.

Representative Walker proposed legislation for a sales tax to renovate school buildings, which did not pass. She successfully acquired state funds for the College Station Civic Center, established the Classified School Employee Minimum Salary Act, and created Senator Hattie W. Caraway Day in Arkansas. Walker cosponsored legislation establishing the Daisy Gatson Bates Holiday and persuaded Governor Mike Huckabee to create by executive order an organizing committee, on which she served two terms.

Walker was honored for her service by the National Council of Negro Women. She was named a Grand Champion for Children by a nonprofit coalition, and the Arkansas Democratic Black Caucus recognized her as an "African American Woman on the Move."

After retiring from Pulaski County School District, Walker opened Wilma's restaurants in Little Rock and Fayetteville. In 2002, she ran unsuccessfully for the state senate. Walker was elected Pulaski County justice of the peace in 2012 and announced as a candidate for Pulaski County judge in 2014 but did not file.

# Sarah Agee

HOUSE: 1999–2004
FROM: Prairie Grove, Washington County
PARTY: Republican
BIRTHPLACE: Fayetteville, Arkansas
DATES: January 2, 1946–
EDUCATION: Fayetteville public schools;
Fayetteville High School, 1964; University
of Arkansas
OCCUPATION: cattle producer, residential
developer

*Photo courtesy of Arkansas Secretary of State.*

Sarah Agee (born Sarah Edith Sonneman) was born into a prominent Fayetteville family that built and operated several landmark businesses in Washington County. Her parents were Gladys Margaret Gosnell and Emil Herman Sonneman, and she was active in the family businesses at a young age. Agee was an honors student in high school and was a member of Quill and Scroll, sang with the Choralettes, and was a maid on the Colors Day Court. After she married Charles Agee, they moved to Prairie Grove and operated Agee Limousin Cattle Farm. She was active in the PTA and was elected to the Prairie Grove School Board, serving almost twelve years. Agee was also appointed to the City's Police Committee.

In 1998, term limits created an open House seat in Agee's district, and she decided to run as a Republican. Although a Republican had never held the seat, Agee won. She was reelected in 2000, and that December she was a presidential elector for George W. Bush. She was unopposed for reelection in 2002.

Governor Mike Huckabee named Representative Agee his deputy floor leader in the House for the 2001–2002 session, and she was chair of the State Agencies and Governmental Affairs Committee during the 2003–2004 session. Agee worked with the Arkansas State Police to enact a number of bills to update traffic laws. She passed legislation that included election law, cosmetology, private career schools, the library of the secretary of state, and restitution for theft of services involving public utilities and enhanced penalties if the theft resulted in environmental contamination. Representative Agee said her philosophy of representation was "that you listen to your constituents," then you inform them and vote the way the majority wishes.

In 2004, Agee lost her Senate challenge to Senator Sue Madison. She returned to Little Rock in 2005 as one of Republican governor Mike Huckabee's legislative liaisons, then she joined the governor's staff in 2006 as assistant for City, County, and Local Affairs and policy advisor for agricultural issues.

Reflecting the bipartisan respect for Agee, Democratic secretary of state Charlie Daniels appointed her in 2006 to a committee to review and make recommendations for improving the state's election software system. She joined the staff of Democratic governor Mike Beebe from 2007–2014, serving as a legislative liaison and as the governor's liaison to the Arkansas Science and Technology Authority and the Arkansas Workforce Investment Board.

# Cecile Bledsoe

HOUSE: 1999–2004, SENATE: 2009–2022
FROM: Rogers, Benton County
PARTY: Republican
BIRTHPLACE: Lyons, Georgia
DATES: June 26, 1944–
EDUCATION: Sidney Lanier Elementary School; Glynn Academy, 1962; University of Georgia, BA in journalism, 1969
OCCUPATION: surgical clinic administrator

*Photo courtesy of Arkansas Secretary of State.*

Cecile Bledsoe (born Cecile Herndon) is the daughter of Bess Clarke, a thirty-year public school teacher, and Cecil E. Herndon, a small-business owner, and grew up in Brunswick, Georgia. She was on the student council every year in high school. After receiving her bachelor's degree in journalism, she took education courses and taught summer Head Start and kindergarten. In July of 1970, she became a case worker for UAMS in Little Rock, where she met Dr. James "Jim" H. Bledsoe. They married in 1972 and had three children. The family moved to Rogers, where she worked as the vice president and assistant office manager for her husband's clinic.

In 1986, Cecile Bledsoe was Rogers's campaign coordinator for Asa Hutchinson's US Senate campaign. She was active in Immanuel Baptist Church, the school board, recreational sports fundraising, Miller Place and

Our Farm, Inc. boards, the Pea Ridge National Military Park Foundation, the Kendrick Fincher Memorial Foundation, Northwest Arkansas Agency on Aging, and the Rogers Police Civil Service Commission. She also served on the Benton County Republican Committee, as a member of Benton County Republican Women, and on the Arkansas Club for Growth Board.

Bledsoe won election to the House of Representatives in 1998 and served three terms until term-limited in 2004. In 2008, she ran unopposed for the Arkansas Senate, and was again unopposed in 2012 and 2014, and in 2018 was reelected in the general election with 61.9 percent of the vote. In 2010, she was an unsuccessful candidate for nomination for Congress from the Third District.

Her favorite part of legislative service has been constituent service and policy decisions. She worked on legislation that included making safe retractable needles available to health-care workers, telemedicine, adoption, medical savings accounts, body piercing, medical student loan programs, tort reform, gun owner rights, lower taxes, mandatory motorcycle helmet use, limiting abortions, additional regulations requiring an ultrasound and offering an image viewing before consent to an abortion, mammography reimbursements, establishment of the Heritage Trails System, sex trafficking, restricting medical marijuana advertising and use, and coverage for early refills of prescription eye drops. She was most proud of the telemedicine legislation and said limiting jury awards in tort cases was her most important legislation. She chaired the Senate Public Health, Welfare, and Labor Committee; and was a member of the Health and Human Services Task Force of the American Legislative Exchange Council (ALEC) and the Human Services and Welfare Committee of the National Conference of State Legislatures.

Bledsoe received the Legislative Excellence Award from the Arkansas Bankers Association, the State Chamber of Commerce Business Matters Leadership Award, Statesman Award from the Family Council, Capitol Caregiver Award from the AARP, Legislator of the Year from the Arkansas Medical Society, and Distinguished Legislator from the Arkansas Municipal League.

# Jo Carson

HOUSE: 1999–2002
FROM: Fort Smith, Sebastian County
PARTY: Democratic
BIRTHPLACE: Norman, Oklahoma
DATES: May 30, 1955–
EDUCATION: Fort Smith Southside
High School, 1973; Westark Community
College, 1976; University of Arkansas, BA
in Communication, 1981, and JD, 1984;
graduate coursework in communication at
University of Arkansas and secondary edu-
cation at Northeastern State University
OCCUPATION: attorney

*Photo courtesy of Arkansas Secretary of State.*

Jo Carson (born Jo Ellen Miles) is the daughter of Gloriette Tsoodle, a public school teacher, and Richard Orville Miles, a petroleum landman. She
became interested in politics in college when she and her husband, Doug
Carson, were senators in the Arkansas Student Congress and debate partners
at Westark Community College. Jo Carson was also a champion debater at
the University of Arkansas.

Active in her community, Carson was a founding board member of the Fort
Smith Children's Emergency Shelter and was president of the local chapter
of Zonta International, an organization empowering women and advocating
that women's rights are human rights. She also taught Sunday school at St.
Bartholomew's Episcopal Church and sometimes did substitute teaching at
Fort Smith and Van Buren public schools.

Carson served as an assistant public defender for Sebastian County, specializing in juvenile cases for eight years. She became active in the Democratic
Party, served on the Sebastian County Election Commission, and was elected
delegate to the Democratic National Convention in 1996 and 2000.

In 1998, Carson ran for the open House seat for District 13, which had
been represented by Republican representative Carolyn Pollan since 1975.
Unopposed in the Democratic primary, Carson won the general election with
53 percent. She was reelected in 2000 with 56 percent in the general election.

Representative Carson, a member of the Apache Tribe of Oklahoma, was
the first Native American woman to serve in the Arkansas General Assembly.

She was chair of the House Aging, Children and Youth, and Legislative and Military Affairs Committee and sponsored legislation to revise the state's juvenile code. Carson also enacted legislation to link and upgrade municipal court computer systems around the state and was the lead House sponsor of legislation to transform Westark Community College into a branch of the University of Arkansas.

After her second term, Carson was a candidate for Congress from the Third District in a 2001 special election, narrowing losing in a runoff for the Democratic nomination. She was also unsuccessful in the general election for a 2002 race for the state Senate and a 2004 contest for a House seat.

Afterwards, Carson continued her political involvement as chair of the Sebastian County Democratic Party and chair of Citizens Alliance for a Progressive Arkansas. She was an adjunct professor of Communication at UA-Fort Smith and was an attorney ad litem representing children in dependency-neglect proceedings.

# Joyce Dees

HOUSE: 1999–2004
FROM: Warren, Bradley County
PARTY: Democratic
BIRTHPLACE: Pattsville, Arkansas
DATES: July 30, 1954–
EDUCATION: Hermitage public schools; Hermitage High School, 1971; University of Arkansas at Monticello, business, 1971–1974
OCCUPATION: banker, financial consultant

*Photo courtesy of Arkansas Secretary of State.*

Joyce Dees (born Joyce Ann Johnson) was raised on a farm in rural South Arkansas. Her mother, Ethel Mattie Trussell Johnson, was a teacher, and her father, Hagard Eddis Johnson, worked at Potlatch Lumber Company. Dees was raised in a close family, her mother made many of her clothes, and she learned to sew from her grandmother, who was a professional seamstress. In high school, she was a cheerleader, was in Beta club, library club, and future teachers, and took piano and voice lessons. Soon after graduation, she married John Dees in 1971. After his deployment with the Arkansas Army National

Guard, they pursued their college educations together. After earning a business degree, Joyce Dees began a twenty-five-year career in banking. They had two daughters.

In 1998, Dees ran for an open House seat. She led two opponents with 40 percent in the Democratic primary, defeated a former county judge in the runoff with 58 percent, and beat the Republican and write-in candidates with 68 percent in the general election. She was unopposed for reelection in 2000 and 2002 and was term-limited in 2004.

Representative Dees's first legislative action was adopting of a resolution to designate House members' private work area as nonsmoking. She passed a resolution celebrating March 8 as International Women's Day and in her second and third terms co-chaired the Women's Legislative Caucus. Representative Dees focused on health, elderly, and children's issues. She passed legislation addressing sexual assault, crimes committed in the presence of a child, adult abuse, child maltreatment, the juvenile code, adoption and guardianship, child welfare, and nurse practice. She also passed legislation addressing personal watercraft safety, information disclosure, highway and road obstruction, alternative fuels, the Workforce Investment Board, the Arkansas Heavy Equipment Operator Training Academy, and the "Cure Breast Cancer" license plates to fund cancer research. Dees was chair of the Aging, Children and Youth, Legislative and Military Affairs Committee, and a member of the Public Health, Welfare, and Labor and Joint Budget Committees.

After being term-limited in 2004, Dees ran for the state senate, losing to the incumbent in the Democratic primary. She served on the board of Warren Bank and Trust and worked at the bank for a short period before becoming Governor Mike Huckabee's health policy advisor for the Department of Health and Human Services in 2005.

# Mary Beth Green

HOUSE: 1999–2004
FROM: Van Buren, Crawford County
PARTY: Republican
BIRTHPLACE: Carlisle, Arkansas
DATES: April 16, 1957–
EDUCATION: Brinkley High School, 1975;
University of Arkansas at Little Rock, BS,
1979; University of Central Arkansas, MS,
1988
OCCUPATION: speech pathologist

*Photo courtesy of Arkansas Secretary of State.*

Mary Beth Green (born Mary Beth Caldwell) is the daughter of Nettie Jean Park Caldwell, an optometrist, and Edgar Eugene Caldwell, who worked at the rice mill, farmed, and was a maintenance engineer. She attended Partee Elementary School, Marion Anderson Junior High, and Brinkley High School. In junior high, she was a volunteer for Winthrop Rockefeller's gubernatorial campaign. In high school, she acted in school plays, attended Arkansas Girls State, became a majorette, and was the 1974 homecoming queen.

Green worked for sixteen years as a speech and language pathologist in the public schools in Monroe, Sebastian, Crawford and Franklin counties, then for Regional Rehab Systems Inc. of Fort Smith before establishing a private practice in speech pathology. In addition to professional organizations, she was a member of the GFWC Van Buren Women's League. In 1996, she married former Crawford County circuit clerk Rick Green.

In 1998, Crawford County Republican Party chair Ruth Whitaker recruited Green to run for the Arkansas House. She was unopposed in the primary and defeated Democrat Lyn Brown in the general election, becoming the first woman and first Republican to represent Crawford County's District 11 in the Arkansas House of Representatives. Green was reelected in 2000, with the endorsement of Governor Mike Huckabee in the Republican primary, and she was unopposed in the general election. In 2002, Green ran for reelection in the newly reapportioned House District 66 and was unopposed in both the primary and general elections.

As a legislator, Green focused on education and human services issues, increasing teachers' salaries and authorizing an increase in school district bond debt. She was the lead sponsor for Governor Huckabee's Omnibus

Quality Education Act of 2003, which authorized the state board of education to consolidate fiscally or academically distressed school districts. Green served as co-chair of the Women's Legislative Caucus, and she was named a Grand Champion for Children by a coalition of child advocacy groups.

After being term-limited in 2004, Rick Green was elected to represent District 66, becoming the first husband to win a wife's seat in the House. Mary Beth Green returned to her private practice and was appointed by Governor Huckabee as a member of the Arkansas Educational Television Commission (2005–2010).

# Brenda Gullett

HOUSE: 1999–2000, SENATE: 2001–2004
FROM: Pine Bluff, Jefferson County
PARTY: Democratic
BIRTHPLACE: Houston, Texas
DATES: July 9, 1948–
EDUCATION: Garfield Elementary; Irving High School and Aldine High School (Houston), 1966; Baylor University; South Texas Junior College; University of Houston, BA, 1970; Centenary College, graduate work in adolescent psychology
OCCUPATION: human resources trainer

*Photo courtesy of Arkansas Secretary of State.*

Brenda Gullett (born Brenda Gale Judice) grew up primarily in Houston, Texas, where her mother, Estelle Dugas, was an administration assistant at a bank and her stepfather, David Bowen, was an accountant at Texaco. She worked numerous jobs during college to earn a degree in communication and English, with a minor in Spanish and a teaching certificate. While in Shreveport, where she was a church youth minister and later directed a drug abuse prevention program in the public schools, she met Dr. Robert Gullett Jr. They married in 1974 and moved to Pine Bluff in 1976.

While raising two sons, Gullett taught parent effectiveness training classes, created a drug program for the Pine Bluff schools, was president of Learning Disabilities of Arkansas, and was appointed to the Arkansas Commission on

People with Disabilities. She was active in Rotary, Chamber of Commerce, Junior League, Leadership Pine Bluff, and Woman's Foundation of Arkansas. In 1981, she started Brenda Gullett Associates, a human resources training organization.

In her first race for public office in 1989, Gullett lost an election for the Pine Bluff School Board, but she was elected to the Jefferson County Quorum Court in 1992 and served three terms (1993–1998). In 1998, Gullett ran for an open seat in the Arkansas House of Representatives, defeating Pine Bluff alderman Dale Dixon in the Democratic primary and being unopposed in the general election.

Representative Gullett served one term in the House, then ran for the Arkansas Senate in 2000, winning a runoff in the Democratic primary. She sponsored Arkansas's largest tobacco tax, was co-chair of the Women's Legislative Caucus, and in 2004, she was vice chair of the Education Committee during the special session on education that addressed the *Lakeview* court decision. Senator Gullett was unopposed in her 2002 reelection campaign but was defeated in the 2004 Democratic primary, as a result of her support for school consolidation.

Gullett was proud of her work on Meningitis vaccine availability, protection of women from insurance and employment discrimination, the Nursing Shortage Commission, increased truck speeding fines, earmarking Arkansas's Tobacco Settlement funds for health-related purposes, and school consolidation. Arkansas Advocates for Children and Families honored Gullett in 2001 for her strong child-focused votes. In 2004, the Arkansas State Board of Nursing made her an honorary registered nurse.

In her last political race, Gullett ran unsuccessfully for mayor of Pine Bluff in 2004. She was appointed trustee for the Arkansas School for the Deaf and Blind (2004–2007) and to the Arkansas State Board of Education (2007–2014).

After her family moved to Fayetteville in 2006, Gullett co-chaired the UA College of Education and Health Related Professions development council and was a member of the UA Eleanor Mann School of Nursing advisory council. In 2014, *AY Magazine* honored her as Woman of the Year in Education. In 2015, Gullett received the National Association of State Boards of Education National Public Service Award. She also served on the Fayetteville Public Education Foundation and Magdalene Serenity House boards.

# Jan Judy

HOUSE: 1999–2004
FROM: Fayetteville, Washington County
PARTY: Democratic
BIRTHPLACE: Fayetteville, Arkansas
DATES: December 11, 1946–
EDUCATION: Elkins public schools; Elkins
High School, 1965; College of the Ozarks;
University of Arkansas, BSW, 1981
OCCUPATION: social worker, restaurant
owner

*Photo courtesy of Arkansas Secretary of State.*

Jan Judy (born Janice Ann Watts) grew up on a farm in Durham, where her parents, Daisy Nell Woods and William Wallace Watts, lived on land that their Cherokee ancestors settled in 1838. As president of the White River 4-H Club, she won the county biscuit-making contest when she was fourteen. In high school, she a member of Future Homemakers and won the home economics award.

Judy attended the College of the Ozarks in Clarksville and worked twenty-hours a week as secretary for the art director. She married Phillip Allen and left college to raise their three children while working in daycare and at the Daisy Air Rifle plant. She finished her college degree at the University of Arkansas in 1981, was a social worker at Abilities Unlimited and Head Start, and was a founding board member of the Single Parent Scholarship Fund.

After a divorce, she married Darrell Judy, a Fayetteville firefighter. They owned and operated the Pizza Junction in Elkins. In 1992, she joined the White River EPA to oppose a landfill on Hobbs Mountain near Durham, becoming the group's vice president and spokesperson. The landfill permit was finally denied in 1996. That same year, *Northwest Arkansas Times* named her Newsmaker of the Year.

Judy served on the Fayetteville Parks and Recreation Board, worked on Charlie Cole Chaffin's campaign for lieutenant governor, and was a member of the Washington County Democratic Central Committee. In 1998, she ran for the Arkansas House of Representatives, led in the Democratic primary, won the runoff with 58 percent, and was unopposed in the general election. Judy ran for reelection in 2000 and won with 68 percent against a Republican opponent. She was unopposed for a third term.

Representative Judy is proud of acquiring funding for restoration of the University of Arkansas's Carnall Hall and funding for the Veterans Home in Fayetteville. She sponsored legislation related to children of incarcerated parents, domestic violence, agriculture, reciprocity protection orders, grandparent rights, breast cancer research, environmental and energy issues, and the state's first methamphetamine law.

Judy was president of the National Foundation of Women Legislators and was active in Women in Government and the Council of State Governments. She ran unsuccessfully for the Third District US House of Representatives seat in 2004. Judy moved back to her family farm in Durham and remained active in Senior Democrats of Northwest Arkansas.

# Barbara King

HOUSE: 1999–2004
FROM: Helena, Phillips County
PARTY: Democratic
BIRTHPLACE: Houston, Texas
DATES: June 3, 1946–
EDUCATION: Port Arthur and Groves public schools; Port Neches-Groves High School, 1964; University of Houston; Lamar University; Phillips County Community College, associate of applied science in graphic communications, 1993
OCCUPATION: Air Force, homemaker, election commissioner

*Photo courtesy of Arkansas Secretary of State.*

Barbara King (born Barbara Jean Bottoms) is the daughter of Marie Carmen Maenza, a beautician, and Durwood Ferris Bottoms, a grocer and refinery employee. In high school, King received the American Legion Citizenship Award, was named Miss School Spirit, and was a member of the National Honor Society, Indianettes drill team, Future Teachers, and Tri-Hi-Y.

After two years of college, King enlisted in the United States Air Force and was stationed at Eglin Air Force Base, working in accounting and finance. While there, she was a troop leader of Girl Scout Cadette Troop 122, played in the Women's Slow Pitch Softball League, and was on the Elginettes team that won the Air Force Systems Command Bowling Championship. After four years, she returned to Texas and worked for the DuPont Chemical Plant. She married James Edwin "Timber" King in 1971, and they moved to Helena, his hometown, where he operated the Timberking Company.

Barbara King raised five children, later returning to college for an associate degree in lithography. She edited the *Crownlet* of the National Association of Junior Auxiliaries and regularly volunteered with the Helena Blues Festival. King was secretary and treasurer of the Phillips County Democratic Central Committee and chair of the Phillips County Election Commission.

In 1998, King ran for the House, facing Helena mayor Joann Smith in the Democratic primary, which ended in a tie. King won the runoff with 55 percent and was unopposed in the general election. King was unopposed for reelection in 2000. Redistricting placed incumbents King and Representative Arnell Willis in the same district in 2002. King won the primary with 51 percent of the vote and was unopposed in the general election.

Much of Representative King's legislation dealt with improving election law, and she passed legislation authorizing the merger of Helena and West Helena. Other major legislation included raising the state sales tax for increased education funding in response to the 2002 *Lake View* decision, and she was the lead House sponsor of the major education formula and funding bill. King proposed a constitutional amendment for a state lottery to fund public education.

In 2004, King ran unsuccessfully for county judge, but she was elected to the Phillips County Quorum Court in 2006. She continued to serve the community as president of the local Chamber of Commerce, attending the UCA Community Development Institute, and volunteering at the Helena Welcome Center.

# Mary Anne Salmon

HOUSE: 1999–2002, SENATE: 2003–2012
FROM: North Little Rock, Pulaski County
PARTY: Democratic
BIRTHPLACE: Fort Smith, Arkansas
DATES: April 9, 1939–
EDUCATION: Waldron High School, 1957; University of Arkansas; Arkansas Polytechnic College (ATU), BA in music education, 1961
OCCUPATION: teacher and business owner

*Photo courtesy of Arkansas Secretary of State.*

Mary Anne Salmon (born Mary Anne Sawyer) is the daughter of Vera Mae Martin, substitute teacher, and Lecil Richard Sawyer, school superintendent. Her grandfather Stephen Sawyer represented Monroe County in the Arkansas House of Representatives (1907–1910, 1925–1928), and her grandfather Jefferson Martin was Scott County treasurer (1925–1930) and judge (1933–1934). Her father was later mayor of Waldron (1975–1983).

After graduating from high school, Salmon attended the University of Arkansas for a year before transferring to Arkansas Tech, where she sang in the choir, played clarinet in the band, edited the Agricola yearbook, and was named to Who's Who. Salmon also met Don Salmon at Tech, and after graduation they married and moved to North Little Rock.

Salmon taught music at Scott Elementary and Sylvan Hills Junior High, then devoted her time to raising two daughters and volunteering for numerous causes and organizations in a "spirit of helping people," instilled by her mother. In addition to thirty years as music director at Park Hill Baptist Church, Salmon was president of the Junior League of North Little Rock and served on the boards of the Metro YMCA, Baptist Health Systems, Central Arkansas Radiation Therapy Foundation, United Cerebral Palsy, and Centennial Bank. Later, Salmon was on the Pulaski Technical College Foundation Board and was chair of the Arkansas Tech University Board of Trustees.

After working for several school millage campaigns, Salmon was the county coordinator for the gubernatorial campaigns of David Pryor in 1974 and Bill Clinton in 1982. She worked on Governor Clinton's staff (1983–1991) and was state coordinator for his presidential campaigns (1992 and 1996), then served as political and public liaison for DNC Arkansas office of President Clinton (1993–1998).

Putting her government experience to work, Salmon ran for the Arkansas House of Representatives in 1998, winning by 61 percent in the Democratic primary and general election. She was reelected with 88 percent in the 2000 Democratic primary and was unopposed in the general election. In 2002, Representative Salmon ran for the Senate, defeating Representative Dean Elliott in the general election, and Senator Salmon was reelected without opposition in 2004 and 2008.

During her fourteen years in office, Salmon was chair of the House Rules Committee, chair of the Senate Children and Youth Committee, vice chair of the Senate Education Committee, and the first female chair of the Legislative Council. Her legislation dealt primarily with issues affecting children, the elderly, and the disabled, ranging from protecting against adult maltreatment in residential facilities to providing insurance and funding to help children

with autism spectrum disorders, which she considered the most important. Senator Salmon was a cosponsor of ratification of the Equal Rights
Amendment and said her biggest disappointment was the legislature's failure
to ratify.

Senator Salmon was named Senator of the Year by the Arkansas Circuit
Judges Association in 2003 and Outstanding Woman Politician of the Year by
*AY Magazine* in 2008. Among numerous awards and honors were the Metro
YMCA Humanitarian of the Year and induction to the ATU Alumni Hall
of Distinction.

# Shirley Borhauer

HOUSE: 2001–2006
FROM: Bella Vista, Benton County
PARTY: Republican
BIRTHPLACE: Chicago, Illinois
DATES: October 2, 1926–December 10, 2013
EDUCATION: Chicago public schools;
Blue Island High School, 1944; Little
Company of Mary School of Nursing, 1948;
Governor's State University (Chicago),
BA, 1974
OCCUPATION: nurse

*Photo courtesy of Arkansas Secretary of State.*

Shirley Borhauer (born Shirley Ursala Czosek) worked at the Dodge Chicago
Aircraft Engine Plant, which made engines for B-29 bombers during World
War II, then joined the US Cadet Nurse Corps. She worked at St. Francis
Hospital and for the Chicago Public Health Department. In 1949, she mar-
ried Bill Borhauer and changed her political affiliation to Republican. After
her daughter began school, she returned to work as a school nurse.

Borhauer was named a fellow of the American School Health Association,
was involved with the Illinois Social Hygiene League, and was active in
community organizations. In 1975, she ran as a Republican for alderman of
Chicago's Nineteenth Ward. She lost, finishing third among four candidates,
and wrote *Shirley Who?* about the experience.

After a thirty-two-year career as a school nurse, Borhauer and her husband
retired in 1987 to Bella Vista, Arkansas, where she became an active community volunteer. She was a member of the AAUW Bentonville/Bella Vista,

volunteered at the Benton County Women's Shelter, served on the Bella Vista Property Owners Association Board, and won a position on the parish council at St. Bernard Catholic Church. In 1996, Shirley Borhauer was elected justice of the peace on the Benton County Quorum Court. In 2000, she was an alternate Bush delegate to the Republican National Convention and won a seat in the Arkansas House of Representatives, defeating two opponents with 54 percent in the Republican primary. She was handily reelected in 2002 and 2004.

At age seventy-four, Borhauer entered the Arkansas legislature in 2001. She worked on issues concerning public health, nursing, the environment, and public safety legislation. She was named one of the Grand Champions for Children by a coalition of nonprofits. Borhauer described herself as "a little old grandma, a Catholic Polish lady from Chicago," and said, "I've always been for the underdog—that's why some people think I'm a liberal or a Democrat, because I try to help people who are poor and disabled, and sick, and seniors."

After her legislative service, Borhauer served a term on the Bella Vista City Council. Her last letter to the editor (in 2010), proclaimed, "We ordinary folks can do a kind act for our elderly neighbors."

# Joyce Elliott

HOUSE: 2001–2006, SENATE: 2009–2022
FROM: Little Rock, Pulaski County
PARTY: Democratic
BIRTHPLACE: Willisville, Arkansas
DATES: March 20, 1951–
EDUCATION: Oak Grove grade school; Willisville High School, 1969; Southern State College (SAU), BA in English and speech, 1973; Ouachita Baptist University, MA in English, 1981; Harvard University, Kennedy School of Government Certified Senior Executives in State and Local Government, 2013
OCCUPATION: teacher and union organizer

*Photo courtesy of Arkansas Secretary of State.*

Joyce Elliott was born to Edna Mae Smith, a nurse's aide, and Marvin Elliott, a laborer. Encouraged by her grandmother Effie Elliott she began a life of political engagement at the age of ten during President John Kennedy's election and her willfully drinking from the county courthouse "white-only" water fountain. Later, Martin Luther King Jr. inspired her when she integrated Willisville High School. In college, Elliott was a member of the Black Student Association, Sigma Tau Delta English honor society, and chief justice of the student government. In 1974, she married Billy Barnes, and they had a son.

During a thirty-one-year teaching career, Elliott taught high school English in Texas, Florida, Minnesota, and eight years in El Dorado, Arkansas, before moving to Little Rock in 1984 to teach at McClellan and Robinson High Schools. She served on the executive committee of the Arkansas Education Association and was president of the Pulaski Association of Classroom Teachers and Arkansas president of the American Federation Teachers. In 2004, she became the regional director of Government Relations for the College Board.

Elliott served on the boards of Accelerate Arkansas, City Year Little Rock, Just Communities Central Arkansas, MacArthur Military Museum, Women and Children First, and the Women's Action for New Directions Education Fund. She was a delegate to the 1984, 2004, 2012, and 2016 Democratic National Conventions, vice chair of the Democratic Party of Arkansas, and Democratic National Committee member.

Elliott was elected to the Arkansas House of Representatives in 2000, winning the Democratic primary runoff with 52 percent, and receiving 83 percent in the general election. She was unopposed for reelection in 2002 and 2004 and term-limited in 2006. Elliott defeated state senator Irma Hunter Brown in the 2008 Democratic primary with 58 percent and was unopposed in the general election. Senator Elliott was reelected in 2012 with 63 percent in the Democratic primary and 86 percent in the general election and was unopposed for reelection in 2014 and 2018.

Representative Elliott chaired the House Education Committee. In the Senate, she was vice chair of the Education Committee and a member of Rules, Joint Budget, Legislative Council, and Joint Audit. She chaired the Arkansas Legislative Black Caucus and served on the executive committee of the National Conference of State Legislatures and was the governor's appointee to the Southern Regional Education Board. Senator Elliott was the Democratic nominee for Congress (AR-2) in 2010 and 2020.

Elliott is known as a legislative leader on issues of public education, labor, and equality. She championed significant legislation for reading education in schools, prisons, and juvenile facilities; created the Arkansas Tutoring Corps Act; and passed legislation establishing the conditions under which a public school district shall be returned to local control. She also passed legislation that included issues of juvenile justice, domestic abuse, sex trafficking, public safety, corporal punishment, school recess, dyslexia, recording of open public meetings, fair housing, public art, website information accuracy, creation of the Arkansas Legislative Arts and Technology Boot Camp; and she was twice the main sponsor of the resolution to ratify the Equal Rights Amendment.

In recognition of her legislative leadership, Elliott won numerous awards, including Civil Libertarian of the Year (ACLU), Democratic Woman of the Year (DPA), Outstanding Legislator (Arkansas AFL-CIO), Arkansas's Top Influencers (*Arkansas Money and Politics*), Women Who Mean Business Award (Arkansas B&PW), Distinguished Legislator Award (Arkansas Municipal League), the State Legislature Arts Leadership Award (Americans for the Arts), Champion for Kids Honor (Arkansas Advocates for Children and Families and Arkansas Kids Count Coalition), and the Ed Fry Award (Arkansas Democratic Party). In 2021, *Arkansas Times* readers voted her Best Arkansan, Little Rocker, Liberal, and Politician.

# Sharon Trusty

SENATE: 2001–2009
FROM: Russellville, Pope County
PARTY: Republican
BIRTHPLACE: Oregonia, Ohio
DATES: August 27, 1945–
EDUCATION: Piketon Elementary School; Kensett Elementary School; Paris High School, 1963; Arkansas Polytechnic College (ATU), business major
OCCUPATION: businesswoman

*Photo courtesy of Arkansas Secretary of State.*

Sharon Trusty (born Sharon Kathleen Steffy) is the daughter of Lenora Maxine Brandenburg, a homemaker, and Frank Alexander Steffy, a tool and die maker. The family moved from Ohio to Kensett and bought a strawberry farm when Trusty was in the fifth grade but returned to Cincinnati for a few years; then, in 1959, they moved to Sorghum Hollow in Logan County. Trusty attended Paris High School, where she was in Future Homemakers, Drama Club, school plays, music programs, and on the basketball team.

Trusty attended Arkansas Tech and married her high school sweetheart, John Thomas Trusty, in 1964. While raising their three daughters, she was involved with the community as chair of the Saint Mary's Regional Medical Center Board and served on the boards of Simmons First Bank, Arkansas River Valley Arts Center, Arkansas Next Step Education Foundation, and Child Development Incorporated. After the death of her husband in 1994, Trusty became vice president of Russellville Steel Company. She published an account of her transition from homemaker to widow to businesswoman, *Widowed: Beginning Again Personally and Financially* (August House 1999).

Trusty began volunteering in politics during the 1970s. She was co-chair of the Arkansas Republican Party, 1984–1986, and was a delegate to the Republican National Conventions of 1984, 1988, 1992, and 2004. Trusty was also state co-chair of President George H. W. Bush's reelection campaign and was a Republican presidential elector in 1992.

In 1996, Trusty narrowly lost a Senate race to Democrat Tom Kennedy. Governor Mike Huckabee appointed her to the Work Force Education Career Opportunities Board in 1997 and to the Arkansas Economic Development Commission in 1998. She also worked as a legislative liaison for Governor Huckabee during the 1999 session. In 2000, Trusty was elected to the state senate with 56 percent in the general election, and she was reelected with 58 percent over Representative Olin Cook in the 2002 general election. She was unopposed for reelection in 2004 and 2008.

Senator Trusty was vice chair of the Transportation, Technology and Legislative Affairs Committee and a member of the Legislative Council. She successfully sponsored legislation related to sales tax exemption for the Arkansas Symphony Orchestra Society, transfer agreements among colleges and universities, employment security law, check-cashing businesses, telecommunications devices for disabled persons, and banning novelty lighters. Trusty voted against ratification of the Equal Rights Amendment. She secured funding for Main Street Russellville, senior activity centers, city parks, the Boys and Girls Club, rural fire departments, the Literacy Council, and Arkansas Tech University.

Senator Trusty resigned on September 1, 2009, citing personal considerations that would require more of her time, and she continued as principal in Trusty and Associates, managing commercial and industrial property. Trusty returned to public service in 2013 when she was appointed to the Arkansas Ethics Commission, serving as chair during her last year in 2017.

# Ruth Whitaker

SENATE: 2001–2012
FROM: Van Buren, Crawford County
PARTY: Republican
BIRTHPLACE: Blytheville, Arkansas
DATES: December 13, 1936–November 10, 2014
EDUCATION: Heber Springs public schools; Heber Springs High School, 1954; Hendrix College, BA in speech with English minor, 1958
OCCUPATION: community activist

*Photo courtesy of Arkansas Secretary of State.*

Ruth Whitaker (born Ruth Reed) was the daughter of Ruth Shipton Weidemeyer, state president of the American Legion Auxiliary, and Lawrence Neill Reed, Blytheville mayor and later Heber Springs municipal judge. Whitaker's uncle, Howard Reed, was Speaker of the Arkansas House (1923–1924), when the first two women representatives served. She attended Heber Springs public schools and Hendrix College, where she was a cheerleader, on the student council and tennis team, a member of Chapel Choir and Hendrix Players, and president of Alpha Psi Omega dramatics honorary. She was chosen Hardest Worker in Who's Who, and received the Vivian Hill Drama Award. She was also chosen Miss Hospitality of Heber Springs.

After college, Whitaker worked for El Dorado's KTVE as the state's first "weather girl," then worked for S. M. Brooks advertising agency in Little Rock. In 1961, she married doctor Dr. Thomas Jefferson Whitaker Jr. They moved to Fort Smith in 1963, and she worked in real estate and other businesses while raising two children.

Whitaker was a committed community volunteer. She was president of the PTA and the Sebastian County Medical Society Women's Auxiliary, served on the board of the Sparks Hospital Guild, and was a fundraiser for numerous health-related charities. Other memberships included Alden Kindred of America, American Association of University Women, Arkansas Federation of Women's Clubs, and National Rifle Association. She also chaired the Sebastian County Park Commission and was vice chair of the Arkansas Educational Television Commission.

Soon after moving to Fort Smith, Whitaker switched parties and became a Republican. She later served as chair of the Crawford County Republican Committee, secretary of the Arkansas Republican Party, and delegate to the 1996 Republican National Convention.

In 2000, while serving her first term on the Cedarville City Council, Whitaker was recruited by the state Republican Party to run for an open state senate seat. She told skeptical rural voters that "having a woman in the Senate is important," and she won the general election with 58 percent. She was unopposed for reelection in 2002, 2004, and 2008.

Senator Whitaker was chair of the Rules Committee, vice chair of the Judiciary Committee, and a member of the Legislative Council. In 2003, she was Governor Huckabee's Senate floor leader, and in 2011 was the first female Senate minority leader. She advocated for issues related to rural development, public safety, property rights, health care, senior citizens, and tax cuts. In the school consolidation efforts, she proposed one school district per county. She voted against ratification of the Equal Rights Amendment.

Senator Whitaker and her husband treasured being named Honorary Parents of the Year by the University of Arkansas student body in 1984.

# Judy Pridgen

SENATE: 2002
FROM: Benton, Saline County
PARTY: Democratic
BIRTHPLACE: Malvern, Arkansas
DATES: August 4, 1947–
EDUCATION: Benton public schools; Benton High School, 1965; Arkansas State University
OCCUPATION: law enforcement

*Photo courtesy of Arkansas Secretary of State.*

Judy Pridgen (born Judy Kay Frost) is the daughter of Hazel Dean Jordan, a high school math teacher, and Carlos Lawrence Frost, owner of Frost's Trading Post. After taking criminal justice classes at Arkansas State University, she married Charles Hass in 1967, and they had two sons. She later married Ed Pridgen, a former police officer.

In 1971, Pridgen joined the Benton Police Department as a civilian clerk.

She became a police officer in 1972 and was in the first class that included women at the Arkansas Law Enforcement Training Academy. She publicly supported ratification of the Equal Rights Amendment and filed two successful sex discrimination suits against the Benton Police Department. After twenty years on the force, Lieutenant Pridgen retired in 1991.

Pridgen ran for Saline County sheriff in 1992. She heard remarks that she would "paint the Sheriff's car pink" and questions whether she could kick in a front door, to which she responded, "My job isn't to kick in a front door, it's to make sure the right front door gets kicked in." With sister Mary Dillard as her campaign manager, she defeated six men in the Democratic primary and won the general election. Pridgen was the first woman in Arkansas history to be elected sheriff. After four terms, she lost in the 2000 general election by 142 votes. That same year, her stepson was elected Van Buren County sheriff.

For three consecutive years, Pridgen was named to *Arkansas Business'* Top 100 Women in Arkansas. She was chair of the Arkansas Commission on Law Enforcement Standards and Training. Pridgen was active in the Golden Kiwanis Club, the Churches Joint Council on Human Needs Board, and the Benton Police Department Pension Board. She was also treasurer of the Saline County Democratic Committee.

In July 2002, Pridgen was elected to fill a state senate seat vacated by Doyle Webb. She defeated Senator Webb's sister, Candis Webb, with 61 percent. Senator Pridgen enjoyed helping constituents with problems, participated on the interim committees, and supported residents seeking to stop developers from damming the protected Middle Fork of the Saline River and threatening aquatic species. She did not run for reelection.

After her Senate service, Pridgen worked five years as chief investigator for prosecuting attorney Robert Herzfeld then as case coordinator for circuit judge Gary Arnold's drug court. She also served on the Benton Civil Service Commission.

# Linda Chesterfield

HOUSE: 2003–2008, SENATE: 2011–present
FROM: Little Rock, Pulaski County
PARTY: Democratic
BIRTHPLACE: Hope, Arkansas
DATES: September 13, 1947–
EDUCATION: Hopewell Elementary
School; Henry Clay Yerger High School,
1965; Hendrix College, BA in history and
political science, 1969
OCCUPATION: teacher, consultant

*Photo courtesy of Arkansas Secretary of State.*

Linda Chesterfield (born Linda Ann Pondexter) was raised by a single mom, Ernestine Pondexter, a factory worker at Champion Parts. Her grandmother Ophilia Dixon Logan instilled a love of reading and politics. She played piano at the First Church of God, and in high school, she was student-council president, president of FBLA, president of the library club, and vice president of the senior class. Chesterfield won several state poetry championships, presenting the works of Langston Hughes.

Chesterfield attended Hendrix College after winning one of the first National Achievement Scholarships for outstanding Black students. She was the first Black student to attend Hendrix, and, in 1969, she earned a degree in history and political science, becoming the college's first Black graduate. She then began a thirty-three-year career teaching world geography, civics, and history in the Pulaski County Special School District.

Chesterfield held professional leadership roles as the first Black woman to serve as president of the Arkansas Education Association and president of the Pulaski County Association of Classroom Teachers, and she was on the executive committee of the National Education Association. She was later president of the Little Rock School Board, and she was honored for her efforts to promote social justice with the NEA Mary Hatwood Futrell Award. In 2001, she married Emry Chesterfield, union president of the Pulaski Association of Support Staff.

Linda Chesterfield ran for the Arkansas House in 2002 and won the Democratic primary with 67 percent over two opponents, was unopposed in the general election, and was unopposed for reelection in 2004 and 2006. Leaving the House due to term-limits in 2008, she became an adjunct professor of government at Arkansas Baptist College. Chesterfield ran for the state senate in 2010, won the Democratic primary with 62 percent, was unopposed in 2014, and was reelected in 2018 with 68 percent in the Democratic primary. She was unopposed for reelection in 2022.

Representative Chesterfield chaired the Committee on Aging, Children and Youth and was a strong advocate for improving the state's Youth Services Division and assisting incarcerated youth with education, training, and rehabilitation. She was a delegate to the 2008 and 2020 Democratic National Conventions, was president and treasurer of the Arkansas Democratic Black Caucus, and was chair of the Arkansas Legislative Black Caucus. She sponsored legislation to improve public schools, serving on the Education Committee and chairing the Desegregation Litigation Oversight Subcommittee. She cosponsored ratification of the Equal Rights Amendment in the House and in the Senate.

Chesterfield's successful education legislation includes appropriations for Historic Black Colleges and Universities, facilitating final resolution to Arkansas desegregation cases, college-remediation rate and workforce readiness, requiring legislative review of consolidation of school districts and State Board of Education assumption of administrative authority, and including nonprofit private colleges or universities in the Arkansas Future Grant Program. She also passed legislation on spousal abuse, for paid breaks for classified school employees, establishing the crime of cyberbullying, providing additional income tax relief to heads of households with two or more dependents, and inclusion of John W. Walker in the curriculum for Black History.

In 2021, Senator Chesterfield was honored by Arkansas Baptist College with the Above and Beyond Award.

# Marilyn Edwards

HOUSE: 2003–2008
FROM: Fayetteville, Washington County
PARTY: Democratic
BIRTHPLACE: Hartman, Arkansas
DATES: August 24, 1938–
EDUCATION: Hartman public schools; Hartman High School, 1956
OCCUPATION: data-processing supervisor, county clerk

*Photo courtesy of Arkansas Secretary of State.*

Marilyn Edwards (born Marilyn Ruby Patterson) was born to Reesie Allide James, a hairdresser and Tyson Foods processing plant worker, and Virgil Lee Patterson, a coal miner. Her grandfather and father worked the coal mines and were stewards in Hartman Local 1934 UMWA, where, as a young girl, she met John L. Lewis. She grew up in a politically aware family, and her mentor was her high school teacher, Ocie Bivens, the third woman to serve as president of the Arkansas Education Association. She married George Dee Edwards from Coal Hill when she was seventeen and lived briefly in Illinois and Pennsylvania, while her husband was in the US Air Force. They later moved with their two children to Bakersfield, California, where she was a data-processing supervisor for keypunch operators at Calcot cotton cooperative.

The Edwards family moved to Fayetteville in 1969, and Edwards was a keypunch operator at the University of Arkansas and Ozark Data Processing before being hired by the Washington County judge to manage transition to a Burroughs L-5000 computer for payroll, purchasing, and inventory. She was deputy county clerk for two years before running for county clerk in 1976. Edwards won the Democratic primary with 68 percent and the general election with 72 percent that year, and she was unopposed for twelve additional terms.

After twenty-six years as Washington County clerk, Edwards ran unopposed for state representative in 2002 and was unopposed for reelection in 2004 and 2006.

Edward's legislation focused on improving municipal and county government and elections, and she always supported working-class issues and the Equal Rights Amendment. She said she didn't run for the legislature to sponsor a lot of legislation but saw her main duty as defeating bad bills.

After being term-limited from the House in 2008, Edwards ran for Washington County judge, winning the general election with 58 percent and becoming the first female county judge in the county's 180-year history. Unopposed in 2010 and 2012, she won a fourth term in 2014, defeating Republican county assessor Jeff Williams. In 2016, Judge Edwards ran for justice of the peace but lost in the Democratic primary. Later that year, the Washington County Democrats bestowed the Marilyn Edwards Lifetime Achievement Award to its namesake. Edwards was honored as one of the 2017 Washington County Women in History.

# Janet Johnson

HOUSE: 2003–2008
FROM: Bryant, Saline County
PARTY: Democratic
BIRTHPLACE: Berryville, Arkansas
DATES: October 25, 1947–
EDUCATION: Berryville public schools;
Berryville High School, 1965; Arkansas
Polytechnic College (ATU), BA in history
and political science, 1970
OCCUPATION: teacher, businesswoman

*Photo courtesy of Arkansas Secretary of State.*

Janet Johnson (born Janet Rae Keeton) is the daughter of Frances Rae Curry, a court reporter, and Julian Francis "Buck" Keeton Jr. a Soil Conservation Service employee. She was "always interested in politics," and her family was politically aware and active. Her grandmother Mattie Ledbetter was an ardent campaigner for women's suffrage, and her father "was a staunch supporter of the Equal Rights Amendment, because he loved me so much he wanted me to go out into the world on an equal playing field." In high school, Johnson was in student council, civic club, class plays, a vice president of Future Teachers, president of Future Business Leaders, on the pom-pom squad, Who's Who, a delegate to Girls State, and an advocate against damming the Buffalo River.

After graduating from college in 1970, she married Jamey Johnson, and they had two sons. In 1973, Johnson began teaching at Bryant public schools. She developed the political science program, was twice a Fulbright Teacher, and worked for educational institutions in China with the Freeman Foundation. Johnson was president of Bryant Classroom Teachers Association and on the board of the American Education Association. She also helped manage her family fireworks company.

Senator Charlie Cole Chaffin, Johnson's teaching colleague, encouraged her to run for the House seat being vacated by House Speaker Shane Broadway, their former student. Johnson won the Democratic primary with 59 percent and won the 2002 general election by 165 votes over Republican Dennis Milligan and an independent candidate. In 2004, she again defeated Milligan and an independent candidate by ninety-three votes. Johnson was unopposed for reelection in 2006.

Representative Johnson was Assistant Speaker Pro Tempore of the House. Her legislation focused on education, including teacher retirement, teacher salaries, academic disparities in the Delta, student health, school employee health benefits, and school choice. She passed legislation allowing teachers to have representation for disciplinary or grievance matters, requiring compliance reports on personnel policy, mandating data on the Department of Education website, creating an advisory committee on student health care, and creating the Public Education Salvage Computer Loan Program. Johnson cosponsored and worked for Arkansas's ratification of the Equal Rights Amendment. Her other legislative issues included prescription drug pricing, residential psychiatric treatment facilities, executive clemency procedures, municipal employee health insurance, environmental standards, and juvenile justice.

After her legislative service, Johnson continued teaching until she retired in 2011.

# Betty Pickett

HOUSE: 2003–2008
FROM: Conway, Faulkner County
PARTY: Democratic
BIRTHPLACE: Detroit, Michigan
DATES: November 2, 1941–
EDUCATION: Riverside Elementary; Fourth Street Junior High; North Little Rock High School, 1959; Hendrix College, BA in social science, 1963
OCCUPATION: retired educator and business owner

*Photo courtesy of Arkansas Secretary of State.*

Betty Pickett (born Betty Lou Bryles) is the daughter of Burnice Samuel Bryles, a welder, and Tennie Rebecca Williams, a "Rosie" at Ford's Dearborn aircraft factory. When Pickett's parents divorced, her mother returned to North Little Rock with her three children and later married William Bell Martin.

In high school, Pickett was student council parliamentarian, president of Thespians, acted in the senior play, and was a member of the drill team, Y-Teens, and other clubs. At Hendrix, she was a cheerleader and member of the government club and Student National Education Association. After graduation, she married John Pickett and supported his graduate education and academic career in Missouri, Hawaii, and Australia by teaching third grade and junior high. They moved back to Conway with two young sons in 1973.

Betty Pickett owned a women's clothing store and was involved in civic affairs, serving on the Conway Civil Service Commission, was president of Faulkner County United Way, and helped found the local League of Women Voters. Pickett was elected as a Democrat to the Faulkner County Quorum Court over four opponents in 1976 and served four years. She was president of the Arkansas League of Women Voters in 1984–1985. Governor Jim Guy Tucker appointed Pickett to the State Board of Education, and she served from 1995 until 2003, including two years as chair.

In 2002, Pickett ran for the Arkansas House of Representatives, leading the Democratic primary with 42 percent, winning the runoff with 54 percent, and being elected with 55 percent in the general election. She was reelected with 65 percent in the 2004 general election and was unopposed in 2006.

Representative Pickett served three terms on the House Education Committee and was also a member of the Rules; Joint Budget; City, County, and Local; and Insurance and Commerce Committees, as well as the Legislative Council. Her legislation focused on public education, including accountability, school athletic expenditures, school board training and management practices. She also passed bills on protective orders, funding public libraries, and auditing economic incentive programs and was a cosponsor of legislation to ratify the Equal Rights Amendment.

After being term-limited in the House, Pickett continued to be actively involved in her community. She worked with the nonprofit Conway Downtown Partnership, was a member of the Faulkner County Election Commission, served on the executive committee of the Democratic Party of Arkansas, and was honored as an "Unsung Shero" by the Arkansas Democratic Party.

# Sandra Prater

HOUSE: 2003–2008
FROM: Jacksonville, Pulaski County
PARTY: Democratic
BIRTHPLACE: Hot Springs, Arkansas
DATES: February 6, 1955–
EDUCATION: Ole Main for elementary and junior high school; Ole Main High School, 1973; Baptist System School of Nursing, LPN, 1975, and RN, 1978
OCCUPATION: nurse and small-business owner

*Photo courtesy of Arkansas Secretary of State.*

Sandra Prater (born Sandra Herriott) is the daughter of Bobbie Jean Massey, a waitress, and Billy Hubert Herriott, a career US Marine Tech Sargent. She grew up in North Little Rock and worked at Kentucky Fried Chicken while attending high school. She was a cheerleader, member of Quill & Scroll and Key Club, and active in Y-Teens and 4-H. She married Kenneth Prater in 1974. She was a nurse at Memorial Hospital North Little Rock, and they owned Prater Auto Sales.

While raising two children, Prater was a Northwood Junior High PTO member and a Pulaski County School District volunteer. She was also chair of the Pulaski Leadership Council, a member of the Little Rock Air Force Base Community Council, a graduate of the Pulaski County Sheriff's Community Police Academy, and a Sunday school teacher at Zion Hill Baptist Church.

In 1998, Prater ran for the Pulaski County Quorum Court, defeating an incumbent and serving four years. In 2002, Prater ran for the Arkansas House of Representatives. She won the Democratic primary by 60 percent and the general election with 53 percent. Prater was unopposed for reelection in 2004 and 2006.

Representative Prater was a member of the Public Health, Welfare, and Labor and the Agriculture, Forestry and Economic Development committees. Coach Frank Broyles spoke on behalf of her successful legislation expanding training for certified nurse assistants for treating Alzheimer's patients. Other legislation included the Automatic External Defibrillator Act of 2007, grade school vision screening, Choices for Living information for senior citizens, and creation of the Arkansas Legislative Task Force on

Traumatic Brain Injury. Representative Prater was a cosponsor of the Equal Rights Amendment.

In 2007, Prater was named Legislator of the Year by the AARP and the Physical Therapy Association, Advocate of the Year by the Advanced Practice Nurses Council, and Nurse of the Year by the Arkansas Nurses Association. She also received the Champion for Children Award from the Arkansas Advocates for Children and Families.

Prater ran unsuccessfully for the Arkansas Senate in 2010 and the Pulaski County Quorum Court in 2014. She served on the Baptist System School of Nursing advisory board, the Pulaski County Bridge Facility Board, and the board of directors for Care Link, Arkansas Prostate Cancer Foundation, Lights for Literacy, and the Arkansas Health Care Access Foundation. Governor Mike Beebe appointed Prater to the Arkansas Dietetics Licensing Board 2013–2018.

# Susan Schulte

HOUSE: 2003–2008
FROM: Cabot, Lonoke County
PARTY: Republican
BIRTHPLACE: Nuremburg, Germany
DATES: February 25, 1957–
EDUCATION: Little Red Schoolhouse Kindergarten; Wheeler Elementary School (Hawaii); Hoover Elementary School (Enid, Oklahoma); Little Rock Central High School, 1974; University of Arkansas at Little Rock
OCCUPATION: real estate appraiser

*Photo courtesy of Arkansas Secretary of State.*

Susan Schulte (born Susan Lynn Grider) is the daughter of Shirley Ann Moore, a homemaker, and Mack Carlton Grider, career US Army, who were both from Warren, Arkansas, but the family traveled often with her father's assignments. Schulte was born in Germany and lived in Hawaii and Oklahoma until moving to Little Rock in 1969. During high school, she worked at the Little Rock Public Library and at Casa Bonita restaurant. At Central High School, she was in the drama club, ecology club, Junior Red

Cross, and Junior Civitans. She attended the University of Arkansas at Little Rock and married Frank Schulte during her freshman year.

Schulte earned her real estate license and worked for Block Realty. She and Frank lived in North Little Rock, and she raised three children and helped with Frank's insurance agency. Randy Minton encouraged her to become a licensed appraiser, and she worked with Minton before becoming an independent appraiser.

Schulte was active in professional service, including as vice chair of the Cabot Planning Commission and the Home Inspector Advisory Board, member of the Lonoke County Board of Adjustments, president of the SCS Residential Appraisal Society, education chair of the Arkansas Appraisal Institute, and founder of the local Business and Professional Women chapter. Governor Mike Huckabee appointed her to the state Home Inspector Advisory Board in 1999. She was on the Cabot Chamber of Commerce Board, a member of the Lonoke County Republican Committee, and active in her church.

Representative Randy Minton recruited Schulte to run for the Arkansas House of Representatives seat he was vacating. After talking with her pastor and much prayer, Schulte decided, "Ok, God. I'm just taking the next step, because I know that this is where you want me." Schulte ran for the House in 2002, winning the general election with 55 percent. She was reelected in 2004 with 68 percent and was unopposed for reelection in 2006.

Representative Schulte actively worked on issues regarding home inspections and appraisals. Her legislation included prohibition of partial-birth abortions, specialty license plates for Choose Life Inc., protecting home appraisers from lawsuits, and the promotion of biofuels. She filed legislation to restrict work-release and furlough programs and advocated charging prisoners for room and board. She opposed school consolidation, weatherization assistance, and opposed in-state tuition for immigrant high school graduates.

After legislative service, Schulte continued her profession as a certified residential licensed appraiser.

# Shirley Walters

HOUSE: 2003–2008
FROM: Greenwood, Sebastian County
PARTY: Republican
BIRTHPLACE: Lonoke, Arkansas
DATES: November 12, 1948–
EDUCATION: North Little Rock High
School, 1966; Arkansas Tech University, BS
in elementary education, 1970
OCCUPATION: teacher, business owner

*Photo courtesy of Arkansas Secretary of State.*

Shirley Walters (born Shirley Ann Dixon) is the daughter of Katherine Beatrice Evans, a homemaker, and Cecil Leo Dixon, an X-ray technician at Fort Roots Veterans Administration Hospital. After graduating from Arkansas Tech, Walters moved to Greenwood in 1970 and taught elementary school. She married Bill Walters, a deputy prosecutor, city attorney, and municipal judge who was a state senator (1983–2000), and they had three daughters. In 1980, Walters left teaching and founded the Sebastian County Abstract and Title Company, which she owned until 2002.

Walters was chair of the River Valley Heart Association and president of the Fort Smith Heart Association Board, and she served on the boards of the Arkansas Humanities Council, the Saint Edward Hospital Auxiliary, the Sebastian County Red Cross, and the Fort Smith Community Foundation. She was a member of the South Sebastian County Humane Society, the Habitat for Humanity Carpenter's Club, and the Greenwood Garden Club.

Having learned the legislative process during her husband's sixteen years in the state senate, Walters ran for the House as a Republican in 2002, defeating incumbent Democratic representative Terry McMellon with 57 percent in the general election. She was unopposed for reelection in 2004 and 2006.

Representative Walters was a member of the House committees on Education and Insurance and Commerce and on the Legislative Council. She was Assistant Speaker Pro Tempore during the 2005 session. Among the legislation she enacted were education bills on required art and music instruction, qualifications for substitute teachers, cyberbullying policies, parental involvement plans, and the state public school computer network. Other legislation addressed designation of scenic highways, specialty license plates for veterans, authorizing charitable bingo and raffles, improving emergency and rescue operations, administration of justice, criminal penalties for obscenity and gambling, and the Arkansas Title Insurance Act. She also sponsored appropriations for libraries, museums, parks, senior centers, community buildings, a community college branch, and rural fire departments in her district.

After being term-limited in 2008, Walters continued her service with community organizations and worked as legislative secretary for state senator Bruce Holland. In 2018, she was appointed to the Advancement Advisory Council for the Arkansas Colleges of Health Education in Fort Smith.

# Pam Adcock

HOUSE: 2005–2010
FROM: Little Rock, Pulaski County
PARTY: Democratic
BIRTHPLACE: Hampton, Arkansas
DATES: August 10, 1961–
EDUCATION: Hampton High School, 1979
OCCUPATION: community center director

*Photo courtesy of Arkansas Secretary of State.*

Pam Adcock (born Pamela Annette Farley) is the daughter of Bobbie Jean Holmes and William Clifford Farley Jr. She married Archie Frank Adcock in 1980, and they had three children.

Active in her community, Adcock was president and founder of the Cloverdale Neighborhood Association, chair of the Little Rock Animal Services Advisory Board, and a member of the Little Rock Planning Commission. She and her husband, a Little Rock police officer, received the neighborhood service award from the Arkansas chapter of National Parents Day. Adcock was director of the Ottenheimer Community Center, providing therapeutic recreational and leisure opportunities for individuals with disabilities.

Adcock ran for an open House seat in 2004. She led two opponents with 44 percent in the Democratic primary, won the runoff with 65 percent, and was unopposed in the general election. She was unopposed for reelection in 2006 and 2008.

Representative Adcock was a member of the Legislative Council and the House Rules Committee. She was appointed Assistant Speaker Pro Tempore and served on the Task Force on Abused and Neglected Children; the Public Health Welfare, and Labor Committee; and the State Agencies and Governmental Affairs Committee. In 2007, she was the only woman on the State Agencies Committee to vote against ratification of the Equal Rights Amendment.

In her first term, Representative Adcock passed general appropriations to the city of Little Rock for a day resource center, animal services, and park improvements, and to the Highway Department for a stoplight in her district. Her second-term legislation included exemptions from the state minimum wage, dispute resolution process for state employees, protection against interfering with breastfeeding mothers, and loan forgiveness for state rehabilitation counselors. In her third term, Adcock was the lead House sponsor for legislation making aggravated animal cruelty a felony. She also passed bills on rabies control, tax exemptions for the Arkansas Search Dog Association, a special license plate for the support of animal rescue and shelters, insurance coverage of hearing aids, and health inspection of concession stands.

After being term-limited from the House, Adcock served as president of Southwest United for Progress, an umbrella neighborhood association of thirty neighborhood groups in southwest Little Rock. In 2014, she was an unsuccessful candidate for Little Rock city director.

# Nancy Duffy Blount

HOUSE: 2005–2010
FROM: Marianna, Lee County
PARTY: Democratic
BIRTHPLACE: Augusta, Arkansas
DATES: January 13, 1949–
EDUCATION: Carver Elementary; Carver High School, 1966; Arkansas Agricultural, Mechanical, and Normal College (UAPB), BA in French and Spanish, 1970; University of Arkansas, MA in foreign languages, 1972
OCCUPATION: coroner, teacher, businesswoman

*Photo courtesy of Arkansas Secretary of State.*

Nancy Duffy Blount was one of thirteen children born to sharecroppers Leona Stith and Octavius C. Duffy in Augusta. She chopped cotton from the time she was five years old, but her parents always encouraged their children to pursue higher education. She attended Arkansas Agricultural, Mechanical, and Normal College, where she was a member of Alpha Kappa Alpha and earned her bachelor's degree in French and Spanish with a minor in English. She then attended the University of Arkansas in Fayetteville with a teaching assistantship for her master's degree in foreign languages, where she studied French one summer in Switzerland and worked as a substitute teacher in Benton County. After graduate school, she began her teaching career with the Lee County School District. In 1975 Nancy Duffy married Samuel Blount, and they have a daughter.

While teaching at Lee County High School, Blount studied Spanish at ILISA Language Institute in Costa Rica. She was president of the Arkansas Foreign Language Teachers Association and president of the local association of the Arkansas Education Association. She and Sam also acquired and ran funeral homes, and she was the Lee County coroner for eight years (1991–1998), the first Black elected county coroner in Arkansas.

After thirty-five years of teaching, Blount ran for the Arkansas House of Representatives, seeing it as an opportunity to improve education, health care, and economic development in the Delta. She won the 2004 Democratic primary with 52 percent and was unopposed in the general election. Representative Blount was reelected without opposition in 2006 and 2008.

Representative Blount filed legislation on issues of education, teacher licensing, literacy, funeral costs, promoting languages in schools, funeral cost assistance, felon voting rights, inmate education, and health care. She cosponsored legislation to ratify the Equal Rights Amendment, and she passed legislation that created a literacy skills component to the Arkansas Academic Challenge Scholarship Program and a pilot program for mobile learning technology in public schools. She received an outstanding legislator award from the Association of Arkansas Counties and was honored for her leadership by the Arkansas Education Association and Alpha Kappa Alpha.

Blount ran unsuccessfully for the Arkansas House of Representatives in 2018, losing to the incumbent in the Democratic primary. Along with her sister, Dr. Cora McHenry, she continues to operate her family's Duffy Scholarship fund for students attending the University of Arkansas at Pine Bluff.

# Dawn Creekmore

HOUSE: 2005–2010
FROM: East End, Saline County
PARTY: Democratic
BIRTHPLACE: St. Charles, Illinois
DATES: February 28, 1965–
EDUCATION: Norphlet High School, 1983;
Pulaski Technical College, coursework in
accounting, 1985–1987; Eaton Beauty Stylist
College, cosmetology license, 1985, and
cosmetology instructor license, 1989; Eaton
Barber Stylist College, barber license, 1986,
and barber instructor license, 1990
OCCUPATION: business owner

*Photo courtesy of Arkansas Secretary of State.*

Dawn Creekmore (born Dawn Marie Jahns) is the daughter of Barbara Ann Carter, a homemaker, and Bruce Martin Jahns, a computer programmer. After her parents divorced when she was in the fourth grade, her mother moved back to Norphlet with her children and attended school to become a home health nurse. In 1984, Dawn married Michael Creekmore, and they have two daughters.

Creekmore worked as a cosmetologist and owned six beauty salons in Arkansas. In 1989, she purchased Eaton Beauty College and Eaton Barber College from her in-laws, where she worked as a financial aid officer. Creekmore held memberships in the National Rifle Association and the Arkansas Hunger Coalition.

After her husband was term-limited from the Arkansas House of Representatives, Creekmore ran for the position and won the 2004 general election with 58 percent of the vote against Justice of the Peace Penny Kemp. Creekmore was reelected with 70 percent in the 2006 general election and was unopposed in 2008.

Representative Creekmore chaired the House Aging, Children and Youth Committee; was a member of the Task Force on the Effect of Alzheimer's Disease in Arkansas; and formed an informal committee of professionals to address problems with the state's sex offender process. She filed legislation prohibiting convicted sex offenders from working with or volunteering with children; and on issues of consumer protection, domestic violence, abuse and neglect, cosmetology, elections, identity fraud, sexual violence, stalking, expanding DNA databases, school bus safety, and Alzheimer's disease. Her legislation included the Domestic Violence Address Confidentiality Act, and she sponsored the Partial-Birth Abortion Ban. Creekmore received awards from the Arkansas Psychological Association and the Arkansas Coalition Against Sexual Assault.

In 2010, Creekmore moved to Bauxite to run for the Arkansas Senate and won the Democratic primary but lost to former representative Jeremy Hutchinson in the general election. Creekmore became director of Imagine Paul Mitchell Partner School in North Little Rock in 2011, and she and her husband opened Battery Giant in Little Rock in 2012. Creekmore was chair of the board of Qsource-Arkansas, a nonprofit health-care assessment firm. She was elected to the Saline County Quorum Court as a Republican (2017–2018).

## Stephanie Flowers

HOUSE: 2005–2010, SENATE: 2011–present
FROM: Pine Bluff, Jefferson County
PARTY: Democratic
BIRTHPLACE: Pine Bluff, Arkansas
DATES: August 8, 1953–
EDUCATION: Pine Bluff High School, 1971; Philander Smith College, BA in political science and English, 1975; Texas Southern University Thurgood Marshall School of Law, JD, 1979
OCCUPATION: attorney

*Photo courtesy of Arkansas Secretary of State.*

Stephanie Flowers was born to Margaret Brown, an elementary school teacher, and William Harold Flowers, a civil rights attorney. As a senior at Pine Bluff High School during the year it was integrated by the merger with Merrill High School, Flowers was elected to the school's Interracial Advisory Board.

Returning to Arkansas after law school in 1979, Flowers became the legal advocate for the Area Agency on Aging of Southeast Arkansas, then a deputy prosecuting attorney for the Jefferson County Juvenile Court. She has been in private practice since 1982. She married LaCurtis Kirk and has a son.

In 1994, Flowers ran unsuccessfully as an independent candidate for Circuit/

Chancery juvenile judge against the Democratic incumbent judge Thomas Brown. She later became active in Jefferson County Democratic Women, served on the Arkansas Democratic Party Executive Committee, and was an Obama delegate to the 2008 Democratic National Convention. Flowers is also on the Mount Pleasant A.M.E. Church Board of Trustees.

Flowers filed for the Arkansas House in 2004, winning the Democratic primary with 58 percent and running unopposed in the general election. She was unopposed for reelection in 2006 and 2008. Representative Flowers ran for the state senate in 2010, defeating Representative David Rainey in the Democratic primary with 56.2 percent. Running for reelection in 2012, Flowers defeated Representative Efrem Elliott in the Democratic primary with 58.5 percent and won the general election with 82.8 percent. She was unopposed for reelection in 2016 and was reelected in 2020 with 74.8 percent in the Democratic primary.

Representative Flowers chaired the City, County, and Local Government Affairs Committee. In the Senate, she was assistant president pro tempore, vice chair of the Judiciary Committee, and on the Legislative Council. Flowers passed bills addressing administration of justice, small-business loans, indigent assistance, school employee policies, parental and community involvement in schools, qualifications of health professionals, child abuse, drainage districts, and concealed handgun licenses. She was a cosponsor of the resolution to ratify the Equal Rights Amendment and sponsored appropriation bills for community improvements and organizations.

In 2019, Senator Flowers received national attention for an impassioned committee speech against limiting debate on gun legislation, noting racial injustice and her fear for Black youths' lives, including her son, due to gun violence. In 2021, she served as vice chair of the Senate Judiciary Committee and passed the resolution remembering Detective Kevin Collins of the Pine Bluff Police Department, who was killed in the line of duty, and recognizing his service to Arkansas.

Senator Flowers was awarded the Democratic Party of Arkansas's Chairman's Heritage Award and the Alpha Kappa Alpha Sorority Social Justice Pioneer Award.

# Wilhelmina Lewellen

HOUSE: 2005–2010
FROM: Little Rock, Pulaski County
PARTY: Democratic
BIRTHPLACE: Woodson, Arkansas
DATES: December 9, 1937–
EDUCATION: Woodson Grade School;
Dunbar High School, 1955; Arkansas
Agricultural, Mechanical, and Normal
College (UAPB), BA in sociology, 1959;
Ouachita Baptist University, MEd
in elementary education, 1975
OCCUPATION: teacher

*Photo courtesy of Arkansas Secretary of State.*

Wilhelmina Lewellen (born Wilhelmina Epps) grew up on a farm south of Little Rock, one of seven children born to Odelle J. Hill, a teacher, and Clifford E. Epps, an agriculture extension agent. Although her family was politically aware, her interest in politics grew after she married John Marshall Lewellen in 1956 and worked in his successful campaigns for the Little Rock City Board, the Pulaski County Quorum Court, and the Arkansas House of Representatives (1999–2004). State Senator Bill Lewellen was their nephew, and their daughter, Patricia, married Congressman William Lacy Clay of Missouri.

As a schoolteacher for thirty-five years, Lewellen was active professionally as a member of the Classroom Teachers Association, the Arkansas Education Association, and the National Education Association. Her community service included serving as president of the Ivy Foundation of Little Rock, president of the Links, and as a leader in the Beta Pi Omega graduate chapter of her sorority Alpha Kappa Alpha.

In politics and government, Lewellen was a member of the Pulaski County Democratic Women and the Arkansas Democratic Black Caucus. She gained a greater understanding of state government as an employee of the Arkansas Senate in 1997 and as a *Legislative Digest* and bill clerk in the Arkansas House in 2001.

In 2004, Lewellen ran for the House seat vacated when her husband was term-limited. She led the Democratic primary with 46 percent over two opponents, won the runoff with 56 percent, and was unopposed in the general election. She was unopposed for reelection in 2006, and she was reelected with 82 percent in the 2008 general election.

Representative Lewellen was a member of the committees on Joint Budget, Insurance and Commerce, and Revenue and Taxation, and she was chair of the Task Force for the Study of the Homeless. As a result of her involvement with Women in Government, she sponsored legislation creating the Cervical Cancer Task Force to coordinate the Department of Health's statewide cervical cancer education, prevention, and treatment programs, and she passed several health-care appropriation bills. Lewellen was a member of the Legislative Black Caucus and the Women's Caucus, and she was a cosponsor of the resolution to ratify the Equal Rights Amendment.

In 2009, Arkansas Citizens First Congress rated her 100 percent on Education, Civil Liberties and Civil Rights, Campaign Finance and Elections, Agriculture and Food, Health and Health Care, and Government Operations.

# Beverly Pyle

HOUSE: 2005–2010
FROM: Cedarville, Crawford County
PARTY: Republican
BIRTHPLACE: Fort Smith, Arkansas
DATES: January 13, 1952–
EDUCATION: Cedarville public schools; Cedarville High School, 1969; Arkansas School of Business, certificate, 1971
OCCUPATION: business owner, mayor

*Photo courtesy of Arkansas Secretary of State.*

Beverly Pyle (born Beverly Roberta Shelly) was the eighth of nine children born to Alice Tina Allen, a homemaker, and Robert Shelly, a factory worker and farmer. A lifelong resident of Crawford County, she was raised on a farm in Natural Dam, went to Cedarville schools, and attended the Arkansas School of Business in Fort Smith. She married William Forrest Pyle in 1970, and they had four children.

After having worked in accounts at Sterling Stores and as secretary to the Cedarville school superintendent, Pyle established and operated the Alice N Wonderland children's clothing boutique in 1978. Later, she owned the Popcorn Patch and Fudge Factory and was co-owner of C&C Catfish Restaurant in Van Buren. Pyle served as secretary of the board of Summit Medical Center in Van Buren and on the boards of the Crawford County Senior Citizens Centers and the Crawford County District 5 Volunteer Fire Department.

Beverly Pyle was a leader in incorporating the city of Cedarville in 1998, and she was elected to the city council. After two months in office, Pyle was elected mayor to fill a vacancy, and reelected as mayor in 2000. After serving six years as mayor, Pyle ran as a Republican for an open seat in the Arkansas House, winning the general election with 58 percent of the vote. She was unopposed for reelection in 2006 and 2008 and was term-limited in 2010.

Representative Pyle's legislation focused on city and county government. She passed legislation clarifying the organization of city councils, making state and city bidding requirements consistent, making recorder-treasurer terms four years, clarifying the procedure for filling a recorder-treasurer vacancy, establishing criteria for municipal police patrol of controlled-access facilities, allowing state funding for municipal recreational purposes, allowing police to issue citations at accident scenes, and requiring support documentation for municipal-fund disbursements. She also passed legislation creating an Arkansas realtors special license plate and designating the Cynthiana grape as the official state grape. Pyle's legislation to allow concealed handguns in churches did not pass.

After her legislative service, Pyle was elected Crawford County treasurer in 2010 and served through 2020. She was a legislative committee board member for the Arkansas County Treasurer's Association.

# Lindsley Smith

HOUSE: 2005–2010
FROM: Fayetteville, Washington County
PARTY: Democratic
BIRTHPLACE: Birmingham, Alabama
DATES: September 8, 1963–
EDUCATION: Birmingham public schools;
Woodlawn High School (Birmingham),
1981; Jefferson State Junior College, AA,
1984; University of West Florida, BA in
public relations and advertising, 1986, and
MA in communication, 1989; University
of Arkansas, JD, 1998; Harvard University,
Kennedy School of Government Executive
Education Program, 2009
OCCUPATION: professor, attorney

*Photo courtesy of Arkansas Secretary of State.*

Lindsley Smith (born Lindsley Farrar Armstrong) is the daughter of Jewel
Dean Ott, a homemaker and office assistant, and Lewis Munn Armstrong, a
civil engineer. While living in Birmingham, she sang in the choir at Stockham
Memorial Methodist Church, was active in community theater, high school
band and choir, all-State Chorus, and played clarinet in the Birmingham
Civic Orchestra. During college, she participated in student government, the
speech and debate team, the Socratic Society, dance team, and theater.

After teaching communication at Ferris State University (1989–1990)
and Clemson University (1990–1994), she married Stephen Smith in 1994
and moved to Fayetteville. While in law school, she was editor of the
*Communication Law Review* and held internships with the prosecuting attorney, a circuit judge, the Arkansas attorney general, the Meiklejohn Civil
Liberties Institute, and the White House. After admission to the bar, she
was a law clerk for the Arkansas Court of Appeals and US Eighth Circuit
Court of Appeals before working at a law firm.

Returning to academia in 2002 as a research assistant professor at the
University of Arkansas, Smith taught legal and political communication. She
was a visiting scholar at Oxford and Cambridge Universities and taught in
summer programs at Yale and Stanford. She served on the board of directors
of the Meiklejohn Civil Liberties Institute and on the board of governors of

Manchester College, Oxford University. In the community, Smith was active in Friends of the Fayetteville Public Library, AFSCME Local 965, Rotary Club, Sierra Club, and American Association of University Women.

After serving as president of the Washington County Democratic Women, Smith ran unopposed for an open House seat in 2004. She won reelection in 2006 with 73 percent in the general election and was unopposed in 2008.

Representative Smith's first bill expanded coverage under the Workers Compensation Act. She passed legislation to enhance citizen participation in government, strengthen the Freedom of Information Act, require utility-net metering for renewable energy sources, establish the Heritage Trails System, reduce domestic violence, require insurance coverage of contraceptive prescriptions, provide for workers compensation neck-injury claims, and provide employee break time and reasonable locations for working mothers expressing breast milk. Although unsuccessful, she was proud of sponsoring resolutions to ratify the Equal Rights Amendment and a bill adding sexual orientation to the Arkansas Civil Rights Act.

Representative Smith was chair of the Joint Performance Review Committee. She was named Center for Policy Alternatives National Legislator of the Month in October 2005 and 2005 Arkansas Sierra Club Legislator of the Year. Other honors include the NWA Workers Justice Center Visionary Leader Award, ERArkansas People's Hero Award, AAUW Mary McDorman Burton Award, Arkansas Coalition Against Domestic Violence Legislative Award, and the Arkansas Business and Professional Women's Service to Women's Equality Honor. In 2013, she was selected as a Washington County Woman in History.

After her House service, Smith served six years as communication director for the city of Fayetteville and in 2015 became president of Oxbridge Research Associates, a research, consulting, and academic publishing firm.

# Sharon Dobbins

HOUSE: 2005–2008
FROM: North Little Rock, Pulaski County
PARTY: Democratic
BIRTHPLACE: Dermott, Arkansas
DATES: March 9, 1965–January 13, 2010
EDUCATION: McGehee public schools;
McGehee High School, 1983; University
of Arkansas; University of Arkansas for
Medical Sciences, BA in nursing, 1987;
Webster University, MA in health service
management, 1996; University of Central
Arkansas, MS in nursing, board certifica-
tion as a family nurse practitioner and adult
nurse practitioner, 2005
OCCUPATION: nurse

*Photo courtesy of Arkansas Secretary of State.*

Sharon Dobbins (born Sharon Elizabeth Beasley) was born and raised in McGehee, Arkansas, where her stepfather, Rev. Frank Martin, was the minister at McGehee Chapel Missionary Baptist Church. At McGehee High School, Dobbins was a cheerleader, basketball player, on the student council and debate team, an honor graduate, and on the homecoming court. She was the first to receive the Desha High School Alumni Scholarship. After attending the University of Arkansas and earning her nursing degree at UAMS, she worked on the staff of the Veterans Administration Hospital in Little Rock. In 1988, she married Dwayne Dobbins, and they lived in North Little Rock.

From a young age, Dobbins wanted to be a nurse. She was First Lieutenant in the United States Army Reserve in the Medical Division, receiving an honorable discharge in 1999. She had a career in medicine for over twenty years, including as a Veterans Administration Hospital advanced practice nurse.

As an active member of Bethel AME Church, Dobbins was on the board of trustees, a youth study teacher, and the health coordinator of the Arkansas Conference Women's Missionary Society. She was also an active member of the NAACP.

Dwayne Dobbins was elected to the Arkansas House in 2002 but resigned as a condition of a plea deal in 2005. Sharon Dobbins ran in a special election to fill the seat. She led two opponents in the preferential primary, won the Democratic nomination in a runoff, and won the general election with 65 percent over her Republican opponent. As a federal employee under the Hatch Act, Dobbins had to resign her nurse practitioner position with the Central Arkansas Veterans Healthcare System, and she took the oath of office on December 16, 2005. She ran unopposed for reelection in 2006.

During the 2007 session, Representative Dobbins's legislative issues included health care, protecting the underprivileged, prisons, children and families, and consumer protection. She was very proud of House Bill 1037 and her efforts to end the shackling of prison inmates when giving birth. It passed the House 83–19 despite objections from the Department of Corrections but died in the Senate State Agencies Committee. The policy was finally enacted in 2019. She cosponsored the Resolution for Arkansas's passage of the federal Equal Rights Amendment.

Representative Dobbins did not seek reelection in 2008. She died of pneumonia a year after the end of her term.

# Toni Bradford

HOUSE: 2007–2012
FROM: Pine Bluff, Jefferson County
PARTY: Democratic
BIRTHPLACE: Hot Springs, Arkansas
DATES: October 31, 1942–
EDUCATION: Rison High School, 1960; University of Arkansas at Monticello; University of Arkansas Pine Bluff, BS in elementary education, 1976, and certification in secondary education
OCCUPATION: teacher

*Photo courtesy of Arkansas Secretary of State.*

Toni Bradford (born Toni Carmen Howell) is the daughter of Maxine Fern Hare, and John Haley Howell, a World War II veteran who died when Bradford was five years old. Her mother later married Harvie Malcolm Attwood, and the family moved from Glenwood to Rison. In high school, Bradford was in Beta Club and student council, a cheerleader, and participated in Girls State, where she was elected to the mock legislature. She married Thomas Bradford in 1961, and they have two children.

Bradford taught ninth-grade civics and high school history and government in the Watson Chapel School District. After twenty-six years at Watson Chapel schools, she retired in 2002. She was vice president and president of the Jefferson County Retired Teachers Association, and a volunteer for the Pine Bluff Military and Veterans Museum and the Red Cross. She was a member of the Arkansas Retired Teachers Association, Jefferson County Democratic Women, and Delta Kappa Gamma. Bradford also operated T & T Bradford Consulting.

During the 2003 and 2005 legislative sessions, Bradford supervised pages in the House. In 2006, she ran for the Arkansas House of Representatives. Bradford won the Democratic primary with 65 percent of the vote and won the general election with 69 percent. She was unopposed for reelection in 2008 and 2010 and was term-limited from seeking reelection to the House in 2012.

Representative Bradford was Assistant Speaker Pro Tempore; vice chair of the Legislative Joint Auditing and the House City, County, and Local Affairs Committees; and she chaired Boys State. Bradford sat in the same House of Representative's chair that she sat in when she participated in high school Girls State. Bradford passed legislation providing clarity for depositing of wills with the court, expanding options for motor vehicle racing facilities, allowing city councils of second-class cities or incorporated towns to serve as a planning commission and board of adjustment, creating consistency in municipal election nominating petitions, broadening the ability for sales of air-conditioning parts, and amending the law for paying licensed speech-language pathologist bonuses. She also filed legislation on municipal public safety, post-conviction expense collection, Seabrook Christian Family Center tax exemptions, and public school safety.

In 2014, Bradford became president of the Arkansas Retired Teachers Association, the year the association celebrated its seventy-fifth anniversary.

# Joan Cash

HOUSE: 2007–2010
FROM: Jonesboro, Craighead County
PARTY: Democratic
BIRTHPLACE: West Point, Mississippi
DATES: January 31, 1941–
EDUCATION: West Point, Mississippi,
public schools; West Point High School,
1959; Memphis Business School, 1961
OCCUPATION: farm-equipment dealer

*Photo courtesy of Arkansas Secretary of State.*

Joan Cash (born Mary Joan Sugg) is the daughter of Mary Ethel Riley, a homemaker, and Harry Calvin Sugg, a landowner and farmer. She grew up in West Point, Mississippi, was active in her church, played tennis and piano, and was active in 4-H. In high school, she was a class officer and member of the yearbook staff, journalism club, and glee club. From 1959 to 1961, she attended Memphis Business School and thereafter worked for a car dealership and an insurance company.

She married Claud Vernon Cash in 1963, and they moved to his hometown of Trumann, Arkansas, in 1966. They had two children, and after thirty years moved to Jonesboro. They operated a farm-equipment dealership and leased farmland. Cash volunteered in her church as the preschool director and vacation Bible school director and was a grade school reading tutor. She served on the boards of the Trumann Museum, Flo and Phil Jones Hospice, Program of All-Inclusive Care for the Elderly (PACE), and St. Bernard's Women's Advisory Council.

Cash's husband served in the Arkansas House (1993–1996) and the Arkansas Senate (2001–2002), and Cash worked as a bill clerk in both chambers. Her husband, her political mentor, died in 2004. After encouragement from friends and former legislators, she ran for an open Arkansas House seat in 2006 and won the general election with 53 percent. She was unopposed for reelection in 2008.

Representative Cash was the first woman legislator elected from Jonesboro. She was vice chair of the House Judiciary Committee and cosponsored the Fair Debt Collection Practices Act and ratification of the Equal Rights Amendment. Cash also secured funding for $10 million in grants for shelters that house victims of domestic violence and their children, and she worked hard to defeat bills that would harm constituents in assisted living. She served on the Governor's Global Warming Commission and sponsored the Energy Efficiency Performance Standards Act of 2009 and other energy-conservation legislation, earning her a 92 percent score from the Citizens First Congress. Cash was defeated in her bid for reelection in the 2010 general election.

After her legislative service, Cash returned to her successful family agriculture business, managing the farmlands and continuing her volunteer service to the community, which includes service on the board of directors of the St. Bernards Foundation. Governor Mike Beebe also appointed her to the Arkansas Agricultural Board, and she served two terms (2011–2018).

# Donna Hutchinson

HOUSE: 2007–2012
FROM: Bella Vista, Benton County
PARTY: Republican
BIRTHPLACE: New Bern, North Carolina
DATES: August 23, 1949–
EDUCATION: Bob Jones University, BS in education, 1971; University of Arkansas, MA in communication, 2002
OCCUPATION: teacher, professional mediator

*Photo courtesy of Arkansas Secretary of State.*

Donna Hutchinson (born Donna Jean King) is the daughter of Thelma Ruth Embody, a teacher, and E. D. King, a career Navy man. The family moved twenty-five times, coast-to-coast and overseas, before Hutchinson graduated from high school, providing an educational environment with great cultural variety. Through her mother, Hutchinson is a voting member of the Blackfeet Tribe of Montana.

While still in college, Hutchinson married Arkansas native Young Timothy Hutchinson. She taught in junior and senior high schools in Missouri and Arkansas, where they moved in 1975. While raising three sons, she was co-owner of Christian-format radio station KBCV in Bentonville, and she was active in Benton County Republican politics as a volunteer and campaign manager for local candidates. Her husband was elected to the Arkansas

House, US Congress, and US Senate; her brother-in-law, Asa Hutchinson, served in Congress and as governor; and two of her sons, Tim and Jeremy, served in the Arkansas legislature.

Hutchinson worked as deputy chief of staff for Congressman John Boozman in Washington, then returned to Arkansas for graduate school. Her master's thesis was on Senator Hattie Caraway. In Bella Vista, her new hometown, Hutchinson volunteered at the public library and Crystal Bridges Museum. She also served on the Arkansas Motor Vehicle Commission and developed a professional mediation practice. Concerned that Northwest Arkansas was not receiving its fair share of highway funding, Hutchinson ran for an open House seat in 2006, winning the general election with 64 percent. She was unopposed for reelection in 2008 and was reelected in 2010 with 73 percent in the general election.

Representative Hutchinson sponsored legislation creating a sales-tax holiday for back-to-school supplies, prohibiting sex offenders from entering school campuses, and prohibiting video voyeurism. She also worked with Representative Johnnie Roebuck on legislation to address remedial college courses. In addition, Hutchinson was an effective advocate with state agencies, securing changes in the foster care program, having K2 classified as a controlled substance, and persuading the Arkansas Highway Commission to fund the I-49 Bella Vista By-Pass.

Following her legislative service, Hutchinson served on the Governor's Appointment Commission, the Arkansas Student Loan Authority Board, and the board of visitors for the Arkansas School for Mathematics, Sciences, and the Arts. She was an officer of the Benton County Republican Women, and she continued to address public issues in letters to local newspapers and speeches to civic groups.

# Tracy Pennartz

HOUSE: 2007–2012
FROM: Fort Smith, Sebastian County
PARTY: Democratic
BIRTHPLACE: Charleston, Arkansas
DATES: June 12, 1948–
EDUCATION: Sacred Heart Elementary
School; Charleston High School, 1966;
University of Central Arkansas, 1966–1967;
University of Arkansas, BA and MA in
communication, 1973 and 1974
OCCUPATION: associate director of
mental-health center, health-care and
management consultant

*Photo courtesy of Arkansas Secretary of State.*

Theresia Pennartz is the daughter of Lenus Nicholas Pennartz, a farmer, and Genevieve Ann Scheuer, who worked as a nurse, managed the farm, and raised five children after her husband's death in 1951. In high school, Pennartz was on the student council, academic team, and annual staff, and in the Beta Club, junior class play, and Library Club. After one year of college, she joined the United States Navy, serving 1967–1970 during the Vietnam era and returning to college to earn her degrees on the GI Bill.

For twenty-five years, Pennartz was associate director of the Western Arkansas Counseling and Guidance Center. She was active in her community as co-founder of Fort Smith Rape Crisis Service and chair of the Arkansas Valley Chapter of the National Foundation of March of Dimes. She served on the boards of the Fort Smith Girls' Shelter, Fort Smith Public Library, Fort Smith Volunteer Connection, YWCA of Fort Smith, Crawford-Sebastian Community Development Council, and the WestArk Retired and Senior Volunteer Program. Pennartz was a volunteer tutor for the America Reads Program and a member of the Fort Smith Literacy Council and the Fort Smith League of Women Voters. She was also a lector and Eucharistic minister at Saint Boniface Catholic Church.

Pennartz was the Democratic nominee for the Arkansas House in 1998 but lost the general election. In 2006, she ran again, uncontested in the Democratic primary and winning the general election with 62 percent. Pennartz won renomination with 74 percent in the Democratic primary and was unopposed in the 2008 general election, and she was unopposed for reelection in 2010.

Representative Pennartz was successful as the lead sponsor of nineteen legislative acts including investment tax credits for the rehabilitation and development of central business districts, creation of regional economic development partnerships, funding for the nursing student loans and nursing education programs, authorizing charitable bingo and raffles, protecting the health of inmates in correctional facilities, funding community mental health centers, funding for the UAFS library, and funding for the US Marshalls Museum. She was also a cosponsor of resolutions to ratify the Equal Rights Amendment in 2007 and 2009.

After being term-limited in the House, Representative Pennartz ran for the state senate, losing the general election to incumbent Bruce Holland. Following her legislative service, Pennartz continued as president of her health care and management consulting firm, Pennartz and Associates, and was an adjunct professor of Communication at the University of Arkansas at Fort Smith. In 2014, she was elected to the Fort Smith Board of Directors, serving 2015–2018.

# Johnnie Roebuck

HOUSE: 2007–2012
FROM: Arkadelphia, Clark County
PARTY: Democratic
BIRTHPLACE: Clarksdale, Mississippi
DATES: December 7, 1942–
EDUCATION: Bobo High School
(Clarksdale, Mississippi), 1960; Belhaven
College; Texas Woman's University, BS
in social work, 1964; Henderson State
University, MSE in guidance and counsel-
ing, 1974; University of Arkansas, EdS in
educational administration, 1988, and EdD
in educational administration, 1990
OCCUPATION: professor, higher education
administrator

*Photo courtesy of Arkansas Secretary of State.*

THE STATESWOMEN

Johnnie Roebuck (born Johnnie Patricia Jones) was raised on a Mississippi Delta cotton farm and is a first-generation college graduate. She was an Outstanding Young Women of America, and after receiving her social work degree, she was a Memphis Juvenile Court probation officer (1964–1966) and from 1967 to 1969 was a mental health center social worker. She focused on special education and was a public school teacher from 1969 until 1985, when she became the special education director for the Dawson Education Cooperative in Arkadelphia. In 1988, she married Dr. Tommy G. Roebuck.

Johnnie Roebuck was president of her own consulting firm, Managerial and Leadership Concepts. She was dean of the Henderson State University Graduate School (1995–1999) and taught educational leadership at HSU (1990–2007). Roebuck was co-founder and charter board member of the Henderson State University Alliance for Continuing Excellence in Teacher Education. She received many honors, including Henderson State University's Excellence in Service Award, Excellence in Scholarly Activity Award, and Excellence in Teaching Award.

Roebuck's extensive community service includes president of the Arkadelphia Education Association; Arkadelphia Chamber of Commerce Board; Arkansas School for Mathematics, Sciences, and the Arts Board of Trustees chair; founding president of the Southwest Federal Credit Union; Charter Board Member of Group Living Inc.; and Arkansas Professors of Educational Administration chair. She was a member of the Arkansas Business and Education Alliance and the Economic Development Corporation of Clark County.

In 2006, Roebuck was unopposed for the legislative seat her husband representative Tommy Roebuck (2001–2006) was vacating due to term limits, and unopposed for reelection in 2008 and 2010. She was vice chair of the House Education Committee, the first female House Majority Leader, the first female representing her district, and the first woman to run for Speaker of the Arkansas House.

Representative Roebuck let her constituents lead her filing of legislation, which included issues of education, litter reduction, officer death benefits, state agency subpoenas, motor vehicle impounding, missing child information, youth services, retirement funds, municipal procedures, infection data, the Arkansas Lottery, and jury selection. She passed legislation creating the Task Force on Higher Education Remediation, Retention, and Graduation Rates and served as its chair, and she cosponsored the Equal Rights Amendment Resolution. She was particularly proud of passing her teacher excellence and support system bill, creating the Health Facility Infection Disclosure Act of 2007, and the Arkansas Professional Licensure Standards Board bill.

Roebuck represented the House in the National Conference of State Legislators Women's Legislative Network and gave several speeches about women in government and running for office. She received many honors, including outstanding legislator awards from the Sierra Club, Arkansas Police Benevolent Association, Arkansas Public Policy Foundation, Arkansas Dental Association, Arkansas Firefighters Association, Arkansas Counseling Association, Arkansas Voices for Children Left Behind, and Arkansas Municipal League.

After legislative service, Dr. Roebuck continued her consulting, community service, and volunteering in Democratic politics. In 2014, the Dr. Johnnie Roebuck Educational Leadership Scholarship was established at Henderson State University. She was elected Arkansas National Committeewoman to the Democratic National Committee in 2020.

# Charolette Wagner

HOUSE: 2007–2012
FROM: Manila, Mississippi County
PARTY: Democratic
BIRTHPLACE: Monette, Arkansas
DATES: August 12, 1946–
EDUCATION: Leachville High School, 1963; Arkansas State University, BSE in English with a speech minor, 1967; University of Kentucky, MA in English, 1975; ASU, Arkansas Administrative Certification; ASU, Gifted and Talented Certification and credits toward a specialist degree in community college; University of Arkansas School of Law
OCCUPATION: retired teacher and public school superintendent

*Photo courtesy of Arkansas Secretary of State.*

Charolette Wagner (born Charolette Jo Green) is the daughter of Flossie Ella Evans and Earl Gordon Green of Monette, Arkansas. At Leachville High School, she was a student council officer and cheerleader captain and was crowned Miss Leachville. After graduation from college, Wagner married

Wayne Wagner, a high school and community college coach from Manila, who later became an attorney, municipal judge, state representative (1987–1998), and mayor of Manila. They had two sons.

Charolette Wagner's extensive work experience included teaching English at Arkansas State University, Southern Baptist College, Mississippi County Community College, and the University of Kentucky. However, the focus of her career was on public education at the Manila School District, where in addition to having taught English, she was coordinator of grants, technology, and gifted and talented education and eventually became superintendent.

More than thirty community, professional, and philanthropical groups benefitted from Wagner's membership and volunteerism. Included in these organizations are the Manila Business and Professional Women, Blytheville and Osceloa Chambers of Commerce, and the Arkansas Education Association. She was a breakfast advocate for the Arkansas Hunger Alliance and served on the boards of the Northeast Arkansas Chapter of the Red Cross, the Cotton Boll Vocational Tech School, the Mississippi County Fine Arts Council, the Arkansas Association of Federal Coordinators, and the Osceloa Out of School Youth. Wagner was also an honorary director of the Arkansas Northeastern College Foundation Board.

In 2006, Wagner was elected state representative, winning the general election with 57 percent of the vote, and she was unopposed for reelection in 2008 and 2010. Representative Wagner's legislation included issues of education, public school employee health insurance benefits, elections, police and fire retirement systems, rural medical practice, health care, economic development, agricultural, and public safety. She cosponsored ratification of the Equal Rights Amendment and was also committed to issues of poverty and hunger relief. In her third session, she chaired the City, County, and Local Affairs Committee. When Wagner was term-limited in 2012, her son, Tyler Wes Wagner, was elected to the legislative seat.

Charolette Wagner has been recognized in Outstanding Young Women of America, Who's Who in Executives and Professionals, Who's Who in the South and Southwest, Who's Who in Politics, Who's Who of Professional Women, and Who's Who in the World, and she received the Albert Nelson Marquis Lifetime Achievement Award.

# Kathy Webb

HOUSE: 2007–2012
FROM: Little Rock, Pulaski County
PARTY: Democratic
BIRTHPLACE: Blytheville, Arkansas
DATES: October 21, 1949–
EDUCATION: Highland Park Presbyterian
Day School (Dallas); Pulaski Heights
Elementary School; Forest Heights Junior
High; Hall High School, 1967; Randolph-
Macon College, BA in political science,
1971; University of Central Arkansas;
Harvard University, Kennedy School of
Government Executive Education Program
OCCUPATION: small-business owner,
nonprofit director

*Photo courtesy of Arkansas Secretary of State.*

Kathy Lynette Webb was born to Atha Mae Williams, a teacher, and Maurice Clive Webb, a Methodist minister and professor. She supported John Kennedy in grade school and later volunteered for Herb Rule, Bobby Kennedy, and George McGovern. In college, Webb was junior class president, on the college council, a member of the basketball and tennis teams, and an anti-war activist. After college, Webb was president of the Pulaski County National Organization for Women (NOW), advocating ratification of the Equal Rights Amendment. She later served on the NOW National Board and was national secretary, 1982–1987.

In Virginia, Webb managed a Domino's and was its first woman named national Manager of the Year. She moved to Chicago in 1994 as regional vice president of Bruegger's Bagel Bakeries and owned the award-winning Hoxie's barbeque. *Today's Chicago Woman* named her in "100 Women Making a Difference." Moving to Memphis in 2000, Webb co-owned Lilly's Dim Sum Then Some restaurant and later opened a Lilly's in Little Rock.

Webb served on the boards of the First United Methodist Church, Arkansas Food Bank Network, Arkansas Hospitality Association, and Planned Parenthood. She was president of the Stonewall Democratic Club and a member of the Pulaski County Democratic Committee and Mayor's Clean Indoor Air Task Force. Webb received the Central Arkansas Library

Youth Services Volunteer of the Year, *Little Rock Monthly*'s "Ten Women We Love," Arkansas Hospitality Association Humanitarian of the Year, and Arkansas Rice Depot Volunteer of the Year.

In 2006, Webb ran for the Arkansas House, winning the Democratic primary with 57 percent against three opponents to win the seat. She was unopposed in 2008 and 2010. Representative Webb was the first openly gay member of the Arkansas General Assembly and first woman House co-chair of the Joint Budget Committee. She cosponsored ratification of the Equal Rights Amendment and worked for legislation strengthening education, the environment, health care, renewable energy and energy conservation, poverty, social justice, economic development, and anti-bullying efforts. Webb sponsored legislation establishing the governor's Commission on Global Warming, and served as its co-chair, and led a study on the Economic Status of Women.

Representative Webb received awards from the Arkansas Kids Count Coalition, Arkansas AIDS Foundation, Sierra Club, Just Communities of Arkansas, and received the Brownie Ledbetter Civic Engagement Award. After legislative service, she became executive director of the Arkansas Hunger Relief Alliance. She served on the Little Rock Airport Commission and was elected to the Little Rock City Board in 2015. In 2020, *Arkansas Money & Politics* named Webb an Arkansas Top Influencer.

# Ann Clemmer

HOUSE: 2009–2014
FROM: Salem, Saline County
PARTY: Republican
BIRTHPLACE: Osceola, Arkansas
DATES: August 10, 1958–
EDUCATION: Keiser Elementary School; American School/International School of Manila, Philippines; Rivercrest High School, 1976; Arkansas State University, BA and MA in political science, 1979 and 1980, and additional graduate work in history, 1983
OCCUPATION: college professor

*Photo courtesy of Arkansas Secretary of State.*

Ann Clemmer (born Carol Ann Veasman) is the daughter of Martha Lee Robinson, a teacher, and Joseph Christian Veasman, a farmer and USAID agriculture advisor. In high school, she was president of the National Honor Society, a cheerleader, a member of the Library Club and Future Homemakers, on the annual staff, acted in musical theatre, and was Miss Rivercrest High School.

Although she was a commuter student who married shortly after beginning college, Clemmer was active in the Model United Nations, president of Pi Sigma Alpha, a member of Pi Gamma Mu, and the outstanding political science graduate. She was also the campus and state chair of College Republicans and on the executive committee of the Republican Party of Arkansas.

Clemmer taught history and political science at Mississippi County Community College (ANU) from 1982 to 1992. While raising three daughters, she was also chair of the Mississippi County Republican Committee, an election commissioner, and a delegate to the Republican National Convention. She would later be a delegate for three more conventions.

In 1992, Clemmer joined the political science faculty at the University of Arkansas at Little Rock, and in 1995 she married Jamie Clemmer. She was president of the Arkansas Political Science Association, a panelist on AETN's "Arkansas Week," a guest on KLRE's "Arkansas Viewpoint," and an election night analyst for local television stations.

Ann Clemmer was elected to the Arkansas House, winning the 2008 general election with 63 percent. She was unopposed for reelection in 2010 and 2012. Term-limited in 2014, Clemmer was an unsuccessful candidate in the 2014 Republican primary for Congress.

Representative Clemmer was vice chair of the Education Committee and a member of the Rules Committee, the Joint Audit Committee, and the Legislative Council. She was also appointed Speaker Pro Tempore in 2013–2014. Clemmer sponsored laws to include home-schooled students for the Arkansas Governor's Scholars Program, to authorize electronic transcripts, and to require the Department of Education and the Department of Higher Education to study and report on remediation issues. She also passed legislation requiring mental health services providers to warn law enforcement of a credible threat by a patient, requiring HIV testing for defendants charged with sex offenses, disposition of Medicaid-reimbursement funds, adoption procedures, and extending time for employers to respond to unemployment-benefits applications. Clemmer said she was proud to lead the House effort to override the governor's veto of the twelve-week abortion ban.

In January 2015, Clemmer left the UALR faculty to take a position at the Arkansas Department of Higher Education, where she became senior associate director for Government Relations. She was appointed by Governor Asa Hutchinson as interim director of ADHE in 2016, to the Women's Suffrage Centennial Commemoration Committee (2018–2020), and to the Arkansas Educational Television Commission in 2020.

# Jody Dickinson

HOUSE: 2009–2014
FROM: Newport, Jackson County
PARTY: Democratic
BIRTHPLACE: Lincoln County, Arkansas
DATES: January 28, 1941–
EDUCATION: Glendale Elementary; Glendale High School; University of Arkansas at Monticello, BSE
OCCUPATION: teacher

*Photo courtesy of Arkansas Secretary of State.*

Jody Dickinson (born Reva Jo Edwards) was born in Lincoln County in 1941 to Betty Ruth Via, a homemaker for five children, and Victor Banks Edwards, who worked several jobs, including school custodian and bus driver. She grew up in the Glendale, Arkansas, which had one general store, and she attended a one-building school that served grades one through twelve. "As a youth I worked to help provide for my family through difficult times. I understood the value of an education and committed myself to this goal. After completing high school, I continued my work experience on a chicken farm, shirt factory, and college cafeteria to obtain a degree in education."

In 1962, she married Thomas O. Dickinson Jr. from Newport, and they had three children. Tommy served three terms as a state representative (2003–2008), and his brother-in-law G. W. "Buddy" Turner also served as a representative (1961–1992).

Jody Dickinson taught elementary school for thirty-four years, and she participated in school- and church-related activities. She was a member of the Newport Business and Professional Women, Newport Service League, National Rifle Association, Retired Teachers Association, Jackson County

Humane Society, Jackson County Farm Bureau, and VFW Ladies Auxiliary. She worked as a receptionist for the House of Representatives during the three sessions in which her husband served.

In 2008, Dickinson ran for the House seat that opened when her husband was term-limited. She campaigned on support of education, rural schools, and economic development. She led three opponents in the Democratic preferential primary with 32 percent and won the runoff by 117 votes. She was unopposed in the general election and was unopposed for reelection in 2010 and 2012.

During her first term, Dickinson passed all the bills and resolutions of which she was primary sponsor. By her third term, she chaired the House Committee on Aging and Legislative Affairs. Her main legislation involved veterans, children, and funding for Arkansas State University in Newport.

Dickinson served until term-limited from office in 2014. She and Tommy moved to Heber Springs and were married for fifty-four years, until his death in 2016.

## Jane English

HOUSE: 2009–2012, SENATE: 2013–present
FROM: North Little Rock, Pulaski County
PARTY: Republican
BIRTHPLACE: Lincoln, Nebraska
DATES: November 9, 1940–
EDUCATION: James Blair High School (Williamsburg, VA), 1958; Arkansas Tech University, BS in economics and finance, 1981
OCCUPATION: economic and workforce development officer

*Photo courtesy of Arkansas Secretary of State.*

Jane English (born Elizabeth Jane Marsden) is the daughter of Mary Jane Righter, homemaker and Red Cross volunteer, and Colonel Henry Howard Marsden Jr., a career Army officer. She married Arkansas native Don Carol English, a career Army officer, in 1960, and they had two children.

English held a number of economic development positions in Arkansas. She was senior project manager with the Arkansas Department of Economic Development (1984–1997), executive director of Fort Chaffee Public Trust

(1997–1998), executive director of the Arkansas Manufacturers Association (1998–2001), executive director of the Arkansas Workforce Investment Board (2001–2004), and workforce advisor to Lieutenant Governor Winthrop Paul Rockefeller (2005).

Governor Mike Huckabee appointed English to the Arkansas Psychology Board. She was also a member of North Pulaski Republican Women, the Community Councils of Little Rock Air Force Base and Camp Robinson/Camp Pike, the Auxiliaries of the Disabled American Veterans and Veterans of Foreign Wars, and the Runyan Acres Volunteer Fire Department Auxiliary.

In 2008, English ran for an open House seat and won the general election with 55 percent. She was unopposed for reelection in 2010. Representative English passed legislation regarding education of military children and leaves of absence for military personnel called to active duty. Other successful bills addressed tax breaks for industrial facilities, assessments for fire-protection districts, property-tax collections, and improvement districts.

After two terms in the House, English won a state senate race, defeating Representative Barry Hyde with 50.4 percent in the 2012 general election. She was renominated with 51 percent over Representative Donnie Campbell in the Republican primary and reelected with 58 percent in the 2016 general election. Running for a third Senate term, English was reelected with 54 percent in the 2020 general election.

Senator English was chair of the Senate Education and the Joint Performance Review Committees, assistant president pro tempore, and a member of the Rules Committee, Joint Budget Committee, and the Legislative Council. She is also a member of the American Legislative Exchange Council (ALEC). English continued to sponsor legislation benefitting military personnel and veterans. Her other legislation includes issues of education, workforce development, tax credits for businesses, election procedures and campaign finance, private school vouchers, requiring water bottle stations in schools, computer science education, allowing alcoholic beverage delivery, addressing child maltreatment, public entity data and information systems security, land donation for school development; and mandating that schools play the national anthem, pledge of allegiance to the flag, and have a moment of silence in classes and at sporting events. As vice chair of the Senate State Agencies Committee, she voted against ratification of the Equal Rights Amendment in 2013.

Senator English received the 2014 Garland Hankins Award for her support of adult education, the 2015 Friend of the Profession Award from the Arkansas Society for Human Resource Management, an award from the Sherwood Police Department, and the Family Council Statesman Award.

# Debra Hobbs

HOUSE: 2009–2014
FROM: Rogers, Benton County
PARTY: Republican
BIRTHPLACE: Horsching, Austria
DATES: July 8, 1955–
EDUCATION: Clarksville Elementary and
Junior High; MacArthur High School
(Aldine, TX), 1973; Southern Nazarene
University; University of Houston; College
of the Ozarks, BS in composite science,
1977; Southwest Missouri State University;
University of Arkansas, MS in counseling
education, 1987
OCCUPATION: teacher, counselor,
business owner

*Photo courtesy of Arkansas Secretary of State.*

Debra Hobbs (born Debra May Soard) is the daughter of Lois P. Wood, a homemaker and chicken plant worker, and John Robert Soard, a brick plant worker. Born abroad while her father was stationed in Germany with the Army, she grew up on a farm on Spadra Creek in Johnson County. Hobbs was an honor graduate, both in high school and in college. While in college, she worked at the Singer Sewing Machine plant and Walmart. She married Ray Hobbs in 1977, and they have two children.

Hobbs worked a number of jobs, including insurance clerk in a medical clinic, bank teller, chemist, and Mary Kay Cosmetics salesperson. Following her husband's career moves with Walmart, she taught school in Claremore, Oklahoma, and Blue Springs, Missouri. When they moved to Rogers in 1985, she was the counselor at Decatur Elementary School. From 2003 to 2007, she was executive director of Students of Arkansas Voter Education.

In the community, Hobbs served on the boards of the Single Parent Scholarship Fund of Benton County, Benton County Boys and Girls Club Foundation, Benton County Sunshine School, North Arkansas District Church of the Nazarene, and Pathway to Freedom, a prison rehabilitation ministry. She was also on the board of Benton County Republican Women and was elected to the Benton County Quorum Court in 2007. Running for an open House seat in 2008, Hobbs was unopposed, and she was reelected without opposition in 2010 and 2012.

Representative Hobbs was co-chair of the Arkansas Legislative Hunger Caucus and a member of the Education, State Agencies, and Joint Performance Review Committees. She was also elected to the Legislative Council and appointed House Republican whip. Her successful legislation included teacher licensing, early childhood education, protection of nursing home residents from maltreatment, adoption, and requiring a moment of silence in public schools. She received the Conduit of Commerce Calvin Coolidge Award for her voting record to decrease the size and scope of government.

In 2013, Hobbs announced as a candidate for governor, but she then became a candidate for lieutenant governor, finishing third of three candidates for the Republican nomination. She was also unsuccessful in a 2016 race for nomination to the Arkansas House, losing to incumbent representative Rebecca Petty. She was elected to the NorthWest Arkansas Community College Board of Trustees in 2017, and she was elected to the Benton County Quorum Court in 2018, serving one term.

# Karen Hopper

HOUSE: 2009–2014
FROM: Lakeview, Baxter County
PARTY: Republican
BIRTHPLACE: Princeton, Kentucky
DATES: September 27, 1960–
EDUCATION: West Side Elementary; Caldwell County High School (Princeton, KY), 1978; Murray State University, BS in journalism and advertising, 1982
OCCUPATION: reporter, congressional staff, university administrator

*Photo courtesy of Arkansas Secretary of State.*

Karen Hopper (born Karen Sue Hopper) is the daughter of Mary Evelyn Glass, a homemaker, and John William Hopper, an Illinois Central Railroad yard clerk. Hopper was in Beta Club and editor of her high school newspaper. While in college, she was a spokesperson for the Murray Center for

Mentally Handicapped Adults and was a staff writer for *Main Street Journal* and *Louisville Courier-Journal*. After graduation from college, she worked for a magazine in Springfield, Missouri, and a radio station in Centerville, Iowa. She married John Frederick Waddell in 1984, and they moved to Arkansas in 1987.

Hopper was a reporter for the *North Arkansas View*, an award-winning reporter for KTLO Radio, and news director for KPFM radio in Mountain Home. From 1993 to 1998, she was senior district representative at the Harrison District Office of US Congressmen Tim and Asa Hutchinson, working on legislative issues and individual constituency matters. Hopper was the public relations coordinator for Baxter Regional Medical Center for two years then began a sixteen-year career at Arkansas State University-Mountain Home, retiring as associate vice chancellor in 2016.

Active in the community, Hopper was president of the Cameo Club (GFWC), vice president of Serenity Domestic Violence Shelter, secretary of Twin River Community Living Board, and a member of the Mountain Home Chamber of Commerce Board of Directors. She was also a member of the Mountain Home Rotary Club, the Baxter County Single Parent Scholarship Committee, and the National Rifle Association. Hopper received the Opal Award for volunteer community service from the Mountain Home Chamber of Commerce.

In 2008, Hopper ran for an open House seat, defeating former senator Gary Hunter with 53 percent in the Republican primary and winning the general election with 61 percent of the vote against the Democratic and Independent candidates. She was unopposed for reelection in 2010 and 2012.

Representative Hopper passed legislation eliminating the requirement that National Guard members pay for a substitute employee when they are on military leave, prohibiting emergency lights and sirens on private vehicles, extending the Freedom of Information Act exemption for water-system security and amending the sex-offender-assessment administrative-appeal procedures. She chaired the House Higher Education Subcommittee and was vice chair of the Arkansas Legislative Council Higher Education Subcommittee. As a member of the Joint Audit Committee, Hopper requested the state audit of the Northwest Arkansas Economic Development District, finding financial mismanagement of General Improvement Funds related to the kickback convictions of several legislators.

Hopper was term-limited from reelection to the House in 2014. In 2017, she returned to radio station KTLO in Mountain Home as an investigative reporter.

# Andrea Lea

HOUSE: 2009–2014
FROM: Russellville, Pope County
PARTY: Republican
BIRTHPLACE: Kittery, Maine
DATES: January 8, 1957–
EDUCATION: Newbury Park High
School (California), 1975; Arkansas Tech
University, BS in emergency administration
and management, 2004
OCCUPATION: justice of the peace, city
alderwoman

*Photo courtesy of Arkansas Secretary of State.*

Andrea Lea (born Andrea Christina Dean) is the daughter of Helen Christina Ring, a homemaker, and Andrew Carnegie Dean, a career Air Force master sergeant, and they moved frequently with his assignments as she was growing up. Lea married Phillip Brent Lea in 1978, and, after his service in the US Navy, they moved from California to Russellville for his work at Entergy's Nuclear One in 1982. They have three children, all graduates of Arkansas Tech University. Lea was the clerk of session at Central Presbyterian Church of Russellville.

Lea ran as a Republican for justice of the peace on the Pope County Quorum Court in 1996, defeating the Democratic incumbent with 51 percent. After three terms on the quorum court, she was elected to the Russellville City Council, serving 2003–2008. Lea ran for an open seat in the Arkansas House of Representatives in 2008, winning the general election with 53 percent of the vote. She was unopposed for reelection in 2010 and 2012.

Representative Lea was chair of the Committee on State Agencies and Governmental Affairs, was a member of the Revenue and Taxation and Rules committees, and was elected to the Legislative Council. She was state co-chair of the American Legislative Exchange Council (ALEC) and was a member of the House Shale Caucus to fight regulations on fracking. Lea sponsored several acts that clarified procedures for local government and the State Land Commissioner. She voted against Governor Mike Beebe's statewide trauma system and the state's private option participation in the federal Affordable Care Act, and she voted to override his vetoes of anti-abortion and voter identification bills that she cosponsored. In 2011, Lea sponsored Act 1212 that made it easier for women to obtain a driver's license or state identification card if their names were changed through divorce or remarriage.

As a candidate for state auditor in 2014, Representative Lea described her voting record in the House as "absolutely against Obamacare" and "100 percent pro-life," and boasted that she had been endorsed by the National Rifle Association and Conservative Arkansas. She won the Republican primary with 68 percent and was elected state auditor with 57 percent in the 2014 general election, and she was reelected in 2018. Lea was also a Romney delegate in 2012 and a Rubio delegate in 2016 at the Republican National Conventions.

# Stephanie Malone

HOUSE: 2009–2014
FROM: Fort Smith, Sebastian County
PARTY: Republican
BIRTHPLACE: Rogers, Arkansas
DATES: March 23, 1978–
EDUCATION: Westside Elementary; Rogers High School, 1996; University of Arkansas, BA in journalism, 2000
OCCUPATION: advertising and marketing director

*Photo courtesy of Arkansas Secretary of State.*

Stephanie Malone grew up in Rogers in a politically active family. Her uncle, Fay W. Boozman III, was a state senator and Arkansas Department of Health Director. Another uncle, John Boozman, served as a US representative and US senator.

Malone was communication director for the Fort Smith Chamber of Commerce for six years, was a media buyer at Advertising Plus, and marketing director for the Fort Chaffee Redevelopment Authority. She was active in the community as an officer of the Junior League and a board member of Abilities Unlimited of Fort Smith and Just Communities Arkansas. She was a member of the Fort Smith Chamber's Young Emerging Leaders and was named to the 2009 Arkansas Business 40 Under 40.

An employer who was active in the Republican Party encouraged Malone to run for the Arkansas House of Representatives. She agreed and ran successful primary and general election campaigns for the seat in 2008. She won reelection in 2010 in the Republican primary and won a general election challenge in 2012.

At age thirty, Malone became the second-youngest woman elected to the legislature, and she was vice chair of the Aging and Legislative Affairs Committee during her first term. Upon taking a seat at a legislative committee table early in the session, a legislative staff member approached a representative sitting next to Malone, informing the legislator that "her daughter" was not allowed to sit at the committee table. Malone smiled and informed the staff member that she was, in fact, a state representative.

Malone successfully sponsored legislation on a variety of issues, including victim compensation, domestic violence, assisting nonprofits, and access to health care. In her third term, Malone was appointed Assistant Speaker Pro Tempore of the House and chaired the House Select Committee on Rules. She carried the Arkansas National Guard's legislative package that session and passed them all. Malone was pleased with her ability to make a difference in her district, "reach across the aisle" in her service, and bring unusual groups together.

After her legislative service, Malone briefly worked at the Arkansas Educational Television Network, then served as director of Policy and Advocacy for Community Health Centers of Arkansas, before becoming the director of Governmental Affairs at Arkansas Advocates for Children and Families. In 2020, Malone became the CEO of the Arkansas Trial Lawyers Association.

# Barbara Nix

HOUSE: 2009–2010
FROM: Benton, Saline County
PARTY: Democratic
BIRTHPLACE: Leavenworth, Kansas
DATES: June 2, 1949–
EDUCATION: Westside Elementary; Benton High School, 1967; University of Central Arkansas, BSE, 1971
OCCUPATION: teacher

*Photo courtesy of Arkansas Secretary of State.*

Barbara Nix (born Barbara Ann Farley) was born in Leavenworth, Kansas, where her mother, Dexter Ruth Bolland was a housewife, and father, Embra Herbert Farley, was a guard in the Army prison at Fort Leavenworth. The family moved to Benton when Nix was three years old, after her father took a position in the chemical division at the Alcoa aluminum plant. Nix grew up in Benton and became politically active working on campaigns, including Joe Purcell's lieutenant governor campaigns. She graduated from Benton High School in 1967 and married Richard Jacuzzi in 1968. Upon graduation from the University of Central Arkansas, she began a thirty-eight-year teaching career in the Benton public schools.

In 1982, Nix married former University of Arkansas Football notable Bobby Nix, and they were married until his death in 2003. She served on the boards of the Athletic Memorial Museum, Arkansas Education Association, Benton Chamber of Commerce, and Habitat for Humanity. Nix was president of the Benton Education Association and a member of the Kiwanis. She taught Sunday school for thirty-one years at the First United Methodist Church. In 2008, Nix was approached by members of Benton's fire department, law enforcement, and public school educators about serving in the Arkansas House of Representatives. Nix ran unopposed in the Democratic primary and beat Republican David McCoy in the general election.

Representative Nix was particularly proud to get a good bill passed on safe transportation of railroad employees. She sponsored a longer look-back period for DWI repeat offenders that made it through the House but not the Senate. She cosponsored many bills and felt accomplished with bills such as the Animal Cruelty Act, graduated license for teens, no-texting bill, and the tobacco tax for the trauma center and health care. With her decades of education experience, Nix helped pass legislation benefitting public education. She and Representative Johnnie Roebuck sponsored legislation benefitting state employees' families by increasing death benefits. For her service, Nix was honored by the Chamber of Commerce and Mothers Against Drunk Driving.

Nix ran for reelection in 2010 but was defeated by Republican opponent Kim Hammer in the general election. Nix ran again for the House seat in 2012 but was defeated by the incumbent in the general election. In 2013, Nix was named a lifetime member of Saline Crossing Inc. and worked to save the 1891 Old River Bridge on the Old Military Road near Benton.

# Tiffany Rogers

HOUSE: 2009–2012
FROM: Stuttgart, Arkansas County
PARTY: Democratic
BIRTHPLACE: Stuttgart, Arkansas
DATES: August 14, 1963–
EDUCATION: St. John's Lutheran School;
Stuttgart High School, 1981; Arkansas State
University, AS in business administration,
1983; University of Arkansas, BSE, 2001,
and MEd, 2003
OCCUPATION: director, continuing-
education development officer

*Photo courtesy of Arkansas Secretary of State.*

Tiffany Rogers (born Tiffany Michelle Blackwell) is the daughter of Loretta Inman, office manager for Layne-Arkansas Company, and Billy Eugene Blackwell, a manager for Riceland Foods. Rogers's second cousin, Wanda Northcutt Hartz, served in the legislature fourteen years and was her political mentor, friend, and neighbor. Rogers was a legal secretary and probation officer for fifteen years. In 1991, she married Circuit Judge Russell Rogers.

Tiffany Rogers was director of Development, Continuing Education, and Workforce Training at Phillips Community College of the University of Arkansas in Stuttgart, and she was a Phillips Community College employee of the year. She has been actively involved in several organizations, including president of the Stuttgart Chamber of Commerce and president of the Stuttgart Kiwanis Club. Rogers was co-chair of the Grand Prairie Health and Wellness Expo, president of the Stuttgart Ladies Golf Association, chair of the Arkansas County Partners in Health, and board member of the Museum of the Arkansas Grand Prairie.

In 2008, Rogers ran for the Arkansas House of Representatives, focusing on education and economic development-related issues, specifically agriculture. She won the Democratic primary and defeated a write-in candidate in the general election in 2008. In 2010, she was unopposed in the Democratic primary and defeated a write-in candidate with 99 percent. When Rogers arrived at the legislature, her freshmen colleagues elected her chair of the Freshman Caucus for the 2009–2010 term. She was proud of her 2009 legislation making spring break dates uniform throughout all Arkansas public schools and 2011 legislation requiring financial institutions to provide signed notice before foreclosure.

While in the legislature, Rogers was on the UAMS Southeast Advisory Board and was a member of Women in Government and the Southern Legislative Council. The Arkansas Municipal League honored Rogers with the Distinguished Legislator Award after her first session in 2009. In 2010, Rogers graduated from the Southern Legislative Conference Center for Advancement of Leadership Skills. In 2011 she was honored with the Arkansas Judicial Council First Branch Award, and in 2012 she received the Phenomenal Woman of Stuttgart Award.

Representative Rogers ran for state senate in 2012 but lost to the incumbent in the general election. After her legislative service, Rogers moved to Hot Springs in 2017 and became executive director of Henderson State University's Hot Springs Academic Initiatives. She served on the boards of Bellpoint Independent Living, Women's Foundation of Arkansas, Garland County Single Parent Scholarship Foundation, Imagination Library of the Ouachitas, and the Greater Hot Springs Chamber of Commerce.

# Mary Lou Slinkard

HOUSE: 2009–2014
FROM: Gravette, Benton County
PARTY: Republican
BIRTHPLACE: Gravette, Arkansas
DATES: August 2, 1943–
EDUCATION: Gravette public schools;
Gravette High School, 1961
OCCUPATION: County Clerk

*Photo courtesy of Arkansas Secretary of State.*

Mary Lou Slinkard (born Mary Lou Duncan) was born in Gravette to Viola Marie Pitts, a homemaker, and William Newton Duncan, a farmer and laborer. She grew up in Gravette, was the eighth-grade spelling bee champion, and graduated from Gravette High School, where she was vice president of the student council and second vice president of Future Homemakers of

America. She married shortly after graduating from high school and had two sons, Jason and Russell Slinkard.

From 1962 to 1980, Mary Lou Slinkard worked as a legal secretary and law office manager for Charles Gocio in Bentonville, assisting in the preparation of legal documents, title searches, wills and trusts, contracts, and real estate closings, and she was a member of the Legal Secretaries Association. In 1980, Joe Yates recruited her to run as a Republican for Benton County clerk, and she defeated the Democratic incumbent, going on to serve fourteen two-year terms (1981–2008). She was treasurer of the Bentonville Kiwanis, and a member of Soroptimists, the Arkansas Association of County Clerks, and the International Association of Clerks, Recorders, Election Officials and Treasurers. Slinkard was appointed to the Federal Election Assistance Commission and the Arkansas State Board of Elections (1999–2008).

In 2008, Slinkard ran for the Arkansas House of Representatives, won the Republican primary with 55 percent, and was unopposed in the general election. She was unopposed for reelection in 2010, and in 2012 won the Republican primary with 68 percent of the vote and faced no general election opponent.

Representative Slinkard used her long experience in local government in her state service, focusing particularly on county government and elections. She filed legislation on issues of city and county government, elections, taxes, child support, and towing. She was House chair of the Advanced Communications and Information Technology Committee, vice chair of State Agencies and Governmental Affairs Committee, and a member of the Judiciary and Legislative Joint Auditing Committees, as well as the Arkansas Lottery Commission Legislative Oversight Committee.

In 2015, Slinkard was an unsuccessful candidate for appointment as Benton County Assessor, but Governor Asa Hutchinson appointed her to fill an unexpired term as a Benton County justice of the peace (2015–2016).

# Linda Tyler

HOUSE: 2009–2012
FROM: Conway, Faulkner County
PARTY: Democratic
BIRTHPLACE: Dallas, Texas
DATES: July 1, 1948–
EDUCATION: Dallas public schools; Lead Hill High School, 1965; University of Central Arkansas, BS in management, summa cum laude, 1980, and MS in community and economic development, 2014; University of Pennsylvania Wharton School of Business Executive Development Program; Birkman International Certified Birkman Consultant
OCCUPATION: human resources director

*Photo courtesy of Arkansas Secretary of State.*

Linda Tyler (born Linda Sue Holloway) was born in Dallas, Texas, to Mary Gladys Faris and Ralph Samuel Holloway. In 1961, she and her family moved to Lead Hill, Arkansas, where she worked in the family's Big D Cafe, gas station, and marine repair shop on Bull Shoals Lake. Her mother was a Boone County justice of the peace. In 1966, Tyler married Hugh Tyler, and they had two children. They lived in Conway, where Tyler graduated summa cum laude from the University of Central Arkansas in management. Her career included management positions with Carrier Air Conditioning, United Broadcasting, and Acxiom.

Tyler's community service was extensive, including chair of the boards of Conway Regional Health System, Conway Regional Foundation, University of Central Arkansas Foundation, Conway United Methodist Church, and board president of the National Kidney Foundation. She was co-chair of the NAACP Project One Voice, president of the Society for Human Resource Management, and served on the boards of the National Heart Association, American Association of Kidney Patients, Falkner County Library, and University of Arkansas School of Business. She was named a Rotary Paul Harris Fellow.

In 2008, Tyler ran for the Arkansas House of Representatives, winning the Democratic primary by twenty-eight votes and the general election with

56 percent. She was reelected in 2010 with 52 percent in the general election. During her second term, she was elected House Democratic leader and chaired the Public Health, Welfare, and Labor Committee. Representative Tyler's legislative work included protection-order violators wearing ankle monitors, establishment and funding of the Arkansas trauma system, local government-funded public transportation, prescription-drug monitoring, water-system fluoridation, Improvement District tax credits, and establishing the Office of Health Information Technology. She was state director for Women in Government. She was the first female majority leader of the Arkansas House of Representatives.

The Arkansas Dental Association honored Tyler for her support. She received the Faulkner County Leadership Institute Award, Arkansas Municipal League Distinguished Legislator Award, Associated General Contractors of America Chapter Award, Disabled American Veterans Chapter Citation of Merit, and Arkansas Kidney Disease Commission Chain of Life Award.

In 2012, Tyler ran unsuccessfully for the Arkansas Senate against the Republican incumbent, then became director of human resources for Target-Smart Communications. She earned a graduate degree in community and economic development in 2014. In 2015, she received the Conway Chamber of Commerce Distinguished Service Award and was a Hillary Clinton delegate to the Democratic National Convention in 2016.

# Lori Benedict

HOUSE: 2011–2012
FROM: Salem, Fulton County
PARTY: Republican
BIRTHPLACE: Chicago, Illinois
DATES: August 4, 1946–
EDUCATION: St. Stephen's Catholic School; St. Ann's High School, 1964
OCCUPATION: cattle and dairy farmer

*Photo courtesy of Arkansas Secretary of State.*

Lori Benedict (born Lorraine Ann Klimala) is the daughter of Gertrude M. Pych, a homemaker, and Joseph Stanley Klimala, a carpenter for the Chicago

Park District and a Democratic precinct captain. During high school, she founded a horseback riding club, acted in school plays, modeled, and worked part time as a check sorter at the Federal Reserve Bank of Chicago. After graduation, she was a payroll clerk for Hines Lumber Company.

Impressed with the Ozarks' natural beauty and an opportunity for country living, Benedict and her family moved to Arkansas in 1972. She opened Corral Western Wear in Mountain Home and a riding stable called White River Trail Rides. She married Don Benedict in 1978 and moved to Salem, where they owned Sunrise Cattle Company and Benedict Dairy Farm. They were named Fulton County Farm Family of the Year.

Benedict has two children, Rick and Sherry, and was a lector of St. Mary of the Mount Catholic Church and on the church council. In 1991, the family established Ozark Regional Flight Service, a fixed-base operation at Baxter Regional Airport, and she was president and general manager. She was named Fulton County Business Woman of the Year and was vice chair of Fulton County Business and Professional Women. She won dozens of shooting championships, including the 2004 Cowboy Mounted Shooting National and World Champion Senior Lady.

Benedict ran for the Arkansas House in 1992, losing to Democratic incumbent Larry Goodwin. She was chair of the Fulton County Republican Committee, on the Fulton County Election Commission, and Governor Mike Huckabee appointed her to the State Board of Election Commissioners. She was an unsuccessful candidate for Fulton County justice of the peace in 2002. Benedict again ran for the House in 2010, winning the Republican primary with 58 percent and the general election with 55 percent. She was defeated for reelection in the 2012 general election. Governor Asa Hutchinson appointed her to an unexpired term on the Fulton County Quorum Court in 2022.

Representative Benedict was a member of the Legislative Council, Joint Performance Review Committee, and House committees on Public Transportation and Aging, Children and Youth. She was the lead sponsor on an act to exempt cottage-food operations, farmers' markets, and similar food sales entities from Department of Health permit requirements.

In 2015, Governor Asa Hutchinson appointed Benedict to the Governor's Advisory Council on Aging. She was an unsuccessful candidate for Fulton County justice of the peace in 2016. She and her husband continued to own Sunrise Cattle Company on a ranch of nearly a thousand acres at Sturkie.

# Linda Collins-Smith

HOUSE: 2011–2012, SENATE: 2015–2018
FROM: Pocahontas, Randolph County
PARTY: Democratic/Republican
BIRTHPLACE: Pocahontas, Arkansas
DATES: April 17, 1962–June 4, 2019
EDUCATION: Williford High School, 1980
OCCUPATION: realtor, motel owner

*Photo courtesy of Arkansas Secretary of State.*

Linda Collins-Smith (born Linda F. Collins) was the daughter of Carolyn Vernice Hunnicutt, a homemaker, and Benny Collins, a farmer. Growing up poor on a gravel road in rural Sharp County, Collins-Smith said she knew "what it is like to carry water from the spring and cut her own firewood." She became a successful realtor and married Philip Smith, then a municipal judge, in 1995. They owned and operated two motels in Pocahontas, and she became involved with regional tourism promotion.

Collins-Smith was on the board of the Rotary Club of Pocahontas, Ozark Gateway Tourism Association, and the Arkansas Hospitality Association and president of the Randolph County Tourism Association and the Arkansas Lodging Association. She was also involved with the Randolph County Heritage Museum and Rock 'n' Roll Highway 67. Collins-Smith was a member of the National Rifle Association, Gun Owners of America, the National Federation of Independent Business, the Randolph County Arkansas Chamber of Commerce, and the Arkansas Federation of Republican Women.

Governor Mike Huckabee appointed Philip Smith to a circuit judgeship in 2001, and Collins-Smith supported Huckabee in his 2004 gubernatorial campaign and his 2008 presidential campaign. She was also a large donor to George W. Bush's 2004 reelection campaign. In 2008, she was appointed to the Arkansas Ethics Commission, resigning in 2009, when she announced as a Democratic candidate for state representative. Collins-Smith won the 2010 Democratic primary with 53 percent and the general election with 52 percent of the vote.

Representative Collins-Smith was state co-chair of the American Legislative Exchange Council (ALEC). Her bills restricting abortion rights and consumer protection failed in committee. After the session, she held a press conference to announce that she was switching to the Republican Party and would run for the state senate. Incumbent Democrat senator David Wyatt defeated Collins-Smith in the 2012 general election; however, she ran again for the open seat in 2014 and was elected with 58 percent in the general election.

Senator Collins-Smith was vice chair of the Judiciary Committee and state director for the National Foundation for Women Legislators. She passed legislation for concealed handguns and revamping the high school history curriculum, but she unsuccessfully opposed Medicaid expansion and failed to pass a "bathroom bill" restricting access by transgendered citizens. Collins-Smith was a Ted Cruz delegate to the 2016 Republican National Convention. She was defeated for reelection in the 2018 Republican primary.

# Mary P. "Prissy" Hickerson

HOUSE: 2011–2016
FROM: Texarkana, Miller County
PARTY: Republican
BIRTHPLACE: Ida, Louisiana
DATES: August 24, 1951–
EDUCATION: Central Elementary;
Arkansas High School; coursework at
Watkins Business Institute in Nashville,
1968–1969, and the University of Tennessee,
1969–1970
OCCUPATION: business manager

*Photo courtesy of Arkansas Secretary of State.*

Mary P. "Prissy" Hickerson (born Mary Priscilla Tinsley) was born in Louisiana to Mary Christine Cater, a bookkeeper and homemaker, and Jessie Durrell Tinsley, an electrician. The family moved to Texarkana, Arkansas, when Hickerson was a baby. Her family actively discussed current events, and she was in her high school's Teenage Republican Group and worked on political campaigns.

In 1968, she married Randall Hickerson. Hickerson was business manager for Randall's dental practice and their real estate partnership. Her extensive volunteer work included the Arkansas Good Roads and Transportation Council, Texarkana Regional Arts and Humanities Council, president of Junior League of Texarkana, and board member of Christus St. Michael Health Care System, Texarkana Resources for the Disabled, Temple Memorial Treatment Center, Women for the Arts, Texarkana Volunteer Center, United Way, Leadership Texarkana, Texarkana Animal League, and Texarkana AR Baseball Association. She was also a graduate of Leadership Texarkana and on the steering committee of the Susan G. Komen Texarkana Race for the Cure.

Involved in politics, Hickerson was director of political operations for Mike Huckabee's 1992, 1993, 1994, and 1996 campaigns; on his gubernatorial transition team in 1996, a Miller County Republican Party state committeewoman, and state secretary of the Republican Party of Arkansas. She was an alternate delegate in 1992 and a delegate in 1996, 2004, and 2008 to the Republican National Conventions.

Hickerson was chair of the Arkansas State Highway Commission, only the third woman ever appointed to the commission. She participated in establishing six new Arkansas Welcome Centers. Hickerson was chair of the Southeastern Association of Highway Officials Commissions and Boards Committee and a member of the I-49 Coalition.

In 2010, Hickerson was elected to the Arkansas House of Representatives. She was unopposed all three terms she ran for the House. Representative Hickerson was the first woman to chair the House Public Transportation Committee. Her legislation focused on insurance, local government, transportation, public safety, mental illness, and providing care of pets under domestic abuse orders. Governor Asa Hutchinson appointed her to the Governor's Task Force on Highway Funding.

Hickerson was honored with the 2015 Christus Health Eagle Award, Leadership Texarkana Idalee Hawkins Leader of the Year, Junior League of Texarkana Sustainer of the Year, and Republican Party of Arkansas Jay Dickey Party Builder Award. After legislative service, she served on the University of Arkansas Hope-Texarkana Board of Visitors, the Christus ArkLaTex Finance Committee, and Life Net Emergency Medical Services Board of Directors.

# Missy Irvin

SENATE: 2011–present
FROM: Mountain View, Stone County
PARTY: Republican
BIRTHPLACE: Little Rock, Arkansas
DATES: February 12, 1971–
EDUCATION: Mount Saint Mary Academy,
1989; Randolph-Macon College, BA in
political science, communications, and
dance, with minor in art history, 1993
OCCUPATION: marketing director

*Photo courtesy of Arkansas Secretary of State.*

Missy Irvin (born Melissa Ann Thomas) is the daughter of Dr. Jerry Lynn Thomas, an orthopedic surgeon, and Evelyn Irene Mertes, an office manager. After graduation from college, she was a news editor at KATV and a marketing director for a Little Rock florist. She married Dr. John Dawson Irvin, and they have four children. After moving to Mountain View in 1996, Irvin was marketing director for Stone County Ironworks and was later an adjunct professor and director of the department of dance at Hendrix College. She then worked as the marketing director for Irvin-Dibrell Clinic.

Irvin's volunteer activities include the American Cancer Society, Human Rights for Kids Organization, Ozark Folk Center, and the Music Roots Program. She was chapter president of PEO and a member of the Heber Springs Rotary Club, Mountain View Chamber of Commerce, Arkansas Farm Bureau, and National Rifle Association. Irvin was president of the Mountain View Youth Soccer Association, vice president of the Arkansas State Soccer Association, and a volunteer soccer coach at Mountain View High School, named 2010 Coach of the Year. She received a President's Volunteer Service Award in 2008.

Irvin's political interest began at age nine, when she volunteered with her mother for Ronald Reagan in Arkansas. She worked for Sheffield Nelson's gubernatorial campaigns in 1990 and 1994, and for her brother, Bob Thomas, who ran for Congress in 2000 and the state senate in 2020. Her own campaigns were more successful, beginning with her 2010 bid for the state senate, when she won the Republican primary with 52 percent and defeated Representative Curren Everett with 58 percent in the general election. At thirty-nine, she was the first woman legislator elected from Stone County and the youngest woman elected to the state senate. Irvin was reelected in 2012 with 65 percent in the general election, and in 2014, she won the Republican primary with 64 percent and was unopposed in the general election. Irvin was unopposed for reelection in 2018 and 2022.

Senator Irvin was chair of the Senate Public Health, Welfare, and Labor Committee; vice chair of the Joint Budget Committee; served one term as assistant president pro tempore; and was chair of the Senate Education Committee. She was also state chair for the American Legislative Exchange Council (ALEC).

Among the legislation passed by Senator Irvin were twenty-three bills related to health-care delivery, insurance, licensing, and payments to physicians. She also passed bills on abortion, firearms, tax exemptions, registered sex offenders, human trafficking, sexual assault, child abuse, domestic violence, school safety, law enforcement, elections, state vehicles, driver education, municipal government, property taxes, body art, unemployment claims, career planning, government reorganization, juvenile justice, distilleries, bicycle safety, and duck stamps. In 2021, she passed sixty-four acts, which included issues of education, public schools, gas rates, safety, law enforcement, health care, local-option elections, collection of a felon's fines, public school nurse professional development, repeal of the Arkansas Pawnbroker Act, increased opportunities for colorectal-cancer screening, prohibiting transgender girls from competing in school sports with other girls, and an overhaul to Medicaid expansion.

Irvin's legislative service led to awards from the Arkansas Rural Economic Development Commission, Arkansas Prosecuting Attorneys Association, Campaign for the Fair Sentencing for Minors, Arkansas Advocate for Children and Families, Health Resources of Arkansas, Arkansas Hunger Relief Alliance, Arkansas Cattleman's Association, Arkansas Medical Society, and the Arkansas Municipal League.

# Sheilla E. Lampkin

HOUSE: 2011–2016
FROM: Monticello, Drew County
PARTY: Democratic
BIRTHPLACE: Rohwer, Arkansas
DATES: August 23, 1945–July 23, 2016
EDUCATION: Dumas High School, 1963;
Arkansas A&M College, BSE, 1966;
University of Arkansas, MEd, 1981
OCCUPATION: teacher

*Photo courtesy of Arkansas Secretary of State.*

Sheilla E. Lampkin taught in the Drew Central and Monticello school districts in a career of more than thirty years teaching math and special education classes, three times being recognized as Monticello Teacher of the Year. After retiring from teaching, she pursued a new career volunteering in numerous civic organizations and historic preservation causes, including chair of the Arkansas History Commission. Lampkin wrote a weekly column on local history for the *Advance-Monticellonian*, published award-winning articles in the *Drew County Historical Journal*, and recorded interviews with more than fifty WWII veterans for the Library of Congress Veteran's Oral History Project. She was named the Monticello-Drew County Chamber of Commerce Woman of the Year, and she received the Historic Preservation Alliance of Arkansas Award for Excellence in Preservation in 2011.

Lampkin was familiar with local politics, as her husband, Damon, was Drew County judge from 2003–2012. She saw politics as a way she could make a difference and announced her candidacy for an open House seat in 2010. Lampkin proved to be a formidable candidate, elected to three terms in the House and being undefeated in six contested elections.

As a freshman legislator, Representative Lampkin attended to local issues. In subsequent terms she addressed issues relating to children and education. She sponsored legislation adding instructional materials and resources to the Free Textbook Act, including coverage of developmentally disabled adult children in state employee children's educational leave, and providing that abused and neglected children could be placed with "fictive kin" rather than in a group home. She also sponsored legislation to create a legislative task force on the Best Practices for Special Education in Arkansas. Lampkin was vice chair of the Education Committee and a member of the Legislative Council in 2015–2016. She also served by appointment of the governor on the Southern Regional Education Board Legislative Advisory Council.

While running for a fourth term in which she would have been unopposed, Lampkin announced on July 19, 2016, that she was withdrawing from the race due to a diagnosis of ovarian cancer, and she died a week later. Just weeks before her death, she proudly showed the 2016 Girls State class the shirt and hat she wore at Girls State more than fifty years before. She loved teaching young women about public service and the importance of civil debate.

# Betty Overbey

HOUSE: 2011–2016
FROM: Lamar, Johnson County
PARTY: Democratic
BIRTHPLACE: Salus, Arkansas
DATES: January 9, 1946–
EDUCATION: Oark High School, 1963
OCCUPATION: state revenue agent

*Photo courtesy of Arkansas Secretary of State.*

Betty Warren Overbey had a thirty-five-year career as the Arkansas state revenue agent for Johnson and Pope Counties. She was active in the community as a member the Order of the Eastern Star of Arkansas and of PEO, an organization that provides scholarships to help women further their education. Overbey also served on the Finance Committee and as a Stephen Minister of the First United Methodist Church in Lamar.

After raising three children and retiring in 2010, Overbey filed for the Arkansas House of Representatives in the position held from 2005–2010 by her husband, George. She won the Democratic nomination in a runoff and was unopposed in the general election.

During her first term, Representative Overbey passed all eight of the bills for which she was the primary sponsor, and every bill she cosponsored also became an act during her first term. Her legislation in this and subsequent sessions reflected her knowledge of municipal affairs and issues related to procedures of state revenue offices.

In her bid for reelection in 2012, Overbey was unopposed in the Democratic primary and won the general election. During her second term, she served on the Committees on Public Health, Welfare, and Labor; State Agencies and Governmental Affairs; and the Joint Committee on Constitutional Amendments. Overbey sponsored Act 1005 of 2013 related to state funding for isolated school districts, the legislation of which she said she was most proud.

Overbey was unopposed for reelection to a third term in 2014. She chaired the City, County, and Local Affairs Committee and served on the Public Health, Welfare, and Labor Committee and the Arkansas Legislative Council. She passed city and county legislation clarifying retention of homestead credit documents, amending the statute concerning officials in certain mayor-council cities, and amending the law concerning organizational procedures of city councils.

Overbey chose not to run for reelection to a fourth term in 2016. In each of her three terms in office, Overbey received a Distinguished Legislator Award from the Arkansas Municipal League for support of local government. During her time in the legislature, she said she treasured "serving with so many wonderful people and working together to solve problems and better our state."

## Leslee Milam Post

HOUSE: 2011–2012
FROM: Ozark, Franklin County
PARTY: Democratic
BIRTHPLACE: Ozark, Arkansas
DATES: October 16, 1973–
EDUCATION: Ozark High School, 1992; University of the Ozarks, BA in communications, 1996
OCCUPATION: nonprofit executive director, farmer

*Photo courtesy of Arkansas Secretary of State.*

Leslee Milam Post (born Leslee Jane Milam) is the daughter of John Charles and Pamela Gay Milam. At Ozark High School, she was a cheerleader and squad captain, junior class officer, student council officer, a member of the yearbook staff, homecoming senior maid, and voted as most school spirited. After graduation from the University of the Ozarks, she married Andrew Post, president of Post Winery, and they have four children.

Post was the executive director of the Crisis Center for Women in Fort Smith. She was president of the Arkansas Coalition Against Domestic Violence and a member of the Arkansas Coalition Against Sexual Assault. Her community service included Leadership Fort Smith Board of Advisors, president of the Altus Area Sunset Rotary Club, an active member of the Altus/Ozark Council of Churches, and a volunteer with the Foothills Little Theatre and the Ozark Public School District.

In 2010, Post ran for the Arkansas House of Representatives. After her Republican opponent was disqualified, she was unopposed and declared the winner. The House of Representatives voted to seat her on a roll-call vote of 61–29, rejecting Republican members' effort to delay or deny her swearing into office.

Representative Post served on the Public Transportation; City, County, and Local Affairs; and Boys State Committees; and the Public School Desegregation Lawsuit Resolution Task Force. She sponsored legislation on domestic abuse, sex offenders, child custody, railroads, criminal law, public office filing, county government, and dump-truck license plates. She was the lead sponsor on legislation creating the Arkansas Wine Trail. She received the Prosecuting Attorneys Association Advocate of Justice Award.

In 2012, Post lost her bid for reelection in the general election. After her legislative service, she continued her work as a consultant in nonprofit management and government relations. She worked for the Arkansas Leukemia and Lymphoma Society, and she became the executive director of the American Diabetes Association (Arkansas-Oklahoma) in 2020.

# Mary Broadaway

HOUSE: 2013–2016
FROM: Paragould, Greene County
PARTY: Democratic
BIRTHPLACE: Jonesboro, Arkansas
DATES: March 19, 1964–
EDUCATION: West Elementary; Annie Camp Jr. High; Jonesboro High School, 1982; Trinity University, BA in history, 1986; University of Arkansas, JD, 1989; Harvard University, Kennedy School of Government Certified Senior Executives in State and Local Government, 2014
OCCUPATION: attorney

*Photo courtesy of Arkansas Secretary of State.*

Mary Broadaway (born Mary C. Lile) is the daughter of Dr. Robert Warren Lile, an oral surgeon, and Wilma Louise Massey, a homemaker. After growing up in Jonesboro and graduating high school, Broadaway enrolled in the honors program at Trinity University in San Antonio, where she was a presidential scholar, selected for Mortar Board, and a member of Gamma Chi Delta sorority. While attending the University of Arkansas Law School, she married Brad Broadaway, with whom she made a home in Paragould and raised three children.

In addition to her private practice, Broadaway was an attorney for the Child Support Enforcement Unit and Corning City Attorney, 2009–2012. Professionally, she served on the boards of the Arkansas Volunteer Lawyers for the Elderly, Legal Aid of Northeast Arkansas, Access to Justice, Court-Appointed Special Advocates, the Greene-Clay Bar Association, the Arkansas Bar Association, and the State Board of Law Examiners. In the community, she served on the boards of the Paragould Rotary Club, Paragould/Greene County Chamber of Commerce, Main Street Paragould, Greene County Community Fund, and the Learning Center.

In 2012, Broadaway was motivated to run for state representative because of her autistic son and the chance to help other children with special needs. She won the Democratic primary with 68 percent and won 54 percent against two opponents in the general election. She considered running for attorney general in 2014 but chose to run for reelection, winning with 56 percent in the general election.

Representative Broadaway was the House chair of the Legislative Audit Committee and a member of the Judiciary; Rules; and Aging, Children and Youth Committees. She was also appointed to the Arkansas Supreme Court Special Task Force on Practice and Procedure in Civil Cases. In addition to sponsoring legislation on public health, administration of justice, and juvenile justice, she passed a package regarding Alcohol Beverage Control enforcement. She was the lead sponsor on passage of the Building Better Futures Program to allow students with intellectual disabilities to broaden their career opportunities through education and job training.

For her legislative service, Representative Broadaway received the ATLA Consumer Advocate Award and was inducted into the Arkansas State Independent Living Council's Circle of Service. She chose not to seek reelection in 2016 but continued working to improve workforce training opportunities for young adults with intellectual disabilities. In 2020, Broadaway was elected as a circuit court judge, Seventh Division, Second Judicial District.

## Charlotte Vining Douglas

HOUSE: 2013–2018
FROM: Alma, Crawford County
PARTY: Republican
BIRTHPLACE: Pasa Robles, California
DATES: February 13, 1952–
EDUCATION: Arkadelphia High School, 1970; Ouachita Baptist University, BSE in science and secondary education, 1974
OCCUPATION: teacher

*Photo courtesy of Arkansas Secretary of State.*

Charlotte Vining Douglas (born Charlotte Ruth Vining) is the daughter of Ann Strickland and William Coleman Vining. Her father was a star athlete at Ouachita Baptist University and later became the university's men's basketball coach. Her mother was the 1946 OBU homecoming queen, and she later assisted her husband with the university's basketball team as "team Mom."

In high school, Douglas was student council secretary, a cheerleader, homecoming maid, Girls State delegate, in the senior class play, and an honors graduate. In college, she was a member of the Delta Kappa Gamma education sorority, a cheerleader, an Upward Bound counselor, a member of the Student Judiciary, and homecoming queen. She married Rickey B. Douglas, and they had three children.

Douglas taught high school science, physics, anatomy, and physiology at Fort Smith Northside, Van Buren (where she was also Medical Academy administrator), Sparkman, and West Memphis. She also taught Sunday school, worked with medical missions providing dental care in Nicaragua and Mexico, and served on the board of Arkansas Children's Advocacy Center. Douglas received awards that include Innovative Teacher of the Year, ING Unsung Heroes, Van Buren Community Service Award, and Academy Teacher of the Year.

Retiring after twenty-seven years of teaching, Douglas ran for an open Arkansas House seat. She was unopposed in the Republican primary and defeated former Democratic representative Steve Breedlove with 58 percent of the vote in the general election. She was unopposed for reelection in 2014 and 2016.

Representative Douglas was Assistant Speaker Pro Tempore of the House, House Education Committee vice chair, co-chair of the Arkansas Legislative Hunger Caucus, and a member of the National Conference of State Legislatures Hunger Partnership. She passed legislation removing gubernatorial power over firearms in disaster emergencies; specifying child maltreatment in the Child Abuse Hotline law; creating "Laura's Card" for victim-rights information; including dating-violence awareness in health curricula; requiring a human-trafficking prevention course for a class A commercial driver's license; and creating the Colin Keady Young Entrepreneur Mentor Program. Douglas received awards from the Arkansas Family Council, Alternative Learning Environment Teachers, Arkansas Chamber of Commerce, Arkansas Education Association, and Arkansas Municipal League.

In 2018, Douglas was term-limited in the House. In 2019, she was a program administrator for the Arkansas Workforce Services' Temporary Assistance for Needy Families and began serving as a consultant to the Winthrop Rockefeller Beyond Civility program. She then joined the staff of United Way of Fort Smith Area as the Crawford County Coordinator for 100 Families.

# Deborah Ferguson

HOUSE: 2013–present
FROM: West Memphis, Crittenden County
PARTY: Democratic
BIRTHPLACE: Parkin, Arkansas
DATES: July 28, 1953–
EDUCATION: Parkin High School, 1971;
University of Mississippi, BA in interior
design, 1976; University of Tennessee
Health Science Center, DDS, 1979
OCCUPATION: dentist

*Photo courtesy of Arkansas Secretary of State.*

Deborah Ferguson (born Deborah Faye Thompson) is the daughter of Faye Martin and Kenneth Eugene Thompson, a farmer, who began with 150 acres of rented land that he built into a forty-thousand-acre farming operation. The family was named the State Farm Family of the Year in 1978. At Ole Miss, Ferguson was a majorette, a member of Kappa Kappa Gamma sorority and the Society of Cwens honor society, and a contestant in the Miss University pageant. After earning her DDS degree in 1979, she married Scott Ferguson, a radiologist.

While operating her own dental clinic in West Memphis and raising three children, Dr. Ferguson was president of the Crittenden County Medical Alliance, treasurer of the Arkansas Medical Alliance, finance chair of the Junior Auxiliary, and a Sunday school teacher at First United Methodist Church. She also served as a court-appointed special advocate for foster children, and Governor Mike Beebe appointed her to the Arkansas Arts Council.

Ferguson's father had served on the Parkin School Board, and her mother-in-law, Joyce Ferguson, was mayor of West Memphis (1975–82). Her husband served two terms as state representative (1995–1998), and she was active in his 1998 campaign for the Democratic nomination for the US Senate. She was elected to the Arkansas House in 2012, winning the general election with 79 percent, and she was reelected with 74 percent in the 2014 general election. She was unopposed for reelection in 2016, 2018, and 2020.

Representative Ferguson was a member of the Legislative Council, the Rules Committee, and the Insurance and Commerce Committee. She served as chair of the Girls State Committee; vice chair of the House Public Health, Welfare, and Labor Committee; and a member of the Health Committees of the National Conference of State Legislators and the Council of State Governments. Ferguson was also the Arkansas State director of Women in Government and treasurer of the House Democratic Caucus.

Ferguson's legislation focused on health-care issues. She was the sponsor of legislation creating the Patient Right-To-Know Act, a maternal mortality review committee, a state diabetes action plan, an action plan to address the prevention of unplanned teen pregnancy, and a Medicaid primary care case management savings pilot program. Other issues she addressed were limiting smoking in long-term care facilities, prohibiting e-cigarettes on college campuses, requiring that denials of dental claims be decided by licensed dentists, medical school admissions, licensing physicians, prior authorization for medication-assisted treatment, and reporting patient transfers from a lay midwife. She cosponsored a resolution to ratify the Equal Rights Amendment, was vice chair of the House Public Health, Welfare, and Labor Committee; and passed a resolution proclaiming April 2021 as autism awareness and acceptance month.

## Charlene Fite

HOUSE: 2013–present
FROM: Van Buren, Crawford County
PARTY: Republican
BIRTHPLACE: Alma, Arkansas
DATES: August 4, 1950–
EDUCATION: Alma High School, 1968; University of Tennessee, BS in deaf education, 1974; University of Arkansas MEd in special education, 1992; Taipei Language Institute
OCCUPATION: school psychology specialist

*Photo courtesy of Arkansas Secretary of State.*

Charlene Fite (born Edna Charlene Harris) is the daughter of Mayme Mae Winborn, a teacher and reading specialist, and Garland Gano Harris, a postal employee, poultry farmer, and disabled veteran of World War II. Growing up and attending Alma public schools, in high school she was on the newspaper staff and student council, a member of the drama club and the National Honor Society, a cheerleader, homecoming queen, and named Miss Alma High School.

From 1981 to 1989, Fite was a Baptist missionary in Taiwan. Returning to Arkansas, she was a special education teacher and school psychology specialist in the Fort Smith Public Schools for more than twenty years and was the educational director for Arkansas Easter Seals for one year. She married Tom Fite in 1994.

In volunteer community service, Fite has been a board member for the Crawford County Library, the Court Appointed Special Advocates in Crawford County, Children's Advocacy Centers of Arkansas, Bost Development Centers, and on the Arkansas Baptist Executive Committee.

Fite was vice chair of the Crawford County Republican Party and had a lifelong interest in government. With the encouragement of her political mentor, former representative Rick Green, Fite ran for an open House seat for District 82, winning the 2012 Republican primary with 54 percent and the general election with 57 percent. She was easily reelected over the Libertarian nominee in 2014 and was unopposed in 2016. In 2018, she won a fourth term with 60 percent over Libertarian and Democratic opponents. She was reelected with 72 percent in the 2020 general election.

Representative Fite served as chair of the House Aging, Children, and Military Affairs Committee, and was a member of the Judiciary and Joint Budget Committees and the Legislative Council. She was prolific and successful with her legislative agenda that provided income tax exemptions for military retirees, tax credits for motion picture production, required photo identification for voters, created the Alzheimer's Disease and Dementia Advisory Council, and others addressing the juvenile justice system, children in the foster care system, domestic violence, child welfare, child abuse and maltreatment, sex offenses, individuals who are hearing impaired, the College and Career Coaches Program, and education renewal zones. She cosponsored several bills limiting both the availability of abortion procedures and restrictions on possession of firearms. In 2019, Representative Fite passed a House resolution Celebrating Women in Public Office Day.

Among the awards Fite received are the Domestic Peace Award from the Arkansas Coalition Against Domestic Violence, Joe T. Robinson Award from the Arkansas National Guard, the Family Council Statesman Award, Champion for the Deaf, 2017 Woman of the Year from Women's Own Worth, 2017 Arkansas Chamber of Commerce Leadership Award, 2019 Arkansas Advocates for Children and Families and Arkansas Kids Count Coalition Champion for Kids, and she was listed among *AY Magazine*'s 2019 Intriguing Women. In 2020, she was named a National Conference of State Legislators Maternal and Child Health Fellow.

# Fonda Hawthorne

HOUSE: 2013–2014
FROM: Ashdown, Little River County
PARTY: Democratic
BIRTHPLACE: Stuttgart, Arkansas
DATES: September 20, 1956–
EDUCATION: Stuttgart Elementary;
Ashdown High School, 1974; Ouachita
Baptist University, sociology major,
1974–1976
OCCUPATION: economic development
officer

*Photo courtesy of Arkansas Secretary of State.*

Fonda Hawthorne (born Fonda Faye Hagan) was born in Stuttgart to home-maker Maylene Caroline Moritz and Chester Crandall Hagan, a farmer and pilot. At Ashdown High School, Hawthorne was co-editor of *Panther Eyes*, a member of the band, and a student newspaper reporter. She attended Ouachita Baptist University as a sociology major for two years and in 1976 married Joseph Stephen Hawthorne. They have two children. She graduated from the US Chamber of Commerce Institute of Organization Management and the Community Development Institute.

Hawthorne worked at Southwestern Electric Power Company (AEP/SWEPCO) and served as executive director of the De Queen/Sevier County Chamber of Commerce and economic development director for the Little River Chamber of Commerce. She was president of the De Queen Lions Club, president of the Ashdown Rotary Club, and director of the Texarkana Regional Initiative. She was on the Domtar Paper Mill Community Advisory Board and Ash Grove Citizens Board. Hawthorne volunteered with the Ashdown Community Auction and Little River County Fair and was a member of the Ash Grove Citizens Committee, Millwood Lake Focus Committee, the Arkansas State Chamber of Commerce, Arkansas Chamber of Executive Directors, and Leadership Arkansas. The De Queen/Sevier County Chamber of Commerce honored Hawthorne with the Steve Pearce Citizen of the Year Award.

Former representative Larry Cowling encouraged Hawthorne's interest and involvement in politics and government. In 2012, Hawthorne ran for the Arkansas House of Representatives, was unopposed in the Democratic primary, and won the general election with 54 percent of the vote.

Representative Hawthorne served on the Legislative Joint Auditing; Public Transportation; and City, County, and Local Affairs Committees. She passed two bills authorizing specialty license plates, one for disabled veterans and one for court-appointed special advocates. Hawthorne also passed legislation requiring health benefit plans to provide corrective surgery and treatment for craniofacial anomaly. Representative Hawthorne knew Wendelyn Osborne from the First Baptist Church in Ashdown, and the new legislation helped Osborne and others like her who were born with a craniofacial overgrowth but were denied corrective surgery coverage from their insurance company.

Hawthorne lost her bid for reelection in 2014 to Republican DeAnn Vaught. Hawthorne continued working as director of the Little River County Chamber of Commerce and ran unsuccessfully against incumbent representative Vaught in 2016.

# Patti Julian

HOUSE: 2013–2014
FROM: North Little Rock, Pulaski County
PARTY: Democratic
BIRTHPLACE: Little Rock, Arkansas
DATES: June 7, 1955–
EDUCATION: North Little Rock Northeast High School, 1973; University of Arkansas, BSBA in accounting, 1977, and JD, 1980
OCCUPATION: attorney

*Photo courtesy of Arkansas Secretary of State.*

Patti Julian (born Patricia Roberts) graduated from law school and married fellow attorney Jim Julian in 1980. Her first job was with Touche Ross in Memphis. In 1983, she returned to Arkansas and worked for one year at the Arkansas Securities Department and five years as a governmental affairs attorney for Arkansas Blue Cross Blue Shield, also serving on the Health Law Committee of the Arkansas Bar Association. In 1989, she retired and focused on raising their daughter, Katy.

Julian was an active community-service volunteer for many organizations, including the Arkansas Race for the Cure, the Penick Boys and Girls Club, the North Little Rock Unit of the American Cancer Society; the Junior League of North Little Rock, of which she was treasurer; and the Cathedral School, where she was a trustee. She also served two terms on the North Little Rock Wastewater Treatment Commission.

Growing up, politics was a family affair. Julian's father, David Roberts, was a state representative from 1973 until 1992. Her sister, Debra, was president of the North Little Rock School Board. Julian developed her political skills as the campaign coordinator for Paul Suskie in his 2006 Democratic primary race for attorney general. Encouraged by Senator Mary Anne Salmon, Julian announced as a candidate for the Arkansas House in 2012. She was unopposed in the Democratic primary and elected over three opponents in the general election.

During the 2013 session, Julian cosponsored legislation to reduce the sales tax on food, and she was most proud of her efforts to help pass Arkansas Works, enabling the state to provide federally funded private health insurance for low-income families. Julian recommended considering diversion and treatment programs rather than building new prisons, and she argued against the twelve-week and twenty-week abortion bans that were later declared unconstitutional. Julian was also an advocate for pay equity for women, contending that "ensuring equal pay isn't just good for women; it's good for our children and our families."

Running for reelection in 2014, Julian was unopposed in the Democratic primary but lost in the general election. She later worked as the legislative lobbyist for the Arkansas Bar Association.

# Sue Scott

HOUSE: 2013–2016
FROM: Rogers, Benton County
PARTY: Republican
BIRTHPLACE: Little Rock, Arkansas
DATES: January 11, 1954–
EDUCATION: Danville High School, 1972; Petit Jean Vocational Technical School (University of Arkansas Community College at Morrilton), business and management, 1973
OCCUPATION: caterer, daycare owner

*Photo courtesy of Arkansas Secretary of State.*

Sue Scott (born Norma Sue Cagle) is the daughter of Glenna Jo Brand and Wesley Marlo Cagle. In high school, Scott was president of Future Business Leaders, an officer of Future Teachers, Future Homemakers, Library Club, and the pep club. She was also cast in class plays, on the staff of the school paper and yearbook, and voted Miss Congeniality in the Miss Danville Pageant. She moved to Benton County in 1976 and married John Russell Scott in 1988. They have four children.

Sue Scott owned and operated Mud Pie Catering and also owned a daycare. She was president of Beta Sigma Phi Sorority and the PTA. Her local political involvement included serving as president of the Bella Vista Republican Women and on the executive board of the Republican Party of Benton County, as well as working on her husband's successful campaign for Benton County circuit judge.

After retirement, Scott ran for a seat in the Arkansas House of Representatives, winning the 2012 general election with 61 percent against an independent candidate. She was reelected in 2014, winning the Republican primary with 55 percent of the vote and defeating the Libertarian candidate in the general election with 82 percent of the vote.

In her first legislative term, Representative Scott was a member of Judiciary; Aging, Children and Youth, Legislative and Military Affairs; Arkansas Health Insurance Marketplace Legislative Oversight; and the Arkansas State Game and Fish Commission Oversight Committees. In her second term, she was vice chair of Girls State and vice chair of Legislative Joint Auditing. She also served on the 2016–2017 Southern States Energy Board Committee on Clean Coal Energy Policies and Technologies. Her legislation included issues of sex crimes, gun open carry, veterans' preference employment, public charter schools, public school choice, motor scooter helmet use, public officials, higher education, and military certification and licensure preferences.

Although endorsed by Governor Asa Hutchinson and the *Arkansas Democrat-Gazette*, Scott was defeated for reelection in the 2016 Republican primary.

# Camille Bennett

HOUSE: 2015–2016
FROM: Lonoke, Lonoke County
PARTY: Democratic
BIRTHPLACE: Pine Bluff, Arkansas
DATES: December 5, 1960–
EDUCATION: Pine Bluff public and private schools; Pine Bluff High School, 1979; University of Arkansas at Little Rock, BS in political science and criminal justice, 1982; University of Missouri, JD, 1995
OCCUPATION: attorney

*Photo courtesy of Arkansas Secretary of State.*

Camille Bennett (born Camille Williams) is the daughter of Willie Merle Hankins, home demonstration agent, and Randall Lee Williams, municipal judge, state representative, and circuit judge. Both parents were active in politics, her mother a Republican and father a Democrat. At Pine Bluff High School, Bennett was a Zebra Prancer and member of Winged Zebra. After receiving her bachelor of science degree in political science and criminal justice, she acquired her law degree. She married Otis Wayne Bennett Jr. in 2005.

Active as a community volunteer, Bennett served on the UAMS Psychiatry Advisory Board, UAMS Consortium Board, and Central Arkansas Rescue Efforts Board. She also served as UAMS Central Arkansas Rescue Efforts Foundation Board president, Scott Connections Executive Board president, All Souls Church Board of Directors chair, and American Heart Association Heart Ball Logistics Committee. She held membership in the Arkansas Bar Association and volunteered for Paws in Prison and various political campaigns.

Bennett was assistant to Commissioner Helen G. Corrothers at the United States Sentencing Commission, manager of corporate affairs of Emergency Medical/Occupational Health Services, an attorney in Kansas City and Little Rock, and an assistant attorney general in the Arkansas Attorney General's Public Protection Department. She also taught courses at the University of Arkansas in Little Rock. From 2007 to 2009, Bennett was a district court judge in Lonoke, and from 2009 to 2014 she was Lonoke city attorney.

When a House seat came open in 2014, Bennett ran for the position. Having previously worked for Senator Max Howell during legislative sessions,

Bennett was knowledgeable on how to work effectively within the legislative process. She was unopposed in the Democratic primary and won the general election with 50.5 percent of the vote.

Representative Bennett's legislation included assisting the Department of Corrections, protecting the separation of powers, helping farmers and rural communities, allowing online publishing of unclaimed property by the state auditor, and protecting and strengthening agricultural programs at the Lonoke extension office. She passed legislation on administration of justice issues on restitution orders, court record retention schedules, filing fees, and DNA collection. Representative Bennett received awards from the Arkansas Municipal League and Farm Bureau. She opposed a "religious freedom" bill, but before its passage she rewrote it to mirror constitutional protections while excluding the discriminatory underpinnings.

Bennett served one term, having lost her bid for reelection in the 2016 general election. She continued practicing law and volunteering in her community.

# Mary Bentley

HOUSE: 2015–present
FROM: Perryville, Perry County
PARTY: Republican
BIRTHPLACE: Nellis Air Force Base, Nevada
DATES: December 26, 1961–
EDUCATION: Plymouth Christian Academy (Duxbury, MA), 1979; Harding University, BSN, 1983
OCCUPATION: registered nurse, business owner

*Photo courtesy of Arkansas Secretary of State.*

Mary Bentley (born Mary Elizabeth Murphy) moved to Arkansas in 1979, when her parents became associated with the Heifer Ranch educational farm in Perryville. After graduating from Harding University, she was a registered nurse for ten years at the Arkansas Children's Hospital in Little Rock. Bentley is the owner of Bentley Plastics, a 100 percent woman-owned business of which she has been the CEO since 2008. She has three grown children and four grandchildren.

Bentley was vice president of Perry County Right to Life and chair of the Perry County Republican Party. She also served on the board of the Safe Place family shelter and was a volunteer firefighter/first responder. The Williams Junction Volunteer Fire Department named her Fireman of the Year.

In 2012, Bentley first ran for an Arkansas House of Representatives seat, losing to Democratic incumbent representative John Catlett in the general election. In 2014, she ran again, unseating Representative Catlett with 51 percent of the vote. In 2016 and 2018, Bentley defeated her Democratic opponents with 76 percent of the general election vote, and she was unopposed in 2020.

Representative Bentley was vice chair of the City, County, and Local Affairs Committee; vice chair of the Legislative Joint Auditing Committee; and a member of the Girls State Committee. She passed legislation that includes issues of nursing licensing, health insurance coverage for metabolic disorders, immunity for volunteer health professionals, public charter school agricultural studies, childcare, orders of protection, drug screening of school employees, rural physician recruitment, property law and state lands, farm-to-school and early childhood education, and the designation of the True Grit Trail. Other acts she passed include additional work requirements for food stamp recipients, enhanced penalties for physician-assisted suicide, limiting the governor's powers during an emergency regarding religious organizations, certifying nurse midwives, set pricing for Arkansas milk, levee districts, parental access to public school sex and gender information, increased abortion facility requirements, significant restrictions on abortion, and stricter requirements for colleges and universities, including disclosure of foreign-source funding and prohibition of contracts with the Confucius Institute, an organization promoting Chinese language and culture in Arkansas.

Among her awards are the Rural Community Alliance Champion of Rural Arkansas Award, Champion of Charity Award from the Foundation of Government Accountability, Arkansas Chamber of Commerce Business Matters Leadership Award, the Family Council Action Committee Statesman Award, National Conference of State Legislators Maternal and Child Health Fellow, and the Governor's Health Policy Award from the Arkansas Minority Health Commission.

# Karilyn Brown

HOUSE: 2015–present
FROM: Sherwood, Pulaski County
PARTY: Republican
BIRTHPLACE: Cape Girardeau, Missouri
DATES: September 19, 1947–
EDUCATION: Jacksonville High School,
1965; University of Arkansas at Little Rock:
BA magna cum laude, 2000; IT certificate,
2001; and MA in professional, technical,
business, and scientific writing, 2007
OCCUPATION: technical writer

*Photo courtesy of Arkansas Secretary of State.*

Karilyn Brown (born Karilyn Mae Boggan) is the daughter of Verna L. Bauchmann and Robert Norfleet Boggan, a career Air Force veteran who served as director of Arkansas Veterans Services under Governor Winthrop Rockefeller. The family moved often, but her father retired to his native state when Brown was in high school. She was employed in a state agency and private business before returning to college to earn undergraduate and graduate degrees in technical writing. After working in customer service for Alltel and as an editor for Arkansas Blue Cross and Blue Shield, she was the community engagement coordinator for Thrivent Financial for Lutherans. In 2005, she married retired Air Force lieutenant colonel Lawrence Lee Brown.

Brown was president of the Arkansas State Veterans Cemetery Beautification Foundation and an associate member of the Eaker Chapter of the Distinguished Flying Cross Society. She was also active in party politics as an officer of the North Pulaski Republican Women, a member of the Arkansas Federation of Republican Women, and an alternate delegate to the 2020 Republican National Convention.

After serving one term on the Pulaski County Quorum Court (2013–2014), Brown ran for an open House seat in 2014. She won the Republican primary with 58 percent and the general election with 57 percent. She was unopposed for reelection in 2016 and was reelected with 54 percent in the 2018 general election. In 2020, she was reelected with 56 percent in the general election.

Representative Brown secured adoption of a resolution finding that the proliferation and accessibility of pornography has created a public health crisis and passed legislation regarding human cloning, acknowledgement of paternity, vacation leave for municipal police, wheelchair transportation, veteran-designation driver's licenses, limiting voter assistants, dual-office holding, tax-deferred tuition savings, and a vehicle-fee exemption. Her other successful legislation includes providing for a differential diagnosis in an investigation involving child abuse, criminal provisions related to rioting and the aggravated assault of first responders, authorizing delivery of alcoholic beverages directly to a consumer, fees for the state veterans' cemetery system, allowing the Child Welfare Agency Review Board to prohibit corporal discipline in licensed facilities, prohibiting persons within one hundred feet of a voting-location entrance, and creating the Arkansas Military Child School Transitions Act.

Representative Brown received the Arkansas Chamber of Commerce Business Matters Leadership Award in 2015, 2017 and 2019 and a 2019 Family Council Legislative Award.

# Jana Della Rosa

HOUSE: 2015–2020
FROM: Rogers, Benton County
PARTY: Republican
BIRTHPLACE: Springdale, Arkansas
DATES: September 16, 1976–
EDUCATION: Springdale High School, 1994; University of Arkansas, BS in industrial engineering, 2000
OCCUPATION: marketing, homemaker

*Photo courtesy of Arkansas Secretary of State.*

Jana Della Rosa (born Jana Leigh Wootton) is the daughter of Aubrey Wayne Wootton, a banker, and Patsy Ann Ritchie, a conservative activist who chaired the Northwest Arkansas Chapter of Family, Life, America, and God (FLAG) and served as executive director of Conservative Arkansas political action committee. When Della Rosa was eight years old, she signed her first political newspaper advertisement supporting the Pro-Life Education Alliance.

After graduating from college, she married Russell Della Rosa, an engineering graduate, and they lived in Fayetteville. Della Rosa's first job was as a sales analyst with Ozark Consulting and Marketing, assisting small businesses to sell their products to Walmart. She then worked twelve years as a national account executive with Church & Dwight, responsible for all laundry product sales to Walmart. The family moved to Rogers in 2006, and Della Rosa became a full-time homemaker after the birth of her second son in 2012.

In politics, Della Rosa volunteered in local campaigns and was a member of the Benton County Republican Women, the Benton County Republican Committee, and the National Rifle Association. She also served on the board of Conservative Arkansas.

Della Rosa ran for the Arkansas House in 2014, defeating two other candidates in the Republican primary with 52 percent of the vote, and she was unopposed in the general election. She was reelected in 2016, receiving 64 percent in the Republican primary against two opponents, including former representative Randy Alexander. In 2018, she prevailed in the Republican primary by three votes after a recount and won the general election with 66 percent. Running for a fourth term in 2020, Della Rosa led in the Republican primary but was defeated in the runoff primary.

Representative Della Rosa was a member of the Education Committee and the City, County, and Local Affairs Committee. As member of the Joint Audit Committee, she instigated the audit of a Planning and Development District associated with kickback schemes that led to the convictions of two Republican legislators and a lobbyist. Della Rosa passed transparency legislation related to campaign advertising, ethics commission investigations, electronic filing of campaign finance reports, and county purchasing law. She also passed education bills affecting school recess periods; the maximum daily number of students taught per teacher; a limit on use of English learners' scores on a state-mandated assessment; grants for students enrolled in Science, Technology, Engineering and Math programs; and community college local board elections.

# Vivian Flowers

HOUSE: 2015–present
FROM: Pine Bluff, Jefferson County
PARTY: Democratic
BIRTHPLACE: Pine Bluff, Arkansas
DATES: September 4, 1969–
EDUCATION: Nathaniel Narbonne High
School (Harbor City, CA), 1987; Howard
University; University of Arkansas at Little
Rock, BA in political science and technical
writing, 2005; University of Arkansas
Clinton School of Public Service, MPS,
2006
OCCUPATION: university administrator

*Photo courtesy of Arkansas Secretary of State.*

Vivian Flowers was born to Mary Yeargin, an office manager, and Dr. John Alonzo Flowers Sr., a pediatrician. She is a fifth-generation Arkansan, and her family has been active in community affairs. State Senator Stephanie Flowers (D-Pine Bluff) is her cousin.

Flowers served on the boards of the Women's Foundation of Arkansas, Common Cause/Arkansas, Committee Against Spouse Abuse Women's Shelter, and she actively volunteered for the Pine Bluff Historic District Commission, Arkansas Mentoring and Networking Association, Arkansas Advanced Initiative for Math and Science, and St. John African Methodist Episcopal Church. She is a life member of the Arkansas Democratic Black Caucus and the Pine Bluff chapter of the NAACP. She worked for Democratic Party organizations and political campaigns, was a Democratic presidential elector in 2016, and was a delegate to the 2020 Democratic National Convention.

With over a decade of legislative and state policy experience prior to her election, Flowers was on the staff of the Bureau of Legislative Research assigned to the Public Health and Agriculture Committees and the House Rules Committee. She was executive director of the Arkansas Legislative Black Caucus and interned with Civicus World Alliance for Civic Participation in South Africa. She also chaired the Arkansas Minority Health Commission. Since 2007, Flowers has worked at the University of Arkansas for Medical Sciences, most recently as chief operating officer of the UAMS Center for Diversity Affairs.

Flowers ran unopposed for an open House seat in 2014 and was reelected without opposition in 2016. She was reelected in 2018 with 89 percent in the general election, and she was unopposed for reelection in 2020.

Representative Flowers was chair of the Arkansas Legislative Black Caucus and a member of the committees on Public Transportation and Agriculture, Forestry, and Economic Development, Girls State, and Legislative Audit. Her legislation has addressed health, education, and justice issues, as well as tourism, family reunification, and fair elections. Flowers was lead sponsor of the Equal Rights Amendment Resolution in 2017. Her legislation includes designating a portion of US Highway 65 as the "Delta Rhythm & Bayous Highway," amending the law concerning rights of incarcerated parents and the termination of parental rights, creating the Voting and Elections Transparency Act of 2017, transferring oversight of the Arkansas Entertainers Hall of Fame, creating additional forms of custody in juvenile delinquency cases, amending the minimum age requirement for marriage, and requiring open public meetings to be recorded.

Flowers holds leadership posts in the National Black Caucus for State Legislatures (NBCSL) and the Women Legislators' Lobby, and she became president of Women of Color Vote political action committee. In 2020 she was honored as the NBCSL Legislator of the Year, and in 2021 she received the Arkansas Municipal League Distinguished Legislator Award.

# Michelle Gray

HOUSE: 2015–2022
FROM: Melbourne, Izard County
PARTY: Republican
BIRTHPLACE: Melbourne, Arkansas
DATES: September 11, 1976–
EDUCATION: Melbourne High School, 1994; Arkansas State University, BS in accounting, 1999
OCCUPATION: chief financial officer

*Photo courtesy of Arkansas Secretary of State.*

Michelle Gray (born April Michelle Harvey) grew up in Melborne and is the daughter of Russell Lee and Phyllis Rose Harvey. She learned from her mother "that a good education, a strong work ethic, an acknowledgement of personal responsibility, and a sense of ownership could make for a better life." After high school, Gray earned an accounting degree and began working in the budget and finance offices at Arkansas State University for three years. She then served for six years as business manager and interim vice president for Finance at Ozarka College.

In 2008, she married Dr. Adam Gray and became clinic manager and chief financial officer for Gray Family Practice Clinic in Melbourne. They have five children. Since 2018, Gray has been director of Provider Operations at White River Health System. She was secretary-treasurer of the Emergency Medical Services Board of Izard County, on the Local Emergency Planning Committee, and treasurer of the Single Parent Scholarship Foundation of Izard County.

After losing races for justice of the peace on the Izard County Quorum Court in 2010 and 2012, Gray ran for the Arkansas House of Representatives in 2014, pledging to lower taxes, practice fiscal conservatism, cap state spending, protect personal property rights, protect the right to keep and bear arms, and "protect the sanctity of life." Unopposed in the Republican primary, she defeated incumbent Democratic representative Tommy Wren with 54 percent of the vote in the general election, becoming the first woman to represent Izard County in the legislature. Gray was unopposed for reelection in 2016, 2018, and 2020. She did not seek reelection in 2022.

Representative Gray served as Assistant Speaker Pro Tempore. She passed legislation that included allowing concealed handguns in vehicles, election law, tax cuts, medical practice, medical marijuana cultivation facilities, speed traps, law enforcement personnel protections, and adding women-owned business enterprises to the Minority Business Economic Development Act. Gray also passed laws related to Medicaid reimbursement and substantial Medicaid expansion. Other legislation includes issues of the attorney general's jurisdiction, violations of probation and parole, licensed chiropractors, duties of inspector general and internal audit of executive agencies, body art, prescription drugs, Arkansas insurance market, and tobacco business.

For her legislative record, Gray received the Arkansas Pharmacists Association Guy Newcomb Award, the Arkansas Chamber of Commerce Business Matters Leadership Award, the Family Council Action Committee's Statesman Award, and an award from the American Conservative Union.

# Robin Lundstrum

HOUSE: 2015–present
FROM: Elm Springs, Washington County
PARTY: Republican
BIRTHPLACE: Fort Benning, Georgia
DATES: December 28, 1962–
EDUCATION: Springdale High School, 1981; University of Arkansas, BS in health sciences, 1985, MEd in community health, 1986, and EdD in health science, 1996
OCCUPATION: property management, small-business owner

*Photo courtesy of Arkansas Secretary of State.*

Robin Lundstrum (born Robin Dale Hall) is the daughter of Margie Lyn Honeycutt, a nurse, and Oscar Maxey Hall, a real estate broker and civil engineer who was a principal in the development of the Springdale Municipal Airport. In 1986, she married Thomas Duane "Tom" Lundstrum, who would serve on the Springdale City Council and Washington County Election Commission and whose father served twelve years on the Washington County Quorum Court. From 1989 to 1998, Robin Lundstrum was an assistant professor at John Brown University. She was owner of ChemStation and president and property manager at Cypress Investments LLC.

Dr. Lundstrum is a member of the Springdale Rotary, Siloam Springs American Legion Auxiliary, Eagle Forum, FBI Citizens Academy Alumni Association, Springdale and Siloam Springs Chambers of Commerce, the 99's International Organization of Women Pilots, National Rifle Association, American Mothers Association, Arkansas Farm Bureau, and Arkansas Family Council. She has been a rape-crisis volunteer and board member.

Politically active, Lundstrum served four years on the Elm Springs City Council. Her other activities include Washington County Republican Women president, vice chair of the Republican Party of Arkansas, and work on numerous Republican campaigns. She has also been a member of the Washington County Tea Party, National Federation of Republican Women Convention delegate, and delegate to the 2008, 2012, and 2016 Republican National Conventions.

In 2014, Lundstrum ran for the Arkansas House, winning the Republican primary with 58 percent of the vote and being unopposed in the general election. She was unopposed in 2016. In 2018, she won the general election with 70 percent of the vote. She was unopposed in the 2020 Republican primary and was reelected with 74 percent in the general election.

Representative Lundstrum was vice chair of the House Insurance and Commerce Committee and majority party whip. She passed legislation that includes financial and tax issues; municipal fire service; unemployment; workforce services; limits on the marketing, sale, and use of medicinal marijuana; restrictions on physicians performing abortions; limiting abortions to eighteen weeks' gestation; restricting abortions in regard to Medicaid funding; limiting eligibility for Supplemental Nutrition Assistance and Medicaid; human trafficking; and banning gender transition treatment for minors. Her sponsored acts also include enhancing the sexual assault collection kit procedure, exemptions from the minimum wage law passed by voters, prohibiting state-mandated coronavirus vaccinations, protecting businesses' liability regarding coronavirus, and prescription drug fairness in cost sharing.

Lundstrum was honored by the Arkansas State Lodge Fraternal Order of Police, received the Family Council of Arkansas's Power of Courage Award and Statesman Award, and received an Arkansas Chamber of Commerce Leadership Award.

# Julie Mayberry

HOUSE: 2015–2016 and 2019–present
FROM: Hensley, Saline County
PARTY: Republican
BIRTHPLACE: Fort Lauderdale, Florida
DATES: July 17, 1971–
EDUCATION: Plantation High School, 1989; Florida State University, 1989–1990; Emerson College, BS in mass communications and broadcast journalism, 1994
OCCUPATION: media and advertising executive

*Photo courtesy of Arkansas Secretary of State.*

Julie Mayberry (born Julie Ann Weidner) was the youngest of five children born to Clarence Julius "Clay" Weidner Jr., owner of a drapery-installation business, and Betty Jo Smith. In high school, Mayberry was president of the

Thespian Society and a member of the Anchor Club, National Honor Society, Social Studies Honor Society, and Drama Club. She received the Hugh O'Brian Youth Leadership Award and was in the Miss Broward County Pageant. She attended Florida State University for one year then transferred to Emerson College, where she worked at the student television station and was selected for Gold Key Honor Society.

Mayberry interned with CNN and worked at television stations in Chattanooga and Atlanta before moving to Little Rock in 1996 for a five-year stint as cohost on KATV's *Daybreak* morning news show. She married Andy Mayberry in 1997, and they have four daughters. They own Mayberry Advertising and publish the *East Ender*, a monthly community newspaper. She also directs the nonprofit I Can! Dance and Resource Center, which provides art and dance activities for children with special needs. She was inducted into the Independent Living Council's Circle of Service and is past president of the Little Rock South Lions Club.

Politics is a family activity for the Mayberrys. Andy Mayberry ran unsuccessfully for Congress in 2006 then served two terms in the Arkansas House (2011–2014). He sought the Republican nomination for lieutenant governor in 2014, and Mayberry ran unopposed for his House seat. After her first term, she decided that being a mother and a legislator was too stressful and declined to run, but her husband again won the position. Two years later, Mayberry decided to return to the House, and she was elected without opposition in 2018 and 2020.

Representative Mayberry enacted legislation to improve public school health and safety, to expand the Arkansas Student Publications Act to include all student media and protect student media advisors, to create the Achieving a Better Life Experience deductible savings program to pay for qualified disability expense, to require and mandate insurance coverage for newborn screening for spinal muscular atrophy, to authorize distribution of organ and tissue donation information in cases of fatal fetal condition, to amend the reproductive health monitoring system, and to restrict administration of the emergency contraception drugs such as mifepristone. In 2021, she passed laws regarding patient visitation rights, the Arkansas Rehabilitation Services loan forgiveness program, the fee collection procedures for the Telecommunications Equipment Fund, contributions to Achieving a Better Life Experience Program Act, professional development for school nurses, Medicaid eligibility, creation of the Public School Americans with Disabilities Act Compliance Committee, and appointments of temporary guardians for children in the event of a parent's death.

Representative Mayberry received a Family Council Action Committee

Statesman Award, the Friend of Scholastic Journalism Award from the Journalism Education Association, and the Conduit for Commerce 2019 Heroes of Liberty Freedom Bill Award.

# Rebecca Petty

HOUSE: 2015–2020
FROM: Rogers, Benton County
PARTY: Republican
BIRTHPLACE: Wichita, Kansas
DATES: April 13, 1970–
EDUCATION: Hatfield High School, 1988; Tulsa Community College, criminal justice, 2005–2008; Arkansas Tech University, BS in criminal justice, 2012; John Brown University, MBA in leadership and ethics, 2017
OCCUPATION: child crime victim advocate

*Photo courtesy of Arkansas Secretary of State.*

Rebecca Petty is the daughter of Carolyn Ann Singleton and Richard Milton Petty. After the 1999 abduction, rape, and murder of her twelve-year-old daughter, Andria Nichole "Andi" Brewer, Petty became an advocate for victims of violent crime and an advocate for children. She wrote and published a book, *Little Girl Stolen*, about losing her daughter to a predatory crime and dealing with grief (DeMauro 2001).

During the next fifteen years, Petty was executive director of the Andi Foundation for Children, a member of the National Center for Missing and Exploited Children's Team HOPE, and a founding member of the Surviving Parents Coalition. She appeared on the *Oprah Winfrey Show* and *Phil Donahue Show*, met with President George W. Bush, and lobbied for the Child Safety Act that created the National Amber Alert system.

After moving to Arkansas from Oklahoma and earning a criminal justice degree from Arkansas Tech, Petty lobbied the Arkansas legislature in 2013 for passage of legislation to allow family members of victims of capital crimes to witness the execution of the person sentenced to death. It passed in the Senate but was defeated in the House.

Motivated to change Arkansas law, Petty ran for an open House seat in 2014. She won the Republican primary with 55 percent and the general election with 58 percent. She was opposed for reelection in 2016 by former representative Debra Hobbs, but defeated Hobbs in the Republican primary and won the general election with 54 percent of the vote. In 2018, Petty was reelected with 56 percent in the general election. Representative Petty chose not to seek reelection to a fourth term in 2020.

Representative Petty was vice chair of the House Judiciary Committee; a member of the Rules Committee; the Committee on Aging, Children and Youth; and the Joint Committee on Legislative Auditing. Her successful legislation dealt almost exclusively with criminal justice issues, including "Andi's Law" to allow victim family members to watch executions, requiring wireless companies to provide cell phone location data to law enforcement, minors' testimony, cause of death entries on certificates of executed felons, crime victims reparations, sexual assault medical legal examinations, national missing and unidentified persons system, no-contact orders, child abduction response teams, probation terms, adult offender supervision, and victims of human trafficking. She received the Advocate of Justice award from the Prosecuting Attorney's Association.

# Laurie Rushing

HOUSE: 2015–2020
FROM: Hot Springs, Garland County
PARTY: Republican
BIRTHPLACE: Hot Springs, Arkansas
DATES: September 10, 1968–
EDUCATION: Fountain Lake High School 1986; University of Arkansas, industrial engineering, 1987–1990; John Brown University, BS organizational leadership, 2020
OCCUPATION: realtor

*Photo courtesy of Arkansas Secretary of State.*

Laurie Rushing (born Laurie Jeanette Nobles) grew up in rural Garland County, Arkansas, and is the daughter of Johnny Leroy Nobles, a painter, and Lorna Jean Pawelczak, a realtor. At Fountain Lake High School in Hot Springs, Rushing was treasurer of Future Homemakers of America, class treasurer and class president, journalism layout editor, a Fountain Lake Singers member, in Beta Club, a cheerleader, and voted Most School Spirited. She married Clifford Lee Rushing, and they had two children.

Rushing's community service included the Charitable Christian Medical Clinic, Garland County Cans for Kids, Habitat for Humanity, Special Olympics, Starting Over Ministries, St. Jude's, Arkansas Children's Hospital, and the Arkansas School for Mathematics, Sciences, and the Arts (ASMSA) Foundation She was also a member of the Greater Hot Springs Chamber of Commerce, Malvern Chamber of Commerce, and the National Association of Professional Women.

In 2002, Rushing joined Trademark Real Estate in Hot Springs, owned by her mother, where she was associate broker and realtor. She was a district vice president of the Arkansas Realtors Association, Hot Springs Board of Realtors president, and the 2009 Arkansas State Realtor of the Year. She graduated from the National Association of Realtors Leadership Academy and was the federal political coordinator for the National Association of Realtors, assigned to lobby US congressmen Tom Cotton and Bruce Westerman. Rushing received the Omega Tau Rho Medal of Service from the National Association of Realtors.

Rushing ran for an Arkansas House seat in 2014, defeating Democratic incumbent representative David Kizzia with 51 percent of the vote in the general election. She was unopposed in 2016, and in 2018, she won the Republican primary with 64 percent and the general election with 61 percent of the vote.

Representative Rushing passed legislation related to real estate issues, including principal brokers, realtor continuing education, real property transfer tax, casualty insurance coverage and mortgage lien protection. She was also lead sponsor on bills addressing deceptive trade practices, brewery licensing, substance abuse treatment, harassing communications, and expanding grandparents' visitation rights. Rushing was awarded the Arkansas Press Association's 2017 Freedom of Information Award, having passed legislation creating the Arkansas Freedom of Information Act Task Force and a resolution honoring Freedom of Information Day in Arkansas. She did not seek reelection in 2020 and continued her work as associate broker for Trademark Real Estate.

# Nelda Speaks

HOUSE: 2015–2022
FROM: Mountain Home, Baxter County
PARTY: Republican
BIRTHPLACE: Norfork, Arkansas
DATES: April 7, 1944–
EDUCATION: Norfork Public School;
Norfork High School, 1962; Draughon's
Business College (Springfield, MO);
Rhema Bible Training College (Broken
Bow, OK), diploma 1993
OCCUPATION: business owner, county
treasurer, justice of the peace

*Photo courtesy of Arkansas Secretary of State.*

Nelda Speaks (born Nelda Gean Adams) is a fifth-generation Arkansan, born in Norfork to Cleo Taylor, a homemaker, and William Eugene Adams, a farmer and small-business owner. She married Benny Speaks in 1963, and they have a daughter. Speaks's father, brother, and sister served on the Norfork School Board; and her father was a member of the Baxter County Democratic Committee. Vada Sheid and Mildred and Dick Holmon influenced her interest and mentored her involvement in politics and government.

Speaks owned and operated Nelda's Boutique, was treasurer of the Norfork School Board, held several positions in banking, and was Baxter County treasurer for sixteen years. Active in organizations, Speaks was treasurer of the Cameo Club and a member of the Mountain Home Chamber of Commerce and the National Rifle Association. She was named Cameo Club Woman of the Year. Governor Mike Huckabee appointed Speaks to the Outdoor Recreation Grants Advisory Committee in 2003.

Active in the Republican Party, Speaks served on the Finance Committee and as legislative liaison for the Republican Party of Arkansas, chair of the Baxter County Republican Committee Candidate Recruiting Committee, and chair of the Twin Lakes Republican Women's Committee. Speaks was an alternate to the 2000 Republican National Convention, and she received the Lifetime Achievement Award from the Baxter County Republican Committee.

While serving her first term on the Baxter County Quorum Court, Speaks ran for a seat in the Arkansas House of Representatives in 2014, winning the general election with 63 percent of the vote against Democrat Willa Mae Sutterfield Tilley. She was unopposed for reelection in 2016 and 2018. Speaks was reelected to a fourth term in 2020, defeating Paige Dillard Evans in the Republican primary with 57 percent of the vote and a Libertarian candidate in the general election with 79 percent.

Representative Speaks passed legislation on county financial operations, county property sales, publication of public school district budgets and bond sales, the Arkansas Public School Computer Network, requiring unopposed candidates to appear on the ballot, district court fees, and the apportionment of fire protection premium tax funds. In 2021, she passed legislation expanding military and veteran special license plates, creating the Higher Education Consumer Guide Act, allowing a school district to receive declining enrollment funding as well as special needs isolated funding, and amending county financial records and operations law.

The Arkansas State Chamber of Commerce honored Speaks with the Business Matters Leadership Award in 2017 and 2019. She also received the Distinguished Legislator Award from the Arkansas Municipal League, and the American Conservative Union honored her with a Conservative Achievement Award.

# DeAnn Vaught

HOUSE: 2015–present
FROM: Horatio, Sevier County
PARTY: Republican
BIRTHPLACE: Ashdown, Arkansas
DATES: January 27, 1970–
EDUCATION: Horatio High School, 1988; Southern Arkansas University, BS in agriculture business, 1991
OCCUPATION: farmer

*Photo courtesy of Arkansas Secretary of State.*

DeAnn Vaught (born DeAnn Kay Stewart) is the daughter of Sharon Kay Napper and James J. Stewart Jr., farmers and real estate brokers. During her first year in college, she married Jonathan David Vaught, and they have three daughters. The Vaughts own Prayer Creek Farm with extensive hog, chicken, and dairy operations. Vaught is a member of the Arkansas Pork Producers Association, the Arkansas Cattlemen's Association, and the Arkansas Farm Bureau Federation. She served on the 2007 Arkansas Farm Bureau task force to address the federal farm bill.

Recruited to run for the House in 2014, Vaught defeated Democratic incumbent Fonda Hawthorne with 59 percent in the general election, and she prevailed again in 2016 against Hawthorne with 73 percent in the general election. Vaught was unopposed for reelection in 2018 and 2020.

Representative Vaught was chair of the House Agriculture, Forestry, and Economic Development Committee; vice chair of the Legislative Joint Auditing Committee; chair of Girls State; and a member of the House Rules Committee.

Vaught passed legislation adding exemptions to the Freedom of Information Act, an "Ag Gag" law with civil penalties for unauthorized access to private property, and legislation making it more difficult for citizens to propose referenda, initiated acts, or constitutional amendments. She passed agricultural legislation related to feral hogs, agricultural extension experiment stations, veterinary licensing, stolen equipment, rural development authorities, veterinary telemedicine, animal artificial insemination, creation of the state meat-inspection program, and processes pertaining to milk and cattle production. Vaught's education legislation includes administrator evaluation, teacher licensing, employee background checks, ethics for school board members, computer science education, requiring public schools to teach the Holocaust, prohibiting males from competing in state-funded school sports that are designated for females, minority teacher and administrator recruitment plans, and creation of the Arkansas Tutoring Corps Act. Other acts include raising speed limits, providing paid maternity leave for state employees, extending a legislative task force on abused and neglected children, environmental compliance, prohibiting pelvic examinations on unconscious or anesthetized patients without prior consent, embalmers and funeral directors' continuing education, health-care coverage, and authorizing legislative review of Presidential Executive Orders.

Vaught received a Leadership Award from the Arkansas Chamber of Commerce, was named a Blue Ribbon Honoree by the Children's Advocacy Centers of Arkansas in 2018, received the 2019 Arkansas Advocates for Children and Families and the Arkansas Kids Count Coalition Legislative Leadership Award, and in 2020 was Healthcare Express's first HCE Hometown Hero.

# LeAnne Burch

HOUSE: 2016–2020
FROM: Monticello, Drew County
PARTY: Democratic
BIRTHPLACE: Stuttgart, Arkansas
DATES: October 7, 1960–
EDUCATION: DeWitt High School, 1979;
Hendrix College, BA, 1982; Memphis
State University School of Law, JD, 1985;
The Judge Advocate General's School,
Army LLM, 1996; US Army War College,
MSS, 2005
OCCUPATION: attorney, brigadier general

*Photo courtesy of Arkansas Secretary of State.*

LeAnne Burch (born LeAnne Pittman) is the daughter of Gail Gateley and Floyd Lee Pittman. In high school, she was senior class president, on the basketball team and annual staff, a cheerleader, in Beta Club, an honor graduate, in Who's Who, and chosen as Most Versatile and Homecoming Maid. After graduating from law school, she began her legal career in the US Army and served on active duty for twelve years. Her military deployments included tours as the senior legal advisor to the Afghan National Army and Afghan Ministry of Defense legal leaders, and legal advisor on NATO issues as part of Operation Joint Guard in Bosnia-Herzegovina. She was awarded the Distinguished Service Medal, the Legion of Merit, and the Bronze Star.

In 1998, she and her husband, Army dentist Dr. Robert (Bobby) Burch Jr., moved to his hometown of Monticello. They each went into private practice and raised two children. Burch joined the Office of Chief Counsel with the Arkansas Department of Human Services in 2002 as a child and adult welfare legal specialist. She remained in the Army Reserve for eighteen years and retired as a brigadier general and commander of the Army Reserve Legal Command. She was the first woman to serve in that position and the second female Army Reservist selected to serve as general officer in the Judge Advocate General's Corps. She also served as a general officer in the Reserve Component Chief Judge, US Army Court of Criminal Appeals.

Burch was the Drew County DHS Employee of the Year in 2012 and a Hendrix College Distinguished Alumna in 2014. Her civic work included the Drew County Master Gardeners, Drew Memorial Hospital Auxiliary,

PEO, Daughters of the American Revolution, Options Inc., the CALL, and the Board of Camp Alliance. Burch received the Monticello Rotary's "Service Above Self" award and was awarded the Joseph T. Robinson Medal of Merit by the National Guard Association of Arkansas.

After the death of Representative Sheilla Lampkin in June 2016, Burch was nominated by the Ninth District Democratic Convention to run to fill the vacancy and for the general election, in which she was unopposed. Burch assumed office on November 16, 2016. She was reelected without opposition in 2018 and was defeated for reelection the 2020 general election, receiving 48 percent.

Representative Burch was co-chair of the House Hunger Caucus; chair of the House Military Caucus; House minority whip; and was appointed to the Arkansas Early Childhood Commission and the Arkansas Supreme Court Commission on Children, Youth, and Families. Her legislation addressed issues concerning children, families, and veterans. Burch was the lead sponsor for "Jacob's Law" that expanded and clarified Arkansas's impaired driving law, and she passed legislation on human services, Arkansas Academic Challenge Scholarship Program eligibility, Arkansas Bar admission, and the creation of the Arkansas Medal of Honor Commission.

Burch was honored with the Arkansas Judicial Council First Branch Award, Arkansas Chamber of Commerce and Associated Industries of Arkansas Business Matters Leadership Award, and twice received the Arkansas Municipal League Distinguished Legislator Award. In 2021, Burch became a member of the Common Ground Arkansas Board.

# Sonia Eubanks Barker

HOUSE: 2017–present
FROM: Smackover, Union County
PARTY: Republican
BIRTHPLACE: El Dorado, Arkansas
DATES: June 22, 1967–
EDUCATION: El Dorado public schools; El Dorado High School, 1985; Southern Arkansas University, BSE in English and French, 1989
OCCUPATION: teacher

*Photo courtesy of Arkansas Secretary of State.*

Sonia Eubanks Barker (born Sonia Eubanks) is the daughter of Gail Williams, a homemaker, and James Troy Eubanks, a human resources manager at Murphy Oil. The family moved from Mt. Holly to El Dorado when she was in the first grade. In high school, Barker was in the National Honor Society, Beta Club, and Brothers and Sisters in Christ. After graduating with honors from college, she was teaching at Westside Christian School in El Dorado when she married John Barker, and they have three children. She teaches French and literacy and is the tennis coach at Smackover High School.

Barker is a member of the American Association of Teachers of French, a lifetime member of the National Rifle Association, and a member of Conservative Arkansas. She is an active member of First Baptist Church in Smackover, where she teaches an adult Sunday school class, sings in the choir, serves on the recreation and finance committees, and frequently travels with youth mission trips.

Although never aspiring to public office, Barker said she "felt a calling" to represent family values, less regulation of business, lower taxes, local control of schools, and unrestricted gun ownership, because "a free people should always have the ability to stand up to tyranny if the situation ever arose." She was elected to an open House seat in 2016, defeating both the Democratic nominee and an Independent candidate with 58 percent in the general election. Barker was unopposed for reelection in 2018 and was reelected in the 2020 general election with 60 percent of the vote. She was unopposed for reelection in 2022.

Representative Barker was vice chair of the House Aging, Children and Youth, Legislative and Military Affairs Committee, and she also served on the House Public Transportation Committee and the Joint Performance Review Committee. A former member of the Education Committee, she was appointed by Governor Asa Hutchinson to the Southern Regional Education Board Legislative Advisory Council.

Representative Barker was lead sponsor on successful legislation to transfer private career education oversight to the Department of Higher Education, exempt an adult services ombudsman from reporting adult or long-term care facility resident maltreatment, require reporting of maternal substance abuse resulting in prenatal drug exposure, and adding restrictions on abortion providers. She also passed legislation regarding transgender girls competing in school sports, adding restrictions for medication abortion services, amending the Child Welfare Agency Licensing Act concerning permitted disclosures of information, and creating a task force to end child abuse.

Representative Barker received a Leadership Award from the Arkansas

Chamber of Commerce and a Statesman Award from the Family Council Action Committee.

# Sarah Capp

HOUSE: 2017–2020
FROM: Ozark, Franklin County
PARTY: Republican
BIRTHPLACE: Elizabethtown, Kentucky
DATES: August 31, 1979–
EDUCATION: H. W. Wilkey Elementary School; Grayson County High School (Leitchfield, KY), 1997; Murray State University, BS in political science and journalism, 2001; University of Arkansas at Little Rock, JD, 2004
OCCUPATION: attorney

*Photo courtesy of Arkansas Secretary of State.*

Sarah Capp (born Sarah Elizabeth Stanton) is the daughter of Kathy S. McClure, an administrative assistant, and Joey F. Stanton, Grayson County jailer who was elected to the office as a Republican. Capp graduated magna cum laude from Murray State University and received a scholarship to attend the UALR Bowen School of Law. She was a law clerk for the Pulaski County prosecuting attorney during law school. In 2004, she married Eric Capp, and they had two children.

In 2006, Capp began the practice of law in Ozark and Russellville, eventually heading her own firm in Ozark. She also worked as a public defender with the Fifteenth Judicial District and served as Altus City attorney. Capp was a member of the Arkansas Bar Association, Leadership Russellville, Rotary International, and the Ozark Area Chamber of Commerce. She was president of Big Brothers Big Sisters Organization for the River Valley Area, finance committee chair of the First United Methodist Church in Ozark, and chapter president of Beta Sigma Phi. Capp was on the Arkansas Access to Justice Foundation Board and served on the Arkansas Access to Justice Commission.

Governor Asa Hutchinson appointed Capp as a special justice of the Arkansas Supreme Court in 2015 and to the Arkansas Development Finance Authority Board in 2016.

In 2016, Capp was nominated by a Republican convention of delegates from Franklin, Madison and Crawford counties, defeating Bobby Ballinger 25–10, to replace Representative Bill Gossage, who resigned to join the staff of Governor Hutchinson. She was unopposed in the general election and was reelected without opposition in 2018.

Representative Capp passed legislation on issues of court procedure, court costs and fees, municipal ordinance codification, county revenue allocation, decedents and estate law, protection of personal information, maltreatment of long-term care patients, tourism, native wines, and venture capital programs. She chaired the House Rules Committee. After visiting with young women at schools in her district and hearing their comments about feeling empowered having a female representative, Capp was the legislative leader in creating #ARGIRLSLEAD, a video series of Arkansas women legislators sharing their personal stories and promoting positive self-image and leadership for young girls across the state. Capp received awards from the Arkansas Chamber of Commerce, the Arkansas Municipal League, and the Arkansas Judicial Council.

In 2020, Sarah Capp was elected to the Arkansas District Court, beginning service in 2021 and becoming the first woman judge in Franklin and Johnson Counties.

# Frances Cavenaugh

HOUSE: 2017–present
FROM: Walnut Ridge, Lawrence County
PARTY: Republican
BIRTHPLACE: Trumann, Arkansas
DATES: December 20, 1962–
EDUCATION: Truman High School, 1981
OCCUPATION: chief finance officer, business owner

*Photo courtesy of Arkansas Secretary of State.*

Frances Cavenaugh (born Frances Marie Wells) is the daughter of Lora Monolia James and Arthur Lee "Hoot" Wells, a farmer and renowned gunsmith. In high school, Cavenaugh was a member of the National Honor

Society, the band, and the band council. After living in Jonesboro, she married Donald Cavenaugh and moved to Walnut Ridge.

Cavenaugh has been president of Collection Pros LLC and the chief financial officer of Cavenaugh Auto Group, with dealerships in Walnut Ridge and Jonesboro. She and her husband also breed and race champion quarter horses. In 2006, the Lawrence County Chamber of Commerce named her business the Industry of the Year, it awarded her the Community Service Award in 2010, and it named her Woman of the Year in 2012.

Professional and community service for Cavenaugh included serving as president of the Arkansas Independent Automobile Dealers Association, the Children's Shelter of Northeast Arkansas, and the Lawrence County Chamber of Commerce. She has served on the boards of the Lawrence Memorial Hospital Foundation and Delta Symphony Orchestra. Cavenaugh was also a member of the Community Revitalization and Beautification Committee and promoted development efforts on Main Street in Walnut Ridge. She organizes the annual Thumperthon race to raise funds for the Northeast Arkansas Humane Society and other area animal rescue groups.

Cavenaugh announced for a seat in the Arkansas House in 2016, running unopposed in the Republican primary and defeating Democratic incumbent representative James Ratliff with 51 percent of the vote. She was unopposed for reelection in 2018 and 2020.

In her first term, Representative Cavenaugh passed a resolution commemorating the integration of Hoxie Public Schools in 1955. In her second term, she was primary sponsor of legislation that created the Government Financial Disclosure and Accountability Act of 2019, prohibited former members of the General Assembly from registering as lobbyists or becoming a director of an educational cooperative or area agency on aging until two years after their term of office, addressed the election of city attorneys in certain mayor-council cities, amended the Rental Purchase Act, and amended the Personal Information Protection Act.

In her third term, Representative Cavenaugh passed legislation concerning providing a sales tax exemption for volunteer fire department protection and emergency equipment; sale and removal of property from a self-service storage facility; clarifying child support obligations; use of administrative subpoenas by the Arkansas State Police investigating internet crimes against a minor; and access to fire protection district information for 911 services. She also passed the joint resolution for a proposed constitutional amendment to allow legislators to call special sessions.

Representative Cavenaugh was honored with a Leadership Award from the Arkansas Chamber of Commerce.

# Carol Dalby

HOUSE: 2017–present
FROM: Texarkana, Miller County
PARTY: Republican
BIRTHPLACE: Decatur, Illinois
DATES: October 2, 1957–
EDUCATION: Arkansas High School,
1975; Ouachita Baptist University, BSE
in English and political science minor,
1979; East Texas State University (Texas
A&M at Texarkana), MS in education
with a business minor, 1982; University of
Arkansas School of Law, JD, 1986
OCCUPATION: teacher and attorney

*Photo courtesy of Arkansas Secretary of State.*

Carol Dalby (born Carol Jan Cannedy) is the daughter of Jeanice White and George Franklin Cannedy, a longtime school board member who also served on the Texarkana Civil Service Commission. At Arkansas High, Dalby was a drum majorette and in NIKE club, all-regional band, student council, senior class play, National Honor Society, Future Teachers, and Teenage Republicans. In college, she was active in student senate, Association of Women Students, Ouachita Student Foundation, EEE women's social club, band, Baptist Student Union, Who's Who, and Kappa Delta Pi education honorary. She was on the Dean's and President's Lists and received the Ouachitonian Leadership Award. She married John L. Dalby, and they have two children.

After teaching seventh-grade English at North Heights Junior High and serving as the public relations officer and director of personnel for the Texarkana School District, Dalby earned a law degree, was a law firm associate, and was appointed by Governor Mike Huckabee as a district judge in Miller County in 2002. For ten years, she served by Huckabee's appointment to the Arkansas Supreme Court as a special associate justice in the Lakeview school funding case. She is an assistant district attorney for Bowie County, Texas, and a member of the Arkansas Bar Association's Professional Ethics Committee.

Dalby was a founding board member of Arkansas Women for Education, Junior League of Texarkana president, president of the Texarkana School

Board, president of the Texarkana Regional Arts Council/Women for the Arts, Red Cross chair, Opportunities Incorporated president, Texarkana Library Commission president, Texarkana Regional Center on Aging Board member, member of the University of Arkansas Alumni Association Board of Directors, and a member of Texarkana Resources for the Disabled. She also teaches Sunday school at the First United Methodist Church.

Dalby ran for a House seat in 2016, winning the Republican primary with 59 percent of the vote and was unopposed in the general election. She was unopposed for reelection in 2018 and 2020.

Representative Dalby is the first woman to chair the House Judiciary Committee. She served on the Girls State Committee. Dalby's legislation included issues of campaign advertising, recording deeds, sex offenders, the Natural Heritage Commission, district courts, civil service eligibility, school safety, law enforcement, juror per diem donation, specialty court program transfers and creating specialty court programs for veterans treatment and driving or boating while intoxicated cases, aggravated assault upon a law enforcement officer or correctional facility employee, and creation of the Uniform Civil Remedies for Unauthorized Disclosure of Intimate Images Act.

Dalby was honored by the Arkansas Prosecuting Attorneys Association with an Advocate of Justice Award due to her support of crime victims, and in 2019 was named an Arkansas High School Distinguished Alumna. She also received a Family Council Action Committee Statesman Award and an Arkansas Chamber of Commerce Leadership Award.

# Breanne Davis

SENATE: 2018–present
FROM: Russellville, Pope County
PARTY: Republican
BIRTHPLACE: Los Angeles, California
DATES: December 26, 1982–
EDUCATION: Russellville High School, 2001; Arkansas Tech University, BS in speech communication, 2007; University of Central Arkansas, MS in community and economic development, 2018
OCCUPATION: account executive, business owner

*Photo courtesy of Arkansas Secretary of State.*

Breanne Davis (born Breanne Deelyte Riley) is the daughter of Jill Deelyte Maloof and David Robert Riley. At Arkansas Tech, Davis was a member of the debate team and College Republicans, and she did internships with KATV in Little Rock and with Congressman John Boozman in Washington, DC. She married John-Paul Davis in 2003, and they have four children.

Davis's first job was as office manager at Impact Management Group, a lobbying and political consulting firm. She later worked as an office assistant for a highway construction firm, a registered lobbyist for Arkansas Tech University, and an account executive for a developer of analytics software before founding the Good Seed Society, a flower and seed partnership that grows and sells its own flowers.

Active in the community, Davis was a Sunday school teacher at Fellowship Bible Church, coached U8 Girls Soccer and Upward Cheerleading, volunteered with Partners Against Trafficking Humans, was a member of the Russellville Area Chamber of Commerce governmental affairs committee, was president of the Russellville School Board, and served on the Russellville Downtown Master Planning Committee. She was selected for the Chamber of Commerce's Leadership Russellville and named 2009 Outstanding Leader of the Year. Davis was appointed by Governor Asa Hutchinson to the Arkansas State Board of Athletic Training.

Politically active since college, Davis was chair of the Pope County Republican Committee, vice chair of the Arkansas Young Republicans, and a member of Pope County Republican Women, River Valley Young Republicans, and the Republican State Committee. She worked for Tom Cotton's campaigns for Congress and US Senate. In November 2017, Davis announced as a candidate to complete the term of Senator Greg Standridge who had died earlier that month. She led the 2018 special Republican primary with 43 percent and won the runoff with 55 percent of the vote, then won the special general election with 77 percent. Davis was unopposed for reelection in 2020.

Senator Davis passed legislation authorizing local governments to provide broadband service, to prohibit female genital mutilation, to clarify applications for casinos, to specify educational measures on school counselors, to allow school resource officers, and to provide a process for reinstating revoked teaching licenses. Davis opposed ratification of the Equal Rights Amendment. Among the legislation she passed in 2021 were laws regarding organ transplants, diabetes, restrictions on gathering signatures for ballot initiatives, treatment of the hearing impaired, health-care facility visitation rights, requiring hepatitis C screening during pregnancy, Medicaid reimbursement of mental health services, domestic violence survivors privacy for voter registration address, concealing nonprofit records, prohibiting state inspection of homemade food sales, prohibiting coronavirus vaccine mandates, electric utilities, law enforcement critical incident debriefing, and creation of the Arkansas Breast Milk Bank. She also passed the joint resolution for a proposed constitutional amendment allowing the legislature to call special sessions.

According to her Senate biography, Senator Davis was the first member of the Arkansas General Assembly to be pregnant and to give birth while in office (fall 2018). She received a 2019 Business Matters Leadership Award from the State Chamber of Commerce, and American Mothers honored her as their 2019 Arkansas Mother of the Year.

# Nicole Clowney

HOUSE: 2019–present
FROM: Fayetteville, Washington County
PARTY: Democratic
BIRTHPLACE: Oklahoma City, Oklahoma
DATES: July 10, 1982–
EDUCATION: Wilson Elementary School; Westminster Day School; Classen School of Advanced Studies, 2000; University of Chicago, BA in classics, 2004; Yale Law School, JD, 2007; University of Kentucky, MA in classics, 2014
OCCUPATION: attorney, professor

*Photo courtesy of Arkansas Secretary of State.*

Nicole Clowney (born Nicole Erin LeFrancois) is the daughter of Elizabeth M. Sperling, a high school special education teacher, and Arthur Gardner LeFrancois, a law professor. Clowney was in the Latin Club and on the Odyssey of the Mind team in high school and won a National Merit Scholarship to the University of Chicago, graduating with a degree in classical studies. She enrolled in Yale Law School and spent one summer working with Northwestern University's Center on Wrongful Convictions. After earning her law degree, she clerked for Chief Judge Robert H. Henry on the United States Tenth Circuit Court of Appeals. In 2008, she married Stephen Clowney, and they have two daughters.

Clowney was a staff attorney for the Children's Law Center, a nonprofit legal service center in Lexington, Kentucky, to protect the rights of children and youth. She completed a master's degree in classics at the University of Kentucky and moved to Fayetteville in 2014, when she and her husband joined the faculty at the University of Arkansas. Clowney is a member of AFSCME Local 965, and she founded the Northwest Arkansas group of Moms Demand Action for Gun Sense in America.

In 2018, Clowney ran for state representative, winning the Democratic primary with 64 percent over Fayetteville alderman Mark Kinion, and she was unopposed in the general election. Clowney was reelected in 2020 with 70 percent over former alderman John LaTour in the general election, and she was also a Democratic presidential elector for Joe Biden in 2020. She was unopposed for reelection in 2022.

Representative Clowney passed legislation extending paid sick leave and clarifying disability retirement for firefighters diagnosed with cancer while in the line of duty, amending the law of aggravated assault, amending the law concerning penalties for violation of an order of protection, and concerning rights and opportunities of inmates who are minors. In 2021, she passed legislation allowing survivors of domestic violence to keep the address on their voter registration private, amending the law concerning intestate succession for a child conceived by assisted reproduction after the death of donor, and creating a cause of action against commercial website operators that post incorrect background information on a person. Clowney was also a cosponsor of the resolution to ratify the Equal Rights Amendment in 2019.

The Arkansas Professional Firefighters Association named Representative Clowney as their 2019 Legislator of the Year, and Arkansas Citizens First Congress rated her record 100 percent on Campaign Finance and Elections, Civil Rights and Civil Liberties, Environment, and Government Operations.

# Cindy Crawford

HOUSE: 2019–present
FROM: Fort Smith, Sebastian County
PARTY: Republican
BIRTHPLACE: Fort Smith, Arkansas
DATES: October 30, 1957–
EDUCATION: Muldrow High School, 1975
OCCUPATION: nonprofit director

*Photo courtesy of Arkansas Secretary of State.*

Cindy Crawford (born Cindy Lee Rogers) grew up in Muldrow, Oklahoma, the daughter of Ott Lee Rogers and Bonnie Blanche Fletcher. In high school, Crawford was a cheerleader, Pep Club officer, Yearbook Queen Attendant, first runner-up to Miss Muldrow High School, ensemble choral member, in Future Homemakers, and in senior chorus. She married Gerald Eugene Crawford in April of 1980, driving off from their wedding on a Harley Davidson motorcycle and continuing to enjoy motorcycle riding together decades thereafter. They have two sons.

Crawford began volunteering at the Pregnancy Crisis Center in 1990 and later became its director. In 1995, she founded and became CEO of the nonprofit organization, Tree of Life Preventive Health Maintenance, Inc. in Fort Smith. It has had grants for ministries in abstinence education and smoking and drug education through the River Valley Drug Free Coalition, and it operates Hannah House, a location for young women who are pregnant or have a crisis situation in their life. Her family also owns Go Ye Employment Services. Crawford's volunteerism includes Restore Hope, a community partnership to facilitate reentry of incarcerated inmates, promote alternative sentencing, and reduce the number of children entering our state's foster care system. She was also treasurer of the Sebastian County Republican Women.

In 2018, Crawford ran for an open seat in the Arkansas House of Representatives, defeating Kelly Proctor Pierce with 51 percent of the vote in the Republican primary to win the legislative seat. In 2020, she was unopposed in the Republican primary and reelected with 71 percent in the general election. She was unopposed for reelection in 2022.

Representative Crawford passed legislation establishing the Life Choices Lifeline Program to provide services for biological or adoptive parents of children under two years of age and legislation to allow persons with non-violent felony convictions to be a guardian for a relative. In 2021, she passed legislation to reorganize the Riverside Vocational and Technical School into the Corrections School System; modify the law on perpetually maintained cemeteries; amend the insolvent Cemetery Grant Fund Act; amend the law concerning the taking of fingerprints and photographs of arrested individuals; and create a restricted lifetime journeyman electrician license.

The Arkansas Chamber of Commerce honored Representative Crawford with a Business Matters Leadership Award, and the Family Council Action Committee awarded her with a 2019 Statesman Award.

## Denise Garner

HOUSE: 2019–present
FROM: Fayetteville, Washington County
PARTY: Democratic
BIRTHPLACE: Dallas, Texas
DATES: December 9, 1956–
EDUCATION: Bradfield Elementary (Highland Park, TX); Lake Highlands Junior High; Lake Highlands High School, 1975; Baylor University, 1975–1977; University of Arkansas for Medical Sciences College of Nursing, BSN/RNP, 1981
OCCUPATION: registered nurse practitioner, small-business owner

*Photo courtesy of Arkansas Secretary of State.*

Denise Garner (born Denise Marie Firmin) is the daughter of Helen Marie Roberts, an educator, and John Thomas Firmin Jr., a business owner. Garner's second cousin, Damon Young, was an Arkansas legislator (1967–1970). In high school, Garner was student council treasurer, on the drill team, and a Key Club sweetheart. She attended Baylor University (1975–1977), where she was Kappa Kappa Gamma Chaplain and chaired "All University Sing."

In August of 1976, she married Hershel (Hershey) Garner, and they moved to Arkansas where he finished law school and medical school. Garner earned her nursing degree at UAMS College of Nursing, where she was in the Sigma Theta Tau honor society. They have two sons. Garner began working at UAMS in 1981 as a nurse in Internal Medicine and as head nurse of the Department of Surgery. From 1982 to 1987, she was a registered nurse practitioner in the Department of Otolaryngology and Head and Neck Cancer at UAMS. In 1990, Garner ventured into a diverse small-business career focused on restaurants, celebration, and friendships. She also founded and chaired Role Call and Feed Fayetteville, and she published *Edible Ozarkansas Magazine.*

Garner is an avid volunteer, community activist, and philanthropist. She held leadership positions with several nonprofit organizations, including the National Museum for Women in the Arts Arkansas Committee, United Way of NWA, Lifestyles, Inc., UAMS Foundation, Arts Center of the Ozarks, Theatre Squared, and the Northwest Arkansas Children's Museum. Garner's service was honored with the Susan G. Komen Power of a Promise National Award, Arkansas Governor's Arts Patrons of the Year Award, Arkansas Women's Foundation Woman in Philanthropy Honoree, *AY Magazine*'s 2010 Powerful Woman, Northwest Arkansas Women in History Award, induction to the Fayetteville Public Education Foundation Hall of Honor, Martin Luther King Lifetime Achievement Award, YouthCan! Shining Star Award, and University of Arkansas Outstanding Alumnae Award.

As a Democratic Party activist, Garner was a member of the Washington County Democratic Women and the county and state Democratic Central Committees, was a delegate to the 2016 Democratic National Convention, and was a Democratic presidential elector in 2016. In 2018, Garner was elected to the Arkansas House of Representatives, defeating the Republican incumbent with 55.4 percent. She was unopposed for reelection in 2020 and 2022.

Representative Garner's legislation focused on gun safety, public education, and health care. She cosponsored legislation that included ratification of the Equal Rights Amendment, ending child marriage, establishing the Maternal Mortality Review Committee, nursing facility staffing standards and reporting requirements, and creating a state meat-inspection program, the Alzheimer's Disease and Dementia Advisory Council, the Arkansas Legislative Arts and Technology Boot Camp, and the Arkansas Tutoring Corps Act. In 2021, she worked on several colleague's bills and sponsored the resolution honoring Fayetteville Public Schools for 150 years of excellence in public education.

# Megan Godfrey

HOUSE: 2019–2022
FROM: Springdale, Washington County
PARTY: Democratic
BIRTHPLACE: Dallas, Texas
DATES: December 5, 1983–
EDUCATION: B. B. Owen Elementary
School; Griffin Middle School; Southwest
Junior High; Springdale High School, 2002;
University of Arkansas, BA in Spanish
and Latin American studies, 2006; Loyola
Marymount University, MA in elementary
education, 2008; University of Arkansas,
PhD curriculum and instruction, 2022.
OCCUPATION: teacher and co-director of
English language learning

*Photo courtesy of Arkansas Secretary of State.*

Megan Godfrey (born Megan Leigh Cardwell) was born in Dallas, Texas, to Cindy Cardwell, a junior high school science teacher, and Gary Cardwell, a sales and marketing executive. When she was in the eighth grade in 1998, Godfrey's father got a promotion that led the family to live in Springdale, Arkansas. She was active in University of Arkansas student government, serving as senator (2002–2004, 2005–2006), chief of staff (2003–2004), and student body secretary (2004–2005). She was also the 2004 University of Arkansas homecoming queen.

After graduating cum laude in 2006, Godfrey moved to Los Angeles, California, participating in Teach for America as a sixth-grade math and science teacher at El Sereno Middle School and earning her master's degree in elementary education at Loyola Marymount University. She returned to Springdale and married Daniel Godfrey in 2008, then began teaching fifth grade at Westwood Elementary School and serving as an English as a second language specialist. In 2014, Megan Godfrey was the ESL curriculum specialist for Springdale Public Schools and in 2017 was Fayetteville Public Schools' co-director of English language learning.

In 2018, while employed with the Fayetteville Public Schools and working toward her doctorate at the University of Arkansas, Godfrey was encouraged to run for a seat in the Arkansas House of Representatives by her college friend Dwayne Bensing, who served as her campaign manager. Godfrey was unopposed in the Democratic primary and defeated the Republican incumbent in the general election with 50.4 percent of the vote. She was reelected with 56 percent in the 2020 general election. Representative Godfrey declined to seek reelection in 2022 after redistricting changed the boundaries of her district to favor Republican candidates.

In her first House term, Representative Godfrey was the main sponsor of legislation amending nursing and teaching licensures. In 2021, she passed legislation allowing campaign funds to be allocated for a candidate's childcare expenses and permitting bilingual instruction and dual-language immersion education in public schools.

Godfrey was the National Association of Social Workers 2019 Legislator of the Year, received the 2019 Change Champion Award for immigrant advocacy, was named a 2019 Northwest Arkansas 40 Under 40 Honoree, was an Arkansas Municipal League 2019 Distinguished Legislator, was an Arkansas Advocates for Children and Families and Arkansas Kids Count Coalition Champion for Kids, received a 2019 Business Matters Leadership Award from the State Chamber of Commerce, and in 2021 was honored as the Champion of Literacy by the Ozark Literacy Council.

# Tippi McCullough

HOUSE: 2019–present
FROM: Little Rock, Pulaski County
PARTY: Democratic
BIRTHPLACE: Carlsbad, New Mexico
DATES: October 1, 1963–
EDUCATION: Lake Hamilton High School, 1981; Garland County Community College, AA in physical education, 1983; Ouachita Baptist University, BSE in physical education and English, 1985; Henderson State University, MSE in English, 1993
OCCUPATION: educator

*Photo courtesy of Arkansas Secretary of State.*

Tippi McCullough is the daughter of Terry McCullough, a car salesman, and Judy Faye Tidwell, a registered nurse. In high school, McCullough was an all-conference basketball player, on the tennis and volleyball teams, a homecoming maid, and participated in Future Homemakers, Beta Club, track, and band. McCullough played basketball and tennis in community college then received a basketball scholarship to Ouachita Baptist University. After graduation, she taught English and coached women's sports for thirty-four years at Arkansas schools located in Kingston, Newport, Mountain Pine, and Little Rock. She was the first woman to serve as president of the Arkansas High School Coaches Association.

In 2013, McCullough married longtime partner Pulaski County deputy prosecuting attorney Barbara Mariani. Mount Saint Mary Academy, where McCullough had taught for fourteen years, immediately forced her resignation. McCullough then began teaching at Little Rock Central High School, where she was sponsor for the Young Democrats, Feminist Alliance, and Gay/ Straight Alliance. She served on the legislative committee of the Arkansas Education Association and the Women's Issues Committee of the National Education Association.

After the employment injustice, McCullough became engaged in politics as chair of the Pulaski County Democratic Party, Democratic Party of Arkansas executive committee, president of the Arkansas Stonewall Democrats, and a Clinton delegate to the 2016 Democratic National Convention. She spoke at the 2017 Women's March at the Arkansas State Capitol and spoke around the nation for the Human Rights Campaign.

McCullough's community involvement includes vice president of the Hillcrest Residents' Association, co-chair of Pridecorps Youth Board, chair of Hillcrest HarvestFest, the Kaleidoscope Film Festival Advisory Committee, Central Arkansas Library System Speaker Series Advisory Committee, and the First United Methodist Church Parish Relations Committee. McCullough received the 2014 ACLU Champion of Liberty Award, was named the *Arkansas Times* 2013 Person of the Year and runner-up for Best Little Rocker, and was Central Arkansas Pride's 2018 Grand Marshal.

Mentored by Senator Joyce Elliott and former representative Kathy Webb, McCullough ran for an open House seat in 2018, winning the Democratic primary with 55 percent of the vote and was unopposed in the general election. She was unopposed for reelection in 2020.

Representative McCullough filed legislation to create the Working Families Tax Relief Act and the Arkansas Equal Pay Act of 2019 and passed legislation that allows a sentence enhancement against a person who commits certain offences in the presence of a child. She also cosponsored a resolution for ratification of the Equal Rights Amendment. In the 2021 regular session, McCullough passed legislation amending the offense of sexual assault in the second and third degrees when committed by a minor, amending requirements for sex offenders having their obligation to register terminated, clarifying rights and duties of operating a bicycle upon a crosswalk, requiring safety hotline information on student identification cards or badges, protecting address confidentiality from an individual convicted of domestic violence, and prohibiting the use of campaign or carryover funds to pay for an ethics violation.

In 2019, McCullough received the Arkansas Municipal League Distinguished Legislator Award and the Arkansas Coalition Against Domestic Violence Domestic Peace Award. She was elected by the House Democratic Caucus as the 2021 Minority Leader of the House.

# Gayla H. McKenzie

HOUSE: 2019–2022
FROM: Gravette, Benton County
PARTY: Republican
BIRTHPLACE: Siloam Springs, Arkansas
DATES: August 12, 1965–
EDUCATION: Gravette High School, 1983; University of Arkansas, BSE in music education, 1987, and JD, 1990
OCCUPATION: attorney, business owner

*Photo courtesy of Arkansas Secretary of State.*

Gayla H. McKenzie (born Gayla Joy Hendren), the daughter of Kim Dexter Hendren and Marylea Hutchinson, grew up in a political family. Both her father and brother, Jim Hendren, served in the Arkansas House and Senate. Her uncle, Tim Hutchinson, served in the Arkansas House and the United States House and Senate; and her uncle, Asa Hutchinson, served in the US Congress and as governor. McKenzie's aunt, Donna Hutchinson, served in the Arkansas House; her cousin, Timothy Hutchinson, served in the Arkansas House; and her cousin, Jeremy Hutchinson, served in the Arkansas House and Senate.

In high school, McKenzie was secretary of the National Honor Society, in all-regional band, on the basketball team, and in senior choir and the senior class play. After receiving her undergraduate and law degrees, McKenzie returned to Gravette and practiced law for one year before forming Hendren Communications, Inc. and became president of KBVA-FM radio for twenty-six years. She married Loyd W. McKenzie, and they have two daughters. In

2017, she sold the radio station, and they established Ozark Stone Designs, a stone veneer manufacturing plant in Gravette.

McKenzie is on the board of Northwest National Bank, a member of Gravette Kiwanis Club, and a volunteer in Gravette Public Schools. She is active in Berean Ministries as pianist, teacher, and youth director.

When her father decided not to seek reelection to the House in 2018. McKenzie ran for the position. She was elected with 71 percent in the 2018 general election, and she was unopposed for reelection in 2020. McKenzie was a candidate for the state senate in 2022.

Representative McKenzie sponsored Act 834 of 2019, allowing college students to retain their state scholarships if they drop to part-time student status in their senior year. In the 2021 session, she sponsored a study of the best practices for reducing the number of children in foster care and passed legislation amending the law concerning the rights of guardians and wards and repealing provisions for rights of relatives.

# Jamie Scott

HOUSE: 2019–present
FROM: North Little Rock, Pulaski County
PARTY: Democratic
BIRTHPLACE: North Little Rock, Arkansas
DATES: March 7, 1982–
EDUCATION: North Little Rock High School, 2000; Arkansas State University, BA in criminology and sociology, 2004, and MA in criminal justice, 2007; Harvard University, Kennedy School of Government Executive Education Program, 2015
OCCUPATION: county youth services director

*Photo courtesy of Arkansas Secretary of State.*

Jamie Aleshia Scott, the daughter of Freddie Bernard Scott and Margie Nell Smith, is the youngest Black woman ever elected to the Arkansas General Assembly. While in high school, she was on the student council, the dance team, the softball team, and the cheerleading squad and worked in her uncle's barbeque restaurant. In college, Scott was selected for Who's Who Among Students in American Universities and Colleges, active in the Black Student Association, Alpha Kappa Alpha Sorority, and worked in the chancellor's office.

After graduate school, Scott worked as a regional field director for the Alliance for Climate Protection, was director of the Upward Bound program at Arkansas Baptist College for five years, and became Pulaski County youth services director in 2015. She also formed the Jamie Scott Group, LLC, a public affairs consulting firm.

Scott has served on the boards of Just Communities of Arkansas, Volunteers in Public Schools, AR Kids Read, Inspire the Vote, and Arkansas Women's Action for New Directions. She is a mentor for Big Brothers Big Sisters of America and is an active member of Alpha Kappa Alpha Sorority and the Junior League of Little Rock. Governor Mike Beebe appointed Scott to the Arkansas Legislative Task Force on Abused and Neglected Children. She has been recognized by the Women of Excellence in Education Award, Arkansas State University Emerging Young Alumni Award, Arkansas Business 40 under 40, and the Presidential Leadership Scholars Program.

Political involvement for Scott began in working for Hillary Clinton's 2008 campaign, and she has worked in numerous state and local campaigns, including serving as 2012 campaign manager for her mentor, senator Joyce Elliott. Scott was a member of the Pulaski County Democratic Committee and the Executive Committee of the Democratic Party of Arkansas, as well as a delegate to Democratic National Convention in 2016 (Clinton) and 2020 (Biden). Scott received the Democratic Party of Arkansas's Emerging Leader Award in 2017.

In 2018, Scott ran for an open House seat, was nominated with 59 percent in the Democratic primary, and was elected unopposed in the general election. She was unopposed for reelection in 2020 and 2022.

Representative Scott's enacted legislation includes prohibiting prostitution charges against minors who are human trafficking victims, limiting the use of solitary confinement as punishment for incarcerated youths, allowing higher education staff to serve as homeless and foster student liaisons, providing prohibitions on solitary confinement or restrictive housing of pregnant or recently pregnant detainees, requiring the Department of Corrections to establish a mammogram and prostate-screening policy for detainees free of cost, school resource officers training, and creating transparency and uniformity in the bail bond process. Scott was also primary sponsor of the resolution to ratify the Equal Rights Amendment. She secured adoption of a resolution honoring the North Little Rock Six.

Scott was named a Legislative Champion by Arkansas Advocates for Children and Families. In 2021, she joined the National Governors Association workgroup to meet social and emotional needs of Arkansas students and families.

# Denise Jones Ennett

HOUSE: 2019–present
FROM: Little Rock, Pulaski County
PARTY: Democratic
BIRTHPLACE: Little Rock, Arkansas
DATES: June 24, 1977–
EDUCATION: Central High School, 1995;
University of Texas at Arlington, BA
in history, 2008; University of Arkansas
at Little Rock, MA in student affairs in
higher education, 2013
OCCUPATION: community advocate

*Photo courtesy of Arkansas Secretary of State.*

Denise Jones Ennett (born Denise Brooke Jones) is the daughter of Beverly
Ann Hood, an attorney, and Dennis Raymond Jones, a Marine Corp offi-
cer and educator. Ennett was an active student at Little Rock Central High
School, where she was on the student council and in the Ladies Club,
TAILS peer counseling group, Spanish Club, yearbook staff, and Accept No
Boundaries. After living in Texas and Oklahoma, Ennett married master ser-
geant Cecil Stephen Ennett, and they moved to Little Rock when he retired
from the United States Air Force in 2010. They purchased the 1907 Gustave
Bruno Kleinschmidt House, Ennett's childhood home in the Pettaway neigh-
borhood, where they are raising three children. The house is listed on the
National Register of Historic Places.

As a parent advocate/mentor at the Center for Exceptional Families,
Ennett works with families to improve the educational opportunities for stu-
dents with disabilities. She is active in the community, serving on the boards
of the Arkansas Parent Teachers Association, Volunteer in Public Schools,
Autism Taskforce, Historic Arkansas Museum Foundation, Mosaic Templars
Cultural Center, Preserve Arkansas, Education of Children with Disabilities,
Carver Magnet Parent Teacher Association, and public radio stations KLRE/
KUAR. Ennett has volunteered with the American Association of University
Women, League of Women Voters, Helping Hands Catholic Charities,
Downtown Neighborhood Association, Quapaw Quarter Association, and
she is a member of the Little Rock Arts and Cultural Commission.

Ennett's political involvement began when she testified on education issues
before the Arkansas Board of Education and committees of the Arkansas

General Assembly, working to return local control for the Little Rock School District. When Representative Charles Blake resigned to serve as Little Rock mayor's chief of staff, Ennett announced for the House seat. After the *Arkansas Democrat-Gazette* identified her as a homemaker, she said, "Yes, I am a homemaker and a leader, a Black woman and a volunteer, a mom and a political activist." Ennett led four male candidates in the August 2019 Democratic primary, won the September runoff with 58 percent of the vote, and was elected without opposition in the November 2019 general election. She won renomination with 70 percent in the 2020 Democratic primary and was unopposed in the general election. Ennett was unopposed for reelection in 2022.

When entering the Arkansas General Assembly in 2020, Representative Ennett served on the Judiciary Committee and Insurance and Commerce Committee. During her first regular session, in 2021, she passed legislation that allows public schools and open-enrollment public charter schools to use funding to provide feminine hygiene products at no charge, amended the law concerning warehouse facilities and municipal port authorities, and passed a resolution recognizing Scipio Africanus Jones and his role in defending men accused in the Elaine massacre of 1919.

# Joy Springer

HOUSE: 2020–present
FROM: Little Rock, Pulaski County
PARTY: Democratic
BIRTHPLACE: Ogemaw, Arkansas
DATES: December 11, 1956–
EDUCATION: Carver Elementary School; Stephens High School, 1974; Henderson State University, BSBA in general business and minor in economics, 1977; University of Arkansas at Little Rock, BSE in elementary education, 1999, and MEd in educational leadership, 2001; Philander Smith College Educator Preparation Program
OCCUPATION: office manager and paralegal

*Photo courtesy of Arkansas House of Representatives.*

Joy Springer (born Joy Dale Charles) was born in Ogemaw, Arkansas, to Bobbie Lee Joshua, a bookkeeper and homemaker, and Eli Charles, owner of

Charles Lumber Company. In high school, Springer was an honor student, class president, a member of the student council, a majorette, member of the championship basketball team, and voted Most Courteous. At Henderson State University, she was elected to the student senate, was an officer in Alpha Kappa Alpha Sorority, and was named to Who's Who. She married Horace L. Springer III in 1983.

Springer was an insurance claims manager before becoming office manager, paralegal, and desegregation monitor for civil rights attorney John W. Walker. She was the lead monitor for Pulaski County School District's compliance with its desegregation plans for over twenty-five years, representing the Joshua Intervenors, Black students in the district. Walker was a mentor and strong influence on Springer's involvement in politics and government. She worked on Walker's successful 2010 campaign for state representative, and Walker backed Springer's successful 2014 election to the Little Rock School Board.

Always active in her community, Springer served on the Executive Committee of the National Association for the Advancement of Colored People's Little Rock Branch, the Executive Committee of Forward Arkansas, and the Clementine Mathis Rouse Scholarship Fund Board. She was a Sunday school teacher, Missionary Society Trustee, and member of the Steward's Board at Ward Chapel African Methodist Episcopal Church. Springer was also a member of the Little Rock School District Magnet Review Committee, Community Advocates for Public Education, and the Wright Avenue Neighborhood Association. In 2017, she received the Social Justice Award from the Little Rock Christian Ministerial Alliance.

When Representative Walker died in 2019, Springer, who had worked alongside Walker for over twenty-five years, announced for his House seat "to continue the legacy." In the special election to complete his term, she led a field of four in the Democratic primary with 43 percent, won the runoff by a single vote, and won the special general election with 78 percent. In her reelection campaign for a full term, Springer won the Democratic primary over two opponents with 64 percent and won the general election with 70 percent of the vote.

Representative Springer served on the House Aging, Children and Youth, Legislative and Military Affairs Committee, as well as the Joint Budget, Joint Performance Review, and House Public Transportation Committees. She was lead House sponsor of legislation in 2021 amending the membership of the Arkansas State Medical Board and the supervision and prescriptive authority of physician assistants.

*Soiree Magazine*, in 2020, honored Springer as one of the Women to Watch.

In 2021, she became president for Alpha Kappa Alpha Sorority, Incorporated®, Beta Pi Omega Chapter, and she received the Humanitarian of the Year award from the Arkansas Martin Luther King Jr. Commission.

# Jill Bryant

HOUSE: 2020
FROM: Rogers, Benton County
PARTY: Republican
BIRTHPLACE: Rogers, Arkansas
DATES: September 10, 1978–
EDUCATION: Rogers Public Schools;
Benton County Christian High School,
1996; John Brown University; NorthWest
Arkansas Community College, AA, 2000;
Campbell University; University of Science
and Arts of Oklahoma, BSBA magna cum
laude, business, 2006
OCCUPATION: property management

*Photo courtesy of Arkansas House of Representatives.*

Jill Bryant (born Barbara Jill Carney) is the daughter of Arlene Rose Carney, a homemaker, and Billy Craig Carney, owner of Dixieland Shoes. Bryant attended Benton County Christian School, an institution where Tim Hutchinson was board president, Asa Hutchinson was a board member, Donna Hutchinson was on the faculty, and Timothy and Jeremy Hutchinson were students. Bryant was a member of the swim team, class treasurer, and salutatorian of her graduating class. She married classmate Joshua Paul Bryant in 1999, and they have two children. Her husband served on the Benton County Quorum Court, 2017–2020, and is a partner with her brother in a general contracting firm. In 2018, Governor Hutchinson appointed her father to the Arkansas Contractors Licensing Board.

Bryant served as treasurer of the Eastside Elementary Parent Teacher Organization in Rogers and is a member of Benton County Republican Women. She is also an avid scuba diver and has four times received the Iron Diver Award from Aggressor Adventures.

When Representative Grant Hodges resigned in July 2020, Jill Bryant filed on August 3 for the open House seat in a special election to fill the term. She was elected without opposition on November 3, 2020, took the oath of office on November 23, 2020, and served for fifty days. Representative Bryant was a member of the House Education Committee and the House Insurance and Commerce Committee. Bryant was succeeded by her husband, who was elected for a full term on the same day she was elected to replace Hodges.

# Delia J. Haak

HOUSE: 2021–present
FROM: Gentry, Benton County
PARTY: Republican
BIRTHPLACE: Phoenix, Arizona
DATES: August 26, 1956–
EDUCATION: Phoenix Christian High School, 1974; Phoenix College; Arizona College of the Bible; NorthWest Arkansas Community College; John Brown University, BS in business administration, magna cum laude, 1990; University of Arkansas, MBA, 1994, and EdD, 1999
OCCUPATION: professor, nonprofit director

*Photo courtesy of Arkansas House of Representatives.*

Delia J. Haak (born Delia Jane Gumm) is the daughter of Ruby Jane "Nova" Terry, a state employee, and Wilford Warren "Bill" Gumm, a bookkeeper and office manager for a car dealership. Often called "Dee Dee" by high school friends, Haak was 1973–1974 National Vice President of Future Homemakers of America (now Family, Career, and Community Leaders of America). She married William B. Haak Jr., in 1976, and they soon moved to a forty-seven-acre farm near Gentry. Their farming operation has grown to 830 acres and includes dairy, beef, hay, and shavings and sawdust sales. The Haak Dairy Farm is one of ten farms statewide in the University of Arkansas Discover Farm Program conducting on-farm research, and the family was honored as the Arkansas Farm Family of the Year. They have two sons and seven grandchildren.

Haak worked for two years as a secretary for the Gentry School System, then continued her own education, earning bachelor's, master's, and doctorate degrees. At John Brown University in Siloam Springs, Haak was an associate professor of business and also served at various times as executive assistant to the president, marketing services coordinator, director for the Soderquist Center for Leadership and Ethics, and director of graduate business programs. Dr. Haak received the 1991 Golden Eagle Service Award, the 2000 JBU Alumnus of the Year award, the 2001 JBU Faculty of the Year Award, and in 2018 published *By These Stones: Biographies and Writings of Former Faculty at John Brown University* with John E. Brown III.

While continuing as an adjunct professor at JBU, Dr. Haak was executive director of the Illinois River Watershed Partnership from 2007 to 2016. She was appointed federal chair of the Arkansas-Oklahoma Arkansas River Compact Commission, and she was appointed by Governor Asa Hutchinson to the Arkansas Forestry Commission (2015–2019) and the Arkansas Pollution Control and Ecology Commission (2019–2020). The Haaks were an International Host Family from 1986 to 2006 for international students from seven countries.

Dr. Haak served on the Gentry Public Library Board, as a member of the Circle of Life Ladies Auxiliary and NWA Fellowship Bible Church, and on the Arvest Bank Board of Siloam Springs. Among her awards were the 2011 Arkansas Water Works and Water Environment Association Educator of the Year Award and the 2014 Rogers-Lowell Chamber of Commerce Spirit Award.

In 2020, Haak ran for the District 91 House of Representatives seat. She placed second among three candidates in the Republican preferential primary, then won the runoff with 54 percent of the vote. She won the 2020 general election with 73 percent of the votes, and she was unopposed in 2022.

Representative Haak passed legislation creating the Safe Trails Act, requiring disclosure of certain sales tax data to governmental subdivisions, authorizing driver's license cards without a photograph, restrictions on medical marijuana advertising, creating the electric vehicle infrastructure grant program, authorizing regulations and taxes on car-sharing programs, and creating sales tax exemptions for coins, currency, and bullion.

Haak received a Distinguished Legislator Award from the Arkansas Municipal League in 2021.

# Ashley Hudson

HOUSE: 2021–present
FROM: Little Rock, Pulaski County
PARTY: Democratic
BIRTHPLACE: Little Rock, Arkansas
DATES: June 17, 1979–
EDUCATION: Paris High School (IL), 1997;
Vanderbilt University, BA in English liter-
ature and political science, 2001; University
of Arkansas, MA in political science, 2007,
and JD, 2007
OCCUPATION: attorney

*Photo courtesy of Arkansas House of Representatives.*

Ashley Hudson (born Ashley Rebecca Welch) is the daughter of Rebecca Ann McCarty, an account executive at Southwestern Bell, and Morgan Eldridge "Chip" Welch, an attorney and later Pulaski County circuit judge. In high school, Hudson played saxophone in the band, acted in class plays, and was a member of the National Honor Society, and in college, she was on the Arts and Science College Council, active in VandyCares, and a member of Pi Beta Phi fraternity. After graduation, she worked production for Country Music Television and USA Network in Nashville and Los Angeles, before returning to Arkansas for graduate and law school.

At the University of Arkansas, Hudson was active in Model Arab League and a graduate assistant in political science while also pursuing a law degree. Her law school activities included note and comment editor of the *Arkansas Law Review*; regional champion and finalist in American Bar Association National Appellate Advocacy Competition; officer in the Arkansas Trial Lawyers Association Student Section, Media, Entertainment and Sports Law Association, and International Law Association; and membership on the Board of Advocates and Phi Delta Phi legal fraternity. In 2006, Hudson married George Clifford Hudson, a Marine infantry squad leader in Iraq and facilities planner at Central Arkansas Veterans Healthcare System, and they have four children.

Hudson began law practice with the Faulkner Firm in 2007 before joining her father in 2008 to form Welch, Brewer and Hudson in North Little Rock. After her father was elected to a judgeship, she joined the firm of Kutak

Rock as an associate in 2012 and became a partner in 2017, specializing in health-care regulation. Active in her profession, Hudson was a member of the Arkansas Association of Women Lawyers, the House of Delegates of the Arkansas Bar Association, and Board of Directors for QLaw Arkansas. She was also on the editorial board for the *Arkansas Lawyer* and received the Maurice Cathey Award in 2016 for contributions to the periodical. *Arkansas Money & Politics* named her among the Legal Elite for Health Care Law.

Among Hudson's community service activities are board chair of the University of Arkansas-Pulaski Tech Foundation and organizer of the Junior League of Little Rock's Downtown Dash 10K fundraiser for food and school supplies. She was named to *Soirée*'s Women to Watch 2017 and a 2018 Elizabeth Dole Caregiver Fellow for her active military and veteran caregiver leadership.

Hudson announced for the Arkansas House in 2019. She was unopposed in the Democratic primary and defeated three-term Republican incumbent representative Jim Sorvillo by twenty-four votes in the 2020 general election. Representative Hudson was vice chair of Girls State. She passed legislation amending procedures for removing commissioners and filling vacancies for suburban improvement districts, and she was lead House sponsor of legislation concerning confidential and privileged records kept by the State Crime Laboratory.

# Bibliographic Essay

A traditional bibliographic essay would be an extended summary of the most important published scholarship on Arkansas women legislators to guide students and scholars approaching additional research. Unfortunately, the lives and public service of most Arkansas women legislators have been undocumented, and the analyses of their political and policy successes have not often been the subject for serious study or publication. The governors of Arkansas and the United States senators and representatives from Arkansas have more often been the focus of historians and political scientists. Federal officers and state executives are more visible and, perhaps, seen as more important than state legislators. Works about US senator Hattie Caraway, for example, far exceed any other elected Arkansas female public official. To be sure, most libraries and archives are more likely to seek and acquire the papers of governors and national politicians for use by scholars, often overlooking the collections of women state legislative, county, and municipal elected officials who have shaped the state's political culture. What we want to do here is to provide a review of the limited literature and a more detailed introduction to the primary materials available in archives and libraries necessary for future research.

A helpful starting place for understanding the warp and woof of the tapestry of Arkansas politics is Diane D. Blair and Jay Barth's *Arkansas Politics and Government* (2nd ed. Lincoln: University of Nebraska Press, 2005). In addition to a helpful overview, the authors include citations to Blair's research on perceptions of power by the men and women in the Arkansas legislature, as well as information regarding the formation and function of the women's legislative caucus and the impact of term limits on the election and retirement of women legislators. The effect of term limits on open seats available for women candidates is also examined in Art English's "Term Limits in Arkansas: Opportunities and Consequences," in *Readings in Arkansas Politics and Government* (edited by Kim U. Hoffman, Janine A. Parry, and Catherine C. Reese. Fayetteville: University of Arkansas Press, 2019, 127–36).

The only book to focus on the Arkansas General Assembly is Jerry E. Hinshaw's *Call the Roll: The First One Hundred Fifty Years of the Arkansas*

*Legislature* (Little Rock: Department of Arkansas Heritage, 1986). Written by a former state representative for the sesquicentennial celebration of Arkansas statehood, it includes the names and dates of service for almost every member of the Arkansas General Assembly serving before 1986 and a brief historical overview that gives some attention to the contributions of women legislators. Hinshaw devotes two pages to the suffrage movement and the first two elected women legislators. The chapter on "Famous Arkansas Legislators of the 20th Century" includes Representative Bernice Kizer along with nineteen male former legislators.

Four women who previously served in the Arkansas General Assembly have written books about their political experiences. The first autobiographical work was Representative Florence McRaven's *Swift Current* (Santa Barbara California: Press of the Schauer Printing Studio, Inc., 1954). It offers a readable account of her family, experiences growing up, life as a clubwoman, work for the state labor department, campaign for office, and service in the Arkansas House. Representative Shirley Borhauer published *Shirley Who?* (New York: Vantage Press, 1977). Written before she moved to Arkansas, it is about her 1975 campaign for the Chicago City Council, but it provides biographical information and political insight to her early career. Vada Sheid produced a lively account of Arkansas politics in the twentieth century, detailing her early life, political influences, and campaigns for county treasurer, state representative, and state senator in her book, *Vada: Nothing Personal, Just Politics; My Life in the Arkansas House and Senate* (Plano, TX: MC2 Graphics, 2008). Her campaign experiences and public service are recounted in detail, and the discussion of her commitment to constituent service and her persistence in securing projects and public services for her district is particularly instructive. Another autobiography is Charlotte Schexnayder's *Salty Old Editor: An Adventure in Ink* (Little Rock: Butler Center Books, 2012). Much of her autobiography is devoted to her professional newspaper career and public service, but there are enlightening stories about her political career and tenure in the Arkansas House. Schexnayder discussed her memoir and the role of women legislators in a talk moderated by Dean Skip Rutherford at the Clinton School of Public Service on June 4, 2012 (available at https://www.youtube .com/watch?v=Le-m1upVAVw).

An essential source of published biographical information on women legislators is the *Encyclopedia of Arkansas*, an ongoing project of the Central Arkansas Library System in Little Rock, edited by Guy Lancaster. It is a free, online "comprehensive reference work for historians, teachers, students, and others seeking to understand and appreciate Arkansas's heritage." Founded in 2006 as the *Encyclopedia of Arkansas History and Culture*, it now includes more than twenty biographies of Arkansas women legislators with selected bibliographic references. Additional entries are being added each year, and the collection is fully searchable from the website at https://encyclopediaof arkansas.net/. Biographical information about the careers and contributions of six women who formerly served in the legislature is included in *Horizons: 100 Arkansas Women of Achievement* (Kitty Sloan, editor. Little Rock: Rose Publishing Co., 1980). The book was a project of the Arkansas Press Women, who solicited nominations, then made the decisions and wrote the biographies. Included are entries on Representatives Rita Clubbs (Hale), Bernice Kizer, Willie Oates, Carolyn Pollan, Charlotte Schexnayder, and Senator Vada Sheid, as well as Jim Searcy Childers, the first woman to be elected chief clerk of the House.

Beyond *Horizons* and the *Encyclopedia of Arkansas*, journal articles about individual Arkansas women legislators and their contributions are rare. A personal account of Representative Erle Chambers was provided by a friend, who had worked closely with her for years at the Tuberculosis Association and on the state sanitorium board. Jefferson M. (Mrs. W. T.) Dorough's "Pulaski Profiles: The First Woman Legislator in Arkansas—A Tribute to Miss Erle Chambers" (*Pulaski County Historical Review* 32 [Summer 1984]: 32–34) is a brief but informative contribution to understanding Chambers and her professional and political career. A well-documented article about Vada Sheid's political persistence is Clement A. Mulloy's "Vada Webb Sheid and the Transformation of North Central Arkansas" (*Arkansas Historical Quarterly* 73, no. 2 [2014]: 192–215). Particular attention is given to Sheid's successful efforts to secure state and federal infrastructure investments in her district, and it also provides a clear look at the changing political culture in Arkansas.

Based on interviews with women legislators in Arkansas and Texas, Diane D. Blair and Jeanie R. Stanley's "Personal Relationships and Legislative Power: Male and Female Perceptions" (*Legislative Studies Quarterly* 16 [1991]: 495–507) provides a look at the concept of legislative power and its relation to communication styles. They found both similarities and differences between male and female legislators. In another study that dispelled the perception women were more likely to voluntarily leave the legislature because of family concerns, Diane Kincaid Blair and Ann R. Henry's "The Family Factor in State Legislative Turnover" (*Legislative Studies Quarterly* 6, no. 1 [1981]: 55–68) found that male legislators in Arkansas voluntarily retiring from legislative service cited family considerations in twenty-seven of the fifty-six cases studied. Another factor often assumed and expressed is that women legislative candidates are discouraged from running and have less success against male opponents because of their inability to raise sufficient campaign funds. The traditional thinking is that women are disadvantaged by a lack of business networks and connections. However, Emily Adair Neff-Sharum's "Who's the Safer Sex? Testing Barbara Burrell's Theory of Campaign Contributions in Arkansas State Legislative Elections" (MA thesis, University of Arkansas, 2002) found "that not only were women able to raise more money than men of similar candidate status, but they were able to raise more money than men in the aggregate."

Janine A. Parry and William H. Miller's "'The Great Negro State of the Country?': Black Legislators in Arkansas: 1973–2000" (*Journal of Black Studies* 36, no. 6 [July 2006]: 833–72) found that the Arkansas Legislative Black Caucus had too few members and held too few leadership positions "to wield much observable influence." The Women's Legislative Caucus was likely handicapped by similar factors. The article included comments from interviews with Representatives Irma Hunter Brown and Lisa Ferrell. In another article, Parry examines the role of the Arkansas Women's Commissions, which always included women legislators, and the role of women legislators regarding ratification of the proposed Equal Rights Amendment (Janine A. Parry, "'What Women Wanted': Arkansas Women's Commissions and the ERA," *Arkansas Historical Quarterly* 59, no. 3 [2000]: 265–98). Another overview of Arkansas women legislators and their roles in the extended unsuccessful effort to ratify the ERA, from 1973 through the twenty-first century, is Lindsley Armstrong Smith and Stephen A. Smith's "Keeping Hope Alive: A Case Study of the Continuing Argument for Ratification of the ERA" (*Frontiers: A Journal of Women Studies*, 38, no. 2 [2017]: 173–207). The study draws on personal experiences of the authors and interviews with women legislators involved in the ratification efforts.

With a relative dearth of scholarly literature addressing the history of women in the Arkansas General Assembly, we relied heavily on contemporaneous newspaper accounts. Perhaps the most extensive microfilm collection of Arkansas newspapers is that held at the Arkansas State Archives (more than three thousand titles published at two hundred fifty different Arkansas locations) and available for public access in the main reading room. In addition, we relied on the microfilm holdings in Mullins Library at the University of Arkansas and utilized several digital collections. The Library of Congress *Chronicling America* project provides free online access to digitized copies of more than seventy Arkansas newspapers and a convenient search engine for content. Additional research relied upon commercial databases with Arkansas newspaper content, including *NewsBank* for the historical and current content of the *Arkansas Gazette* from 1820, *Arkansas Democrat* from 1947, and *Arkansas Democrat-Gazette* from 1991; *NewspaperArchive.com*, which provides searchable content from Arkansas newspapers published at Fayetteville, Blytheville, Benton, Camden, Harrison, Hope, and Gentry; Gale's *Nineteenth Century U.S. Newspapers* has digital content from the *Arkansas Gazette* (1819–1898), *Arkansas Democrat* (1846–1899), the *Arkansas State Gazette* (1836–1865), and the *Morning Republican* (Little Rock, 1867–1875); and *Newspapers.com* has more than two-million pages from newspapers in forty-five Arkansas counties. We also used the *Internet Archive Wayback Machine* (https://archive.org/web/), a free online search engine for archived webpages, which was helpful in recovering the past campaign websites of women candidates for the Arkansas House and Senate.

There has been no concerted effort to collect and archive the papers of Arkansas women legislators or to document the challenges they faced in state politics. Libraries and archives have accepted donations in a few cases but often seem unaware of this potential source of our state's political history. Few appear to have collection policies that encourage the donation of papers documenting women's political participation in politics and government, overlooking women legislators' papers even when soliciting other political collections. For that and other reasons, women legislators did not appreciate the fact that their papers and political materials would have historical value for research and generally have been unaware of opportunities to preserve their papers and make them accessible in archives and research libraries. We are encouraged that a few archives have overcome the previous bias and lack of awareness regarding the value of women's political and legislative papers.

The Arkansas State Archives, Little Rock, holds the *Frances M. and Sidney J. Hunt Letters, 1892–1936* (MG03814–MG03815), and an extensive collection of photographs of women legislators is in its Shrader Studio State Legislator photographs, the Ernie Dean photographs, and the historic House and Senate composite photographs. Readers cards are available for research in the main reading room, and the staff will respond to online requests.

Special Collections at Mullins Library, University of Arkansas, has several significant collections related to Arkansas women legislators. One is the *Willie Oates Papers* (MC 732). Willie Oates (1918–2008) served as a member of the Arkansas House from 1959 to 1960. The collection includes correspondence, programs, clippings, photographs, scrapbooks, and other papers. The *Charlotte and Melvin Schexnayder Papers: 1939–2013* (MC 1944) pertain to the personal and professional papers of journalists Melvin and Charlotte Schexnayder, owners and editors of the *Dumas Clarion*. Significant portions are related to the political career of Charlotte Schexnayder (1923–2020) as an Arkansas state representative from 1985 through 1998 and include sponsored legislation, ethics filings, campaign expense reports, personal observations, and committee materials. Another is the *Vada Webb Sheid Papers* (MC 930). Vada Sheid (1916–2008) served as Baxter County treasurer and as a member of the Arkansas House of Representatives and the state senate. The collection includes legislative research files, speeches, scrapbooks, photographs, and other papers, including materials related to her autobiography. Additional materials related to Vada Sheid and Judy Petty can be found in the *Arkansas Archives of Public Communication* (MC 942). Audiotape interviews with Representatives Carolyn Pollan, Gloria Cabe, and Wanda Northcutt and with Senator Charlie Cole Chafin are held in the Gender and State Legislature Project: Arkansas General Assembly Interviews, January 28, 1989–March 9, 1989, and related Research Notes in Box 2, Series 4, 3 folders, *Diane D. Blair Papers: 1874–2000* (MC 1632). Also, the *Arkansas Historical Association's Gingles and Westbrook Contest Entries Papers* (MC 757) includes Harold Coogan's 1986 original research essay, "Mary Ellen Blackburn Wigstrand, 1858–1927, The First and Only Woman Representative from Polk County," in Box 1, Folder 8.

The research files for *Stateswomen* by Lindsley Armstrong Smith and Stephen A. Smith can be found in the *Lindsley Armstrong Smith Papers* (MC 1910) in Special Collections, Mullins Library, University of Arkansas, Fayetteville. In addition to Representative Smith's correspondence, campaign materials, photographs, speeches, newspaper clippings, legislative notes, and other materials documenting her political and professional career, the Arkansas Women Legislators Project series contains the individual files on all 146 women who have served in the Arkansas General Assembly. These include the paper and digital research materials used in research for this book. Also, the *Lindsley Smith Arkansas Women Legislators Oral History Project Records* in Special Collections (MC 1775), Mullins Library, University of Arkansas, Fayetteville, includes transcripts and digital copies of forty-eight videotaped interviews with women legislators and fourteen audiotape interviews with women legislators and their family members: Bernice Kizer; Carolyn Pollan; Irma Hunter Brown; Judy Petty Wolf; Peggy Long Hartness; Charlie Cole Chaffin; Myra Jones; Wanda Northcutt Hartz; Charlotte Schexnayder; Christene Brownlee; Jacqueline Roberts; Judy Smith; Josetta Wilkins; Ann Bush; Evelyn Ammons; Lisa Ferrell; Peggy Jeffries; Becky Lynn; Sue Madison; Pat Bond; Sandra Rodgers; Martha Shoffner; Wilma Walker; Sarah Agee; Cecile Bledsoe; Joyce Dees; Mary Beth Green; Brenda Gullett; Jan Judy; Barbara King; Mary Anne Salmon; Shirley Borhauer; Ruth Whitaker; Judy Pridgen; Linda Chesterfield; Marilyn Edwards; Janet Johnson; Betty Pickett; Sandra Prater; Susan Schulte; Lindsley Smith; Sharon Dobbins; Donna Hutchinson; Johnnie Roebuck; Kathy Webb; Henry Jones III interview about grandmother Frances Hunt; George Anna

Tow, daughter of Ella B. Hurst; Doris McCastlain Hinkle (audio); Shirley Meacham (audio); Nancy Duffy Blount (audio); Beverly Pyle (audio); Betty Pickett (audio); Dawn Creekmore (audio); Marian Owens-Ingram (audio); Kathy Webb (audio); Ann Sugg on Ella B. Hurst (audio); Ann Lane re Helen Buchanan (audio); Marilyn Horn re Helen Buchanan (audio); Sue Eroh on Helen Buchanan (audio); Neva Buchanan, Helen Buchanan's sister (audio). Additional videotape materials include the ERA Resolution debate in the House State Agencies and Governmental Affairs Committee in 2007; Cecile Bledsoe's announcement for Congress on February 13, 2010; Women's Legislative Day honoring Arkansas women legislators on March 31, 2010; and Charlie Cole Chaffin campaign events in 1986 and 1988. Copies of the transcripts and digital copies of the video interviews with women legislators also were donated by Representative Smith to the David and Barbara Pryor Center for Arkansas Oral and Visual History at the University of Arkansas, Fayetteville, which is making them available online.

The Butler Center for Arkansas Studies, Bobby L. Roberts Library of Arkansas History and Art, Central Arkansas Library System, Little Rock, holds the *Willie Oates Papers* (BC.MSS.05.04), containing biographical information about Representative Willie Oates and her extensive involvement with more than fifty organization in which she held leadership roles. The Butler Center's political photograph collection (BC.PHO.25) includes photographs of state senator Peggy Jeffries, state representative Ann Bush, state representative Prissy Hickerson, and others.

Another major depository for Arkansas women's history, including women legislators, is the University of Arkansas at Little Rock's Center for Arkansas History and Culture, Arkansas Studies Institute. It holds the papers of Representatives Johnnie Roebuck, Kathy Webb, and Judy Petty. *Kathy Webb Papers, 1991–2013* (UALR.MS.0236) contains the legislative papers of Representative Kathy Webb, emphasizing her work for children, education, the environment, and health. *Johnnie Roebuck Papers, 1992–2013* (UALR.MS.0247) contains materials related to Roebuck's service in the Arkansas House of Representatives from 2007 to 2013, especially strong on education-related issues. *Judy Petty Papers, 1964–1974* (UALR.MS.0277) contains correspondence relating to Petty's work for the Arkansas Republican Party and as a staff member for Governor Winthrop Rockefeller. Files on Representatives Rita Clubbs (Hale), Bernice Kizer, Willie Oates, Carolyn Pollan, and Charlotte Schexnayder; Senator Vada Sheid; and Chief Clerk of the House Jim Searcy Childers are among the biographical information files, Series II, Boxes 1 and 2, in UALR.MS.0037, from Kitty Sloan, editor, *Horizons: 100 Arkansas Women of Achievement* (Little Rock: Rose Publishing

Co., 1980). The *Women in Arkansas Photograph Collection* (UALR.PH.0067), UALR Center for Arkansas History and Culture, also holds photographs of women legislators, including Florence McRaven, Frances Matthews Jones Hunt, Erle Chambers, Vada Shied, Judy Petty, Irma Hunter Brown, Carolyn Pollan, and Shirley Meacham.

The UCA Archives, Torreyson Library, University of Central Arkansas, Conway, holds the *State Representative Betty Pickett Collection* (M13–02). Representative Pickett was a member of the Arkansas House from 2003 to 2008 and previously served as a member of the Arkansas State Board of Education from 1995 to 2002. Series III of the collection includes her correspondence, speeches, campaign materials, photos, and newspaper clippings. The files are especially valuable regarding her work on education and environmental issues. The UCA Archives *Small Manuscript Collection* contains a number of papers written by senior seminar history majors, including UCA SMC #865: Jennifer Sims, "Florence McRaven: A Woman Arkansas Should Be Proud of," *HIST 4300, Seminar*—December 11, 1995; SMC #896: Sherry Harris, "Erle Chambers," *HIST 4300, Seminar*—Summer 1993; and SMC #1449: "Depiction of Progressivism by Florence McRaven," n.d.

The *Southern Women Legislators Collection* (MUM00422), Archives and Special Collections, J. D. Williams Library at the University of Mississippi, contains files on thirty of the thirty-four Arkansas women legislators who served before 1986. The collection was created by University of Mississippi faculty members Joanne V. Hawks and Carolyn Ellis, who received grants from the National Endowment for the Humanities to study the role of women in southern state legislatures. They donated research files containing secondary biographical information, newspaper clippings, political ephemera, completed questionnaires, correspondence, and oral interviews on cassette tapes, and they published articles about women legislators in Alabama, Florida, Mississippi, and South Carolina.

The files related to Arkansas are in Series II of the *Southern Women Legislators Collection* and include Folder 1–24, General information on Arkansas Women Legislators; Folder 1–25, Clippings; Folder 1–26, Dorathy M. Allen; Folder 1–27, Nancy Crain Balton; Folder 1–28, Irma Hunter Brown; Folder 1–29, Maude R. Brown; Folder 1–30, Helen May Buchanan; Folder 1–31, Gloria Burford Cabe; Folder 1–32, Charlie Cole Chafin; Folder 1–33, Erle Rutherford Chambers; Folder 1–34, Ethel Cole Cunningham; Folder 1–35, Mattie Hackett; Folder 1–36, Peggy Long Hartness; Folder 1–37, Frances R. M. J. Hunt; Folder 1–38, Ella B. Hurst; Folder 1–39, Myra Lee Jones; Folder 1–40, Bernice Kizer; Folder 1–41, Doris McCastlain; Folder 1–42, Florence McGraw McRaven; Folder 1–43, Shirley T. Meacham; Folder 1–44, Dove Toland

Mulkey; Folder 1–45, Wanda L. Northcutt; Folder 1–46, Willie Oates; Folder 1–47, Gladys Oglesby; Folder 1–48, Judy Petty; Folder 1–49, Carolyn Pollan; Folder 1–50, Lera Jeanne Rowlette; Folder 1–51, Charlotte T. Schexnayder; Folder 1–52, Vada M, Sheid; Folder 1–53, Elizabeth H. Thompson; Folder 1–54, Mary B. Wigstrand; Folder 1–55, Alene Word. Series XI, Cassette Tapes of Oral Interviews, includes recorded interviews with two Arkansas legislators. Irma Hunter Brown was interviewed by Carolyn Ellis Staton and Joanne V. Hawks on February 22, 1985. The audio recording is in two parts (31:17 and 13:26). They interviewed Peggy Long Hartness on February 21, 1985 (31:16). Digital copies of these interviews are in the *Southern Women Legislators Digital Collection* (https://egrove.olemiss.edu/swl/).

These resources should be helpful to scholars researching and writing about women in Arkansas politics and informative for anyone interested in Arkansas history generally. What is needed is a concerted effort to collect and preserve the papers of Arkansas women legislators to document the challenges they faced in state politics and to celebrate their successes. Libraries and archives in the state must make collecting and preserving women's political history a priority in their development policies and practices. Those who undertake the writing of Arkansas history and telling the state's story must also give greater attention to the role that women played in every aspect of that history. Additional scholarship on Arkansas women in public office at the city, county, and state levels would be a welcome contribution to a better understanding of Arkansas politics.

# Appendices

## Appendix A:
## Women in the Arkansas General Assembly

| General Assembly | Years | Women in Legislature | Total % Women | Women in Senate | Women in House |
|---|---|---|---|---|---|
| 93rd | 2021–2022 | 31/135 | 23 | 7/35 | 24/100 |
| 92nd | 2019–2020 | 35/135 | 25.9 | 7/35 | 28/100 |
| 91st | 2017–2018 | 26/135 | 19.3 | 8/35 | 18/100 |
| 90th | 2015–2016 | 28/135 | 20.7 | 7/35 | 21/100 |
| 89th | 2013–2014 | 23/135 | 17 | 6/35 | 17/100 |
| 88th | 2011–2012 | 30/135 | 22.2 | 8/35 | 22/100 |
| 87th | 2009–2010 | 32/135 | 23.7 | 7/35 | 25/100 |
| 86th | 2007–2008 | 28/135 | 20.7 | 6/35 | 22/100 |
| 85th | 2005–2006 | 23/135 | 17 | 6/35 | 17/100 |
| 84th | 2003–2004 | 22/135 | 16.3 | 7/35 | 15/100 |
| 83rd | 2001–2002 | 19/135 | 14.1 | 5/35 | 14/100 |
| 82nd | 1999–2000 | 20/135 | 14.8 | 0/35 | 20/100 |
| 81st | 1997–1998 | 23/135 | 17.0 | 1/35 | 22/100 |
| 80th | 1995–1996 | 18/135 | 13.3 | 1/35 | 17/100 |
| 79th | 1993–1994 | 15/135 | 10.4 | 1/35 | 14/100 |
| 78th | 1991–1992 | 10/135 | 7.4 | 1/35 | 9/100 |
| 77th | 1989–1990 | 10/135 | 7.4 | 2/35 | 8/100 |
| 76th | 1987–1988 | 10/135 | 7.4 | 1/35 | 9/100 |
| 75th | 1985–1986 | 10/135 | 7.4 | 1/35 | 9/100 |
| 74th | 1983–1984 | 8/135 | 5.9 | 2/35 | 6/100 |
| 73rd | 1981–1982 | 6/135 | 4.4 | 1/35 | 5/100 |
| 72nd | 1979–1980 | 5/135 | 3.7 | 1/35 | 4/100 |

| General Assembly | Years | Women in Legislature | Total % Women | Women in Senate | Women in House |
|---|---|---|---|---|---|
| 71st | 1977–1978 | 3/135 | 2.2 | 1/35 | 2/100 |
| 70th | 1975–1976 | 3/135 | 2.2 | 0/35 | 3/100 |
| 69th | 1973–1974 | 3/135 | 2.2 | 1/35 | 2/100 |
| 68th | 1971–1972 | 3/135 | 2.2 | 1/35 | 2/100 |
| 67th | 1969–1970 | 4/135 | 3 | 1/35 | 3/100 |
| 66th | 1967–1968 | 5/135 | 3.7 | 1/35 | 4/100 |
| 65th | 1965–1966 | 4/135 | 3 | 1/35 | 3/100 |
| 64th | 1963–1964 | 5/135 | 3.7 | 0/35 | 5/100 |
| 63rd | 1961–1962 | 4/135 | 3 | 0/35 | 4/100 |
| 62nd | 1959–1960 | 2/135 | 1.4 | 0/35 | 2/100 |
| 61st | 1957–1958 | 0/135 | 0 | 0/35 | 0/100 |
| 60th | 1955–1956 | 0/135 | 0 | 0/35 | 0/100 |
| 59th | 1953–1954 | 1/135 | 0.7 | 0/35 | 1/100 |
| 58th | 1951–1952 | 0/135 | 0 | 0/35 | 0/100 |
| 57th | 1949–1950 | 0/135 | 0 | 0/35 | 0/100 |
| 56th | 1947–1948 | 1/135 | 0.7 | 0/35 | 1/100 |
| 55th | 1945–1946 | 3/135 | 2.2 | 0/35 | 3/100 |
| 54th | 1943–1944 | 2/135 | 1.4 | 0/35 | 2/100 |
| 53rd | 1941–1942 | 0/135 | 0 | 0/35 | 0/100 |
| 52nd | 1939–1940 | 0/135 | 0 | 0/35 | 0/100 |
| 51st | 1937–1938 | 0/135 | 0 | 0/35 | 0/100 |
| 50th | 1935–1936 | 1/135 | 0.7 | 0/35 | 1/100 |
| 49th | 1933–1934 | 1/135 | 0.7 | 0/35 | 1/100 |
| 48th | 1931–1932 | 1/135 | 0.7 | 0/35 | 1/100 |
| 47th | 1929–1930 | 2/135 | 1.4 | 0/35 | 2/100 |
| 46th | 1927–1928 | 2/135 | 1.4 | 0/35 | 2/100 |
| 45th | 1925–1926 | 3/135 | 2.2 | 0/35 | 3/100 |
| 44th | 1923–1924 | 2/135 | 1.4 | 0/35 | 2/100 |
| 43rd | 1922 | 2/135 | 1.4 | 0/35 | 2/100 |

## Appendix B:
## Women Legislators by County Population

| Rank | County | Population | Women in Senate | Women in House |
|------|--------|-----------|-----------------|----------------|
| 1 | Pulaski County | 392,967 | 5 | 30 |
| 2 | Benton County | 265,759 | 1 | 11 |
| 3 | Washington County | 232,289 | 1 | 10 |
| 4 | Sebastian County | 127,591 | 1 | 7 |
| 5 | Faulkner County | 123,624 | | 2 |
| 6 | Saline County | 119,415 | 2 | 4 |
| 7 | Craighead County | 107,345 | 1 | 1 |
| 8 | Garland County | 98,555 | | 2 |
| 9 | White County | 78,762 | | |
| 10 | Lonoke County | 72,528 | | 2 |
| 11 | Jefferson County | 69,282 | 2 | 7 |
| 12 | Pope County | 63,761 | 2 | 1 |
| 13 | Crawford County | 62,739 | 1 | 4 |
| 14 | Crittenden County | 48,672 | | 2 |
| 15 | Greene County | 44,937 | | 1 |
| 16 | Miller County | 43,572 | | 3 |
| 17 | Mississippi County | 42,126 | | 5 |
| 18 | Baxter County | 41,427 | 1 | 3 |
| 19 | Union County | 39,449 | | 1 |
| 20 | Independence County | 37,427 | | |
| 21 | Boone County | 37,331 | | |

| Rank | County | Population | Women in Senate | Women in House |
|------|--------|-----------|-----------------|----------------|
| 22 | Hot Spring County | 33,597 | | |
| 23 | Carroll County | 27,965 | | |
| 24 | Johnson County | 26,372 | | 1 |
| 25 | St. Francis County | 25,900 | | |
| 26 | Cleburne County | 25,100 | | 1 |
| 27 | Poinsett County | 23,896 | | 1 |
| 28 | Ouachita County | 23,830 | | 1 |
| 29 | Columbia County | 23,776 | | |
| 30 | Clark County | 22,386 | | 1 |
| 31 | Hempstead County | 21,842 | | 1 |
| 32 | Logan County | 21,668 | | |
| 33 | Yell County | 21,464 | | 1 |
| 34 | Conway County | 20,858 | | |
| 35 | Ashley County | 20,270 | | |
| 36 | Polk County | 20,094 | | 1 |
| 37 | Phillips County | 18,606 | | 2 |
| 38 | Drew County | 18,417 | | 3 |
| 39 | Grant County | 18,126 | | |
| 40 | Arkansas County | 17,914 | | 2 |
| 41 | Franklin County | 17,738 | | 2 |
| 42 | Randolph County | 17,695 | 1 | 1 |
| 43 | Sharp County | 17,139 | | |
| 44 | Sevier County | 17,081 | | 1 |

| Rank | County | Population | Women in Senate | Women in House |
|------|--------|-----------|-----------------|----------------|
| 45 | Jackson County | 17,027 | | 2 |
| 46 | Cross County | 16,824 | | |
| 47 | Van Buren County | 16,642 | | |
| 48 | Lawrence County | 16,549 | | 1 |
| 49 | Marion County | 16,476 | | |
| 50 | Madison County | 16,211 | | |
| 51 | Clay County | 14,889 | | |
| 52 | Izard County | 13,570 | | 1 |
| 53 | Lincoln County | 13,455 | | |
| 54 | Howard County | 13,311 | | 1 |
| 55 | Stone County | 12,475 | 1 | |
| 56 | Little River County | 12,347 | 1 | 2 |
| 57 | Fulton County | 12,231 | | 1 |
| 58 | Desha County | 11,709 | | 1 |
| 59 | Bradley County | 10,874 | | 3 |
| 60 | Pike County | 10,756 | | 1 |
| 61 | Chicot County | 10,615 | | |
| 62 | Scott County | 10,376 | | 1 |
| 63 | Perry County | 10,355 | | 1 |
| 64 | Lee County | 9,194 | | 1 |
| 65 | Montgomery County | 8,950 | | |
| 66 | Nevada County | 8,351 | | 1 |
| 67 | Prairie County | 8,189 | | |

| Rank | County | Population | Women in Senate | Women in House |
|---|---|---|---|---|
| 68 | Cleveland County | 8,128 | | |
| 69 | Searcy County | 7,908 | | |
| 70 | Newton County | 7,812 | | |
| 71 | Dallas County | 7,279 | | |
| 72 | Monroe County | 7,050 | 1 | 3 |
| 73 | Lafayette County | 6,800 | | 2 |
| 74 | Woodruff County | 6,533 | | |
| 75 | Calhoun County | 5,192 | | |

*United States Census Bureau. Annual Estimates of the Resident Population. May 2020.*
*http://www.census.gov/.*

# Appendix C:
## Home Counties of 137 Women
## Arkansas State Representatives

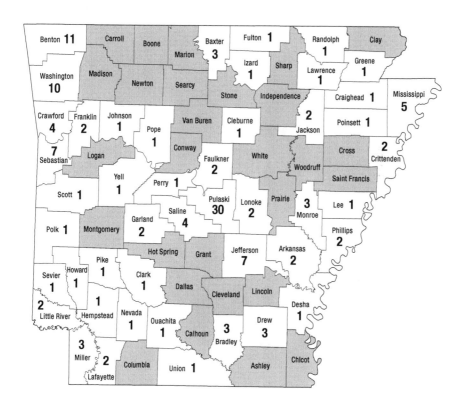

# Appendix D:
## Home Counties of 21 Women
## Arkansas State Senators

# Notes

1. In addition, all of our research files on individual women legislators are available in "Arkansas Women Legislators Project," Lindsley Armstrong Smith Papers, MC 1910, Mullins Library Special Collections, University of Arkansas, Fayetteville. A collection of audiotape and videotape interviews with women legislators is also held in MC 1755, Lindsley Smith Arkansas Women Legislators Oral History Project Records, Mullins Library Special Collections, University of Arkansas, Fayetteville.

2. "Women in State Legislatures 2021," Center for American Women and Politics, Eagleton Institute of Politics, Rutgers University, https://cawp.rutgers .edu/women-state-legislature-2021.

3. Adam McCann, "Best & Worst States for Women's Equality," *WalletHub*, August 24, 2020, https://wallethub.com/edu/best-and-worst-states-for -women-equality/5835.

4. State of Arkansas, *Debates and Proceedings of the Convention* (Little Rock: J. G. Price, 1868), 701.

5. State of Arkansas, *Debates and Proceedings of the Convention*, 702–5. Delegate Robert Smith Gantt was a lawyer from Prairie County. An Alabama native who settled at Brownsville in 1857, he had been a captain of Company G, the "Brownsville Rifles," Fifth Arkansas Infantry CSA, and he had served as Arkansas attorney general (1865–1866) and in the state senate (1866–1867).

6. State of Arkansas, *Debates and Proceedings of the Convention*, 705.

7. State of Arkansas, *Debates and Proceedings of the Convention*, 707–8. Jesse Newton Cypert Jr. (1823–1913), a Tennessee native, was a lawyer from Searcy, White County, who had been captain of Company A, the "Searcy Greys," Desha's 7th Arkansas Infantry Battalion, CSA. He would later serve as a delegate to the 1874 Constitutional Convention and as a circuit judge, 1874–1882.

8. Miles L. Langley to Susan B. Anthony, March 5, 1868, reprinted in "Letter from Arkansas," *The Revolution* 1.12 (26 March 1868): 181.

9. *Report of the Woman's Rights Convention, Held at Seneca Falls, New York, July 19th and 20th. Proceedings and Declaration of Sentiments* (Rochester, NY: John Dick at the North Star Office, 1848), 3.

10. Article III, §1. *Proposed Arkansas Constitution of 1918. Arkansas Gazette*, September 21, 1918: 9.

11. Article II, §§1, 3. *Proposed Arkansas Constitution of 1980. Arkansas Gazette*, August 11, 1980: 30.

12. A 2007 poll of Arkansas voters showed 73 percent favoring and 18 percent opposing ratification of the federal Equal Rights Amendment. Janine A.

Parry, *The Arkansas Poll, 2007 Summary Report* (Fayetteville: University of Arkansas Diane D. Blair Center of Southern Politics and Society, 2007), 6. For the history of unsuccessful ratification efforts in the Arkansas legislature, see Lindsley Armstrong Smith and Stephen A. Smith, "Keeping Hope Alive: A Case Study of the Continuing Argument for Ratification of the ERA," in *Readings in Arkansas Politics and Government*, 2nd ed., edited by Kim U. Hoffman, Janine A, Parry, and Catherine C. Reese (Fayetteville: University of Arkansas Press, 2019), 323–50.

13. Robert Bradshaw Walz, "Migration into Arkansas, 1834–1880," PhD diss., University of Texas, 1958.

14. S. Charles Bolton, "Slavery and the Defining of Arkansas," *Arkansas Historical Quarterly* 58, no. 1 (1999): 1–23; Donald P. McNeilly, *The Old South Frontier: Cotton Plantations and the Formation of Arkansas Society, 1819–1861* (Fayetteville: University of Arkansas Press, 2000); Cheryl Elman, Barbara Wittman, Kathryn M. Feltey, Corey Stevens, and Molly Hartsough, "Women in Frontier Arkansas: Settlement in a Post-Reconstruction Racial State," *Du Bois Review: Social Science Research on Race* 16.2 (Fall 2019): 575–612.

15. This connection was not limited to white women. Formerly enslaved and free Black women were active in both the abolition movement and the woman suffrage movement in the antebellum period, and Black women continued to fight for both civil rights and suffrage in the late-nineteenth and twentieth centuries. See Rosalyn Terborg-Penn, *African American Women in the Struggle for the Vote, 1850–1920* (Bloomington: Indiana University Press, 1998).

16. Gordon E. Finnie, "The Antislavery Movement in the Upper South Before 1840," *Journal of Southern History* 35.3 (August 1969): 319–42; Susan Wyly-Jones, "The Antiabolitionist Panic: Slavery, Abolition, and Politics in the United States South, 1835–1844," PhD diss., Harvard University, 2000; and Gerda Lerner, *The Grimké Sisters from South Carolina: Pioneers for Women's Rights and Abolition* (Chapel Hill: University of North Carolina Press, 2009).

17. *Arkansas Gazette*, July 20, 1848, p. 1; *Arkansas Gazette*, October 11, 1849, p. 3.

18. Arkansas Act of November 22, 1850, codified in *Gould's Digest*, Chapter 51, part VI, art. IV, §3 (1858).

19. While class is often ignored in discussions of Arkansas political history and is sometimes conflated with race, the economic disparities and official hostility to working-class union organizing are a continuing political disability in the state. See Nancy Isenberg, *White Trash: The 400-Year Untold History of Class in America* (New York: Viking, 2016); Matthew Hild and Keri Leigh Merritt, eds., *Reconsidering Southern Labor History: Race, Class, and Power* (Gainesville: University Press of Florida, 2018); and Michael Goldfield, *The Southern Key: Class, Race, and Radicalism in the 1930s and 1940s* (New York: Oxford University Press, 2020).

20. Lindsley Armstrong Smith and Stephen A. Smith, "Keeping Hope Alive: A Case Study of the Continuing Argument for Ratification of the ERA,"

323–50; Jeannie Roberts, "Bid to Ratify ERA Comes Up Short: Equal-Rights Measure Fails to Make It Out of Senate Committee," *Arkansas Democrat-Gazette*, March 8, 2019: 7.

21. James G. Gimpel, Nathan Lovin, Bryant Moy, and Andrew Reeves, "The Urban–Rural Gulf in American Political Behavior," *Political Behavior* 42 (2020): 1343–68.

22. Ninth Census (1870): Volume 1. The Statistics of the Population of the United States (Washington: Government Printing Office, 1872).

23. Eleventh Census (1900): Volume 1. Population, Part 1 (Washington: Government Printing Office, 1901); Idaho was only 6.2 percent urban in 1900, but by 1910 it was 21.5 percent urban, compared with 12.9 percent for Arkansas.

24. *Report of the Woman's Rights Convention, Held at Seneca Falls*, 9.

25. "The Examination of Mrs. Anne Hutchinson at the Court at Newtown," in Thomas Hutchinson, *The History of the Province of Massachusetts-Bay: from the Charter of King William and Queen Mary, in 1691, until the Year 1750* (Boston: Thomas and John Fleet, 1767), 484–85.

26. Luther Lee, *Woman's Right to Preach the Gospel: A Sermon, Preached at the Ordination of the Rev. Miss Antoinette L. Brown, at South Butler, Wayne County, N.Y., Sept. 15, 1853* (Syracuse, NY: by the author, 1853).

27. "Olympia Brown: An Autobiography," *Universalist Historical Society Annual Journal* 4 (1963): 3.

28. See Sue Tolleson Rinehart and Jerry Perkins, "The Intersection of Gender Politics and Religious Beliefs," *Political Behavior* 11.1 (March 1989): 33–56; Robert Wuthnow and William Lehrman, "Religion: Inhibitor or Facilitator of Political Involvement among Women?" in *Women, Politics, and Change*, ed. Louise A. Tilly and Patricia Gurin (New York: Russell Sage Foundation, 1990), 300–22.

29. Jean E. Friedman, *The Enclosed Garden: Women and Community in the Evangelical South. 1830–1900* (Chapel Hill: University of North Carolina Press, 1985); Jean E. Friedman, "Piety and Kin: The Limits of Antebellum Southern Women's Reform," in *Women and the Structure of Society*, ed. Barbara Harris and Jo Ann McNamara (Durham, NC: Duke University Press, 1984); Anne Firor Scott, "Women, Religion, and Social Change in the South, 1830–1930," in *Religion and the Solid South*, ed. Samuel Hill (Nashville: Abingdon Press, 1972).

30. Michael B. Dougan, "The Arkansas Married Woman's Property Law," *Arkansas Historical Quarterly* 46.1 (Spring 1987): 26.

31. Jeannie M. Whayne, Thomas A. DeBlack, George Sabo, and Morris S. Arnold, *Arkansas: A Concise History* (Fayetteville: University of Arkansas Press, 2019), 231–33.

32. "Sixteenth Governor, James Philip Eagle, 1889–1893," in C. Fred Williams, Timothy P. Donovan, Willard B. Gatewood Jr., and Jeannie M. Whayne,

eds., *The Governors of Arkansas* (Fayetteville: University of Arkansas Press, 1995), 90–94; C. Fred Williams, "Eagle, James Philip," in Nancy A. Williams and Jeannie M. Whayne, eds., *Arkansas Biography: A Collection of Notable Lives* (Fayetteville: University of Arkansas Press, 2000), 91–92.

33. Two other Arkansas women, Margaret Francis Owen Searcy (1841–1913), executive board of the Arkansas Women's Missionary Union and wife of Rev. James Bryant Searcy, and Jennie C. Jordan Clark (1844–1907), vice president of the Women's Missionary Union and wife of Rev. William Allen Clark, D.D., had been elected as delegates but did not attend the SBC meeting.

34. Marshall Daniel Early (1846–1918) joined the Mt. Bethel Baptist Church in 1865 and was ordained in 1871 at Bethel-Union Church in Clark County, so he would have been a colleague of Miles Ledford Langley. He was a pastor at Lonoke in 1883–1885 and Little Rock Second Baptist in 1886–1888. Rev. Early was a candidate for Senate chaplain in 1885, was corresponding secretary of the Baptist State Convention, Arkansas vice president of the Southern Baptist Convention Home Mission Board, and on the board of trustees for Ouachita College, 1886–1887. He was awarded a Doctor of Divinity degree by Oklahoma Baptist College. See Marshall E. Kuykendall, "Marshall Daniel Early," *Arkansas Family Historian* 29.4 (December 1991): 171–79.

35. Jones is the subject of a chapter in Charles Reagan Wilson, *Baptized in Blood: The Religion of the Lost Cause, 1865–1920* (Athens: University of Georgia Press, 1980), 119–38.

36. For more on Hawthorne's views opposing women in public life, see David B. Parker, "Satanic Spiders in Atlanta: Rev. J. B. Hawthorne, the New Woman, and the Lost Cause," *Journal of the Georgia Association of Historians* 36 (2020): 67–86.

37. This account of the SBC debates is drawn from the excellent work of J. Michael Raley, "'On the Same Basis as the Men': The Campaign to Reinstate Women Messengers to the Southern Baptist Convention, 1885–1918," *Journal of Southern Religion* 7 (2004), http://jsreligion.org/Volume7/Raley2.htm.

38. *Arkansas Methodist*, April 18, 1885, p. 1.

39. J. R. Moore, "Woman's Sphere," *Arkansas Methodist*, June 10, 1891, pp. 4–5.

40. Hattie E. Copeland, "Woman's Sphere," *Arkansas Methodist*, July 8, 1891, p. 2.

41. J. R. Moore, "Woman's Sphere," *Arkansas Methodist*, July 15, 1891, p. 1. That ended the exchange, because Harriet Elizabeth Gentry Copeland died on the day Moore's rebuttal was published.

42. Boone Keeton, "Woman Suffrage," *Arkansas Methodist*, September 16, 1891, p. 1.

43. J. R. Moore, "If She wants to, Let Her," *Arkansas Methodist*, September 23, 1891, p. 4.

44. "Equal Suffrage," *Arkansas Gazette*, April 30, 1893, p. 13.

45. Bishop R. K. Hargrove, "Woman's Work in the Church," *Methodist Review* 43.1 (March-April 1896): 6–7.

46. Walter Vernon, *Methodism in Arkansas, 1816–1976* (Little Rock: Joint Commission for the History of Arkansas Methodism, 1976), 351.

47. J. J. Mellard, "Shall Women Preach?" *Arkansas Methodist*, October 20, 1897, p. 4.

48. W. J. Hearon, "Shall Women Preach?" *Arkansas Methodist*, November 17, 1897, p. 3.

49. W. P. Whaley "Shall Women Preach?" *Arkansas Methodist*, November 10, 1897, p. 4.

50. J. R. Moore, "Shall Women Preach?" *Arkansas Methodist*, November 10, 1897, p. 2.

51. *Arkansas Gazette*, September 5, 1872, p. 4. After a split in the Restoration Movement by 1906, the Churches of Christ now have more than ten times more congregations and adherents in Arkansas than the Christian Church (Disciples of Christ).

52. "Women Speaking in Church," *Queries and Answers by Lipscomb and Sewell, Being A Compilation of Queries with Answers by D. Lipscomb and E. G. Sewell, Covering a Period of Forty Years of Their Joint Editorial Labors on the Gospel Advocate*, ed. M. C. Kurfees (Nashville, TN: Gospel Advocate Company, 1921), 729. In addition, Lipscomb said the arguments for women preaching originated in the same hotbed of rationalistic infidelity with easy divorce, free love, and the repugnance to childbearing. David Lipscomb, *Queries and Answers* (Nashville: McQuiddy, 1910), 453.

53. David Lipscomb, *Civil Government: Its Origin, Mission, and Destiny, and the Christian's Relation to It* (Nashville: McQuiddy, 1913), 103; *Gospel Advocate*, February 13, 1913, pp. 155–66; *Gospel Advocate*, January 19, 1911, pp. 78–79.

54. "Women and Expedients," *Queries and Answers by Lipscomb and Sewell, Being A Compilation of Queries with Answers by D. Lipscomb and E. G. Sewell, Covering a Period of Forty Years of Their Joint Editorial Labors on the Gospel Advocate*, ed. M. C. Kurfees (Nashville, TN: Gospel Advocate Company, 1921), 739. See also *Gospel Advocate*, July 3, 1913, p. 635.

55. Elizabeth H. Flowers, *Into the Pulpit: Southern Baptist Women and Power since World War II* (Chapel Hill: University of North Carolina Press, 2012); Mary J. Henold, *Catholic and Feminist: The Surprising History of the American Catholic Feminist Movement* (Chapel Hill: University of North Carolina Press, 2008); and for the Churches of Christ, "Women in the Church," *Christian Chronicle*, https://christianchronicle.org/women/.

56. "Methodists to Welcome New Arkansas Bishop," *Arkansas Democrat-Gazette*, September 14, 1996, 3B; *The Leading Women: Stories of the First Women Bishops of the United Methodist Church*, compiled by Judith Craig (Nashville, TN: Abingdon Press, 2004). See also Nancy Britton, *Two Centuries of Methodism in Arkansas, 1800–2000* (Little Rock: August House, 2000), 238–43.

57. "Baptist Convention Opposes ERA, Urges Pastors to 'Warn the Flock,'" *Arkansas Gazette*, November 10, 1978, p. 8; Janet Allured, "Arkansas Baptists

and Methodists and the Equal Rights Amendment," *Arkansas Historical Quarterly* 43.1 (Spring 1984): 55–66.

58. In addition, those official legislative websites employ biographical categories such as veteran status that include fewer women members, while ignoring those more favorable to women, such as educational attainment and community service organizations. See the individual biographical sketches at https://www.arkleg.state.ar.us/Legislators/List

59. This is true beyond the borders of Arkansas and long recognized in the larger historiography. See, for example, Mary R. Beard, *Woman as Force in History: A Study of Traditions and Realities* (New York: Macmillan, 1946). Our approach is informed by Gerda Lerner, *The Majority Finds its Past: Placing Women in History* (Chapel Hill: University of North Carolina Press, 2005).

60. Joan Scott, "Gender: A Useful Category of Historical Analysis," *American Historical Review* 91.5 (December 1986): 1070.

61. See Michael W. Apple and Linda K. Christian-Smith, *The Politics of the Textbook* (New York: Routledge, 1991), 1–21; David Tyack, "Monuments between Covers: The Politics of Textbooks," *The American Behavioral Scientist* 42.6 (1999): 922–32; Christiane Olivo, "The Exclusion and Inclusion of Women in American Government Textbooks," in *The New Politics of the Textbook: Problematizing the Portrayal of Marginalized Groups in Textbooks*, ed. Brad J. Porfilio (Rotterdam: SensePublishers, 2012), 149–72.

62. Joan Kelly, "The Doubled Vision of Feminist Theory: A Postscript to the 'Women and Power' Conference," *Feminist Studies* 5.1 (1979): 225.

63. John H. Moore, *A School History of Arkansas* (Little Rock: Bunyan and Moore, 1924), 229.

64. Fay Hempstead, *A History of the State of Arkansas: For the Use of Schools* (New Orleans: F. F. Hansell, 1889).

65. Josiah Hazen Shinn, *The History of Arkansas: A Textbook for Public Schools, High Schools, and Academies* (Little Rock: Wilson and Webb, 1898; Richmond, VA: B.F. Johnson publishing Co., 1900, 1905), 14–15, 136, 161, 272–73, 288–94.

66. John Hugh Reynolds, *Makers of Arkansas History*, rev. ed. (New York: Silver, Burdett and Company, 1930).

67. "Suffragists Organize," *Arkansas Gazette*, April 18, 1917, p. 4.

68. Dallas T. Herndon, *The Highlights of Arkansas History*, 2nd ed. (Little Rock: Arkansas History Commission, 1922).

69. John H. Moore, *A School History of Arkansas* (Little Rock: Bunyan and Moore, 1924). Ten editions published between 1924 and 1928.

70. Faith Yingling Knoop and James Richard Grant, *Arkansas: Yesterday and Today: A History of Arkansas for Elementary Grades* (Philadelphia: J. B. Lippincott Co, 1935/1947). Faith Yingling Knoop (Mrs. Werner C. Knoop) to Audrey D. Anderson, January 18, 1950, in Audrey D. Anderson, "Arkansas' Contribution to Juvenile Literature," MA thesis, University of Wyoming, 1950, p. 65.

71. O. E. McKnight and Boyd W. Johnson, *The Arkansas Story* (Oklahoma City: Harlow, 1955).

72. Walter Lee Brown, *Our Arkansas* (Austin: Steck-Vaughn, 1958). Third edition published in 1969.

73. John L. Ferguson and James Harris Atkinson, *Historic Arkansas* (Little Rock: Arkansas History Commission, 1966).

74. Fred Arthur Bailey, "Free Speech and the 'Lost Cause' in Arkansas." *Arkansas Historical Quarterly* 55.2 (1996): 143–66; and Fred Arthur Bailey, "The Textbooks of the 'Lost Cause': Censorship and the Creation of Southern State Histories," *Georgia Historical Quarterly* 75.3 (1991): 507–33. See also Carl H. Moneyhon, "Conflicting Civil War Historical Memory and Cultural Divides in Arkansas," in *Competing Memories: The Legacy of Arkansas's Civil War*, ed. Mark K. Christ (Little Rock: Butler Center Books, 2016). Bailey found historians David Y. Thomas, John Hugh Reynolds, and Dallas T. Herndon to be complicit with the United Daughters of the Confederacy censorship program. Other Arkansas history textbooks he included were Walter Scott McNutt, O. E. McKnight, and George Allen Hubbell. *A History of Arkansas* (Little Rock: Democrat Printing and Lithographing Co., 1932); Walter Scott McNutt, *An Elementary History of Arkansas* (Little Rock: Democrat Printing and Lithographing Co., 1935); Hazel Presson and David Y. Thomas, *The Story of Arkansas* (Little Rock: Democrat Printing and Lithographing Co., 1942); and O. E. McKnight, *Living in Arkansas* (Oklahoma City: Harlow Pub. Corp, 1951/1959).

75. For elaboration of the cult of true womanhood, see Barbara Welter, "The Cult of True Womanhood: 1820–1860," *American Quarterly* 18.2 (Summer 1966): 151–74.

76. The contemporary controversy regarding Confederate monuments and efforts to remove them is addressed in Karen L. Cox, *No Common Ground: Confederate Monuments and the Ongoing Fight for Racial Justice* (Chapel Hill: University of North Carolina Press, 2021); and Adam H. Domby, *The False Cause: Fraud, Fabrication, and White Supremacy in Confederate Memory* (Charlottesville: University of Virginia Press, 2020).

77. *Report of the Woman's Rights Convention, Held at Seneca Falls*, 8–9, 12.

78. Joan Kelly, "The Doubled Vision of Feminist Theory: A Postscript to the 'Women and Power' Conference," *Feminist Studies* 5.1 (1979): 216–27; Joan Kelly, *Women, History, and Theory: The Essays of Joan Kelly* (Chicago: University of Chicago Press, 1984), 51–64.

79. Caroline K. Sherman, "Characteristics of the Modern Woman," in *The Congress of Women Held in the Woman's Building, World's Columbian Exposition, Chicago, U.S.A., 1893*, ed. Mary Kavanaugh Oldham Eagle (Chicago: W. B. Conkey, 1894), 766.

80. Anne Firor Scott, "On Seeing and Not Seeing: A Case of Historical Invisibility," *Journal of American History* 71.1 (June 1984): 9.

81. Even in the twenty-first century, it seems that relatively few Arkansas women are recognized as business leaders. Since 1999, only five women (two jointly with their husbands) are among the ninety inductees in the Arkansas Business Hall of Fame, which purports to recognize Arkansas residents who have made a significant impact as a business leader with managerial success, the highest level of ethics, and a concern for improving the community as a business leader. https://walton.uark.edu/abhf/inductees.php.

82. Jim Yong Kim, president of the World Bank, argues that gender equality and economic development are inextricably linked. The persistent constraints and deprivations that prevent many women from achieving their potential have huge consequences for individuals, families, communities, and nations, and men and boys stand to gain from gender equality that improves the economic and psychological well-being of all household members. "Foreword," *Voice and Agency: Empowering Women and Girls for Shared Prosperity* (Washington, DC: World Bank Publications, 2014), ix.

83. Bernadette Cahill, "Carved Only with Her Name: Clara McDiarmid and Woman Suffrage in Arkansas," *Pulaski County Historical Review* 64 (Summer 2016): 69–73.

84. *The Woman's Journal*, January 18, 1890, p. 18; *The Woman's Journal*, March 8, 1890, p. 74; Lura E. Brown, *On the Track and Off the Train: A Revision of the Sketches Recently Published as a Serial* (Little Rock: The Press Printing Company, 1892), 209–10; Mary Kavanaugh Oldham Eagle, *The Congress of Women Held in the Woman's Building, World's Columbian Exposition, Chicago, U.S.A., 1893. With Portraits, Biographies and Addresses* (Philadelphia: International Publishing Co., 1895), 723; *Little Rock, Arkansas, City Directory* (Little Rock: R. L. Polk, 1895).

85. *The Woman's Journal*, July 11, 1891, p. 222; Mrs. S. S. Wassell, "History of Equal Suffrage Movement in Arkansas," *Arkansas Gazette*, February 9, 1919, p. 30.

86. "A Good Investment," *Arkansas Democrat*, June 8, 1880, p. 4; "Perpetual Profits," *Arkansas Gazette*, September 26, 1884, p. 5; *Arkansas Democrat*, May 17, 1890, p. 4; *Chicago Tribune*, June 18, 1893, p. 30.

87. This difficulty was, of course, not limited to Arkansas, but it was generally more challenging in the South. For an extended discussion of the issue, see Barbara J. Harris, *Beyond Her Sphere: Women and the Professions in American History* (Westport, CT: Greenwood Press, 1978).

88. "Smiles," *Fayetteville Weekly Democrat*, August 28, 1869, p. 1.

89. [Catherine Campbell Cunningham], "Arkansas," *History of Woman Suffrage*, ed. Susan B. Anthony and Ida Husted Harper (Indianapolis: The Hollenbeck Press, 1902), vol. 4: 477.

90. *Arkansas Gazette*, May 19, 1893, p. 2; "Pharmacy for Women," *The Woman's Journal*, July 15, 1893, p. 220; *Arkansas Gazette*, July 14, 1895, p. 4; *American Druggist and Pharmaceutical Record*, 27 (1895): 81.

91. "Arkansas Women Druggists," *Fort Smith Times*, November 19, 1903, p. 4;

*Fort Smith Times*, March 22, 1904, p. 5; *Arkansas Democrat*, May 12, 1904, p. 6. See also, David M. Moyers, "From Quackery to Qualification: Arkansas Medical and Drug Legislation, 1881–1909," *Arkansas Historical Quarterly* 35 (Spring 1976): 3–26.

92. Velda Brotherton, "Virginia Maud Dunlap Duncan," *Arkansas Biography: A Collection of Notable Lives*, ed. Nancy A. Williams and Jeannie M. Whayne (Fayetteville: University of Arkansas Press, 2000), 89–90; Elsa Vaught, "That All-Woman Government in Winslow, 1925–1927," *Flashback* 8 (October 1958): 45–56; Robert G. Winn, "Winslow's Petticoat Government, 1925–27," *Flashback* 28 (August 1978): 33–36.

93. Dallas T. Herndon, *Centennial History of Arkansas* (Chicago: S. J. Clarke, 1922).

94. For examples of the early resistance to women in the medical professions, see "Women in Dentistry," *Ohio State Journal of Dental Science* 6.6 (1886): 266–73; "About Woman: She Should Not Be a Doctor (Or Dentist)," *Western Dental Journal* 5 (1891): 214–15; and Mary Roth Walsh, *"Doctors Wanted-No Women Need Apply": Sexual Barriers in the Medical Profession, 1835–1975* (New Haven: Yale University Press, 1977).

95. "A Kentucky Lady Dentist," *Lexington Herald-Leader*, March 18, 1891, p. 8; *Arkansas Gazette*, May 10, 1891, p. 2; "Unique Reception," *Arkansas Democrat*, November 21, 1891, p. 6; "Women in Dentistry," *Arkansas Gazette*, September 11, 1895, p. 6; "Leading Dentists," *Arkansas Gazette*, February 8, 1903, p. 25.

96. "Female Doctors," *Washington Telegraph*, February 27, 1850, p. 1. For the original editorial by Addison Sanders, see "Feminine Doctors," *Evansville Daily Journal*, January 9, 1850, p. 2.

97. See Conevery A. Bolton, "'A Sister's Consolations': Women Health, and Community in Early Arkansas, 1810–1860," *Arkansas Historical Quarterly* 50.3 (1991): 271–91. Sarah Jackman Embree (1783–1837), mistress of Rob Roy Plantation in Jefferson County, settled there in 1815 while it was still part of Missouri Territory. Herndon counts her as one of the ten most famous women in Arkansas history, because "she had uncanny wisdom for the detection and application of medicinal properties possessed by the many herbs which she found growing in forest and field; that she used her knowledge with such skill and success that she acquired the reputation of a wonder worker with the sick." Dallas T. Herndon, "Ten Most Famous Women in Arkansas History," in *The Arkansas Handbook 1937–1938* (Little Rock: Arkansas History Commission, 1938), 70.

98. *Arkansas Democrat*, March 6, 1882, Page 1; "The Official M.D.s," *Arkansas Gazette*, May 26, 1882, p. 4; *Arkansas Gazette*, February 5, 1883, p. 4; *Arkansas Gazette*, November 25, 1883, p. 5.

99. Lizzie Dorman Fyler, "Arkansas Report," *Woman's Journal*, November 21, 1885, 369–70; *Arkansas Gazette*, October 9, 1887, p. 4.; *Arkansas Gazette*, April 3, 1887, p. 4.

100. "Mrs. Helena Maxwell Cady," *A Woman of the Century*, ed. Frances Elizabeth Willard and Mary Ashton Rice Livermore (Chicago: Charles Wells Moulton, 1893), 145–46. At various times between 1898 and 1911, Dr. Cady maintained residences in Edinburgh, Washington, DC, and Chicago.

101. Fred O. Henker, "From Other Years—Ida Josephine Brooks, M.D.," *Journal of the Arkansas Medical Society* 80.12 (1984): 599; Fred O. Henker, "Brooks, Ida Josephine," in *Arkansas Biography: A Collection of Notable Lives*, ed. Nancy A. Williams and Jeannie M. Whayne (Fayetteville: University of Arkansas Press, 2000), 40–41.

102. "The 'First Ladies' of Arkansas Medicine: Dedicated Pioneers in a Male-Dominated World," *Journal of the Arkansas Medical Society* 104.1 (2007): 14.

103. *Bradwell v. State of Illinois*, 83 U.S. 130 at 141 (1873).

104. Albert Pike, Sam. C. Roane, and William McK. Ball, *Revised Statutes of the State of Arkansas: Adopted at the October Session of the General Assembly of Said State, A.D. 1837* (Boston: Weeks, Jordan, 1838), 128; William W. Mansfield's *A Digest of the Statutes of Arkansas, Embracing All Laws of a General and Permanent Character in Force at the Close of the Session of the General Assembly of One Thousand Eight Hundred and Eighty-three* (Little Rock: Mitchell and Bettis, 1884), Chap. 11, Sect. 406, p. 238.

105. *Proceedings of the Arkansas State Bar Association* (Little Rock: Gazette Printing Co., 1883), 29.

106. Lockwood's experience is detailed in Belva A. Lockwood, "My Efforts to Become a Lawyer," *Lippincott's Monthly Magazine*, February 1888, pp. 215–29. The *Arkansas Gazette* reprinted Lockwood's 1884 speech accepting the nomination of the Equal Rights Party, promising "a fair distribution of public offices to women" and "to appoint a reasonable number of women as district attorneys, marshals, and judges of the United States, and would appoint some competent woman to any vacancy that might occur on the United States supreme bench." "Belva for President," *Arkansas Gazette*, September 5, 1884, p. 2.

107. *Proceedings of the Arkansas State Bar Association* (Little Rock: Gazette Printing Co., 1882–188), 46.

108. *The Woman's Journal*, December 6, 1884, p. 391.

109. *The Woman's Journal*, November 21, 1885, p. 379; *Eureka Springs Times*, quoted in *Arkansas Ladies' Journal*, December 5, 1885; *The Woman's Journal*, December 12, 1885, p. 397; Frances Mitchell Ross, "100 Years of History: Arkansas Women and the Law," *Arkansas Lawyer*, October 1984, pp. 178–83; and Frances Mitchell Ross, "Reforming the Bar: Women and the Arkansas Legal Profession," *University of Arkansas at Little Rock Law Review* 20.4 (1998): 869–90. Fyler's relation to Sarah Ridge is mentioned in her mother's obituary, *Mounds Enterprise*, March 22, 1907, p. 1.

110. National Woman Suffrage Association, *Report of the Sixteenth Annual Washington Convention, March 4th, 5th, 6th and 7th, 1884, With Reports of the Forty-Eighth Congress. In right conditions the interests of man and woman are*

essentially one; but in false conditions they must ever be opposed, ed. Elizabeth
Cady Stanton and Susan B. Anthony (Rochester, NY: Charles Mann, 1884),
58–62; *National Republican* (Washington, DC), March 8, 1884, p. 1.

111. *Fayetteville Weekly Democrat*, April 16, 1885, p. 3.

112. *El Dorado Eagle*, April 2, 1885, cited in *Arkansas Gazette*, April 4, 1885, p. 4.

113. *Arkansas Methodist*, April 11, 1885, p. 1; *Arkansas Methodist*, April 18, 1885, p. 1.

114. "St. Paul and the Women," *Arkansas Democrat*, April 18, 1885, p. 1.

115. *Quitman Light*, quoted in *Arkansas Democrat*, April 21, 1885, p. 1.

116. *Arkansas Democrat*, February 23, 1898, p. 8; *Arkansas Democrat*, October 4,
1898, p. 8.

117. Stephen A. Smith, "Erle Rutherford Chambers," unpublished manuscript,
Stephen A. Smith Papers, MC 1686, Mullins Library Special Collections,
University of Arkansas, Fayetteville.

118. *Biographical Sketch of Laura "Lollie" Davis Fitzhugh*, written by Patricia Bruno,
included in *Part III: Mainstream Suffragists—National American Woman
Suffrage Association*.

119. Karen Venturella, "Fuller, Minnie Ursula Oliver Scott Rutherford (1868–
1946), Reformer and Suffragist," *American National Biography*, February 1,
2000.

120. "Should Women Practice Law," *Pine Bluff Daily Graphic*, April 13, 1911, p. 3.

121. "Women May Practice Law," *Arkansas Democrat*, February 27, 1913, p. 11.

122. *Arkansas Gazette*, January 23, 1915, p. 3; Minnie Rutherford Fuller, "Important
Bills in the Legislature," *Arkansas Gazette*, January 31, 1915, p. 34.

123. Beebe Thompson Chapin, "Indifference Dues Not Alter Rights," *Arkansas
Gazette*, September 17, 1916, p. 46.

124. *Arkansas Democrat*, February 1, 1917, p. 2; *Arkansas Gazette*, February 17, 1917,
p. 6; *Arkansas Gazette*, February 18, 1917, p. 16; *Arkansas Gazette*, February 28,
1917, p. 3.

125. Our understanding is drawn from the insightful work of Linda K. Kerber,
"Separate Spheres, Female Worlds, Woman's Place: The Rhetoric of Women's
History," *Journal of American History* 75.1 (June 1988): 9–39.

126. George W. Burnap, *Lectures on the Sphere and Duties of Woman* (Baltimore:
John Murphy, 1841), ix, 47–48, 68. Even before the Seneca Falls Convention,
Rev. Burnap had already pronounced arguments for women's rights and
woman suffrage to be flawed and unwise.

127. Barbara Welter, "The Cult of True Womanhood: 1820–1860," *American
Quarterly* 18.2 (1966): 151–52.

128. Eileen Hunt Botting and Sarah L. Houser, "'Drawing the Line of Equality':
Hannah Mather Crocker on Women's Rights," *American Political Science
Review* 100.2 (2006): 265–78.

129. Hannah Mather Crocker, *Observations on the Real Rights of Women, with Their
Appropriate Duties, Agreeable to Scripture, Reason, and Common Sense* (Boston:
printed for the author, 1818), 6, 15–16, 20.

130. See Kelly Houston Jones, "Bondwomen on Arkansas's Cotton Frontier: Migration, Labor, Family, and Resistance among an Exploited Class," and Rebecca A. Howard, "Women of the Ozarks in the Civil War: 'I Fear We Will See Hard Times,'" in *Arkansas Women: Their Lives and Times*, ed. Cherisse Jones-Branch and Gary T. Edwards (Athens: University of Georgia Press, 2018), 27–45, 72–92; and Barbara Wittman, Kathryn M. Feltey, and Molly Hartsough, "Women in Frontier Arkansas: Settlement in a Post-Reconstruction Racial State," *Du Bois Review* 16. 2 (Fall 2019): 575–612.

131. Matilda Fulton to William S. Fulton, February 9, 1832, in Conevery A. Bolton, "'A Sister's Consolations': Women, Health, and Community in Early Arkansas, 1810–1860," *Arkansas Historical Quarterly* 50.3 (Autumn 1991): 289; Jessica Parker Moore, "'Bursting to Speak My Mind': How Matilda Fulton Challenged the Boundaries of Womanhood in Frontier Arkansas," PhD diss., Texas Christian University, 2014; Jessica Parker Moore, "'Keeping All Hands Moving': A Plantation Mistress in Antebellum Arkansas," *Arkansas Historical Quarterly* 74.3 (2015): 257–76.

132. Michael S. Kimmel, "Men's Responses to Feminism at the Turn of the Century," *Gender and Society* 1.3 (September 1987): 262.

133. See, for example, Angie Maxwell and Todd Shields, "The Impact of Modern Sexism on the 2016 Election," *Blair Center Poll Report* (June 2017), https://blaircenter.uark.edu/the-impact-of-modern-sexism/; Laurie A. Rudman and Peter Glick, "Prescriptive Gender Stereotypes and Backlash toward Agentic Women," *Journal of Social Issues* 57.4 (2001): 743–62; Alice H. Eagly and Steven J. Karau, "Role Congruity Theory of Prejudice Toward Female Leaders," *Psychological Review* 109.3 (July 2002): 573–98; and Andrea L. Miller and Eugene Borgida, "The Separate Spheres Model of Gendered Inequality," *PloS One* 11.1 (2016): e0147315-e0147315.

134. This understanding of standpoint theory is informed by Sandra G. Harding, *The Science Question in Feminism* (Ithaca: Cornell University Press, 1986) and Joan Wallach Scott, *Gender and the Politics of History* (New York: Columbia University Press, 1999).

135. Cherisse Jones-Branch, "The Arkansas Association of Colored Women and Early Twentieth-Century Maternalist Political Activism," *Arkansas Historical Quarterly* 79.3 (2020): 218–30; Kelly Houston Jones, "Race, Gender, and the Struggle for Suffrage in Arkansas," *Arkansas Historical Quarterly* 79.3 (2020): 177–92. The Arkansas Federation of Women's Clubs determined to withdraw from the national General Federation of Women's Clubs if it "decides to eliminate the color line," *Arkansas Democrat*, April 18, 1902, p. 4. The Arkansas Federation of Colored Women's Clubs was founded in 1907. For discussion of Black women's individual and organizational contributions, see Martha S. Jones, *Vanguard: How Black Women Broke Barriers, Won the Vote, and Insisted on Equity for All* (New York: Basic Books, 2020); Susan Ware, *American Women's Suffrage: Voices from the Long Struggle for the Vote 1776–1965* (New

York: Library of America, 2020); Beth Kruse, Rhondalyn K. Peairs, Jodi Skipper, and Shennette Garrett-Scott, "Remembering Ida, Ida Remembering: Ida B. Wells-Barnett and Black Political Culture in Reconstruction-Era Mississippi," *Southern Cultures* 26.3 (2020): 20–41; Rosalind Rosenberg, *Jane Crow: The Life of Pauli Murray* (New York: Oxford University Press, 2017); and Stacey Abrams, *Our Time Is Now: Power, Purpose, and the Fight for a Fair America* (New York: Henry Holt, 2020).

136. For conclusions not dissimilar to those regarding the influence of women legislators, see the excellent study by Janine A. Parry and William H. Miller, "'The Great Negro State of the Country?': Black Legislators in Arkansas: 1973–2000," *Journal of Black Studies* 36.6 (July 2006): 833–72. Furthermore, we must "recognize that being a woman is, in fact, not extractable from context in which one is a woman—that is, race, class, time." Elsa Barkley Brown, "What Has Happened Here: The Politics of Difference in Women's History and Feminist Politics," *Feminist Studies* 12.2 (Summer 1992): 300.

137. *Acts of 1875*, p. 206.

138. "The Three-Mile Law," *Arkansas Gazette*, June 14, 1889, p. 2.

139. *Blackwell v. State*, 36 Ark. 178 (1880) at 184; *Wilson v. State*, 35 Ark. 414 (1880) at 422, 429.

140. *The Woman's Journal*, December 1, 1883, p. 384.

141. *Arkansas Democrat*, June 9, 1879, p. 4.

142. *Minutes of the National Woman's Christian Temperance Union at the 11th Annual Meeting in St. Louis* (Chicago: Woman's Temperance Publication Association, 1884), 34–35; *Woman's Journal*, January 2, 1886, p. 5.

143. The symbiosis between the WCTU and suffrage groups in Arkansas is discussed in Ben F. Johnson, "The Staunchest of the Stout-Hearted Women: The Woman's Christian Temperance Union and the Varieties of Reform in Arkansas," *Arkansas Historical Quarterly* 79.3 (2020): 193–217.

144. For additional information on the role and contributions of women's clubs, see Janie Synatzske Evins, "Arkansas Women: Their Contribution to Society, Politics, and Business, 1865–1900," *Arkansas Historical Quarterly* 44.2 (1985): 118–33; and Marilyn Martin, "From Altruism to Activism: The Contributions of Literary Clubs to Arkansas Public Libraries, 1885–1935," *Arkansas Historical Quarterly* 55.1 (1996): 64–94. See also Frances Mitchell Ross, "The New Woman as Club Woman and Social Activist in Turn of the Century Arkansas," *Arkansas Historical Quarterly* 50.4 (1991): 317–51.

145. *Our Famous Women: Comprising the Lives and Deeds of American Women Who Have Distinguished Themselves in Literature, Science, Art, Music, and the Drama, Or are Famous as Heroines, Patriots, Orators, Educators, Physicians, Philanthropists, etc., with Numerous Anecdotes, Incidents, and Personal Experiences* (Hartford, CT: A. D. Worthington, 1884); *Arkansas Gazette*, November 16, 1890, p. 14; January 12, 1890, p. 1; January 30, 1890, p. 5; February 15, 1890, p. 2. For the rhetorical power of such public presentations,

see Kate White, "Inherent Contradictions: The General Federation of Women's Clubs Use of Patriotic Pageants as Civic Education during the Americanization Era," *College English* 77.6 (July 2015): 512–29.

146. *Woman's Journal*, February 4, 1893, p. 34.

147. Mary Kavanaugh Oldham Eagle, ed., *Congress of Women Held in the Woman's Building, World's Columbian Exhibition, Chicago. 1893* (New York: Wilson, 1894).

148. See Clara B. Eno, "Some Accomplishments of Arkansas Federation of Women's Clubs," *Arkansas Historical Quarterly* 2.3 (1943): 255–58; and Frances Mitchell Ross, "The New Woman as Club Woman and Social Activist in Turn of the Century Arkansas," *Arkansas Historical Quarterly* 50.4 (1991): 317–51.

149. *Arkansas Democrat*, January 5, 1899, p. 2.

150. *Woman's Journal and Suffrage News*, May 15, 1915, p. 151, and May 22, 1915, p. 163.

151. *The Woman's Journal*, October 22, 1881, p. 337. The starting point for the history of woman suffrage in Arkansas is A. Elizabeth Taylor, "The Woman Suffrage Movement in Arkansas," *Arkansas Historical Quarterly* 15.1 (1956): 17–52. See also Kristen L. Thompson, "From the Parlour to the Polls: Arkansas and the Women's Suffrage Question," Master's thesis, University of Arkansas, 2003; and Bernadette Cahill, *Arkansas Women and the Right to Vote: The Little Rock Campaigns, 1868–1920* (Little Rock: Butler Center Books, 2015).

152. Bernadette Cahill, "Carved Only with Her Name: Clara McDiarmid and Woman Suffrage in Arkansas," *Pulaski County Historical Review* 64 (Summer 2016): 69–73.

153. *Arkansas Gazette*, February 26, 1911, p. 1; *Batesville Daily Guard*, March 16, 1911, p. 2; *Arkansas Democrat*, October 13, 1914, p. 8; *Arkansas Democrat*, April 4, 1917, p. 4; *Arkansas Democrat*, December 3, 1919, p. 1; *Arkansas Democrat*, December 3, 1919, p. 1.

154. *Arkansas Gazette*, January 1, 1870, p. 1.

155. *Arkansas Gazette*, March 9, 1876, p. 4 and March 15, 1876, p. 4; Mary Ashton Rice Livermore, *What Shall We Do with Our Daughters? Superfluous Women, And Other Lectures* (Boston: Lee and Shepard, 1883).

156. *Arkansas Gazette*, February 24, 1877, p. 4; *Arkansas Gazette*, March 3, 1877, p. 3; "The S.C.T.U," *Southern Standard*, February 4, 1882, p. 2; *Arkansas Gazette*, February 22, 1889, p. 4.

157. *Arkansas Gazette*, February 11, 1883, p. 5; *Arkansas Democrat*, January 31, 1884, p. 4.

158. *Arkansas Gazette*, April 17, 1896, p. 3; *Arkansas Gazette*, April 19, 1911, p. 7; *Arkansas Gazette*, October 11, 1912, p. 9; *Arkansas Democrat*, March 14, 1914, p. 5; *Arkansas Democrat*, September 30, 1913, p. 8; *Arkansas Gazette*, October 1, 1913, p. 1; *Arkansas Democrat*, October 1, 1913, p. 6; *Arkansas Gazette*, November 18, 1914, p. 14; *Arkansas Democrat*, January 25, 1916, p. 7; *Arkansas Gazette*, March 29, 1916, p. 9.

159. "St Paul and Women in the Ministry," *Arkansas Democrat*, March 24, 1907, p. 16; "Woman's Place in the World," *Arkansas Gazette* March 4, 1907, p. 2; Martha Williamson Rimmer, "A Southern Woman's Place in the Pulpit: Athalia Johnson Irwin Hears the Call of Universalism," *Journal of Unitarian Universalist History* 30 (2005): 71–104.

160. *Arkansas Democrat*, April 4, 1906, p. 1, 3; *The Woman's Journal*, May 12, 1906, p. 75.

161. *Pine Bluff Graphic*, October 18, 1913, p. 1; *Hot Springs New Era*, November 19, 1914, p. 5. For an analysis of the technique, see Mary Chapman, *Making Noise, Making News: Suffrage Print Culture and U.S. Modernism* (New York: Oxford University Press, 2014).

162. *Arkansas Gazette*, May 3, 1914, p. 1.

163. "Lillian Russell Is a Suffragette," *Arkansas Gazette*, December 11, 1913, p. 7.

164. *Arkansas Gazette*, February 26, 1911, p. 9

165. *Arkansas Gazette*, May 29, 1914, p. 2. Nora M. Brown (1895–1960) would later serve as the president of the Arkansas Federation of Business and Professional Women.

166. *Arkansas Gazette*, April 18, 1915, p. 2.

167. *Woman's Journal*, September 12, 1885, p. 293.

168. *Woman's Chronicle*, March 3, 1888, p. 1. See also, Dorsey D. Jones, "Catherine Campbell Cunningham, Advocate of Equal Rights for Women," *Arkansas Historical Quarterly* 12 (Summer 1953): 85–90.

169. "Fine Press Work in States," *Woman's Journal*, December 30, 1911, p. 411.

170. *Arkansas Gazette*, July 12, 1914, p. 30; *Arkansas Gazette*, July 19, 1914, p. 27 *Arkansas Gazette*, August 2, 1914, p. 32; *Arkansas Gazette*, August 9, 1914, p. 28.

171. *Arkansas Gazette*, August 9, 1914, p. 30.

172. *Arkansas Constitution of 1874*, Article II, §3.

173. *Arkansas Constitution of 1874*, Article III, §§1, 2, 5, 6; Article XIX, §1.

174. Marcus LaRue Harrison to Governor Isaac Murphy, September 25, 1866, published in *Arkansas Gazette*, October 3, 1866, p. 2.

175. Post Office Department, *Postal Laws and Regulations*, Chapter I, §3 (Washington: Government Printing Office, 1866).

176. Post Office Department, *Postal Laws and Regulations*, Chapter I, §4 (Washington: Government Printing Office, 1866).

177. Cameron Blevins, "Women and Federal Officeholding in the Late Nineteenth-Century U.S.," *Current Research in Digital History* 2 (2019): https://crdh.rrchnm.org/essays/v02-08-women-and-federal-officeholding/.

178. *U.S., Southern Claims Commission Master Index, 1871–1880*, p. 441. Approved claim for $387 in 1872 ($8,255 in 2021). *Arkansas Gazette*, December 10, 1872.

179. "The Mails Again," *Arkansas Gazette*, September 16, 1870, p. 4.

180. "Items of State News," *Morning Republican*, June 13, 1872; *Arkansas Gazette*, June 13, 1872, p. 4. Bayne moved to Illinois in 1876 and became editor of the *Decatur Daily Review*. In July 1880, he was expelled from his church "on

the charge of gross immoral conduct in connection with boys and young men," resigned from the newspaper, and left town under cover of darkness to avoid arrest on a state warrant. *Decatur Daily Republican*, July 16, 1880, p. 3; "Skipped Out," *Decatur Daily Republican*, July 22, 1880, p. 1.

181. *Arkansas Gazette*, February 9, 1870, p. 2.

182. *Journal of the Executive Proceedings of the Senate of the United States of America, Vol. 18 (1871–1873)* (Washington: Government Printing Office, 1901), 387–88, 392–93, 405, 410.

183. "The Removal of the Postmaster at this Place," *Fort Smith New Era*, February 28, 1873. John G. Price, the editor of the *Little Rock Republican* and a staunch Clayton supporter, called Dell "an alleged republican at Fort Smith, who has never been in accord with the party, and upon all important issues which afforded the least excuse for the weak-kneed element of the party to fly off on a tangent, he could always be found at the extreme end of it." *Arkansas Democrat*, July 20, 1880, p. 1.

184. The effect of Shumard's commission and the Senate's motion to recall is discussed in dicta and footnotes of Justice Brandeis's opinion in *United States v. Smith*, 286 U.S. 6 (1932).

185. Dell served two years as postmaster, made an unsuccessful campaign for Congress, then was appointed US Marshall by President Rutherford B. Hays, much to the chagrin of Judge Isaac Parker, who warned Hays that Dell was "ill-natured, irascible, impractical, and tyrannical, a friend of bad and reckless men who want an opportunity to filch money from the government." Fred Harvey Harrington, *The Hanging Judge* (Norman: University of Oklahoma Press, 1996), 60–61. In 1882, Dell was indicted by a federal grand jury for fraud and embezzlement of government funds intended for maintenance of inmates. "Defendant Jacket Files for US District Court Western Division of Arkansas, Fort Smith Division, 1866–1900, Record Group Number 21," National Archives and Records Administration, Fort Worth, Texas.

186. *Arkansas Gazette*, February 28, 1889, p. 6; *Arkansas Gazette*, June 6, 1889, p. 4. Emma Clayton was commissioned during the Senate recess; her formal nomination was made by President Harrison on December 16 and confirmed by the Senate on December 19, 1889. *Journal of the Executive Proceedings of the Senate of the United States* (Washington: Government Printing Office, 1909), vol. 29, part 1 (1893–1895): pp. 116, 236, 280; *Congressional Record–Senate*, December 20, 1889, p. 329

187. "A Black Eye for the Boss," *Arkansas Gazette*, August 21, 1889, p. 4; *Hot Springs Sentinel*, August 19, 1889, reprinted in "A Democratic Victory," *Arkansas Gazette*, August 21, 1889, p. 4; "Hot Springs Republicans Mad," *Southern Standard*, August 23, 1889, p. 2; "How It Hurts," *Arkansas Gazette*, August 22, 1889, p. 5.

188. *St. Louis Globe-Democrat*, September 22, 1888, p. 11; June 22, 1889, p. 15; *The Courier-Journal*, August 18, 1889, p. 2; *Arkansas Gazette*, August 18, 1889, p. 1;

*Indiana State Sentinel*, August 28, 1889, p. 8; *Arkansas Gazette*, August 30, 1889, p. 4; *St. Louis Globe-Democrat*, September 14, 1889, p. 13; Marshall Cushing, *The Story of Our Post Office* (Boston: Thayer, 1893), p. 449; *Journal of the Executive Proceedings of the Senate of the United States* (Washington: Government Printing Office, 1909), vol. 29, part 1 (1893–1895): pp. 116, 236, 280.

189. *St. Louis Globe-Democrat*, Nov 12, 1893, p. 2; Frances Elizabeth Caroline Willard and Mary Ashton Rice Livermore, *American Women: Fifteen Hundred Biographies with over 1,400 Portraits; A Comprehensive Encyclopedia of the Lives and Achievements of American Women during the Nineteenth Century* (New York: Mast, Crowell & Kirkpatrick, 1897) 1:374; Marshall Cushing, *The Story of Our Post Office* (Boston: Thayer, 1893), p. 449; and *Indianapolis Journal*, June 6, 1894, p. 6.

190. "Women Not Wanted," *New York Times*, November 9, 1902, p. 3; "Marriage and Federal Jobs," *New York Times*, November 28, 1902, p. 8; "Women Clerks Who Wed," *Washington Post*, November 25, 1902, p. 2. Today, more than 60 percent of the nation's postmasters are women.

191. George B. Cortelyou, "The Postmistress," *The Delineator* 68.1 (January 1906): 69–71.

192. *Arkansas Gazette*, December 23, 1906, p. 12.

193. *Arkansas Gazette*, November 21, 1874, p. 4; *Arkansas Gazette*, November 28, 1874, p. 4.

194. The idea that a good "republican mother" could vicariously participate in the political sphere while remaining in the home and educating virtuous sons to be active and informed American citizens was first advanced in Linda Kerber, "The Republican Mother: Women and the Enlightenment—An American Perspective," *American Quarterly* 28.2 (1976): 187–205.

195. *Arkansas Gazette*, November 8, 1874, p. 1.

196. *Arkansas Gazette*, November 21, 1874, p. 4; *Arkansas Gazette*, March 5, 1875, p. 4; *Arkansas Gazette*, January 7, 1877, p. 4; *Arkansas Gazette*, January 9, 1877, p. 4.

197. *Arkansas Democrat*, January 11, 1879, p. 4.

198. *Arkansas Democrat*, April 2, 1887; Eagle, *Congress of Women* (1894): 733–34.

199. *Pine Bluff Daily Graphic*, December 6, 1913, p. 1.

200. *Arkansas Gazette*, January 13, 1895, p. 2.

201. *Arkansas Gazette*, January 10, 1899, p. 5.

202. *Forrest City Times*, December 14, 1894, p. 3.

203. *Arkansas Gazette*, January 14, 1885, p. 2.

204. *Arkansas Democrat*, February 12, 1891, p. 1.

205. *Woman's Chronicle*, February 28, 1891, p. 1. Editor Catherine Campbell Cunningham was the sister of House Enrolling Clerk Bessie Cockrell.

206. *The Osceola Times*, February 16, 1895, p. 2. Committee clerks were employees but not considered to be officers of the House. *Arkansas Gazette*, April 27, 1897, p. 5.

207. *Washington Telegraph*, February 15, 1895, p. 1.

208. *Arkansas Gazette*, January 16, 1897, p. 2.

209. *Arkansas Gazette*, January 16, 1897, p. 2; *Arkansas Gazette*, January 22, 1897, p. 2.

210. *Southern Standard*, January 29, 1897, p. 1; *Arkansas Gazette*, January 23, 1897, p. 2.

211. *Arkansas Gazette*, January 23, 1897, p. 2. Other Representatives speaking against the Witt bill and for postponing consideration indefinitely were Julius H. Amacker, a Springdale lawyer; Alphonso Curl, Hot Springs attorney; Robert Fuller, former circuit judge and attorney of Princeton; Newton Yancey Wadsworth, a Drew County farmer; Theodore F. Potts, attorney from Paris, former State Senator and Logan County judge; and James H. Van Hoose, former Fayetteville mayor. No one spoke in support of passing it.

212. Editorial, *Arkansas Gazette*, January 22, 1897, p. 4.

213. An Old Woman, "Women Clerks," Letter to the Editor, *Arkansas Gazette*, January 24, 1897, p. 4.

214. *Helena Weekly World*, January 27, 1897, p. 2.

215. "A Needed Reform," *Fort Smith Times*, January 21, 1899, p. 1.

216. "Lady Clerks Barred," *Arkansas Democrat*, January 21, 1899, p. 1; "Sullivan Anti-Female Bill," *Arkansas Gazette*, January 22, 1899, p. 2.

217. "In Favor of Women," *Arkansas Democrat*, January 24, 1899, p. 1.

218. *Arkansas Gazette*, January 25, 1899, pp. 3, 8.

219. *Arkansas Democrat*, January 27, 1899, p.1; *Arkansas Gazette*, January 28, 1899, p. 3.

220. *Conway Log Cabin*, January 22, 1901, p. 1; *Arkansas Gazette*, January 10, 1899, p. 5.

221. *Arkansas Gazette*, December 23, 1906, p. 12.

222. *Arkansas Democrat*, April 13, 1916, p. 5, and April 16, 1916, p. 10; Kaye Lundgren, "Biographical Sketch of Julia Burnelle 'Bernie' Smade Babcock," included in "Part III: Mainstream Suffragists—National American Woman Suffrage Association," *Women and Social Movements in the United States, 1600–2000*, Alexander Street, https://documents.alexanderstreet.com/d/1010026843.

223. Mrs. S. S. Wassell, "History of Equal Suffrage Movement in Arkansas: An Account of the Patient, Persistent Efforts for the Emancipation of Women, From Pioneer Days to the Present," *Arkansas Gazette*, February 9, 1919, p. 30, and February 23, 1919, p. 5. Renee Pinkston, "Biographical Sketch of Elizabeth McConaughey Wassell," included in "Part III: Mainstream Suffragists—National American Woman Suffrage Association," *Women and Social Movements in the United States, 1600–2000*, Alexander Street, https://documents.alexanderstreet.com/d/1010111746. Renee Pinkston, "Elizabeth McConaughey (Bettie) Wassell (1859–1923)," *Encyclopedia of Arkansas*, https://encyclopediaofarkansas.net/entries/elizabeth-mcconaughey-wassell-14531.

224. *Arkansas Democrat*, April 1, 1916, p. 4.

225. "Mere Men Defeat Woman Suffrage," *Arkansas Gazette*, April 13, 1911, p. 3.

226. *Arkansas Democrat*, May 12, 1909, p. 3.

227. *Pine Bluff Daily Graphic*, March 12, 1915, p. 1.

228. *Arkansas Democrat*, January 12, 1915, p. 9.

229. *Arkansas Democrat*, May 16, 1917, p. 5.

230. *Arkansas Democrat*, January 9, 1923, p. 10.

231. "Girl Enters Race for Senate Page, *Arkansas Gazette*, January 7, 1915, p. 5.

232. Henry N. Dorris (AP), "Legislative Sidelights," *Hope Star*, January 15, 1931, p. 1.

233. *Appointment of Female Senate Pages. Hearing, Ninety-second Congress, First Session. Senate. Committee on Rules and Administration. Ad Hoc Subcommittee to Consider the Appointment of Female Pages*, March 4, 1971; *The Daily Oklahoman*, May 22, 1973, p. 59.

234. *Act 17 of 1874*, §1 (December 16, 1874); Samuel W. Williams, Leonidas Polk Sandels, and Joseph Morrison Hill, *A Digest of the Statutes of Arkansas: Embracing All Laws of a General Nature in Force at the Close of the Session of the General Assembly of One Thousand Eight Hundred and Ninety-Three*. (Columbia, MO: Press of E. W. Stephens, 1894), chapter 113, §5389, p. 1225.

235. All persons are citizens of the United States and the state where they reside, *United States Constitution. Amend XIV, §1*.

236. Governor James Philip Eagle (1837–1904) had served as a colonel in the 5th Arkansas Infantry and the 2nd Arkansas Mounted Rifles, CSA, and was president of the Arkansas Baptist Convention. Although not active in the suffrage movement, he had introduced Susan B. Anthony two years earlier and was in the audience when she lectured on "Woman Suffrage" at the Capital Theater in Little Rock on February 21, 1889. "Miss Anthony," *Arkansas Gazette*, February 22, 1889, p. 4. Eagle was the great-uncle of Representative Lucile Sullivan Autry, elected to the Arkansas House in 1968.

237. "No Women Need Apply," *Arkansas Gazette*, January 22, 1891, p. 3.

238. Daniel Webster Jones (1839–1918) had been a colonel in the 3rd Infantry Regiment, Arkansas State Troops, CSA, and he had served as a state representative, prosecuting attorney, and Arkansas attorney general before being elected governor.

239. "Women for Office," *Arkansas Gazette*, February 4, 1897, p. 5.

240. *Arkansas Democrat*, November 2, 1899, p. 2.

241. *Arkansas Gazette*, April 17, 1897, p.2; August 17, 1897, p. 6; May 6, 1897, p. 6; October 22, 1898, p. 5; February 4, 1897, p. 5; February 11, 1897, p. 5; August 19, 1897, p. 7; January 16, 1900, p. 6; January 18, 1900, p. 3; *Arkansas Democrat*, March 1, 1900, p. 1.

242. *Arkansas Gazette*, November 7, 1897, and January 18, 1900, p. 3; *Arkansas Democrat*, September 21, 1898, p. 8, and November 25, 1899, p. 6.; *Helena Weekly World*, February 17, 1897, p. 4.

243. "George W. Murphy, attorney general, to Jefferson Davis, governor of the State of Arkansas," reprinted in *Arkansas Gazette*, February 3, 1901, p. 4. Attorney General Murphy's daughter, Jennie Murphy (1885–1938), would

become an active member of the Political Equality League and a frequent debater on women's rights at meetings of the League's Morning Study Club. See "Local Suffragists Endorse Militants," *Arkansas Gazette*, July 9, 1914, pp. 1, 7.

244. *Arkansas Democrat*, February 6, 1901, p. 4.

245. *Arkansas Gazette*, February 1, 1901, p. 4.

246. "No Female Notaries," *Arkansas Gazette*, February 1, 1901, p. 4; *Arkansas Democrat*, November 20, 1900, p. 1.

247. "Gov. Robinson Names a Woman Notary," *Pine Bluff Daily Graphic*, January 21, 1913, p. 3.

248. "Will Test Rights of Women Today," *Arkansas Gazette*, January 23, 1913, p. 1. George Basil Rose (1860–1943) was a former president of the Arkansas Bar Association. His daughter-in-law, Zilla Ward Rose, was an active suffragist and a member of the Political Equality League.

249. "Rights Test Case Lost by Mrs. Gray," *Arkansas Gazette*, February 2, 1913, p. 17; "Women Lose Another Fight," *Arkansas Gazette*, February 22, 1913, p. 3.

250. *State ex rel. Gray v. Hodges*, 107 Ark. 272, 275–76 (1913).

251. *Arkansas Gazette*, January 21, 1917, p. 16; "Suffragists to Work for New Constitution," *Pine Bluff Daily Graphic*, January 25, 1917, p. 1.

252. Arkansas Gazette, February 17, 1917, p.7.

253. *Hot Springs New Era*, January 31, 1917, p. 1; *Arkansas Gazette*, January 31, 1917, p. 1. See also Stephanie Haught Wade, "John Andrew Riggs and the Primary Suffrage Bill," *Arkansas Historical Quarterly* 79.3 (Autumn 2020): 254–77.

254. Haught Wade, "John Andrew Riggs and Arkansas's Primary Suffrage Bill."

255. *Arkansas Gazette*, March 11, 1917, p. 37.

256. *Arkansas Gazette*, March 8, 1917, p. 5.

257. Opinions 110, 111, 112, 113, 114, and 115. *Biennial Report of the Attorney General, 1917–18*, pp. 249–253.

258. "Suffrage Has Supporters Here," *Pine Bluff Daily Graphic*, December 6, 1913, p. 1; "Are Women People?" *Hot Springs New Era*, March 9, 1917, p. 8. Land would soon be elected to three terms as Jefferson County treasurer, 1925–1928.

259. "Mrs. S.S. Wassell First Woman Voter," *Arkansas Democrat*, March 19, 1917, p. 10.

260. Ida Husted Harper, *The History of Woman Suffrage* (New York: National American Woman Suffrage Association, 1922), 20–24; *Arkansas Gazette*, July 12, 1918, p. 10; *Arkansas Gazette*, June 2, 1920, p. 1.

261. *Arkansas Democrat*, April 28, 1920, p. 6; *Little Rock Daily News*, May 31, 1920, p. 1. In 1892, the Prohibition Party had elected three women delegates to the national convention. *Arkansas Gazette*, May 6, 1892, p. 2. Ida Callery was a delegate to the 1912 Socialist Party Convention, and Fannie Crowell was a founding delegate to the 1919 Communist Labor Party Convention.

262. "New Constitution for State Drafted," *Arkansas Gazette*, June 19, 1918, p. 9.

263. All seven House members voted Aye; Senator Kirby voted Aye, and Senator

Robinson was paired Aye. In 1915, before Arkansas women had primary suffrage rights, the Arkansas delegation in the House of Representatives voted unanimously against the proposed suffrage amendment.

264. *Arkansas Democrat*, November 1, 1920, p. 4. The suffrage amendment to the Arkansas Constitution was first declared lost, despite receiving overwhelming popular support. It was finally added after the decision in *Brickhouse v. Hill*, 167 Ark. 513 (1928), ruled it required only a majority of the votes cast upon the question rather than a majority of the votes cast in the election.

265. Opinion of Attorney John D. Arbuckle to Hon. Charles H. Brough, governor; Hon. Tom J. Terral, secretary of state, "The Woman's Suffrage Amendment to the Constitution of the United States Does Not Give to Women in this State the Right to Hold Office until at Least Some Action Is Taken Warranting the Same by the Legislature of the State," October 9, 1920.

266. *Little Rock Daily News*, January 12, 1921, p. 6.

267. *Arkansas Democrat*, August 9, 1920, p. 15; *Arkansas Gazette*, June 6, 1920, p. 16.

268. *Arkansas Gazette*, January 16, 1921, p. 30.

269. Act 59 of 1921, *General Acts and Joint and Concurrent Resolutions and Memorials and Proposed Constitutional Amendments of the Forty-Third General Assembly of the State of Arkansas Passed at the Session Held at the Capitol, in the City of Little Rock, Arkansas, Commencing on the 10th day of January, 1921, and Ending on the 10th day of March, 1921* (Little Rock: Democrat Printing and Lithographing Co., 1921), 65–66.

270. Judge Morris S. Arnold, "Lois Dale: The First Women to Serve on the Bench in Arkansas," *The Arkansas Lawyer* 54.1 (Winter 2019): 50–52.

271. Florence McRaven, "What I Think of the Arkansas Legislature," *Dixie Magazine* 3.2 (February 1927): 33.

272. Elizabeth Hooper Thompson, *Songs and Sonnets of a Solon* (Helena, AR: Bradford Printing Co., 1926).

273. "Women Legislators, Past and Present, Agree State Would Do Well to Send More of Them to Assembly," *Arkansas Gazette*, January 20, 1935, pp. 1, 14. Considerable research on women and politics confirms that women elected officials still work to represent women's perspectives on issues more than do their male colleagues, reflecting their experiences and responsibilities in the private sphere. See Sarah Poggione, "Exploring Gender Differences in State Legislators' Policy Preferences," *Political Research Quarterly* 57. 2 (June 2004): 305–14; John M. Carey, Richard G. Niemi, and Lynda W. Powell, "Are Women State Legislators Different?" in Sue Thomas and Clyde Wilcox, eds., *Women and Elective Office: Past, Present, and Future* (New York: Oxford University Press, 1998), 87–102; Irene Diamond, *Sex Roles in the State House* (New Haven, CT: Yale University Press, 1977); and Shelah Gilbert Leader, "The Policy Impact of Elected Women Officials," in Louis Maisel and Joseph Cooper, eds., *The Impact of the Electoral Process* (Beverly Hills, CA: Sage, 1977).

274. *Arkansas Gazette*, January 20, 1935, p. 14; Sarah A. Fulton, "Running

Backwards and in High Heels: The Gendered Quality Gap and Incumbent Electoral Success," *Political Research Quarterly* 65.2 (2012): 303–14.

275. *Arkansas Gazette*, January 15, 1933, p. 20.

276. *Arkansas Gazette*, April 13, 1911, p. 3.

277. *Arkansas Gazette*, January 20, 1935, p. 14.

278. *Arkansas Gazette*, April 30, 1929, p. 8.

279. *Arkansas Gazette*, January 20, 1935, p. 14. The classic analysis of survey research in the 1950s seemed to confirm this pessimism, finding that most American women had "lower levels of political efficacy, political involvement, and political conceptualization than men and concluded that most women simply followed their husbands' lead when it came to voting." Angus Campbell, Philip E. Converse, Warren E. Miller, and Donald E. Stokes, *The American Voter* (New York: Wiley, 1960), 483–93. However, by the early twenty-first century, research found that women "were now fully part of the electorate, being more involved in politics and voting at higher levels" than men. Michael S. Lewis-Beck, William G. Jacoby, Helmut Norpoth, and Herbert F. Weisber, *The American Voter Revisited* (Ann Arbor: University of Michigan Press, 2008), 426. For a discussion of the political impact of second-wave feminism, see Judith Evans, *Feminist Theory Today: An Introduction to Second-Wave Feminism* (Thousand Oaks, CA: Sage Publications, 2013); and Barbara Molony and Jennifer Nelson, *Women's Activism and "Second Wave" Feminism: Transnational Histories* (London: Bloomsbury Publishing, 2017).

280. "Recognition of Right to Political Power Woman's Chief Goal," *Arkansas Gazette*, December 5, 1937, p. 34.

281. *Arkansas Gazette*, January 12, 1943, p. 7; *Arkansas Gazette*, February 10, 1943, p. 10.

282. *Arkansas Democrat*, January 1, 1950, p. 32; *Arkansas Democrat*, April 23, 1950, p. 57; *Arkansas Democrat*, April 15, 1951, p. 9.

283. *Arkansas Democrat*, August 17, 1952, p. 24.

284. *Arkansas Democrat*, January 11, 1953, p. 5; *Arkansas Gazette*, February 4, 1953, p. 6.

285. *Arkansas Gazette*, March 13, 1963, p. 18. For a discussion of the important role played by women's caucuses, see Anna Mitchell Mahoney and Christopher J. Clark, "When and Where Do Women's Legislative Caucuses Emerge?" *Politics & Gender* 15.4 (2019): 671–94.

286. *Arkansas Democrat*, September 5, 1965, p. 7.

287. Sara Murphy, "Distaff Note: The Ladies of the Legislature," *Arkansas Gazette*, January 29, 1967, p. 5E.

288. Murphy, "Distaff Note: The Ladies of the Legislature."

289. Diane D. Blair and Jeanie R. Stanley, "Personal Relationships and Legislative Power: Male and Female Perceptions," *Legislative Studies Quarterly* 16 (1991): 497–98.

290. Murphy, "Distaff Note: The Ladies of the Legislature."

291. Vada Sheid, *Vada: Nothing Personal, Just Politics* (Plano, TX: MC2 Graphics, 2008), 24–25. In addition to Sheid's book, see the excellent article by Clement A. Mulloy, "Vada Webb Sheid and the Transformation of North Central Arkansas," *Arkansas Historical Quarterly* 73.2 (2014): 192–215.

292. Sheid, *Vada: Nothing Personal, Just Politics*, 13, 222.

293. *Arkansas Gazette*, October 22, 1983, p. 4.

294. Judy Petty Wolfe interview with Lindsley Smith, September 14, 2007.

295. *Arkansas Gazette*, November 19, 1961, p. 12.

296. *Arkansas Democrat*, February 8, 1963, p. 5; *Arkansas Gazette*, August 28, 1963, p. 17; Robert Thompson, "Barefoot and Pregnant: The Education of Paul Van Dalsem," *Arkansas Historical Quarterly* 57 (1998): 377–404.

297. Carrie Rengers, "Sweetie? Actually, She's a Legislator and a Lawyer," *Arkansas Democrat-Gazette*, April 4, 1995, p. 1E; Becky Lynn interview with Lindsley Smith, March 10, 2006.

298. Stephanie Malone, Biographical Information Sheet for Arkansas Women Legislators Project, 13 January 2020, Lindsley Armstrong Smith Papers, MC 1910, Mullins Library Special Collections, University of Arkansas, Fayetteville; Stephanie Malone, "Women on Both Sides of the Aisle Are Paving the Way for Arkansas's Future Female Leaders, *Arkansas Blog*, March 3, 2020, https://arktimes.com/arkansas-blog/2020/03/03/women-on-both-sides-of-the-aisle-are-paving-the-way-for-arkansass-future-female-leaders.

299. These changes reflected evolving characteristics of women legislators in other states as well. See Emmy E. Werner, "Women in the State Legislatures," *Western Political Quarterly* 21.1 (1968): 40–50; Kathleen Dolan and Lynne E. Ford, "Change and Continuity among Women State Legislators: Evidence from Three Decades," *Political Research Quarterly* 50.1 (1997): 137–51.

300. Ruth Whitaker interview with Lindsley Smith, April 28, 2008.

301. Jacqueline Roberts interview with Lindsley Smith, October 19, 2006.

302. Joyce Dees, Legislative Biography, n.d., "Arkansas Women Legislators Project," Lindsley Armstrong Smith Papers, MC 1910, Mullins Library Special Collections, University of Arkansas, Fayetteville.

303. Barbara Nix, Biographical Information Sheet for Arkansas Women Legislators Project, January 13, 2020, Lindsley Armstrong Smith Papers, MC 1910, Mullins Library Special Collections, University of Arkansas, Fayetteville.

304. Jacqueline Roberts interview with Lindsley Smith, October 19, 2006.

305. Copies of the event program, Representative Smith's keynote address, and photographs of the event are in "Arkansas Women Legislators Project," Lindsley Armstrong Smith Papers, MC 1910, Mullins Library Special Collections, University of Arkansas, Fayetteville.

306. John Moritz, "Female Lawmakers Start Video Project to Empower Young Women," *Arkansas Democrat-Gazette*, October 19, 2017, pp. 7, 9. https://

www.youtube.com/channel/UCm3k5ppoYWCGvXghpogfHCw/videos; Facebook: https://www.facebook.com/argirlslead/; Twitter: @ARgirlslead; Email: argirlslead@gmail.com.

307. Kay Lehman Schlozman, Nancy Burns, Sidney Verba, and Jesse Donahue, "Gender and Citizen Participation: Is There a Different Voice?" *American Journal of Political Science* 39.2 (1995): 267–93.

308. Wanda Northcutt, "Women in Arkansas Politics," Women's History Month speech, p. 17. Speech transcript in "Arkansas Women Legislators Project," Lindsley Armstrong Smith Papers, MC 1910, Mullins Library Special Collections, University of Arkansas, Fayetteville.

# Index

*Italicized page numbers refer to photographs.*

Adams, William Eugene, 305
Adcock, Archie Frank, 230
Adcock, Pam, *156, 163, 165, 230,* 230–31
Agee, Charles, 199
Agee, Sarah, *156, 164, 199,* 199–200
Aging, Children, and Youth Committee, 188, 195, 203, 204, 221, 233, 270, 281, 285, 289, 303, 310, 330
Agriculture, Forestry, and Economic Development Committee, 144, 182, 226, 297, 307
Alexander, Bill, 183
Alexander, Randy, 295
Allen, Alice Tina, 237
Allen, Dorathy, 79, 85, 88, *88, 126,* 126–28
Allen, Martha, 44
Allen, Phillip, 208
Allen, Tom, 127
Allison, Ed, 130
American Anti-Slavery Society, 8
American Association of University Women (AAUW), 92, 116–17, 120, 188, 212, 217, 240, 328
American Legislative Exchange Council (ALEC), 139, 179–80, 201, 257, 261, 271, 275
American Woman Suffrage Association Executive Committee, 26
Ammons, Evelyn, *11, 181,* 181–82
Anderson, Mattie Crenshaw Winston, 27
"Andi's Law," 303

Andrews, Prince R., 76
Anthony, Susan B., 40, 44
anti-slavery movement, 8
Apache Tribe of Oklahoma, 202
Arbuckle, John R., 74, 75
#ARGIRLSLEAD, 96, 312
Arkansas Association of Pharmacists, 27
Arkansas Bar Association, 31–32, 280, 287–88, 290, 311, 314, 335
Arkansas Democratic Black Caucus, 198, 221, 236, 296
Arkansas Early Childhood Commission, 133, 309
Arkansas Equal Suffrage Association, 15, 25, 40, 42–43
Arkansas Federation of Women's Clubs, 21, 22, 34, 41, 48, 73, 76–77, 79, 366n135; and legislators, 103, 104, 106, 107, 118, 120, 128, 178, 217
Arkansas Health Insurance Marketplace Legislative Oversight Committee, 289
*Arkansas Ladies' Journal,* 47
Arkansas Legislative Black Caucus, 137, 151, 153, 214, 221, 237, 296–97
Arkansas Legislative Council, 127, 182, 211, 214, 216, 218, 225, 229, 231, 235, 254, 257, 259–61, 270, 277–78, 283, 285
Arkansas Legislative Hunger Caucus, *172,* 259, 282, 309
Arkansas State Game and Fish Commission Oversight Committee, 182, 289

*The Arkansas Story* (McKnight and Johnson), 22

Arkansas Supreme Court Commission on Children, Youth, and Families, 309

Arkansas Supreme Court Special Task Force on Practice and Procedure in Civil Cases, 281

Arkansas Wine Trail, 279

Arkansas Women's Legislative Day (2010), 96, *156*, *166*

Arkansas Women's Political Caucus, 138–39, 183, 186

Arkansas Women's Primary Suffrage Centennial Day, *158*

*Arkansas Yesterday and Today* (Knoop and Grant), 21–22

Armstrong, Lewis Munn, 239

Arnold, Gary, 219

Ashley, Frances "Fannie" Ann, 57

Askew, Benjamin Franklin, 32

Assistant President Pro Tempore (Senate), 235, 257, 275

Assistant Speaker Pro Tempore (House), 224, 229, 231, 243, 263, 282, 298

Associate Speaker Pro Tempore (House), 133

Atkinson, William E., 70, 103

Attwood, Harvie Malcolm, 242

Autry, Lilburn Hardy, 130

Autry, Lucile, *129*, 129–30

Axum, Donna, 23

Babcock, Bernie, 30, 40, 41, 65

Babcock, Elnora Monroe, 46

Babcock, Sarah Martha, 15

Baker, James B., 60

Ballinger, Bobby, 312

Balton, John Collins "Jake," 143

Balton, Nancy Crain, *69*, *97*, 115, *143*, 143–44, *156*

Barker, John, 310

Barker, Sonia Eubanks, *161*, *170*, *309*, 309–11

Barnes, Billy, 214

Barnett, Eva Ware, 21

Barnett, James Russell, 103

Barry, William Henry, 52

Barton, Ruth, 177

Basson, Lucia, *80*

Basye, Faith Margaret, 132

Bates, Daisy, 23

Bauchmann, Verna L., 293

Bayne, William H., 50

Beattie, Mary "Mollie" Melbourne Borland, 58

Beauchamp, Virginia "Jennie" Carter Halstead, 41

Beavers, Lenora, 65

Beavers, Lucy Houston, 64–65

Beebe, Mike, *167*, 200, 227, 245, 283, 327

Bell, Elbert Wesley, 179

Bell, John Henry, 124

Bellard, Agnes Watson, 153

Benedict, Don, 270

Benedict, Lori, *269*, 269–70

Benedict, Rick, 270

Benedict, Sherry, 270

Bennett, Bertie Edgar, Jr., 176

Bennett, Camille, *171*, *290*, 290–91

Bennett, Dee, *11*, *156*, *176*, 176–77

Bennett, Otis Wayne, Jr., 290

Bensing, Dwayne, 322–23

Bentley, Mary, *161*, *170*, *171*, 291–92

Bingham, John Alden Partridge, 60

Bivens, Ocie, 222

Black, Edith, 71

Blackburn, Breckenridge Flournoy, 108

Blackburn, Joseph, 108

Blackburn, Luke, 108

Blackburn, Percy, 109

Blackfeet Tribe of Montana, 245

Blackwell, Alice Stone, 47

Blackwell, Antoinette Louisa Brown, 11

Blackwell, Billy Eugene, 265

Blackwell, Elizabeth, 28
Blackwell, Henry, 47
Black women legislators. *See* Bennett, Dee; Blount, Nancy Duffy; Brown, Irma Hunter; Brownlee, Christene; Chesterfield, Linda; Dobbins, Sharon; Elliott, Joyce; Ennett, Denise Jones; Flowers, Stephanie; Flowers, Vivian; Lewellen, Wilhelmina; Roberts, Jacqueline; Scott, Jamie; Smith, Judy; Springer, Joy; Walker, Wilma; Wilkins, Josetta
Blair, Carl, 141
Blake, Charles, 329
Bledsoe, Cecile, *161, 164, 200*, 200–201
Bledsoe, James "Jim" H., 200
Blount, Nancy Duffy, *156, 162, 166, 231*, 231–32
Blount, Samuel, 232
Board of Cosmetic Therapy, 102
Board of Lady Managers, 20, 41
Boggan, Robert Norfleet, 293
Bolland, Dexter Ruth, 264
Bond, Pat, *164, 190*, 190–91
Bond, Tommy, 190
Bond, Will, 191
Boozman, Fay W., III, 262
Boozman, John, 246, 262, 316
Borhauer, Bill, 212
Borhauer, Shirley, *164, 212*, 212–13
Bost, John Lewis, 135
Bost, Sarah Jane, *135*, 135–36
Bottoms, Durwood Ferris, 209
Bowen, Davis, 206
Boyce, Grace, 76
Boyce, Margaret, 76
Boykin, John B., 60
Boys State Committee, 243, 279
Bradford, Thomas, 242
Bradford, Toni, *156, 242*, 242–43
Bradley, Joseph, 31
Bradwell, Myra, 30–31
Brand, Glenna Jo, 289

Brandenburg, Lenora Maxine, 215
Brandon, Doug, 134
Breedlove, Steve, 282
Brewer, Andria Nichole "Andi," 302
Brewer, William, 109
Bright, James, 102
Bright, John, 102
Brizzolara, Stella Zanone, 74
Broadaway, Brad, 280
Broadaway, Mary, *171, 280*, 280–81
Broadway, Shane, 223
Brooks, Ida Josephine, 20, 28, 29, 30, 75
Brooks, Mary Burt, 28, 47
Brooks, Thomas D., 64
Brough, Charles, 36, 73, 75, 104, 110
Brown, Amanda Rivers, 32–33, 58
Brown, George Franklin, 35
Brown, Henry Epps, 32
Brown, Irma Hunter, *11*, 79, *80*, 90, 96, *136*, 136–38, *156, 163, 167*, 214
Brown, Jesse, 110
Brown, John E., III, 333
Brown, Karilyn, *161, 170, 171*, 293, 293–94
Brown, Lawrence Lee, 293
Brown, Lura, 28
Brown, Lyn, 205
Brown, Margaret, 234
Brown, Maude, *82*, 82–83, *109*, 109–10
Brown, Nora M., 47
Brown, Olympia, 11
Brown, Roosevelt, 137
Brown, Thomas, 235
Brownlee, Billy Earl, 150
Brownlee, Christene, *150*, 150–51
Broyles, Frank, 226
Bruce, Annie Elizabeth, 64
Bryant, Jill, *331*, 331–32
Bryant, Joshua Paul, 331
Bryles, Burnice Samuel, 224
Buchanan, Helen, 84, *115*, 115–16, 132
Buchanan, Leslie, 115

Bumpers, Dale, 128, 131, 183
Burch, LeAnne, *157, 161, 171, 172, 308,*
*308*–9
Burch, Robert "Bobby," Jr., 308
Burford, William Alexander, 134
Burgess, Ivison Cleveland, 35
Burnap, George, 36
Burnham-Packham, Olive, 183
Burrow, Napoleon Bonaparte, 8
Bush, Allen, 177
Bush, Ann, *11, 177,* 177–78
Bush, George, 139
Business Women's Club, 71
Butler, Blanche Olive, 74

Cabe, Gloria, 91, *134,* 134–35
Cabe, Robert, 134
Cady, Helena Mellia Maxwell, 28–29,
*30,* 40
Cady, Henry, 28
Cagle, Wesley Marlo, 289
Cahoon, Haryot Holt, 47
Caldwell, Edgar Eugene, 205
Caldwell, Henry, 44
Caldwell, Nettie Jean Park, 205
Calhoun, Billy, 132
Campbell, Donnie, 257
Campbell, Ida McBee, 189
Campbell, Kate, 51
Cannedy, George Franklin, 314
Capp, Eric, 311
Capp, Sarah, 96, *161, 170, 311,* 311–12
Capps, John Paul, 191
Caraway, Hattie, 22, 27, 34, 108, 121,
131
Cardwell, Cindy, 322
Cardwell, Gary, 322
careers and economic opportunities,
24–25; educators, 26–27; family con-
nections, importance of, 54–55, 57–59,
64–65, 70–71; health professionals,
27–30; lawyers, 30–36; legislative offi-
cers, 54–69, 101, 103, 110; legislative

pages, *69;* notaries public, 69–72, 74,
76; postmasters, 49–54; post-suffrage
rights, public office, 78–79
Carl-Lee, Elmo M., 34, 35, 72
Carney, Arlene Rose, 331
Carney, Billy Craig, 331
Carson, Doug, 202
Carson, Jo, *164,* 202, 202–3
Carter, Barbara Ann, 233
Cash, Claud Vernon, 244
Cash, Joan, *156, 167, 244,* 244–45
Cater, Mary Christine, 272
Catholic Church, 17
Catlett, John, 292
Catt, Carrie Chapman, 45
Cavenaugh, Donald, 313
Cavenaugh, Frances, *161, 170, 171, 312,*
312–13
Cazort, Rachel, *82*
Celebrating Women in Public Office
Day, 96–97, 285
*Centennial History of Arkansas*
(Herndon), 27–28
Chaffin, Charlie Cole, *93, 142,* 142–43,
*156,* 223
Chambers, Erle Rutherford, 33, *45,* 76,
78, *78,* 79, 81, *82,* 104, *104,* 106, 121;
recognition of, 80–81
Chambers, Thomas, 104
Chaney, John Totty, 138
Charles, Eli, 329–30
Cherry, Francis, 190
Chesterfield, Emry, 220
Chesterfield, Linda, *156, 158, 220,* 220–
21
Childers, Jim Jennie Searcy, 69
Childers, Marvin, 178
Christianity: and gender roles, 11–18;
and ordination of women, 10–11,
45–46
Chunn, Fannie, 12, 40
Churches of Christ, 16–18
Citizens' Improvement Union, 46

City, County, and Local Affairs
   Committee, 137, 188, 191, 200, 243, 251,
   278, 279, 287, 292, 295
civil rights movement: resistance to, 119
Clark, Rex, 132
Clarke, Bess, 200
Clarke, James P., 23
Clay, William Lacy, 236
Clayton, Emma, 51–52
Clayton, Powell, 51–52
Clemmer, Ann, *156, 165, 253,* 253–55
Clemmer, Jamie, 254
Clerget, Gus, 34
Cleveland, Kate Delaney, 33
Clinton, Bill, 91, *97,* 120, 129, 132, 134–35,
   141, 145, 150, 151, 176, 192, 211
Clinton, Hillary Rodham, *95,* 135, 142
Clowney, Nicole, *155, 161, 170, 317,* 317–18
Clowney, Stephen, 317
Clubbs, Bennett, 192
Cockrell, Elizabeth "Bessie"
   Cunningham, 59
Cole, John, 142
Cole, Marie Lizzie Squires, 27
Collins, Benny, 271
Collins, Blanche, 83
Collins, Kevin, 235
Collins-Smith, Linda, *271,* 271–72
Columbian Clubs, 40–41
Columbian Exposition (1893), 20, 26,
   40–41, 58
Colvin, Gertrude, 152
Colwell, Emma R., 40
Committee on Confederate Soldiers
   and Widows, 102
Committee on Congresses, 41
Compton, America Frances, 124
Compton, James, 126
Confederacy, 49–50
Confederate Soldiers Monument, 23
Conservative Arkansas, 262, 294–95,
   310
Cook, Edith Mae, 131

Cook, Olin, 216
Cooper, Fannie Matthews, 28
Cooper, Thomas Y., 28
Cope, Hattie, 14
Corbin, Don, 126
Cornelison, Lewis Franklin, 139
Cornwell, Sylvia Ann Hindsman, 69
Corrothers, Helen G., 290
corruption, 260, 295
Cortelyou, George, 53–54
Cotnam, Florence Brown, 41, *42, 44,*
   47, 68, 85
Cotnam, Nell, 85
Cotton States and International
   Exposition in Atlanta (1895), 59
Couzins, Phoebe, 32, 43–44
Covington, Webb, 35
Cowling, Jim, 124
Cowling, Larry, 286
Craig, Annie May, 65
Craig, Lawrence, 198
Crain, James H. "Jim," 115
Crain, John Enochs, 143
Crater of Diamonds, 189
Crawford, Augustus A., 118
Crawford, Cindy (Rep.), *161, 170, 171,*
   *172, 319,* 319–20
Crawford, Gerald Eugene, 319
Crawford, Olevia, 118
Creekmore, Dawn, *165, 233,* 233–34
Creekmore, Michael, 233
Crocker, Hannah Mather, 37
Culler, Opal Shirley, 121
cult of true womanhood, 36
Cunningham, Benjamin, 111
Cunningham, Catherine "Kate"
   Campbell, 47, 59
Cunningham, Ethel Cole, 81, *82,* 83, *111,*
   111–12
Cunningham, Margaret Murphy, *44*
Curry, Frances Rae, 223
Cutting, Herwald, 30
Cypert, Jesse, 6

Dalby, Carol, *161, 170, 314,* 314–15
Dalby, John L., 314
Dale, Lois, 78–79
Daniel, William Elvis, 180
Daniels, Charlie, 200
Daughters of the American Revolution (DAR), 21, 22
DaVila, Isabella, 22
Davis, Breanne, *161, 315,* 315–17
Davis, Hazel Oletta, 179
Davis, Jeff, 71, 109
Davis, John-Paul, 316
Davis, Nora Lee, 114
Davis, Sallie Calvert, 34
Day, Walter, 178
Dean, Andrew Carnegie, 261
Deaton, Helen V., 196
Declaration of Sentiments and Grievances, 6, 10, 24
Dees, John, 203–4
Dees, Joyce, 95, *156, 164, 203,* 203–4
Dell, Valentine, 51
Della Rosa, Jana, *171, 294,* 294–95
Della Rosa, Russell, 294
Democratic Caucus, 284, 325
Dickey, Jay, 154
Dickinson, Jody, *156, 255,* 255–56
Dickinson, Thomas O., Jr., 255
Dillard, Mary, 219
Dixon, Dale, 207
Dobbins, Dwayne, 241–42
Dobbins, Sharon, *241,* 241–42
Dollison, Della, 70–71
Dolphus, Frank, 176
Dolphus, Jeanne, 176
Douglas, Charlotte Vining, *171, 281,* 281–82
Douglas, Rickey B., 282
Drake, Lota West, *44*
Duffy, Octavius C., 232
Dugas, Estelle, 206
Dunaway, Clarice, 68
Duncan, Elsie Fay, 194

Duncan, Maud Dunlap Pearce, 27
Duncan, William Newton, 266
Dunlap, Sarah, 20

Eagle, James Philip, 12–13, 44, 70, 130
Eagle, Mary Kavanaugh Oldham, 12–13, 20, 40–41, *41*
Eakin, John Rogers, 32, 44
Eakin, Lillian, 58
Early, Daniel Marshall, 12–13
Edgerton, Mrs. R. A., 20
Education Committee, 147, 207, 211, 214, 221, 225, 229, 249, 254, 275, 282, 295, 310, 332
Edwards, George Dee, 222
Edwards, James Wesley, 174
Edwards, Jean, 175
Edwards, Marilyn, *156, 167, 221,* 221–22
Edwards, Victor Banks, 255
Elaine massacre, 329
Ellington, Alice Sankey, 41, 43, *44*
Elliott, Dean, 211
Elliott, Effie, 214
Elliott, Efrem, 235
Elliott, Joyce, 137, *158, 161, 213,* 213–15, 324, 327
Elliott, Marvin, 214
Ellis, E. Newton, 36
Ellis, Oscar E., 35
Embody, Thelma Ruth, 245
Emerson, Molly, 70
English, Don Carol, 256
English, Jane, *161, 256,* 256–57
Ennett, Cecil Stephen, 328
Ennett, Denise Jones, *169, 328,* 328–29
Epps, Clifford E., 236
Equal Rights Amendment, 7, 8, 18, 91, 128, 132, 134–35, 138, 144, *167, 173,* 180, 188, 197, 212, 215, 216, 218, 219, 221, 222, 224, 225, 227, 231, 232, 235, 237, 240, 242, 244, 248, 251, 252–53, 284, 297, 316, 318, 324, 327
Etter, William, 28

Eubanks, James Troy, 310
Evans, Dillard, 306
Evans, Flossie Ella, 250
Evans, Katherine Beatrice, 229
Everett, Curren, 274

Faber, Georgia Lydia Knox, 57
families, politically active or well con-
    nected, 102, 105, 108, 111, 124, 126, 130,
    142, 211, 222, 223, 236, 245–46, 262, 283,
    288, 290, 296, 301, 325
Faris, Mary Gladys, 268
Farley, Embra Herbert, 264
Farley, William Clifford, Jr., 230
Farrar, John Perrin, 71–72
Faubus, Alta, 88
Faubus, Orval, 123, 125, 127, 196
Faust, Katherine Clarissa, 65
Fein, Mary Augustine, 27, 76, 77
Ferguson, Deborah, 161, 170, 171, 283,
    283–84
Ferguson, Joyce, 283
Ferguson, Scott, 283
Ferrell, Lisa, 11, 183, 183–84
Ferrell, William Alfred, 183
Firmin, John Thomas, Jr., 320
Fite, Charlene, 96, 161, 168, 170, 171, 284,
    284–85
Fite, Tom, 284
Fitzhugh, Laura "Lollie" Davis, 34
Fletcher, Bonnie Blanche, 319
Fletcher, Mary, 43, 47
floor leaders, 199, 218
Flowers, John Alonzo, Sr., 296
Flowers, Stephanie, 162, 234, 234–35, 296
Flowers, Vivian, 170, 171, 296, 296–97
Flowers, William Harold, 234
Forney, Benjamin F., 39
Fortnightly, 46
Foster, Robert F., 64
Fowler, Joe, 181
Freeman, Laura Bridgette, 174
Freshman Caucus, 265

Friedell, Emile, 34–35
Frost, Carlos Lawrence, 218
Fulbright, Roberta, 119
Fuller, Margaret, 44
Fuller, Minnie Ursula Oliver Scott
    Rutherford, 34–36, 43, 44, 73
Fulton, Matilda Nowland, 37
Fulton, William S., 37
Futrell, Tera, 82
Fyler, Eliza Ada "Lizzie" Dorman, 12,
    29, 31–32, 39, 42

Galloway College, 27
Gantt, Cora Reid, 58
Gantt, Robert, 5–6
Garcia, Karen, 167
Garner, Denise, 161, 170, 171, 172, 320,
    320–21
Garner, George W., 118
Garner, Hershel "Hershey," 321
Gateley, Gail, 308
Gatling, Olive, 43
gay women legislators. See McCullough,
    Tippi; Webb, Kathy
Gibson, Cliff, 141
Gilbert, Alfred Eugene, 149
Girls State, 143, 180, 205, 223, 242, 243,
    277, 282
Girls State Committee, 147, 283, 289,
    292, 297, 307, 315, 335
Glasgow, Charles, 135
Glass, Mary Evelyn, 259
Godfrey, Daniel, 322
Godfrey, Megan, 155, 161, 170, 171, 322,
    322–23
Goode, Earnestine Marie, 176
Goodman, Jack, 178
Goodson, John W., 117
Goodwin, Larry, 270
Gordon, Jean, 44
Gordon, Kate, 44–45
Gosnell, Gladys Margaret, 199
Gossage, Bill, 312

Governor's Task Force on Highway
  Funding, 273
Grace, William P., 61–62
Graham, Nathan, 126
Grant, James R., 22
Gray, Adam, 298
Gray, Aurelius Gilbert, 61
Gray, Mary Carter Baird, 72
Gray, Michelle, *157, 161, 171, 297*, 297–98
Green, Earl Gordon, 250
Green, Mary Beth, *164, 205*, 205–6
Green, Rick, 205, 206, 285
Greenwood, Myrtle C., 139–40
Greer, Amos, 198
Grider, Mack Carlton, 227
Grimke, Angelina, 8
Grimke, Sarah, 8
Gullett, Brenda, *206*, 206–7
Gullett, Robert, Jr., 206
Gumm, Wilford Warren "Bill," 332

Haak, Delia J., *332*, 332–33
Haak, William B., Jr., 332
Hackett, Mattie, 85, *86, 118*, 118–19, 126
Hackett, William T., 118
Hagan, Chester Crandall, 286
Hale, James W., 192
Hale, Rita, *191*, 191–92
Halford, Elijah Walker, 52
Hall, Oscar Maxey, 299
Hall, William, 102
Halliburton, William Henry, 60
Hammer, Kim, 264
Hampton, Wayne, 146
Hankins, Willie Merle, 290
Hare, Maxine Fern, 242
Hargrove, Robert Kennon, 15
Harper, Zella, 78
Harris, Garland Gano, 284
Harris, Joe, Jr., 151
Harrison, Benjamin, 52
Harrison, Marcus LaRue, 49
Hart, Belle, 27

Hart, G. Neill, 27
Hartness, Bill, 141
Hartness, Peggy Long, *140*, 140–41
Hartz, Jake, 147
Harvey, Phyllis Rose, 297–98
Harvey, Russell Lee, 297
Hass, Charles, 218
Hawes, Flora New Harrod, 52, *54*
Hawthorne, Fonda, *286*, 286–87, 307
Hawthorne, James Boardman, 13
Hawthorne, Joseph Stephen, 286
Hayden, Carl, 34
Hayes, Albert, *87*
Hayes, Thomas W., 61
Hays, George, 104
Hearon, William Jasper, 16
Hempstead, Fay, 19
Hendren, Jim, 325
Hendren, Kim Dexter, 325, 326
Hendrix, Bobbie L., *189*, 189–90
Hendrix, Gerald C., 189
Hendrix, Olen, 189
Henry, Catherine Vanson, *44*
Herndon, Cecil E., 200
Herndon, Dallas T., 27–28
Herring, Byron L., 103
Herriott, Billy Hubert, 226
Herrn, Thomas, 64
Herzfeld, Robert, 219
Hickerson, Mary P. "Prissy," *171, 272*,
  272–73
Hickerson, Randall, 272
*The Highlights of Arkansas History*
  (Herndon), 21
Hightower, Hubert D., 135
Hildebrand, Alfred Louis, 146
Hill, Jim, 125
Hill, Odelle J., 236
Hill, Thomas, 102
Hillhouse, George, 64
Hinkle, Carl, 123
*Historic Arkansas* (Ferguson and
  Atkinson), 22–23

*The History of Arkansas* (Shinn), 19–20
*A History of the State of Arkansas* (Hempstead), 19
Hobbs, Debra, *156, 258,* 258–59, 303
Hobbs, Ray, 258
Hocker, Willie Kavanaugh, 21, 58–59
Hodges, Earl, 72
Hodges, Grant, 331
Hoeltzel, Emma Reichardt, 67–68, 84
Hoeltzel, Pauline, 84
Hogue, Bobby, 178, 182
Holland, Bruce, 248
Hollingsworth, Eunice, 149
Holloway, Ralph Samuel, 268
Holmes, Bobbie Jean, 230
Holmes, John Acton, 177
Holmon, Dick, 305
Holmon, Mildred, 305
Honey, Willie Pascal, 59
Honeycutt, Margie Lyn, 299
Hood, Beverly Ann, 328
Hopper, John William, 259
Hopper, Karen, *156, 259,* 259–60
Horn, Barbara, *11, 160, 164, 179,* 179–80
Horn, Hoye, 179
House Military Caucus, 309
House Resolution 1056, 96–97
Howell, John Haley, 242
Howell, John William, 52
Howell, Max, 290
Huckabee, Mike, 133, 143, 151, 154, *164,* 178, 179, 185, 198, 199, 204, 206, 216, 228, 257, 270, 271, 273, 305, 314
Hudgins, Holder Hightower, 112
Hudson, Ashley, *334,* 334–35
Hudson, Dianne, *193,* 193–94
Hudson, Freddie D., 193
Hudson, George, 334
Huie, Janice Riggle, 18
Hunger Caucus (House), 309
Hunnicutt, Carolyn Vernice, 271
Hunt, Frances, 68, *77,* 78, *78,* 79, *101,* 101–2; as House postmistress, 65; recognition of, 80–81
Hunter, Everne, 18
Hunter, Gary, 260
Hurst, Ella B., 66–67, 81–82, *82,* 83–84, *84, 112,* 112–13, 116
Hurst, George Abner, 81–82, 112
Hutchinson, Anne, 10–11
Hutchinson, Asa, 200, 246, 255, 260, 267, 270, 289, 310, 311, 325, 331
Hutchinson, Donna, *156, 245,* 245–46, 325, 331
Hutchinson, Jeremy, 234, 246, 325, 331
Hutchinson, Marylea, 325
Hutchinson, Timothy (son), 246, 325, 331
Hutchinson, Tom, 260
Hutchinson, Young Timothy (husband), 245–46, 325, 331
Hyde, Barry, 257

Ingram, Marian Owens, *11, 180,* 180–81
Ingram, Marlin Perry, 181
Inman, Loretta, 265
Insurance and Commerce Committee, 182, 225, 229, 283, 329, 332, 237300
Irvin, John Dawson, 274
Irvin, Missy, *161, 274,* 274–75
Irwin, Athalia Johnson, 45–46, *46*

Jackson, Tom Edward, 150
"Jacob's Law," 309
Jacobson, Charles, 34, 67
Jacobson, Laura B., 67
Jacuzzi, Richard, 264
Jahns, Bruce Martin, 233
James, Lora Monolia, 312
James, Reesie Allide, 222
Jarman, Josephine Moore, 78
Jeffries, Peggy, *95, 184,* 184–85
Jensen, Allison, *171*
Johnson, Beatrice, 153
Johnson, Ethel Mattie Trussell, 203

Johnson, Hagard Eddis, 203
Johnson, Jamey, 223
Johnson, Janet, *156, 223,* 223–24
Johnson, Josephine, 106
Johnson, Osie, 152
Joint Budget Committee, 147, 197, 204, 214, 225, 237, 253, 257, 275, 285, 330
Joint Committee on Constitutional Amendments, 125, 278
Joint Performance Review Committee, 240, 257, 259, 270, 310, 330
Jones, Amos Walter, 108
Jones, Bob, 145
Jones, Daniel Webster, 70
Jones, Dennis Raymond, 328
Jones, Guy "Mutt," 128
Jones, Henry P., III, 96, 102, *156*
Jones, Henry Pearce, 101
Jones, John William, 13
Jones, Julia Hughes, 196
Jones, Myra, *11, 144,* 144–45, *156, 165, 166*
Jones, Rose Mattie, 130
Jones, Scipio Africanus, 329
Jones, William D., 52
Jordan, Hazel Dean, 218
Jordan, Roberta Fern, 119
Joshua, Bobbie Lee, 329
Judiciary Committee (House), 114, 184, 192, 195, 244, 266, 281, 285, 289, 303, 315, 329
Judiciary Committee (Senate), 218, 235, 272
Judy, Darrell, 208
Judy, Jan, *156, 164, 208,* 208–9
Julian, Jim, 287
Julian, Katy, 287
Julian, Patti, *287,* 287–88

Keel, John H., 34
Keeton, Boone, 14
Keeton, Julian Francis "Buck," Jr., 223
Kelley, Florence, 44
Kelly, Jonathan, 117

Kemp, Penny, 233
Kennedy, Tom, 216
Kimbell, John D., 62
King, Barbara, *156, 164, 209,* 209–10
King, E. D., 245
King, Jacob, 61
King, James Edwin "Timber," 210
King's Daughters Service Club, 29, 40
Kinion, Mark, 318
Kirk, LaCurtis, 234
Kizer, Bernice, 85, 88, *88, 121,* 121–22, 132
Kizer, Harlan, 121
Kizzia, David, 304
Klimala, Joseph Stanley, 269–70
Knoop, Faith Yingling, 21–22
Ku Klux Klan, 21, 106, 107, 176

Labor Committee, 105
Ladies Benevolent Association, 26
Ladies Building Association, 25
Lamb, George Bernard "Buddy," 189
Lampkin, Damon, 276
Lampkin, Sheilla E., *171, 276,* 276–77, 309
Land, Franke Lampedo Van Vulkenburgh, *44,* 74
Langley, Miles Ledford, 5–6, 48–49, 75
Latigue, Mark, 153
LaTour, John, 318
Lea, Andrea, *156, 161, 261,* 261–62
Lea, Phillip Brent, 261
League of Women Voters, 76, 77, 79, 91, 92, 104, 106, 109, 121, 122, 134, 188, 225, 247, 328; founding of, 43
Ledbetter, Mattie, 223
LeFrancois, Arthur Gardner, 317
Legislative and Military Affairs Committee, 203, 204, 285, 289, 310, 330
Legislative Joint Auditing Committee, 123, 182, 214, 243, 254, 260, 267, 281, 287, 289, 292, 295, 297, 303, 307
Lemming, Jo Stein, 138

Lewellen, Bill, 236
Lewellen, Clifford E., 236
Lewellen, John Marshall, 236
Lewellen, Patricia, 236
Lewellen, Wilhelmina, *156, 162, 163, 167,*
  *236,* 236–37
Lewis, John L., 222
Lewis, Mary, 23
libraries, 9
Lichty, Ernest Christian, 121
Lile, Robert Warren, 280
Lincoln, Blanche, 153
Linz, Charles Richard, 186
Lipscomb, David, 16–17
Lipton, John, 181
Little Rock Eclectic Society, 44
Livermore, Mary, 44
Lockwood, Belva, 31
Logan, Ophilia Dixon, 220
Long, Harry Lee, 119
Lonsdale, John, 117
lost cause, myth of, 37
Lotus, 46
Loughborough, Jean "Jenty" Moore, 58
Loughborough, Mary Ann Webster, 47
Lowe, Herald, 50
Lowe, Mary Murphy, 50
Lundstrum, Robin, *161, 170, 171, 299,*
  299–300
Lundstrum, Thomas Duane "Tom," 299
Lynn, Becky, *11,* 92–93, *186,* 186–87
Lynn, Terry, 186

Mack, Nellie B., 58, 77, 79, *102,* 102–3
Mack, William Francis, 103
Madison, Bernard, 187–88
Madison, Sue, *11, 156, 163, 167, 187,*
  187–88, 200
Madzongwe, Edna, *80*
Maenza, Marie Carmen, 209
*Makers of Arkansas History* (Reynolds),
  20
Malone, Stephanie, 93, *172, 262,* 262–63

Maloof, Jill Deelyte, 316
Mansfield, Arabella Babb, 30
Mariani, Barbara, 324
Marinoni, Rosa, 23
marriage: and loss of rights, 24, 49–50;
  and office holding, perceptions of, 53
Marsden, Henry Howard, Jr., 256
Marshall, Mary Ellen Campbell, 66
Martin, Alfred C., 34
Martin, Faye, 283
Martin, Frank, 241
Martin, Harry, 125
Martin, Jefferson, 211
Martin, Vera Mae, 211
Martin, William Bell, 224
Martin Luther King Jr, Commission,
  175, 176
Martin Oglesby, Gladys, 85, 87, 88, *88,*
  *125,* 135–36
Massey, Bobbie Jean, 226
Massey, Wilma Louise, 280
May, Hillman, 116
Mayberry, Andy, 301
Mayberry, Julie, *300,* 300–302
McCarty, Rebecca Ann, 334
McCastlain, Doris, 85–87, *87, 88, 122,*
  122–23, 131
McCastlain, Hugh Marvin "Ted," 123
McChesney, Robert, 50
McClure, Kathy S., 311
McCormic, Mary, 23
McCoy, David, 264
McCulloch, Arlene, 180
McCullough, Terry, 323
McCullough, Tippi, *161, 170, 171, 323,*
  323–25
McDiarmid, Clara Alma Cox, 12, 25,
  *26,* 28, 40–41, *42*–43
McDiarmid, George W., 25
McFerrin, Ben, 35
McGraw, Daniel, 107
McHenry, Cora, 232
McKenzie, Gayla H., *161, 325,* 325–26

McKenzie, Loyd W., 325

McMath, Sid, 84–85

McMellon, Terry, 229

McRae, Thomas C., 27, 75–77, 79, 101, 103, 104

McRaven, Florence, 66, 80, 107, 107–8, 109

McRaven, John, 107

Meacham, Kirby, 131

Meacham, Shirley, 97, 131, 131–32

Meahl, Robert, 116

Meeks, Flossie, 122

Mellard, Jesse James, 15–16

Meriwether, Lide Parker Smith, 44

Mertes, Evelyn Irene, 274

Methodist Church, 13–16, 17–18

Middlebrook, Lonnie, 151

Milam, John Charles, 278

Milam, Pamela Gay, 278

Miles, Richard Orville, 202

Miles, Travis, 185

Miller, John, 129

Miller, Josephine, 74

Milligan, Dennis, 223

Mills, Wilbur, 139

Minton, Randy, 228

Monument to Confederate Women, 23

Moore, James Robert, 13–14, 16

Moore, John H., 21

Moore, Shirley Ann, 227

Moose, William Lewis, 103

Moritz, Maylene Caroline, 286

motivations for seeking office, 134, 222, 280, 302, 310, 324, 330. See also families, politically active or well connected; special election to fill husband's vacant seat

Mulkey, Dove Toland, 59, 85, 124, 124–25

Mulkey, Faust Everett, 124

Munger, Rhoda Philena, 26, 44

Murphy, George W., 71

Murphy, Nap, 92–93

Murphy, Sara Alderman, 87–89

Murrell, Mary Belle Mizell, 25–26, 57

NAACP, 241, 268, 296, 330

Napper, Sharon Kay, 306

National Conference of State Legislatures Hunger Partnership, 282

National Order of Women Legislators (OWL), 85

National Rifle Association, 217, 233, 255, 260, 262, 271, 274, 295, 299, 305, 310

Native American women legislators. See Carson, Jo; Hutchinson, Donna

Naylor, George, 62

Neill, Clare, 71

Nelson, Minnie Ola, 125

Nelson, Sheffield, 123, 274

New, John C., 52

Newland, Nancy Howard Tate, 50

Newland, Robert C., 50

Nicholson, Bill, 144

Nineteenth Amendment, ratification of, 75

Nix, Barbara, 95, 156, 263, 263–64

Nix, Bobby, 264

Nobles, Johnny Leroy, 303

Norman, George William, 39

Northcutt, Carl, 146

Northcutt Hartz, Wanda, 11, 97, 98, 146, 146, 156, 165, 265

Norton, Martha Cummings, 191

notaries public, 27

Nyama, Koti, 80

Oates, Gordon, 120

Oates, Willie, 85, 86, 119, 119–20

Oglesby, Gladys Martin. See Martin Oglesby, Gladys

Oglesby, Lowman, 126

Oldfield, Pearl Peden, 22

Osborne, Thomas S., 73

Osborne, Wendelyn, 287

Ott, Jewel Dean, 239

*Our Arkansas* (Brown), 22
Overbey, Betty, *171, 277,* 277–78
Overbey, George, 277
Owen, Eva Elizabeth, 134
Owens, Wayne, 180–81

pageants, 127
Pan American Conference of Women, 106
Parker, Isaac, 121
Parker, Jamie, 121
party leaders, 144, 218, 249, 269, 325
party whips, 259, 300, 309
Patterson, Virgil Lee, 222
Patton, Nick, 126
Paul, Alice, 45, *45*
Pawelczak, Lorna Jean, 303, 304
Payne, Henry, 53
Pennartz, Lenus Nicholas, 247
Pennartz, Tracy, *156, 162, 247,* 247–48
Pennington, Julia Ward, 75, 78
Perry, Bessie, 59
Pettigrew, Annie B., 58, 60
Petty, Ella B., 112
Petty, John Dandridge, 138
Petty, Judy, 90–91, *91, 138,* 138–39
Petty, Rebecca, *161, 170, 171,* 259, *302,* 302–3
Petty, Richard Milton, 302
pharmacists, 27
Phillips, Ella, 70
Phillips, Kate, 71
Pickett, Betty, *163, 167, 224,* 224–25
Pickett, John, 225
Pierce, Kelly Proctor, 319
Pittman, Floyd Lee, 308
Pittman, John Middleton, 32
Pitts, Viola, 266
Political Equality League, 41, 43, 46–47, 65, 66, 67, 74, 104
Pollan, Carolyn, *11, 132,* 132–33, *159, 162,* 202
Pollan, Cee Cee, *159*

Pollan, George, 132
Pondexter, Ernestine, 220
Post, Leslee Milam, *278,* 278–79
Prater, Kenneth, 226
Prater, Sandra, *156, 163, 167,* 226, 226–27
Pridgen, Ed, 218
Pridgen, Judy, *218,* 218–19
Pryor, David, 137, 148, 211
Public Health, Welfare, and Labor Committee, 182, 195, 201, 204, 226, 231, 269, 275, 278, 283–84, 296
Public Health and Practice of Medicine Committee, 120, 124
Public School Desegregation Lawsuit Resolution Task Force, 279
Public Transportation Committee, 144, 150, 182, 270, 273, 279, 287, 297, 310, 330
Pugh, Elizabeth C., 71
Pure Elections Law, 83, 113
Pych, Gertrude M., 269–70
Pyle, Beverly, *156, 166, 237,* 237–38
Pyle, William Forrest, 237

Rainey, David, 235
Rankin, Lydia Alice, 59
Ratliff, James, 313
Ray, Donald, 196–97
Reagan, Ronald, 274
reapportionment, 89
Reed, Howard, 217
Reed, Lawrence Neill, 217
Reichardt, Eva, 67
Reid, Charles C., 55
Reid, Sarah Ann "Sallie" Robertson, 55–57, *56*
Reinhardt, Ellen, 71
Rembert, Erma Lee, 198
Republican Caucus, 151
"republican motherhood," explanation of, 371n194
Reyenga, James Martin, 194
Reynolds, Gertrude, 128

Reynolds, John Hugh, 20
Reynolds, Margaret Harwood, 20
Richardson, Arthur Ralph, 110
Ridge, Sarah Northrup, 32
Riggs, John A., 73
Riggs Primary Suffrage Act, 68, 73–74
Righter, Mary Jane, 256
Riles, David Robert, 316
Riley, Mary Ethel, 244
Ring, Helen Christina, 261
Ritchie, Patsy Ann, 294
Roane, Bethunia Lea, 58
Roberts, Curley, 152
Roberts, David, 288
Roberts, Debra, 288
Roberts, Helen Marie, 320
Roberts, Jacqueline, *11*, 94–95, *152*,
    152–53, *156*, *167*
Roberts, J. P., 60
Roberts, Vernon, 141
Robertson, James T., 35
Robinson, Martha Lee, 254
Robinson, Pat, 118–19
Rockefeller, Winthrop, 125, 127, 138, 143
Rodgers, Danny Paul, 195
Rodgers, Sandra, *156*, *164*, *194*, 194–95
Roebuck, Johnnie, *156*, *167*, *169*, 246,
    *248*, 248–50, 264
Roebuck, Tommy G., 249
Rogers, Anthony A. C., 51
Rogers, Ott Lee, 319
Rogers, Tiffany, *156*, *169*, *265*, 265–66
Rogers, Mrs. W. C., 20
Rorex, Sam, 35
Rose, George B., 72
Rose, Uriah M., 23
Ross, Mike, 154
Rotenberry Anti-Evolution Bill, 80, 108
Rothrock, Irvin R., 113
Rowell, Alexander Hendrix, Jr., 191
Rowlette, Lera Jeanne, 85, *116*, 116–17
Royston, Stella, 64
Rules Committee, 117, 123, 147, 211, 214,

218, 225, 231, 254, 257, 261, 263, 281, 283,
    296, 303, 307, 312
Rushing, Clifford Lee, 304
Rushing, Laurie, *161*, *171*, *303*, 303–4
Russell, Lillian, 47
Rutherford, Minnie U. *See* Fuller,
    Minnie Ursula Oliver Scott
    Rutherford
Rutledge, Leslie, *161*

St. Paul, 13–14, 32, 45
Salmon, Don, 211
Salmon, Mary Anne, *156*, *164*, *167*, 210,
    210–12, 288
Sanders, Lucy, 71
Sawyer, Lecil Richard, 211
Sawyer, Stephen, 211
Scheuer, Genevieve Ann, 247
Schexnayder, Charlotte, *11*, 96, *97*, *147*,
    147–49, *156*, *165*
Schexnayder, Melvin, 148
Schlafly, Phyllis, *173*
*A School History of Arkansas* (Moore), 21
school segregation and integration, 148,
    214, 234
Schulte, Frank, 228
Schulte, Susan, *156*, *163*, *227*, 227–28
Scott, Fannie, 20
Scott, Freddie Bernard, 326–27
Scott, Jamie, *161*, *170*, *171*, *326*, 326–27
Scott, Sue, *288*, 288–89
Scruggs, Martha Lula, 68
Seneca Falls Convention, 6, 10, 24
separate spheres, 36–37, 38. *See also*
    careers and economic opportunities
Shaw, Anna Howard, 11
Sheffield, John, 106
Sheid, Carl, 128
Sheid, Vada, 87, *90*, *128*, 128–29, 305
Shelly, Robert, 237
sheriff, 219
Sherman, Bill, 186
"Sheroes of Arkansas History," 96

Shinn, Josiah, 19–20
Shipman, Jerry, 150
Shoffner, Irma, 196
Shoffner, James Edwin, 196
Shoffner, Martha, 96, *156, 167, 196,*
    196–97
Shoppach, Ann Adelia Annette Ryerse
    Cutting, 29–30
Shoppach, James Henry, 30
Shug, Andy, 150
Shumard, George Getz, 51
Shumard, Isabella Clark "Belle"
    Atkinson, 51
Siler, Mary Edith, 143
Simpson, Cleda Maria, 146
single-member districts, 89
Singleton, Carolyn Ann, 302
Slater, Rodney, 175
Slinkard, Jason, 267
Slinkard, Mary Lou, *156, 266,* 266–67
Slinkard, Russell, 267
Smead, Lamar, 76
Smith, Betty Jo, 300
Smith, Edna Mae, 214
Smith, James E., 62
Smith, Joann, 210
Smith, Judy, *153,* 153–54, *156*
Smith, Lindsley, 96, *156, 163, 167, 173,*
    *239,* 239–40
Smith, Margie Nell, 326–27
Smith, Philip, 271
Smith, Stephen, 239
Smith, Sylvester Lee, 154
Smith, Walker, 73
Smith, William Wright, 31
*Songs and Sonnets of a Solon* (Thompson),
    80–81, 106
Sonneman, Emil Herman, 199
Sorvillo, Jim, 335
South, Jerry C., 61–62
Southern Baptist Convention, 12–13,
    17–18
*Southern Ladies Journal,* 47, 58

Southern States Energy Board
    Committee on Clean Coal Energy
    Policies and Technologies, 289
Speaker Pro Tempore (House), 254
Speaks, Benny, 305
Speaks, Nelda, *158, 161, 170, 171, 172, 305,*
    305–6
special election to fill husband's vacant
    seat, 241–42; death of husband, 78,
    115, 123, 127, 130, 131, 140, 150, 174, 179,
    189–90
Sperling, Elizabeth M., 317
Springer, Horace L., III, 330
Springer, Joy, *329,* 329–31
standpoint theory, 38–39
Standridge, Greg, 316
Stanton, Joey F., 311
Stark, Jerry, 186
Starr, Belle, 22–23
State Agencies and Governmental
    Affairs Committee, *173,* 188, 197, 199,
    231, 261, 267, 278
Steffy, Frank Alexander, 215
Stewart, James J., Jr., 306
Stith, Leona, 232
Stone, Lucy, 5, 47
Strickland, Ann, 281
suffrage movement: legislation, 73, 75;
    and press, use of, 47–48; and public
    speaking, 43–47; roots of, 8, 39–41;
    suffrage organizations, 42–43
Sugg, Harry Calvin, 244
Sullenger, Charles E., 114
Sullivan, Henry Hays, 130
Sullivan, James Osgood Andrew, 63–64
Susan B. Anthony Amendment, 8

Taylor, Cleo, 305
Taylor, Vaney Elizabeth, 110
Teague, James, 142
temperance organizations, 39–40. *See
    also* Woman's Christian Temperance
    Union

Terral, Thomas J., 74, 75, 106
Terry, Adolphine Fletcher, 33, 48
Terry, Bertha Elizabeth, 147
Terry, Ruby Jane "Nova," 332
Terry, Tommy Lee, 131
textbooks: history, erasure of women's contributions, 18–24
Thanet, Octavia, 23
Thomas, Bob, 274
Thomas, Jerry Lynn, 274
Thompson, Elizabeth, 48, 78, 80, *105,* 105–6
Thompson, Frank, 106
Thompson, Irene, 68–69
Thompson, Kenneth Eugene, 283
Thompson, Norma, *139,* 139–40
Thompson, William Henry, 140
"Three Mile Law," 39
Thrower, Christopher, 31
Tidwell, Judy Faye, 323
Tillar, Jewel Stephen, 147
Tilley, Willa Mae Sutterfield, 306
Tinsley, Jessie Durrell, 272
Toland, Margaret Thomas "Tompie," 59
Toland, William Henry, 124
Toney, Hardin Kimbrough, 64
True Grit Trail, 292
Trusty, John Thomas, 216
Trusty, Sharon, *164, 215,* 215–16
Tsoodle, Gloriette, 202
Tucker, Jim Guy, 177, 183, 225
Turner, G. W. "Buddy," 255
Turner, Henry "Champ," 117
Turner, Sarah Emily, 135
Tyler, Hugh, 268
Tyler, Linda, *156, 169, 268,* 268–69

United Daughters of the Confederacy, 21, 23, 37
United States Daughters of 1812, 21
US Post Office employees, 49–54
US Supreme Court, 30–31

Van Dalsem, Paul, 92
Vaught, DeAnn, *157, 161, 170, 171,* 287, *306,* 306–7
Vaught, Jonathan David, 306
Veasman, Joseph Christian, 254
Vernon, Mable, *45*
Via, Betty Ruth, 255
Vining, William Coleman, 281

Waddell, John Frederick, 260
Wagner, Charolette, *156, 250,* 250–51
Wagner, Earl Leonel, 122
Wagner, Tyler Wes, 251
Wagner, Wayne, 250–51
Walker, John W., 330
Walker, Melvin, 198
Walker, Wilma, *164, 197,* 197–98
Wall, Fannie Murray, 150
Walters, Bill, 229
Walters, Shirley, *156, 163, 229,* 229–30
Ward, Francis Leon "Frank," 125
Wassell, Elizabeth "Bettie" McConaughey, 65–66, 74
Watson, Edmond Penn, 75
Watson, Gladys, *149,* 149–50, *160*
Watson, Tom, 149–50
Watts, William Wallace, 208
Weatherly, Dalton, 140
Weatherly, John, 140
Webb, Candis, 219
Webb, Clara, 59–60
Webb, Doyle, 219
Webb, John William, 128
Webb, Kathy, *156, 165, 169, 252,* 252–53, 324
Webb, Maurice Clive, 252
Weidemeyer, Ruth Shipton, 217
Weidner, Clarence Julius "Clay," Jr., 300
Welch, Morgan Eldridge "Chip," 334
Wells, Arthur Lee "Hoot," 312
Whaley, William Pearson, 16
Whitaker, Ruth, 94, *156, 168,* 205, *217,* 217–18

Whitaker, Thomas Jefferson, Jr., 217
White, Jeanice, 314
White, John, 188
White, Thomas C., 35
Wigstrand, Fred, 109
Wigstrand, Mary B., *108,* 108–9
Wilkins, Henry, 152
Wilkins, Henry, III, 152, 174–75
Wilkins, Henry "Hank," IV, 175
Wilkins, Josetta, *11, 167, 174,* 174–75
Willard, Frances, 15, 40, 44
Williams, Atha Mae, 252
Williams, Gail, 310
Williams, Jeff, 222
Williams, Peggy Jean, 186
Williams, Randall Lee, 290
Williams, Tennie Rebecca, 224
Willis, Arnell, 210
Wilson, Mabel Irene Fowler, 77
Winborn, Mayme Mae, 284
Winfield, Augustus R., 13, 32
Wingo, Effiegene Locke, 22
Winthrop, John, 10–11
Witt, Almus J., 60–63
Wolf, Robert H., 139
Woman's Christian Temperance Union
    (WCTU), 17, 21, 25, 29, 34, 40, 41, 65,
    101, 103
*Woman's Chronicle,* 25, 28, 43, 47–48, 60
Woman's Foundation of Arkansas, 145,
    207, 266, 296
*Woman's Journal,* 25, 26, 42, 43, 47–48
Woman Suffrage Association: Arkansas
    chapter, 26, 32, 34, 39, 42, 43, *44,* 73;
    national organization, 26, 32, 45, 46,
    47, 65; other chapters, 29, 44

Women in Government, 209, 237, 266,
    269, 284
women legislators: appearances, public
    preoccupation with, 85; demographic
    trends, 94; gendered expectations for,
    88–89; and male-dominated culture
    of General Assembly, 90–93, 94–95;
    numbers of, 5, 79, 82–88, 89–90,
    93–94, 116, 185, 347–54; and political
    parties, 94; structural obstacles for,
    25–26; urban versus rural recruitment
    of, 10; voluntary public service, his-
    tory of, 4; and women's perspective
    on issues, 81, 84–85
Women's History Month, 96, *156*
Women's Legislative Caucus, 85, 90,
    96, 145, 147, 151, *163, 164,* 184, 192, 204,
    206, 207, 237
Women's Medical Club, 29
Women's Suffrage Centennial
    Commemoration Committee, 255
Wood, Lois P., 258
Wood, Roy Lee, 187
Woods, Daisy Nell, 208
Wootton, Aubrey Wayne, 294
Word, Alene, 84, *114,* 114–15, 116
Word, Percy B., 114
Wren, Tommy, 298
Wyatt, David, 272

Yadon, Thomas, 62
Yates, Joe, 267
Yates, Lynda Camille, 187
Yeargin, Mary, 296
Young, Damon, 320
Young, Dennis, 179

**Lindsley Armstrong Smith** earned a JD from the University of Arkansas School of Law and served as research assistant professor of communication at the university. From 2005 to 2010, she was a member of the Arkansas House of Representatives.

**Stephen A. Smith** is professor emeritus of communication at the University of Arkansas. He was a member of the Arkansas House of Representatives (1971–1974), chief of staff to the Arkansas attorney general, and executive assistant to Governor Bill Clinton. During his legislative career, Smith served with Senator Dorathy Allen, Representative Vada Sheid, and Representative Bernice Kizer. He is the author of nine books, including *Myth, Media, and the Southern Mind.*